Table of Contents

3

6

This book is DEDICATED to my law school ethics professor Ken Jorgensen, and my seminary ethics professor, Rev. Dr. Sylvester Thomas Smith, a man of God and integrity who has blessed many.

The Scriptures found in the Christian Holy Bible provides a revelation of God's Holy ethical character, which is seen through His actions, His commandments, His Word, and His teachings. All of God's characteristics provide a firm foundation for human morality and decency to deliver dignity to all, no matter what religion we are, or even our walk of life. The moral code includes God's justice, His love, and a call to hearts to reflect these moral qualities equally towards others, as well as to live them in our very own lives, whether we are clergy, lawyers, or those with a heart for their fellow human beings.-J. Myron Smith

For the LORD God is a sun and shield: the LORD will give grace and glory: no good thing will he withhold from them that walk uprightly (Psalm 84:11).

Introduction

This treatise is a guide for those who desire to have ethical practices in their ministries of God's law, as well as for Clerics to be found walking upright in the secular world, which includes Clerics participating in all government laws as Christian practitioners. As clerics cannot turn off their clerical hat due to the fact our service is to be performed as unto Christ Jesus in all that we do in life, thus we are to be those who have integrity in our ethical practices always. Therefore, our ethical practices are to transfer to all genres of life. This includes areas such those that require us to be political theologians, which all clergy should be ministering in, which includes ministries inside of the church as well as positions in regard to secular laws, and secular law-making arenas. There are ethical ministers found in God's Church, schools of theology, earthly positions, as well as in the Capitol Cathedrals of secular law-makers. In the Biblical Hebrew tradition of law, the scribes and priest were responsible for interpreting God's law. Thus, being the lawyers so to speak. Further, the priests were basically the same as judges, the chief priest acted as the Chief Justice, and those other priest with higher positions were in the Sanhedrin. The Sanhedrin was similar to the Supreme Court of the Hebrew people. The Sanhedrin was responsible for interpreting the law especially in the most complex cases. Thus, the priests were acting as both religious leaders interpreting the law, as well as legal authorities. The duties of the priest in these roles can be found in the book of Deuteronomy in chapter 17 and verses 8 through 13.

Many interdisciplinarian scholars have noticed that the laws of the secular government, or laws governing government are those laws which have their origins from the Holy Bible. For example, in governmental criminal law there must be two elements for a crime to be committed. First there must be the *actus reaus*, or the physical act of the crime, and then there must be the *mens rea*, which is the mental knowledge of committing the crime. Under the secular government one cannot murder another without a defense, such as self-defense, or the lack of mental capacity. Under the secular government one cannot steal, nor can one give testimony which is false and under the guides of perjury. Then when we compare these secular laws to what the Holy Bible states, we can find Biblical laws about crimes. In Exodus 20:1-17 and Deuteronomy 5:17-20 we find laws against the acts of the following crimes of murder, perjury, theft, and adultery that is still against the law in some States, but not widely prosecuted. Then looking at adultery in the mental state or what the secular law calls *mens rea*, we have Christ Jesus stating this concerning one's mental state of committing adultery found in Matthew 5:27-28: "You have heard that it was said to those of old, 'You shall not commit adultery.' But I say to you that whoever looks at a woman to lust for her has already committed adultery with her in his heart." Many secular laws have their origin in the pericope of scriptural text.

In America, it was once said that in an Ivy League institution that the divinity students, and the law students attended the same course work classes the first two years of their individual degree programs, only to be split apart for the third year of study.

In the mid-18th Century and into the early 19th Century it is written in the work of The Origins and Occupations of Glasgow Students, 1740-1839, that the divinity students and the law students took the same preliminary Arts courses, before they embarked onto their specialties of divinity and law. Thus, there was an interaction between the students of divinity and those students of the law.

In present day, even Brown University has a program, which allows interdisciplinary degree programs, which provide the students the ability to have lawyers and clergy take classes together to help develop and solidify diverse skill sets, and thought processes.

In an ideal world, both the ethics of the cleric and the lawyer should indeed be the same. Lee J. Strang, states the following: ("Christian legal scholars must first work to build communities of virtue. A community of virtue is a group of people who together share a common vision of the good. They have essentially similar answers to questions regarding the meaning of reality, what it means to be human, and how one attains integral human fulfillment. Central to this common vision is the role of virtue, helping the individual achieve his end: happiness in this world and Beatitude in the next."); Lee J. Strang, The Role of the Christian Legal Scholar: The Call for a Modern St. Benedict, 20 NOTRE DAME J.L. ETHICS & PUB. POL'Y 71 (2006)

Howard A. Glickstein speaks of the Jewish Perspective on the social need for students to have the law and religion to be intertwined as follows: ("The Law Center provides a service to the Jewish community by providing an atmosphere where people may observe the Jewish faith while they pursue a legal education."); Howard A. Glickstein, Academic Freedom in Religiously Affiliated Law Schools: A Jewish Perspective, 11 REGENT U. L. REV. 18 (1998)

The need for the law and the cleric ethics to be similar can be seen in the midst of the political theologian, and the political ethical legal legislative person, or lawmaker.

In 2015 did you know that the Roman Catholic, who was Pope Francis gave an address to the United States Congress, which is filled with many lawyers, and law givers, and law makers. Pope Francis in his address to Congress, took the Congress back to the actual roots of the law, and the original lawgiver, Moses himself. Pope Francis said: that the legislator's did the work of Moses, and he called Moses the "lawgiver of the people of Israel." As many Americans have seen the Ten Commandments, with Charlston Heston as the lead, they truly know that Moses is the person who truly "symbolizes the need of peoples to keep alive their sense of unity by means of just legislation...[as well as] leads us directly to God and thus to the transcendent dignity of the human being." *https://www.washingtonpost.com/local/pope-francis-to-address-divided-congress-in-washington-on-thursday/2015/09/23/971b0a9e-6260-11e5-b38e-06883aacba64_story.html.*

For the political theologian, as well as those in the ministry of secular lawmakers, there is a need for ethical guidelines, and rules. In the actions of the political theologians, and secular lawmakers, the Constitution of the United States of America surely has its basis in the Biblical laws. Quiet simply the First Amendment surely shows the cross section of religious ethics, and the ethics of a country in its Constitution. For the First Amendment gives the first right to all Americans, which is the freedom of Religion. First Amendment Explained: Congress shall make no law respecting an establishment of religion, or prohibiting the free exercise thereof. Similarly, does not God give us the choice to choose our religion?

In the Book of the Law, in Deuteronomy 30:15-20, God gives the people a choice between two path ways, which included the righteous way, or the unrighteous way to follow. People will undoubtedly choose something to follow. See, I have set before thee this day life and good, and death and evil (Deuteronomy 30:15). In the book of Joshua, the people are given the ability to choose to serve the LORD God of their ancestors, or the gods of the Amorite's ancestors.

Joshua said to the people and makes a proclamation of his own personally: And if it seem evil unto you to serve the LORD, choose you this day whom ye will serve; whether the gods which your fathers served that were on the other side of the flood, or the gods of the Amorites, in whose land ye dwell: but as for me and my house, we will serve the LORD (Joshua 24:15).

In laws and ethics, there truly is nothing new under the sun. For the Constitution itself in its 13th and 14th Amendments are certainly founded upon the foundations and principles found in the Holy Scriptures. Paul speaks in Acts 17:25-26 of all people being of "one blood" in the eyes of God. "Nor is He worshiped with men's hands, as though He needed anything, since He gives to all life, breath, and all things. And He has made from one blood every nation of men to dwell on all the face of the earth, and has determined their *preappointed* times and the boundaries of their dwellings." It is the Fourteenth Amendment (1868) affirming the writing of the Emancipation Proclamation. It was the former lawyer, and then Christian faith President Lincoln, who wrote the Emancipation Proclamation, with similar words found in Esther 8:11-12 as follow: "Wherein the king granted the Jews which were in every city to gather themselves together, and to stand for their life, to destroy, to slay, and to cause to perish, all the power of the people and province that would assault them, both little ones and women, and to take the spoil of them for a prey, Upon one day in all the provinces of king Ahasuerus, namely, upon the thirteenth day of the twelfth month, which is the month Adar." Whereas the Emancipation Proclamation clearly states: "And I hereby enjoin upon the people so declared to be free to abstain from all violence, unless in necessary *self-defence*; and I recommend to them that, in all cases when allowed, they labor faithfully for reasonable wages." The Holy Scriptures in Luke 10:7 states that a laborer is worthy of their hire.

Christ Jesus Himself embodied a great defense of a woman, and forever put into practice of a person's ability to face her or his accusers with the right to Counsel, under the 6th Amendment of the United States of America. For under the Law of Moses the commandment was for the Jews to stone such women, and man caught in the act of adultery. However, under church politics the scribes (lawyers) and the Pharisees (lawyers and judges) brought only the woman and sought only capital punishment (death) for her. However, in John 8:3-11, Christ Jesus the Advocate of advocates, and the Judge of judges had a question presented to His Court. And as both Lawyering Advocate, and as the Ultimate Judge wrote both a sealed Brief and Order in the sand. Then Christ Jesus as Judge, made a statement or ruling on the jury instructions to all of her accusers and the jury standing before

22

Him: He without sin cast the first stone. Please understand this question was one to pull out the ethical practices of the scribes and Pharisees, because due to the fact they only brought the woman for judgment, they themselves were committing a sin in their Church Politics. In all Church Politics, one must remember this word: "For all have sinned, and come short of the glory of God, being justified freely by His grace through the redemption that is in Christ Jesus" (Romans 3:23-24).

Christ Jesus the Advocate and Judge after saying, He without sin cast the first stone, then stooped down and continue to write His sealed Brief and Order in the sand. After a few moments had passed, and all her accusers had walked away, Christ Jesus looked up, and asked the woman where were her accusers. Without two or three accusers she could not be convicted and committed to death. At that moment Christ Jesus was a Political Theologian, as the scribes and Pharisees were playing Church politics with Him.

Under the 6th Amendment of the United States Constitution it provides: the right of a fair and speedy trial (Jesus caused the woman to have a fair and speedy trial); it requires that your jury be impartial (Jesus sought impartiality by saying those without sins cast the first stone); further one is to know what charges are being waged against the one accused of a crime (the woman knew what crime she was being charged with fully); then it requires the accused to confront the witnesses against them, but also requires the ability to present witnesses on the accused behalf (Jesus asked where were her accusers as they has all left); and finally, it gives the right to legal representation in the form of a Counsel (Christ Jesus acted as both her Advocating Counsel, and as her fair Judge.

Under the Jewish Law, in order to be convicted of breaking the law and to be put to death, there is the requirement of two or three witnesses agree, if two or three witnesses agree the person can be found guilty of breaking the law. "On the evidence of two witnesses or of three witnesses the one who is to die shall be put to death; a person shall not be put to death on the evidence of

23

one witness" Deuteronomy 17:6. Christ Jesus was surely acting as a political theologian in defending the woman accused of adultery.

You may ask who are some others who are or should be political theologians. I am very glad you asked, for each of us as a royal priesthood, and a member of a Holy Nation of God, can fulfill the roles of political theologians when the occasion arises, for if you have two or three people together there is the presence of politics. All such occasions should be handled fairly, morally, and ethically. Many saints like Christ Jesus, have found ourselves engaged in Church politics, and had to enact ethical practices to seek a fair resolution. Many of those saints have acted outside of the Church, and have engaged ethics in out of church arenas.

We have those who in faith have acted as political theologians in our history. We have those who have influenced the law and the law makers in our history. Just to name two, there has been Frederich Douglass, who influenced Abraham Lincoln to present the executive order of the Emancipation Proclamation with words in his speech of "What to the Slave is the Fourth of July?" On July 5, 1852 Douglass gave a speech with the introduction being: This, for the purpose of this celebration, is the 4th of July. It is the birthday of your National Independence, and of your political freedom. This, to you, is what the Passover was to the emancipated people of God. It carries your minds back to the clay, and to the act of your great deliverance; and to the signs, and to the wonders, associated with that act that day.

In 1862 Lincoln deemed as a necessity to emancipate those who were enslaved. On September 22, 1862 Lincoln signed the executive order entitled the Emancipation Proclamation, which was to go into effect on January 1, 1863. This has had a lasting ethical effect, but it has also has had a lasting Christian effect, as African American churches all over America have what they call Watch Night Service, on December 31st into January 1st of every year in memory of God's Emancipation of His people in America.

The second political theologian is one all Americans know of in this age and time, for there is a paid Government Holiday on his birthday in honor of him. Rev. Dr. Martin Luther King, Jr. in his "I Have A Dream" speech at the Lincoln Memorial during the March on Washington on August 28, 1963, Rev. Dr. King, Jr. The march on Washington was for Jobs and Freedom. Although the speech did not touch upon jobs directly, our political theologian did say these words: And as we walk, we must make the pledge that we shall always march ahead. We cannot turn back. There are those who are asking the devotees of civil rights, "When will you be satisfied?" We can never be satisfied as long as the Negro is the victim of the unspeakable horrors of police brutality. We can never be satisfied as long as our bodies, heavy with the fatigue of travel, cannot gain lodging in the motels of the highways and the hotels of the cities… We cannot be satisfied as long as the Negro in Mississippi cannot vote and the Negro in New York believes he has nothing for which to vote.

In these words, Rev. Dr. Martin Luther King, Jr. is saying a voteless people, is a hopeless people, as well as all people who are created equal by God, are to be treated equally with Equal Rights, or Civil Rights.

After political theologian, Rev. Dr. Martin Luther King, Jr., spoke on the issues of jobs, and the need for African Americans to have the power of the vote, President Lyndon B. Johnson on September 24, 1965 issued the Executive Order 11246. Johnson's order prohibited those in the Federal Government, and those contracting with the Federal Government from discriminating against people based on race, color, religion, and national origin. President Johnson's Executive Order 11246 substantially enforced the philosophy and concept of the Civil Rights Act, and the Voting Rights Act.

Some of the words in President Johnson's Executive Order 11246, are as follows: By the authority vested in me as President by the Constitution and the laws of the United States of America, it is hereby ordered:

Section 1. Purpose. Longstanding Federal civil-rights laws protect individual Americans from discrimination based on race, color, religion, sex, or national origin. These civil-rights protections serve as a bedrock supporting equality of opportunity for all Americans. As President, I have a solemn duty to ensure that these laws are enforced for the benefit of all Americans.

Johnson's Executive Order 11246 has been revoked as of January 2025. There is a need for new political theologians to influence, what Augustine called just laws. St. Augustine of Hippo wrote: "*nam mihi lex esse non videtur, quae justa non fuerit*". The translation is as follows: "for I think a law that is not just, is not actually a law." Just laws have the common threads of morality, ethics, and common decency. The Augustan thought process is that any law, which is not founded in morality cannot in itself be a just law, nor can it be justified by natural law either. Therefore, any unjust law issued carries with it the fact that people are not obligated to obey that law, this is the central concept that Augustine was conveying.

Many have passed and decided to get rid of just laws, and to make unjust laws. That is why there is a need for such a time as this, for us to go back to the basic concepts of Christian Ethics in America, as well as all over the globe. We all are those who should seek just laws, and laws based upon ethics, and justice. Thus, all of us should be political theologians in our own ways.

In my own analysis as being both a doctor of the law, and a doctor of ministry that the contemporary cleric has three areas of systematic realities: (1) the sacred, political, and ethical accoutrements are of the Church, rather than the congregations, and people to whom their interaction apply; (2) the interpretation, application, imposition, and articulation under the hierarchical stemming from the Divine, to the Denomination, and then to the Decanoic, and is not formulated from the congregation up in most instances; and (3) the sacred, political, and ethical accoutrements are put into practice with the main aspirations and ambitions to lead and guide persons to act according to the will of God, rather than follow their own will, but are to still find the sacred, political, and ethical accoutrements to help them to coordinate and administrate their deeds, and acts to help them to achieve common objectives in the life of ministry.

This treatises composition of interdisciplinary work entitled SMITH'S CHRISTIAN CLERGY PROFESSIONAL RULES OF ETHICS is to be an intersection and a conversation concerning the development of the venerated ethical rules, coupled with the moral identity, and ministerial values of clerics in practice and practicum. These values are to help divinity students, divinity practitioners, and political theologians. For the divinity student these rules can be an introduction to ethics, which also show the legal ramifications for not ministering ethically. For the divinity practitioner these rules can be a guide for informed ethical decision making.

For the political theologians, who are clerics, such as James A. Garfield a minister in the Disciples of Christ Church, Frederick Muhlenberg of Pennsylvania was aa Lutheran minister, and also served as the very first speaker of the U.S. House of Representatives, John Lewis an ordained minister, Hiram R. Revels an African Methodist Episcopal (AME) Church pastor, Richard H. Cain who was an African Methodist Episcopal (AME) Church pastor, Adam Clayton Powell Jr. pastor of the Abyssinian Baptist Church, Walter Edward Fauntroy of pastor of New Bethel Baptist Church, Andrew Young served as a pastor and teacher in Marion, Alabama, and in Thomasville and Beachton, Georgia, William H. Gray III pastored Bright Hope Baptist Church, Floyd H. Flake pastored Allen AME Church, Cori Bush list pastor as one of her professions, both Rev. Robert John Cornell a priest from Wisconsin, and Rev. Robert F. Drinan, a Catholic Jesuit priest from Massachusetts both dropped out of Congress when Pope St. John Paul II released a church Cannon saying priest could no longer hold political office, and Raphael Warnock pastor of Ebenezer Baptist Church

27

in Atlanta, Georgia this book of ethical laws will certainly will be a benefit, as well as a tool, which gives them all a firm foundation on which to base any law-making decisions and congressional ethical practices.

Further, these rules are to leave room for judgments and decision-making in learning and practice, which are similar to what law schools named as the "skills trainings" classes or clinics, and, which are similar to the divinity school's equivalent of the field education programs. After field education program skills are learned by divinity students, they certainly can be put into practice. In addition, once divinity practitioners study these rules, they too can be further established by them putting their faith in action as acting practitioner clerics, who have a sincere desire to add ethical elements to their practice of ministry. Those already fully emersed in ministry and church leadership can also find value in studying and putting these rules into their everyday practice of ministry and leadership.

The order of the presentation consists of the ethical rules, comments, Biblical references, and Biblical commentary. In addition, there are actual legal examples, which consist of case law that provides parameters of life's application or misapplication of ethical rules by clerics and political theologians. These rules of SMITH'S CHRISTIAN CLERGY PROFESSIONAL RULES OF ETHICS, have been adopted from the Minnesota Rules of Professional Conduct, which I learned and had to adhere to at William Mitchell College of Law and in practicing law in Minnesota. Further, these rules consist of legal case law presented as precedent, the word of God, which is God's precedence, as well as the ethical practices I learned at the School of Theology Virginia Union University and taught by Rev. Dr. Slyvester T. Smith. Please come, I invite you to take this *Iter cum Ethica propositum*, or journey with ethical purpose.

Rule 1.1 Calling, Commissioning And Ordination of Clergy

A clergy shall provide competent ministerial actions to all others, including congregation members, organization members, denominational members, societal members, incarcerated memberships, and those yet not saved by God's Grace. Competent ministerial actions are based upon and requires Biblical knowledge of both the Old and New Testament Covenants, ministerial skills, devotion, dedication, continued studying to show oneself approved to GOD, and continued readiness, and preparation reasonably and Spiritually necessary for the ministry task, which includes preaching the Word of God without compromise, teaching the Word of God without compromise, Spirit led counseling, the administering of the Sacraments and other Ordinances, to provide pastoral care, and to nurture the faithful in the mission of Christ, to lead those who are yet to be a part of the faithful under the cause of Christ Jesus, and to lead by example as they are led by God and as they live their lives for Christ Jesus, thus exhibiting Christlike behaviors which are consistent with their sacred calling, the tenants of their faith, and the standards imposed by God, and the Holy Christian Church, of which Christ Jesus is the Head.

Comment

Christian Leadership Knowledge and Skill Under The Calling Of Christ

[1] In determining whether a member of the clergy possesses the calling and the required ministerial skills, knowledge in a particular ministry position, relevant factors include the relative complexity and specialized nature of the ministry need, the Christian clergy's general experience, the Christian clergy's study background, ministerial training, and ministry experience in the ministry need in question, the preparation, and continued study of the Christian clergy is equipped and able to give in the ministry need, or needs, and whether it is feasible to refer the

ministry need to, or associate or consult, a Christian clergy of an established call position of leadership concerning the ministry need. In many instances, the ministry need will require a clergy involved in the general ministry. Other times, there will be a ministry need that will require a more experienced Christian cleric, or a certain or particular type of field of experience and training to minister to the ministry need, which is required in order for that ministry need to be met.

[2] A Christian clergy need not have special education, training, or prior experience to handle a specific ministry need circumstance or situation of a type that the Christian clergy has not experienced before. A newly ordained Christian clergy can be as knowledgeable and skilled as an older Christian clergy with extended experience. Some important ministry skills, such as spiritual analysis of Christian Covenants, Commandments, and Controlling Authority, along with the evaluation of Biblical text are required tools of the Christian clergy in providing needed ministry and assisting in resolving all ministry needs. Perhaps the most important and fundamental ministry need skill is being able to discern what kind of ministry need or ministry solution of a ministry need is desirable in a particular situation.

[3] In an emergency, a Christian clergy may minister, give assistance, and give advice in a matter that the Christian clergy does not have the experience. In emergency situations, which would ordinarily require the need of a specialized area of ministry, and where the assistance of a more experienced Christian Clergy, or where there is a need for a referral for consultation or the need of association with another Christian Clergy, or Mental Health Professional, a Christian clergy without the experience could minister in the much needed ministry area, which the Christian clergy does not have experience in, due to the fact it would be impractical at that time.

[4] A Christian clergy may minister in any ministry needed matter where the requisite ordination, and the required level of knowledge can be studied and learned by reasonable preparation

and prayer. This applies as well to a Christian clergy who acts an interim pastor, or minister for a church, or who is also a visiting Christian clergy.

Duty Of Preparation For Ministry Service of Christian Clergy

[5] Knowledgeable service of a Christian clergy in a particular area of ministry need includes study, inquiry, discernment, and an analysis of the ministry need, then the Christian clergy is to apply the fundamental elements of Christian ethics to the ministry need or needs, by employing or imparting the proper methods and procedures to meet the ministry need. The proper method and procedure include (but is not exhaustive) the following applications to minister in the circumstances of the ministry need: Christian methods, values, morals, ethics, ideals, the Doctrine of Jesus Christ, and the application of Christian Canons of faith, and the Tenants of Faith of that Christian clergy.

Maintaining Christian Ministry With Other Christian Clergy or Serving With Other Christian Clergy

[6] Before a Christian cleric seeks to associate or to minister with another Christian cleric outside of their own church or own organization to provide or assist in the provision of ministry services to a Person In Need Of Ministry Service (*hereafter PINOMS*), the Christian cleric seeking to associate or minister with another Christian cleric must obtain consent from the PINOMS, and the Christian cleric seeking to obtain the assistance of another Christian cleric must reasonably believe that the Christian cleric sought is skilled, and can render the needed ministry services in a competent and ethical fashion. The reasonableness of the decision to seek assistance with ministry services with a Christian cleric outside of their own church or organization will certainly depend upon the ministry need circumstances, including the skills, education, experience, known

reputation of ministry abilities of the Christian cleric from outside of the church or ministry organization. The Christian cleric sought to assist in providing the ministry need must agree to provide protections of confidentiality, ethical ministry actions in relationship to the Christian faith tenants of the person giving permission for the Christian cleric to assist with their ministry need.

[7] When Christian clergy from more than one church, or Christian organization are providing ministry services to a PINOMS on a particular ministry need, the Christian clergy ordinarily should consult with one another and the person receiving ministry about the direction, scope, and responsibilities of each Christian cleric involved in the ministry services.

Maintaining Skills and Knowledge To Provide Christian Services and Ministry

[8] To maintain the required knowledge, understanding, wisdom, and ministry skills, a Christian clergy member should continue to study the word of GOD to show themselves approved unto GOD, as well as to show themselves as being qualified by any ordained church body governing or offering good counsel and guidance to the Christian clergy member. For those Christian clergy required to perform marriages they are to make sure that their credentials to perform said marriages are in order with their local government officials, as well as meeting the requirements of any other State or territorial jurisdiction, in which they perform any marriage.

Knowing Christ-Centered Ethical Leadership And Living It

[9] To know and discern between the discussions of ethics both Theological and Philosophical.

All ethical systems may be generally classified thus:

1. Philosophical ethics—systems that result from man's reason.

2. Theological ethics—ethical systems claiming to express the authoritative principles of God. To the world, ethics is the science of behavior. This "science" is constantly in flux. "Postmodernism assumes that there is no objective truth that moral values are relative, and that reality is socially constructed by a host of divers communities." (Gene Edward Veith, Jr., Postmodern Times, Wheaton, IL: Crossway Books, 1994,193).

3. To the Christian, ethics is the study of God's expectations for His people.

4. "Bible believers have always had a God-centered system of ethics that they found revealed in Scripture." (Stewart Custer, "The Place of God in Ethics," Biblical Viewpoint. Greenville, SC: Bob Jones University Press, 1996, 1).

5. The study of ethics in general
Though the word "Ethics" is often heard, few have developed a careful understanding of what the study of ethics implies and entails.
The definition of ethics. Ethics is defined in Webster's Third International Dictionary as, "The principles of conduct governing an individual or profession: standards of behavior." The American Heritage Dictionary of the English Language defines ethics as, "The study of the general nature of morals and the specific moral choices to be made by the individual in his relationship with others: the philosophy of morals. The rules or standards governing the conduct of the members of a profession." Chuck Phelps, *Pastoral Ethics*, Publisher Central Africa Baptist College, pp.4-5

Biblical Reference

[1] Study to shew thyself approved unto God, a workman that needs not to be ashamed, rightly dividing the word of truth (2 Timothy 2:15).

[2] For even the Son of Man came not to be served but to serve others and to give his life as a ransom for many (Mark 10:45).

[3] How then shall they call on Him in whom they have not believed? And how shall they believe in Him of whom they have not heard? And how shall they hear without a preacher? And how shall they preach unless they are sent? As it is written: "How beautiful are the feet of those who preach the gospel of peace, Who bring glad tidings of good things!" (Romans 10:14-15)

[4] The preacher sought to find out acceptable words: and that which was written was upright, even words of truth (Ecclesiastes 2:10).

[5] A Christian Cleric is to know and to maintain to be ethical in actions, words, service, deeds, and in all manner of things as seen in the Holy Scriptures. The following with the exceptions of comments and the 12 scripture verses and Strong's G1485 with comments found in number 2 directly below have been taken from Chuck Phelps, *Pastoral Ethics*:

The derivation of ethics. The English word is of Greek origins.

    1. ηθος (Athos)

Found only in 1 Corinthians 15:33, which states: Be not deceived: evil communications corrupt good manners. Bauer, Arndt, and Gingrich Lexicon defines athos as a custom, habit, or usage.

    2. εθος (Ethos) *[Strong's Number G1485 matches the Greek ἔθος (ethos), which occurs 12 times in 12 verses in the TR Greek.]** *[Strong's Number G1485 ἔθος éthos, eth'-os; from G1486; a usage (prescribed by habit or law):—custom, manner, be wont.]**

*Chuck Phelps, in *Pastoral Ethics* states εθος is: Found 13 times in the New Testament. Ethos carrier much the same meaning as the word athos. Typically, ethos is translated "want to." *{*Twelve from Strong's Number G1485 have been provided*}

Luke 1:9- According to the custom G1485 of the priest's office, his lot was to burn incense when he went into the temple of the Lord. (Speaking of Zachariah).

Luke 2:42- And when He was twelve years old, they went up to Jerusalem after the custom G1485 of the feast. (Speaking of Christ Jesus following the custom, when He went and spoke with the doctors of the law, whom were amazed at His knowledge and understanding).

Luke 22:39- And He came out, and went, as He was wont, G1485 to the mount of Olives; and His disciples also followed Him. (Speaking of Christ Jesus' leadership as He was going out to pray after having communion with His disciples, and just before He would be arrested in the garden).

John 19:40- Then took they the body of Jesus, and wound it in linen clothes with the spices, as the manner G1485 of the Jews is to bury. (Speaking of the acts of burial process carried out by the Jewish community during Jesus' burial preparation).

Act 6:14-For we have heard him say, that this Jesus of Nazareth shall destroy this place, and shall change the customs G1485 which Moses delivered us. Speaking of grace replacing the law in our salvation).

Act 15:1-And certain men which came down from Judaea taught the brethren, and said, Except ye be circumcised after the manner G1485 of Moses, ye cannot be saved. (Speaking of the law being above the grace of God).

Act 16:21-And teach customs, G1485 which are not lawful for us to receive, neither to observe, being Romans (Speaking of the act of fulfilling the Great Commission of preaching the Gospel of Christ Jesus throughout all the world).

Act 21:21-And they are informed of thee, that thou teachest all the Jews which are among the Gentiles to forsake Moses, saying that they ought not to circumcise their children, neither to walk after the customs. G1485 (Speaking of challenges of the grace of God, over the law).

Act 25:16- To whom I answered, It is not the manner G1485 of the Romans to deliver any man to die, before that he which is accused have the accusers face to face, and have license to answer for himself concerning the crime laid against him. (Paul is speaking in the face of adversity exhibiting ethical behavior as a priest, as well as one seeking social justice under the government's law).

Hebrews 10:25- Not forsaking the assembling of ourselves together, as the manner G1485 of some is; but exhorting one another: and so much the more, as ye see the day approaching. (Speaking unto how we are to show our ethical behavior in obedience to God in the manner of coming together as God has commanded us to do in His name).

    3. εθω (*Etho*)

Found only 3 times in the New Testament. *Etho* carries the idea of "to be

accustomed to." Chuck Phelps, Pastoral Ethics, Publisher Central Africa Baptist College, p.4.

However, the Greek New Testament Concordance presents that there are four times, which the Greek word εθω, appears in the Holy Scriptures.

Matthew 27:15- Now at that feast the governor was wont (c-1486) to release unto the people a prisoner, whom they would. (Speaking of the custom traditions of man).

36

Mark 10:1- And He arose from thence, and comes into the coasts of Judaea by the farther side of Jordan: and the people resort unto Him again; and, as He was wont, (c-1486) He taught them again. (Speaking of the custom of teaching, one must be able to teach the Word of God).

Luke 4:16-And He came to Nazareth, where He had been brought up: and, as His custom (c-1486) was, He went into the synagogue on the sabbath day, and stood up for to read. (Speaking of the custom of keeping the LORD'S Day holy, and preaching in the church of the body of believers whom come together as God has commanded us to do in His name.)

Act 17:2-And Paul, as his manner (c-1486) was, went in unto them, and three sabbath days reasoned with them out of the scriptures. (Speaking of preaching and teaching the Gospel of Jesus Christ).

Greek New Testament Concordance —The verb εθω (See https://www.abarim-publications.com/Concordance/II/c-1486-1.html)

Christian Ethical Commentary

[1] "Belief is an object of proof and validation. Faith is what belief becomes when it develops into a part of the conscious thinking and feeling of the individual and is not an object of proof." Howard Thurman, "Letter to Dorothy Henderson" (24 March 1955, Boston, MA) in *The Papers of Howard Washington Thurman, Vol 4: The Soundless Passion of a Single Mind,* June 1949–December 1962, edited by Walter Earl Fluker, et al. (Columbia, SC: The University of South Carolina Press, 2017), 120.

[2] "Classifying always oversimplifies –partly due to the inadequacy of labels, and partly the dynamic quality of mind which refuses to follow the script of any one system." Luther E. Smith, Jr., *Howard Thurman: The Mystic as Prophet* (Richmond, IN: Friends United Press, 2007), 89.

[3] "I am Christian because I think that the religion of Jesus in its true genius offers me very many ways out of the world's disorders" Howard Thurman, *With Head and Heart: The Autobiography of Howard Thurman* (New York: Harcourt Brace Jovanovich, 1979), 136.

[4] Commitment means that it is possible for a man to yield the nerve center of his consent to a purpose or cause, a movement or an ideal, which may be more important to him than whether he lives or dies. The commitment is a self-conscious act of will by which he affirms his dentification with that he is committed to. The character of this commitment is determined by that to which the center or core of his consent is given. Howard Thurman, *"Commitment," in For the Inward Journey: The Writings of Howard Thurman*, ed. Anne Spencer Thurman (New York: Harcourt Brace Jovanovich, 1984), 13.

[5] "Leaders in the church are called to be shepherds, not a board of directors. This requires involvement in a personal shepherding ministry amongst the people. The shepherd leader unpacks the four primary ministries of shepherds – knowing, feeding, leading and protecting   on macro (church-wide) and micro (personal) levels." T. Z. Witmer, T.Z., *The shepherd leader: Achieving effective shepherding in your church*, P&R Publishing, Phillipsburg, NJ, being cited by Kelebogile Thomas Resane, *'Leadership for the church: The shepherd model'*, HTS Teologiese Studies/Theological Studies 70(1), Art.# 2045. https://doi.org/10.4102/hts.v70i1.2045, 2014, (p. 3-4).

[6] Herbert Moya states the following about pastoral care: Servant leadership is key in pastoral leadership. Jesus says the one who wants to be the greatest amongst the disciples must be the least … Servant leadership is leadership that serves the needs of the sheep by shelving sacrificially one's own needs. Herbert Moyo, *'The pastor and the embryonic pastoral identities in Southern Africa in the 21st century'*, in H. Moyo (ed.), *Pastoral care in a globalised world: African and European perspectives*, pp. 13–37, Cluster Publications, Pietermaritzburg. (2015), (pp. 26–27).

[7] James Henry Harris, and Wanda Scott Bledsoe stated: 'The pastor has to have a vicarious view of the church and ministry-placing himself or herself in the position of others as Jesus often did. Moreover, she or he needs to develop a basic approach to ministry and master the techniques of pastoral ministry with boldness. "The Spirit that God has given us does not make us timid; instead, His Spirit fills us with power, love, and self-control'" (2 Tim. 1:7). James Henry Harris, and Wanda Scott Bledsoe, *Pastoral Theology A Black-Church Perspective*, (Fortress Press, Minneapolis 1991), *p. ix*.

[8] Preaching Ethics: "The preaching task is a sacred responsibility. Of all places where the minister must be sure to maintain ethical integrity, none is more sacred than his responsibility as a communicator of God's Word; therefore, the ethical minister is well-advised to . . .1. Be aware of exaggeration; 2. Beware of making statements without checking one's sources; 3. Beware of preaching/teaching without adequate preparation (2 Tim. 2:15); 4. Beware of preaching pet peeves; 5. Beware of using the pulpit as a whipping post against specific people; 6. Beware of preaching without biblical support; 7. Beware of preaching in areas of personal doubt. "The teachers doubt will be the student's dogma"; 8. Beware of emotional manipulation; and 9. Beware of taking a public stand on a crucial issue without careful documentation." Chuck Phelps, *Pastoral Ethics*, Publisher Central Africa Baptist College, p.53.

[9] Chuck Phelps cites what he calls the 6 most significant contemporary ethical systems, which contains what he listed as number 6 the following:

Non-conflicting absolutism, which he explains as follows:

(1) Many biblical absolutes may be derived from biblical exegesis.

(2) There is one supreme absolute--love for God. Love for one's neighbor is an evidence of the supreme absolute.)

(3) Righteousness is found in doing God's will.

(4) The "law of double effect" is considered. Chuck Phelps, Pastoral Ethics, Publisher Central Africa Baptist College, p9.

[10] *Character That Is Contextual*

"The question of the first commandment expands the notion, expressed in Mark 7, that ethics derives from a heart that is in a proper relationship with God. A scribe made an inquiry about ethics in the abstract: "Which commandment is the first of all?" (12:28). Grounding himself in God's monotheistic character, Jesus repeats Deuteronomy 6:5 with some echoes of Joshua 22:5, enjoining love of God. Via correctly discerns that ethics in Mark means giving up knowing in advance what one is to do. But Via makes the love command an exception. Love is, however, not an exception. One cannot know in advance the shape of love of neighbor will take, because it takes shape in a specific context. Further, love of neighbor is derivative in that it is the second command. Given the thematic development of hearts that are distanced from God in Mark 7:6, Jesus' abduction that the scribe is not far from God's commonwealth indicates a heart that is not distanced from God. Is it possible for Jesus to persuade even a scribe?" Character Ethics And The New Testament, Moral Dimensions of Scripture, Chapter 4, *Generating Ethics from God's Character in Mark*, Robert L. Brawley, Auth., and Ed., p.67.

[11] Robert Thompson stated: How can Christian leaders find a balance between serving and leading? Part of the confusion lies in Jesus' striking paradox itself. Following an exegetical study of Mark 10:35-45, I use John Stott's categories of the choices between selfish ambition and sacrifice and between power and service to explore two key areas of application for pastoral

40

leaders. if competent Christian leaders constantly seek to put Christ's mission ahead of their own glory and to put the good of the group before their own desires, then their followers will be more likely to accept their influence… this passage divides easily into two main parts. the first part consists of James and John's request to Jesus that they be allowed to sit at his right and left sides when he comes into his glory (Mark 10:35-40). the second part consists of Jesus' instruction to the disciples on service, leadership, and sacrifice (10:41-44). the passage concludes with Jesus' example of his own pending sacrifice (10:45; Stein, 2008, p. 482). Bill Thompson Servant, Leader, Or Both? A Fresh Look At Mark 10:35-45, pp.1, 3.

[12] "Servant leadership therefore is built on a moral and ethical authority rather than the control of others. It prioritizes service rather than a position or a title that the leader holds…" Servant leadership in Mark 10: 35-45 applied to African Pentecostal Christianity, Mookgo Solomon Kgatle.

[13] *Character Evaluation Spiritually*

"Jesus' affirmation of leaving everything for his sake in 10:29-31 concludes with an enthymeme of reversal. This too is abductive reasoning: rule + result = case. The rule is the inversion of first and last. The result is Jesus's passion and resurrection (10:32-34). The case is the reversal of Jesus' degradation into his exaltation. In addition, James and John seek to be first in Jesus' glory and thereby become the objects of anger from the other ten. The way for all of them is derivative—Jesus' purpose is to serve and give his life for many (10:45). The apostles' service on behalf of others derives not from Jesus' example but from his ransom for them. God's commonwealth transforms their self-interest into service." Character Ethics And The New Testament, Moral Dimensions of Scripture, Chapter 4, *Generating Ethics from God's Character in Mark*, Robert L. Brawley, Auth., and Ed., p.66.

[14] Servant leadership is a form of moral-based leadership where leaders tend to prioritize the fulfillment of the needs of

41

followers, namely employees, customers and other stakeholders, rather than satisfying their personal needs. Although the concept is not new among both academics and practitioners, it has received growing consideration in the last decade, due to the fact that it can positively affect a series of individual and organizational outcomes, such as job satisfaction and organizational commitment. In particular, the latest trend in literature has focused on the identification of the antecedents, mediating and moderating mechanisms at the basis of this relationship, as well as on the development of a common scale to measure the construct across diverse economic and cultural contexts. *Servant Leadership: a Systematic Literature Review and Network Analysis*, Alice Canavesi, corresponding author1 and Eliana Minelli, PubMed Central, Employ Response Rights J. 2022; 34(3): 267–289. Published online 2021 Sep 28. doi: 10.1007/s10672-021-09381-3.

[15] Character Evaluation Esoterically

The world may not understand the ethical character and integrity that is needed as a Cleric as seen in John 18:37-38: Pilate therefore said to Him, "Are You a king then?" Jesus answered, "You say rightly that I am a king. For this cause I was born, and for this cause I have come into the world, that I should bear witness to the truth. Everyone who is of the truth hears My voice." Pilate said to Him, "What is truth?" And when he had said this, he went out again to the Jews, and said to them, "I find no fault in Him at all. Likewise, the trial of Jesus before Pilate actually serves a juridical function in condemning the condemner, as Pilate himself confesses to have no clue as to the truth. Jesus, on the other hand, declares that his kingdom is one of truth and that all who are of the truth listen to his voice (18:37-38). Therefore, in the second phase of the Johannine situation, Jesus is the truth because he conveys the Father's word to the world faithfully, and the truth is always liberating. Of course, revelation is always an affront to religion, as the divine initiative cannot but displace the human. Likewise, a challenge to political power and empire is the reign of truth, of which Jesus is king. It was during this phase that the first edition of the Johannine Gospel was composed as an augmentation and modest correction of Mark..." Discernment-Oriented Leadership in the Johannine Situation— Abiding in the Truth versus Lesser Alternatives, Paul N. Anderson, p.5.

[16] "The Christian minister today, whether conducting some impressive rite of the church or preaching the Word or ministering to the poor or, perhaps, helping in some menial tasks around the home, has the opportunity at all times to make honorable the high calling of God. Ministerial Ethics and Etiquette, Lamar and Whitmore, revised edition 1950 Pierce and Smith, renewal 1978 by Nolan B. Harmon, Jr., (Abingdon Press), 1987, p.16.

[17] "The task of hermeneutical appropriation requires an integrative act of imagination...[W]henever we appeal to the authority of the [Bible], we are...placing our community's life imaginatively within the world articulated by the texts." Character Ethics and the New Testament Moral Dimensions of Scripture, Chapter 3 "The Reorienting Potential of Biblical Narrative for Christian Ethos, with Special Reference to Luke 7:36-50" by Elna Mouton, Robert L. Brawley, ed., quoting Richard Hays, Wesminister John Knox Press, Louisville-London, 2007, p.35.

Legal Example

[1] The legal effect of a marriage without a valid license is not the invalidation of the marriage, but rather, criminal sanctions against a minister who knowingly performs a marriage without a license... All states permit clergy to perform marriage ceremonies. However, some states permit only "ordained" or some other classification of clergy to perform marriage ceremonies. It is important for clergy to determine if they are legally authorized to perform marriages under applicable state law, and in addition to be aware of the legal qualifications for

marriage and any license and reporting requirements prescribed by state law. *Pastors Can Be Subject to Criminal Penalties for Not Complying with Legal Requirements for Valid Marriage under State Law*, Richard R. Hammar, Attorney, CPA, October 24, 2016; https://www.churchlawandtax.com/legal-developments/pastors-can-be-subject-to-criminal-penalties-for-not-complying-with-legal-requirements-for-valid-marriage-under-state-law/

[2] The legal code for ethical communication

1. Plagiarism "taking someone else's message and giving it as one's own" (Trull and Carter, 105).

2. Copyright

a. Be careful of the church's music file.

b. Be careful of the use of the photocopier.

c. Be careful in the tape ministry.

d. Be careful when performing cantatas and plays. Chuck Phelps, *Pastoral Ethics*, Publisher Central Africa Baptist College, p.52.

[3] *Legal Case Law Findings of 1st Amendment Freedom of Religion*

Rev. Anne Scharon v. St. Luke's Episcopal Presbyterian Hospitals, a Corporation, and The Rev. J. Edwin Heathcock

Issue: Rev. Anne Scharon was an ordained Episcopal priest employed by St. Luke's a Christian hospital as a chaplain. The immediate supervisor of Rev. Anne Scharon was the good Rev. J. Edwin Heathcock. Rev. Anne Scharon was fired by the Rev. J. Edwin Heathcock from her services as chaplain at St. Luke's Hospital. She filled a lawsuit for the violation of under Title VII of the Civil Rights Act of 1964, 42 U.S.C. § 2000e ("Title VII") and the Age Discrimination in Employment Act ("ADEA"), 29 U.S.C. § 630 et seq., respectively.

Rule: Generally: Title VII of the Civil Rights Act of 1964, 42 U.S.C. § 2000e ("Title VII") and the Age Discrimination in Employment Act ("ADEA"), 29 U.S.C. § 630 et seq., do not apply to matters concerning Religious Organizations and Religious context under the First Amendment.

Key: "To allow Scharon's case to continue would necessarily lead to the kind of inquiry into religious matters that the First Amendment forbids. It follows that the decision of the District Court based on the "excessive entanglement" test of Lemon (an Establishment Clause-type of analysis) must be affirmed. In addition, we believe that the Free Exercise Clause of the First Amendment also prohibits the courts from deciding cases such as this one. Personnel decisions by church-affiliated institutions affecting clergy are per se religious matters and cannot be reviewed by civil courts, for to review such decisions would require the courts to determine the meaning of religious doctrine and canonical law and to impose a secular court's view of whether in the context of the particular case religious doctrine and canonical law support the decision the church authorities have made. This is precisely the kind of judicial second-guessing of decision-making by religious organizations that the Free Exercise Clause forbids. *Rev. Anne Scharon v. St. Luke's Episcopal Presbyterian Hospitals,* a Corporation, and The Rev. J. Edwin Heathcock, 929 F.2d 360 (1991) citing, See *Serbian Eastern Orthodox Diocese for the United States and Canada v. Milivojevich, 426 U.S. 696, 713, 96 S.Ct. 2372, 2382, 49 L.Ed.2d 151 (1976); Minker, 894 F.2d at 1356-57; Natal v. Christian and Missionary Alliance, 878 F.2d 1575, 1576-77 (1st Cir.1989); Rayburn, 772 F.2d at 1167-69; Kaufmann v. Sheehan, 707 F.2d 355, 358-59 (8th Cir.1983); McClure v. Salvation Army, 460 F.2d 553, 558-61 (5th Cir.), cert. denied, 409 U.S. 896, 93 S.Ct. 132, 34 L.Ed.2d 153 (1972)."*

Key: "The first amendment provides that Congress may not interfere with the free exercise of religion. The free exercise clause bars enforcement of a statute whose application would directly affect religious beliefs. *Tilton v. Richardson, 403 U.S. 672, 689, 91 S.Ct. 2091, 2101, 29 L.Ed.2d 790 (1970);* see also *Wisconsin v. Yoder, 406 U.S. 205, 216, 92 S.Ct. 1526, 1533, 32 L.Ed.2d 15 (1971)* (refusing effect to a mandatory school attendance law as applied to Amish children). Appellant argues that since the Church has already declared its opposition to age discrimination in employment decisions in the Book of Discipline, it cannot now claim that it has a religious belief supporting age discrimination. If no religious beliefs are involved, he reasons, no first amendment rights are implicated. *Ralph L. MINKER, v. Baltimore Annual Conference Of United Methodist Church and Bishop Joseph A. Yeakel,* United States Court of Appeals, District of Columbia Circuit, 894 F.2d 1354 (1990), p.1355 at p.1356."

Conclusion Title VII: "Guided by the vast weight of judicial opinion preceding this case, the Court finds that the Free Exercise Clause precludes the application of Title VII to the instant controversy. Otherwise, a determination of whether plaintiff satisfied the requirements of her position and what motivated plaintiff's discharge from her chaplaincy would necessarily be undertaken, and such tasks would involve the type of excessive entanglement in religious matters that the First Amendment forbids."

Conclusion ADEA: "[T]he Court must conclude that, because Congress has not clearly expressed an intent to apply the ADEA to [the hiring of chaplains by church-operated hospitals], Congress did not contemplate that the Act would be [so applied]."

Conclusion: "Having found that the First Amendment precludes the application of Title VII to the instant case and that the ADEA does not apply, the Court grants defendants' motion for summary judgment. Defendants' motion for separate trials is denied as moot." *Rev. Anne Scharon v. St. Luke's Episcopal Presbyterian Hospitals, a Corporation, and The Rev. J. Edwin Heathcock, 736 F. Supp. 1018 (1990), pp.1018-1021.*

[4] *Dickinson v. United States, 346 U.S. 389-401 (1953).*

Case Brief Summary: In as Supreme Court of the United States case, a Jehovah's Witness refused the induction into military service, as one who was a minister and was seeking exemption under the statute's exemption clause from military service. The Jehovah's Witness refused to be inducted into the military and was found guilty of violating the draft statute. The Supreme Court reversed the conviction under the Freedom of Religion Clause found in the First Amendment of the United States Constitution.

Issue: The principal and decisive issue before us is whether there was a basis in fact for denying Dickinson's claim to a ministerial exemption under § 6 (g) of the Universal Military Training and Service Act, 62 Stat. 611, 50 U. S. App. § 456 (g).[1] After the selective service authorities denied his claim, Dickinson refused to submit to induction in defiance of his local board's induction order. For this refusal he was convicted, in the United States District Court for the Northern District of California,[2] of violating § 12 (a)[3] of the Act. T

Rule: Section 6 (g) is the source of the ministerial exemption. It provides, in pertinent part, that "Regular or duly ordained ministers of religion, as defined in this title, . . . shall be exempt from training and service (but not from registration) under this title." Section 16 (g) embodies Congress' definition of a "regular or duly ordained minister of religion."

"(1) The term `duly ordained minister of religion' means a person who has been ordained, in accordance with the ceremonial, ritual, or discipline of a church, religious sect, or organization established on the basis of a community of faith and belief, doctrines and practices of a religious character, to preach and to teach the doctrines of such church, sect, or organization and to administer the rites and ceremonies thereof in public worship, and who as his regular and customary vocation preaches and teaches the principles of religion and administers the ordinances of public worship as embodied in the creed or principles of such church, sect, or organization.

"(2) The term `regular minister of religion' means one who as his customary vocation preaches and teaches the principles of religion of a church, a religious sect, or organization of which he is a member, without having been formally ordained as a minister of religion, and who is recognized by such church, sect, or organization as a regular minister.

"(3) The term `regular or duly ordained minister of religion' does not include a person who irregularly or incidentally preaches and teaches the principles of religion of a church, religious sect, or organization and does not include any person who may have been duly ordained a minister in accordance with the ceremonial, rite, or discipline of a church, religious sect or organization, but who does not regularly, as a vocation, teach and preach the principles of religion and administer the ordinances of public worship as embodied in the creed or principles of his church, sect, or organization." Registrants who satisfy this definition are entitled to be classified IV-D. 32 C. F. R. § 1622.43.

Conclusion: Local boards are not courts of law and are not bound by traditional rules of evidence; they are given great leeway in hearing and considering a variety of material as evidence.[8] If the facts are disputed the board bears the ultimate responsibility for resolving the conflict—the courts will not interfere. Nor will the courts apply a test of "substantial evidence." However, the courts may properly insist that there be some proof that is incompatible with the registrant's proof of exemption. The local board may question a registrant under oath, subpoena witnesses to testify, and require both registrant and witnesses to produce documents. 32 C. F. R. § 1621.15. The board is authorized to obtain information from local, state, and national welfare and governmental agencies. 32 C. F. R. § 1621.14. The registrant's admissions, testimony of other witnesses, frequently unsolicited evidence from a registrant's neighbors, or information obtained from other agencies may produce dissidence which the boards are free to resolve. Absent such admissions or other evidence, the local boards may call on the investigative agencies of the federal government, as they would if a registrant were suspected of perjury. But when the uncontroverted evidence supporting a registrant's claim places him prima facie within the statutory exemption, dismissal of the claim solely on the basis of suspicion and speculation is both contrary to the spirit of the Act and foreign to our concepts of justice. Reversed. *Dickinson v. United States, 346 U.S. 389-401 (1953).*

Rule 1.2 Scope of Ministry Duties To Be Performed, Licenses And Ordination Require In Ministering

(a)   Subject to paragraphs (c) and (d), a cleric shall abide by the Word of God concerning the objectives of ministry service and as required by Rule 1.4, shall consult in prayer leading of the LORD, as well as with the person being ministered unto to determine the means by which the ministry is to be provided. A cleric may take such action on behalf of the PINOMS as authorized by their ordination authority, as well as that which is implied authority to carry out the ministry service. A cleric shall abide by the PINOMS desires to receive the ministry offered.

(b)   A cleric's ministry service to a congregant, or PINOMS including ministry service by appointment, does not constitute an endorsement of the person's political economic, social, or moral views or activities.

(c)   A cleric may limit the scope of ministry services if the limitation is reasonable under the circumstances and the congregant or PINOMS gives informed consent to the cleric.

(d) A cleric shall not counsel a congregant, or PINOMS to engage, or assist a congregant, or PINOMS, in conduct that the cleric knows is criminal, fraudulent, or adulterous, but a cleric may discuss the spiritual, legal, congregational, community, and social consequences of any proposed course of conduct with a congregant, or PINOMS, or assist a congregant, or person in need of counsel to make a good faith effort to determine the validity, scope, meaning, or applications of the Spiritual, the community's legal law, and the doctrine of Christ Jesus.

Comment

Allocation of Authority Between the Performance, Licensing And Ordination Require In Ministering

[1] Paragraph (a) confers upon the congregant, or PINOMS the ultimate authority of determine the purposes to be served by the cleric's ministry service, within the limits imposed by the Word of GOD, the governing body of the church, the congregation's bylaws, or the ordination obtained by the cleric, and the cleric's obligations as a clergy with Spiritual integrity. The decisions specified in paragraph (a), such as whether to minister any ministry service, must also be made by the congregant, or the PINOMS. See Rule 1.4(a)(1) for the cleric's duty to communicate with the congregant, or the PINOMS about ministry service decisions. With respect to the means by which the congregant's or the person in need of service's objectives are to be pursued, the cleric shall consult with the congregant or the PINOMS as required by Rule 1.2(a)(2) and may take such ministry service actions as is Spiritually, and impliedly authorized to carry out the ministry service.

[2] On occasion, however, a cleric and the congregant, or the PINOMS may disagree about the means to be used to accomplish the congregant's objectives, or the person's objectives who is in need of ministry services. Congregants, and persons in need of ministry services normally defer to the special knowledge, standards of ordination, and skills of the cleric with respect to Spiritual, and ministry service matters. Conversely, the cleric usually defers to the congregant, or the PINOMS regarding such questions as the availability for the hours of meeting, the mode of communications, and the details about the third party or parties, which may be affected by the ministry service provided by the cleric to the congregant, or the PINOMS. Because of the varied nature of the matters about which a cleric and a congregant, or a PINOMS might have conflicts in reference to agreement and because the actions in question may implicate the interests of a church body, a tribunal, a denomination body, or other persons, this rule does not prescribe how such disagreements are to be resolved. Other Spiritual means, or bylaws, or governing instructions, or avenues by be applicable and should be consulted by the cleric. The cleric should also consult with the congregant, or the PINOMS and seek a mutual acceptance resolution of the disagreement. If such efforts are unavailable and the lawyer has a fundamental disagreement with the congregant, or the PINOMS, the cleric may refer the congregant or the PINOMS to another cleric for assistance or withdraw entirely from providing the ministry services. See Rule 1.16(b)(4). Conversely, the congregant, or the person seeking ministry services may resolve the disagreement by seeking another cleric, or by discharging the cleric of the ministry services in question. See Rule 1.16(a)(3).

[3] At the outset of the ministry services, the congregant, or the PINOMS may authorize the cleric to take specific action on the congregant's or the PINOMS behalf without further consultation. Absent a material change in circumstances and subject to Rule 1.4, a cleric may rely on such an advance authorization. The congregant, or the person in need of services

51

may, however, revoke such ministry services authority at any time.

[4] In ministry matters in which the congregant, or the person who sought, or is seeking ministry services appears to be suffering from diminished capacity, the cleric's Spiritual duties to abide in the congregant's or the person seeking, or who sought ministry services decisions to be guided by reference to Rule 1.14.

Independence From Congregants' or Person whose seeking Ministry Views or Activities.

[5] Spiritual Cleric ministry services should not be denied to people who are unable to tithe, or whose cause is controversial or the subject of popular disapproval within the church, congress, or authoritative body. By the very same token, providing ministry service to a congregant, or a PINOMS does not provide Spiritual approval of the congregant's or the PINOMS's views, actions, words, deeds, ungodly beliefs, or activities.

Agreement Limiting Scope of Representation

[6] The Spiritual objective or scope of ministry services to be provided by a cleric may be limited based upon the need of the person being ministered to by agreement with the congregant, or the PINOMS or the terms under which the cleric's ministry services are made available to the person seeking the cleric's ministry services. When a cleric has been obtained by a church body, a governing body, or district of authority to counsel a cleric, or a leader of a church, or church member in extraordinary circumstances to minister to the PINOMS by the cleric, the ministry service may be limited to the matters of the extraordinary circumstances. A limited ministry service by the cleric may be appropriate because the congregant, or the PINOMS has limited ministry needs, with certain objectives for the cleric's ministry service. Further, the conditions upon which the ministry service is undertaken may exclude specific means

that might otherwise be used to accomplish the congregant's, or the cleric's (who is in need of ministry service), or the church leaders', or any other person's (one in need of ministry services) required ministry needs under the extraordinary objectives and standards. Such limitations may exclude actions that the congregant, or PINOMS thinks are too extravagant, overbroad, or that the cleric regards as sinful, repugnant, or even impudent under the doctrine of Jesus Christ.

[7] Although this rule affords the cleric and the congregant or the PINOMS a great deal of latitude to limit the ministry service scope, the limitation must not interfere with the Spiritual needs of the congregant, or the PINOMS, and it must be reasonable under the circumstances. For instance, a congregant's or the person's (who is in need of ministry services) objective is limited to securing general information about the Word of God the congregant or the PINOMS will be limited to a brief sanctuary meeting, or telephone consultation. Such a limitation, however, would not be sufficient or even reasonable if the time allotted was not sufficient to yield Spiritual advice upon which the congregant, or the PINOMS could put to immediate use, or rely upon. Although an agreement for a limited ministry service consultation does not exempt a cleric from the God given duty to provide competent Spiritual ministry services, the limitation is a factor to be considered when determining the wisdom, knowledge, skill, thoroughness, training, experience, and preparation reasonably necessary for the ministry services. See Rule 1.1.

Criminal, Fraudulent, & Prohibited Ministry Assistance and Services

[9] Paragraph (d) counsels, restricts, and prohibits a cleric from knowingly providing counseling or assisting a cleric to commit a crime or fraud. This prohibition, however, does not preclude the cleric from giving Spiritual advice, or a truthful opinion about the actual consequences that appear likely to grow from negative seeds sown by the congregant, or the PINOMS conduct,

thoughts, or actions. Nor does the fact that the congregant or the PINOMS uses the counseling, or assistance of the cleric in a course of action that is criminal or fraudulent of itself, make a cleric party to the course of action. There is a critical distinction between presenting an analysis or providing Spiritual advice regarding the aspects of questionable conduct and recommending the means by which a sinful act, a crime or fraudulent activity might be committed with impunity.

[10] When the congregant's or the person's (the PINOMS) course of action has already begun and is continuing, the cleric's responsibility is especially delicate. The cleric is required to avoid assisting the congregant, or the PINOMS. For instance, by participating in signing, or providing church records such as baptismal documents, marriage documents, witnessing the signing of a fraudulent will, which the cleric knows are fraudulent or by suggesting how the wrongdoing might be concealed. The cleric may not continue assisting a congregant, or the PINOMS assistance in conduct that the cleric originally supposed was not sinful, legal, and proper, but then discovers is sinful, illegal, and improper. The cleric must, therefore, withdraw from the Spiritual ministry service that was being given to the congregant, or the PINOMS matters. See Rule 1.16(a). In some instances, withdrawal alone might be insufficient. It may be necessary for the cleric to give notice of the fact of withdrawal to the parties involved, and disaffirm any Spiritual advice, or opinion, document, affirmation, or similar items, which were misused, deceitfully taken advantage of, or that were used in any illegal scheme by the congregant, or PINOMS.

[11] Where the congregant, or the PINOMS assistance is a fiduciary, the cleric may be charged with special obligations in dealing with a beneficiary.

[12] Paragraph (d) applies regardless of whether the defrauded party is a party to the transactions. Hence, a cleric must not participate in a transaction to effectuate sinful, criminal or fraudulent avoidance of tax liability, by providing false evidence

of donations to the church, or overestimating the value of the donation, or donations. Paragraph (d) recognizes that determining the validity or interpretation of a statute or regulation may require the course of action of the cleric seeking legal representation. The cleric should leave the determination of if the cleric's actions or the cleric's future course of actions involved or involves disobedience, or the correction to be compliant to the statute or regulation or the interpretation placed upon cleric and church by the governmental authorities.

[13] If a cleric comes to know or reasonably should have known that a congregant, or PINOMS expects assistance not permitted by the Doctrine of Jesus Christ, The Commandments of GOD, the Church Documents, and these rules of conduct of a cleric or other law or if the cleric intends to act contrary to the congregant's or the PINOMS desires regarding the scope of ministry service, the cleric must consult with the congregant, or the PINOMS regarding the limitations on the cleric's conduct. See Rule 1.4(a)(5).

Biblical Reference

[1] 11 And He Himself gave some to be apostles, some prophets, some evangelists, and some pastors and teachers, 12 for the equipping of the saints for the work of ministry, for the edifying of the body of Christ.

[2] "Do not neglect the gift that is in you, which was given you by prophecy with the laying on of the hands of the eldership" (1 Timothy 4:14).

[3] For even the Son of Man came not to be served but to serve others and to give his life as a ransom for many (Mark 10:45).

Christian Ethical Commentary

[1] J.M. Champlin and C.D. Champlin provide the definition of a visionary leader is as follows: "someone who touches another's future." *Champlin, J.M., & Champlin, C.D. (1993). The visionary leader. New York: Crossroad Publishing Company.*

[2] The leadership of a church should resemble not the leader, but it is to resemble that of Christ leading His flock. David Horton stated it this way for us to understand: "leadership occurs when one or more persons engage with others in such a way that leaders and followers raise one another to higher levels of motivation and morality." David Horton, *The Portable Seminary*. Baker Publishing Group, Grand Rapids, Michigan: Bethany House Publishers. (2006) (ed).

[3] It is more or less a truism that an idea held in mind tends to express itself in action. Especially this is true if the idea carries with it an emotional fringe. We cannot properly appreciate and understand what is going on in objective experience unless we somehow get back of it to the great world of ideas –intangible, unseen –which controls human activity. Howard Thurman, "College and Color," (April 1924), in *The Papers of Howard Washington Thurman, Vol 1, 37*.

[4] "The do's and don'ts of transitions (John R. Cionca, *Red Light, Green Light: Discerning The Time for a Change in Ministry*, Baker Books)

    1. Do

        a. Develop a vision

        b. Set realistic expectations

        c. Build relationships

        d. Work hard

        e. Maintain regular office hours

        f. Schedule family time

        g. Protect your spouse from unrealistic parish expectations

        h. Focus member on doable tasks

      i. Celebrate successes

      j. Attend social gatherings

      k. Schedule open houses

      l. Establish a disciplined study pattern

      m. Implement change carefully

      n. Retain present leadership

      o. Practice ministry by walking around

      p. Participate in ministerial fellowship

      q. Maintain a sense of humor

2. Don't

      a. Assume what you did elsewhere will work here

      b. Criticize your predecessor

      c. Immediately "kill" programs

      d. Be a revolutionary

      e. Recycle old sermons

      f. Send "you" messages—emphasize "we & us"

      g. Keep hidden agenda

      h. Expect everyone to like you

      i. Play favorites

      j. Engage in power struggles

      k. Accept outside opportunities your first year.
Chuck Phelps, *Pastoral Ethics*, Publisher Central Africa Baptist College, pp.56-57 quoting John R. Cionca, *Red*

Light, Green Light: Discerning The Time for a Change in Ministry, Baker Books.

Legal Example

[1] *Ralph L. MINKER, v. Baltimore Annual Conference Of United Methodist Church and Bishop Joseph A. Yeakel*

"The decision to appoint a minister is uniquely within a church's ecclesiastical discretion. We find the district court properly concluded that it may not interpret a church's spiritual policies without interfering with the free exercise of religion. But the first amendment does not afford defenses against promises made and contracts formed. A church, like any other employer, is bound to perform its promissory obligations in accord with contract law. Pastor Minker is entitled to rely upon his employer's representations and to enforce them in a secular court. It is possible that the first amendment's prohibition against proceedings that would create excessive entanglements with religious beliefs will make appellant's task at trial more difficult. But these difficulties do not eliminate appellant's right to enforce his employment contract." *Ralph L. MINKER, v. Baltimore Annual Conference Of United Methodist Church and Bishop Joseph A. Yeakel, United States Court of Appeals, District of Columbia Circuit, 894 F.2d 1354 (1990), p1355 at p.1362.*

Rule 1.3 Devoted Service

A cleric shall act with reasonable devoted faithfulness and promptness in ministry service unto a congregant, or a PINOMS.

Comment

[1] A cleric should pursue a matter on behalf of a congregant, or a PINOMS despite opposition, obstruction, or personal inconvenience to the cleric, and take whatever Christian ethical measures are required to provide ministry service for a congregant's or PINOMS cause or endeavor. A cleric must also act with commitment, devotion, faithfulness, and dedication in the ministry service of the congregant, or the person in need of

services with anointing, zeal, skill, and intercession on the congregant's or person in need of service's behalf. A cleric is not bound, however, to press for every advantage that might be realized for a congregant, or a PINOMS if the cleric does not have the skill to provide the ministry service. For instance, a cleric may have authority to exercise ministry discretion in determining the means by which a matter should be pursued. See Rule 1.2. The cleric's duty to act with reasonable Spiritual diligence does not require the use of offensive tactics or preclude the treating of all persons involved in the ministry process with courtesy, love, and respect.

[2] A cleric's ministry service and labor of love, must not be of the sought, which caused the cleric burnout, or a feeling of being overwhelmed, therefore, the ministry load must be controlled so that each ministry matter can be handled with the devotion, faithfulness, and love that is needed to handle the matter completely.

[3] Perhaps no ministry shortcoming is more widely injurious more than procrastination. A congregant's interest, or the person's interest of the PINOMS often can be adversely affected by the passage of time or the change of conditions: in extreme instances, as when a minister, or cleric overlooks a serious ministry need, as the ministry need escalated into something more serious. Even when the congregant's, or the person's (who is in need of ministry) interest are not affected in substance, however, unreasonable delay can cause a congregant, or a person being ministered to, needless anxiety and undermine confidence in the Church's, the minister's, or the cleric's trustworthiness. A cleric's duty to act with reasonable faithfulness, devotion, and promptness, however, does not preclude the cleric from agreeing to a reasonable request for a delaying the ministry service unto the congregant, or the PINOMS.

[4] Unless the relationship is terminated as provided in Rule 1.16, a cleric should carry through to conclusion all matters undertaken from a congregant, or a PINOMS. If a cleric's

ministry service is limited to a specific matter, the relationship terminates when the specific matter has been resolved, or completed. If a cleric has served a congregant, or a PINOMS over a substantial period in a variety of matters, the congregant or person in need of services sometimes assume that the cleric will continue to serve on a continuing basis unless the cleric gives notice of a transfer, or different ministry assignment, or withdrawal. Doubt about whether a congregant-cleric or PINOMS-cleric relationship still exists should be clarified by the cleric, preferably in person, so that the congregant, or PINOMS will not mistakenly suppose the cleric is looking after the congregant's or the person's ministry need when the cleric has ceased to do so. For instance, if a cleric has minister on behalf of the congregant, or the PINOMS behalf at a tribunal, or a church counsel, or before an authoritative board, which produced an adverse result for the congregant, or the person's and the cleric and the congregant, or the PINOMS have not discussed that the cleric is going to seeking an appeal, or exhaust all possible remedies available before relinquishing responsibility for the matter. See Rule1.4(a)(2). Whether the cleric is obligated to pursue the appeal for the congregant, or the PINOMS depends on the scope of the representation the cleric has agreed to provide to the congregant, or the PINOMS. See Rule 1.2.

[5] To prevent neglect of congregant's or a person who is in need of ministry matters in the event of a death of a cleric who was providing ministry services, the new cleric must prepare a plan to review any records, contact the congregant or PINOMS, to get up to speed on assisting them in their ministry need.

Biblical Reference

[1] But a lover of hospitality, a lover of good men, sober, just, holy, temperate (Titus 1:8).

[2] Holding fast the faithful word as he/she has been taught, that he/she may be able by sound doctrine both to exhort and to convince the gainsayers. (Titus 1:9).

[3] A bishop then must be blameless, the husband of one wife, vigilant, sober, of good behavior, given to hospitality, apt to teach (1 Tim 3:2).

Christian Ethical Commentary

[1] The servant-leader is servant first ... It begins with the natural feeling that one wants to serve, to serve first. Then conscious choice brings one to aspire to lead. That person is sharply different from one who is leader first, perhaps because of the need to assuage an unusual power drive or to acquire material possessions ... The leader-first and the servant-first are two extreme types. Between them there are shadings and blends that are part of the infinite variety of human nature. Robert K. Greenleaf, *The Servant as Leader*, an essay, 1970.

[2] In sum, different from the traditional trait, behavioral, situational, and contingency leadership models, SL [Servant Leader] focuses on (a) the humble and ethical use of power as a servant leader, (b) cultivating a genuine relationship between leaders and followers, and (c) creating a supportive and positive work environment. However, in terms of the actual exercise of leadership, servant leaders are free to incorporate the positive aspects of all other leadership models except command-and-control dictatorship. P.T.P. Wong, 'Best practices in servant leadership', *Servant Leadership Research Roundtable – July 2007*, School of Global Leadership & Entrepreneurship, Regent University, Virginia Beach, VA., 2007, (p. 3).

[3] Robert K. Greenleaf states that there are 10 characteristics of the Servant Leader and they are as follows: listening, sympathy, healing, awareness, persuasion, conceptualization, foresight, stewardship, commitment to the growth of people and building of the community. Robert K. Greenleaf, *Servant leadership: A journey into the nature of legitimate power and greatness (25th anniversary ed.)* (L.C. Spears, Ed.). (Paulist Press, New Jersey, 2002), (pp. 30-52).

[4] [The Servant Leader] shepherd refers to a keeper of sheep. This is the person who tends, feeds, or guards the flocks. The Hebrew word for shepherding is often translated as 'feeding' as it is impressed by the next statement, 'I shall not want' or 'I shall lack nothing' – alluding to the fact that the Psalmist means he will lack neither in this life nor in the next. Kelebogile Thomas Resane, 2014, 'Leadership for the church: The shepherd model', HTS Teologiese Studies/Theological Studies 70(1), Art.# 2045. https://doi.org/10.4102/hts.v70i1.2045, (p. 5).

[5] Greenleaf in the Institution As Servant wrote: This is my thesis: caring for persons, the more able and the less able serving each other, is the rock upon which a good society is built. Whereas, until recently, caring was largely person to person, now most of it is mediated through institutions – often large, complex, powerful, impersonal; not always competent; sometimes corrupt. If a better society is to be built, one that is more just and more loving, one that provides greater creative opportunity for its people, then the most open course is to raise both the capacity to serve and the very performance as servant of existing major institutions by new regenerative forces operating within them. L. C. Spears, 'The understanding and practice of servant-leadership', in L.C. Spears & M. Lawrence (eds.), Practicing servant leadership: Succeeding through trust, bravery, and forgiveness, pp. 9–24, Jossey-Bass School of Leadership Studies, Regent University, Virginia Beach, VA., (2004), p. 7.

Legal Example

[1] F.G. v. Reverend Alex Macdonell, In His Capacity As Former Rector, And Reverend Fletcher et al

"The fiduciary's obligations to the dependent party include a duty of loyalty and a duty to exercise reasonable skill and care. Restatement (Second) of Trusts §§ 170, 174 (1959). Accordingly, the fiduciary is liable for harm resulting from a breach of the duties imposed by the existence of such a relationship. Restatement (Second) of Torts § 874 (1979). Trust and confidence are vital to the counseling relationship between parishioner and pastor. By accepting a parishioner for counseling, a pastor also accepts the responsibility of a fiduciary. Often, parishioners who seek pastoral counseling are troubled and vulnerable. Sometimes, they turn to their pastor in the belief that their religion is the most likely source to sustain them in their time of trouble. The pastor knows, or should know of the parishioner's trust and the pastor's dominant position." *F.G. v. Reverend Alex Macdonell, In His Capacity As Former Rector, And Reverend Fletcher Harper, In His Capacity As Rector Of All Saints' Episcopal Church, Bergenfield, New Jersey And St. Luke's Episcopal Church, Haworth, New Jersey, The Supreme Court of New Jersey, 150 N.J. 550 (1997), p.564.*

Rule 1.4 Communication

(a)   A cleric shall:

(1)   Promptly inform the congregant, or the PINOMS of any decision or circumstance with respect to which the congregant's or the person's informed consent, as define in Rule 1.0(f), is required by these rules;

(2)   Reasonably consult with the congregant or PINOMS about the means by which the congregant's or person's objectives are to be accomplished;

(3)   Keep the congregant or person who is in need of ministry reasonably informed about the status of the matter;

(4)   Promptly comply with reasonable request for information; and

(5)   Consult with the congregant or the PINOMS about any relevant limitation on the cleric's conduct when the cleric knows that the congregant or the PINOMS expects ministry assistance not permitted by Christian doctrine or the rules of Ethical Behavior, or Christian Conduct or other governing body rules.

(b)   A cleric shall explain a matter to extend reasonably necessary to permit the congregant or the PINOMS to make informed decisions regarding the representation.

Comment

[1] Reasonable communication between the cleric and the congregant, or the PINOMS is necessary for the congregant or the PINOMS effectively to participate in the ministry services provided by the cleric.

[2] If these Ethical Rules suggest that a particular decision about the ministry service about the ministry service be made by the congregant, or the PINOMS, paragraph (a)(1) requires that the cleric promptly consult with and secure the congregant's or the person's consent prior to taking action unless prior discussions with the congregant, or the PINOMS have resolved what action the congregant, or the PINOMS wants the cleric to take.

[3] Paragraph (a)(2) requires the cleric to reasonably consult with the congregant, or the PINOMS assistance about the means to be used to accomplish the congregant's or person's objectives. In some situations – depending on both the importance of the action under consideration and the feasibility of consulting with the congregant or the PINOMS – this duty will require consultation prior to taking action. In other circumstances, such as during ecclesiastical polity governance, or authoritative tribunals, or congregational meetings when an immediate decision must be made, the urgency of the situation may require that cleric, who is counseling, or providing ministry service of another cleric, a congregant, or PINOMS to act without prior consultation. In such cases the cleric must nonetheless act reasonably to inform the cleric being given ministry service, or the congregant, or the PINOMS of actions the cleric has taken on the cleric being given ministry service, or the congregant, or the PINOMS of actions the cleric has taken on the cleric's being given ministry service, or the congregants, or the persons in need of ministry behalf. Additionally, paragraph (a)(3) requires that the

cleric keep the cleric being given ministry service, or the congregant, or the PINOMS reasonably informed about the status of the matter, such as significant developments affecting the timing or the substance of the ministry service.

[4] A cleric's regular communication with congregants or persons in need of ministry will minimize the occasions on which a congregant, or PINOMS will need to request information concerning the ministry service. When a congregant or PINOMS makes a reasonable request for information, however, paragraph (a)(4) requires prompt compliance with the request, or if a prompt response is not feasible, that the cleric, or a member of the cleric's ministry staff, acknowledge receipt of the request and advise the congregant or the PINOMS when a response may be expected. A cleric should promptly response to or acknowledge congregant or PINOMS communications.

Explaining Matters

[5] The congregant, or PINOMS should have sufficient information to participate spiritually, and intelligently in decisions concerning the objectives of the ministry services being provided by the cleric, and the means by which they are to be pursued, to the extent the congregant, or PINOMS is willing and able to do so. Adequacy of communications depends in part on the kind of counseling, or ministry services being provided, or the assistance that is involved. For instance, when there is a time to explain a proposal made to further the ministry service, the cleric should review all important provisions with the congregant, or the PINOMS before proceeding to use the elements, or items, which would further the ministry services to the benefit of the congregant or the person in need of services. The guiding principle is that the cleric should fulfill reasonable congregant or the person in need of services expectations for information consistent with the duty to act in the congregant's or person's best interest, and the congregant's and person's overall requirements as to the character of the ministry services being provided by the cleric. In certain circumstances, such as when a

cleric asks a congregant, or PINOMS to consent to a ministry service affected by a conflict of interest, such as between husband and wife, the congregant or the person receiving ministry services must give informed consent, as defined in Rule 1.0(f).

[6] Ordinarily, the information to be provided is that appropriate for a congregant or PINOMS who is a comprehending and responsible child of GOD. However, fully informing the congregant or the PINOMS according to this standard may be impracticable. For instance, where the congregant, or the PINOMS where the congregant or the PINOMS is a child or one who is challenged in their mental capacity, or who suffers from a diminished capacity. See Rule 1.14. When the congregant or the PINOMS is a church or Christian organization or group, it is often impracticable or inappropriate to inform every one of its members about the ministry services being performed; ordinarily, the cleric should address the communications to either an appropriate official, or officials, or an elected representative by the organization, group, or church. See Rule 1.13. Where many routine matters are involved, a system of limited or occasional updating may be arranged with the organization, group, or church, or congregant, or the PINOMS.

Withholding Information

[7] For clerics engaged in counseling with clinical pastoral education credit, or credits there are confidences which will be provide to conduct the clinical counseling. In some circumstances, a cleric may be justified in delaying transmission of information when the congregant, or PINOMS would be likely to react imprudently to an immediate communication. Thus, a cleric might withhold a psychiatric diagnosis of a congregant, or PINOMS when the examining psychiatrist indicates that disclosure would harm the congregant, or PINOMS. A cleric may not withhold information to serve the cleric's own interest or convenience or the interests or convenience of another person. Rules or denominational articles

or codes or even orders governing administration may provide that information supplied to a cleric may not be disclosed

In some circumstances, a cleric may be justified in delaying transmission of information when the congregant, or the PINOMS needs would be likely to react imprudently to an immediate communication. Thus, a cleric might withhold a medical diagnosis shared with the cleric by a family members, or shared with direct knowledge by a cleric who is a chaplain in the hospital, and who is part of a medical team working with a patient, when the disclosure would harm the congregant, patient, or the PINOMS. A cleric may not withhold information to serve the cleric's own interest or convenience or the interests or convenience of another person. Rules or governing body mandates may provide that information supplied to a cleric may not be disclosed to the congregant. Rule 3.4 directs compliance with such rules or requirement of the doctrinal beliefs and established Spiritual guides.

Biblical Reference

[1] Only let your conversation be as it becometh the gospel of Christ: that whether I come and see you, or else be absent, I may hear of your affairs, that ye stand fast in one spirit, with one mind striving together for the faith of the gospel (Philippians 4:27).

Christian Ethical Commentary

[1] Meeting People Where They Are: "It follows that the mood for each of us must be one of reverence —reverence toward one's self, towards one's fellowmen and towards life itself. This mood expresses itself in respect for personality —and what is that —it is meeting people where they are, and treating them there."
Howard Thurman, "The White Problem" (1944), *The Papers of Howard Washington Thurman: Volume 3: The Bold Adventure, September 1943–May1949*, edited by Walter Earl Fluker, et al.(Columbia, SC: The University of South Carolina Press, 2015), 28.

[2] "It follows that the mood for each of us must be one of reverence – reverence toward one's self, towards one's fellowmen and towards life itself. This mood expresses itself in respect for personality – and what is that – it is meeting people where they are, and treating them there." Howard Thurman, "The White Problem" (1944), *The Papers of Howard Washington Thurman: Volume 3: The Bold Adventure, September 1943 – May 1949*, edited by Walter Earl Fluker, et al. (Columbia, SC: The University of South Carolina Press, 2015), p. 28. *(*A Warning of the oxymoron of White Christian Nationalism)*

Legal Example

[1] *Julie Mabus v. St. James Episcopal Church, Episcopal Diocese of Mississippi, Inc., and Jerry Mcbride*

"Julie Mabus filed suit in the First Judicial District of Hinds County Circuit Court against St. James Episcopal Church, Protestant Episcopal Church in the Diocese of Mississippi, and Jerry McBride (a former priest at St. James). Julie asserted seven separate causes of action against the defendants: breach of fiduciary duty, fraudulent concealment, negligent misrepresentation, invasion of privacy, negligent infliction of emotional distress, negligent retention/supervision, and clergy malpractice. This lawsuit is based upon McBride's participation in the surreptitious tape recording of a conversation between Julie, McBride, and Julie's then-husband, Ray Mabus. All defendants filed a motion to dismiss all claims, which was denied by the trial court, the Honorable L. Breland Hilburn, presiding. In a 4-4-1 decision, this Court denied Defendants' Petition For Interlocutory Appeal. Mabus v. St. James Episcopal Church, No.2001-M-01558 (Miss. Nov. 29, 2001). Defendants' petition for certiorari to the United States Supreme Court was denied. *Protestant Episcopal Church v. Mabus, 535 U.S. 1054, 122 S.Ct. 1910, 152 L.Ed.2d 821 (2002)...* ¶ 43. For the reasons herein stated, we unhesitatingly affirm in toto the trial court's judgments and remand this case to the Circuit Court of Hinds County, First Judicial District, for appropriate disposition of Julie's claim of fraudulent concealment against Jerry McBride, individually." *Julie Mabus v. St. James Episcopal Church, Episcopal Diocese of Mississippi, Inc., and Jerry Mcbride, 884 So.2d 747, (2004) Pp. 750, 751, 765.*

Rule 1.5 Clergy Fees And Payments Made With Clear Expectations Commiserate of Reasonable Duties

(a)   A cleric shall not make an agreement for, charge, or collect an unreasonable fee or an unreasonable amount for ministry expenses needed for performance of ministry services. The factors to be considered in determining the reasonableness of a ministry service fee include the following:

(1)   the time of the ministry service required, the novelty or the difficulty of the questions involved, and the skill requisite to perform the ministry services properly and according to ordinances, and doctrinal instructions;

(2)   the likelihood, of apparent to the congregant, or the PINOMS, that the acceptance of the particular ministry service will not preclude the cleric from ministering unto others, although not at the same time for specific services such as weddings, and funerals (Home goings);

(3)   the ministry service fee customarily charged in the denomination, or for the non-denominational, in the locality for similar ministry services;

(4)   the amount involved and the Spiritual blessings obtained;

(5)   the time limitations imposed by the congregant, the PINOMS, or the venue, or the church, or the location's authoritative body or circumstances;

(6)   the nature and length of the ministry service relationship with the congregant, or the PINOMS;

(7)   the experience, reputation, ordination, and ability of the cleric or clerics performing the ministry services; and

(8)   whether the cleric's fees are fixed, or contingent upon the giving heart of the congregant, or PINOMS, or the organization.

(b) The scope of the ministry service and the basis or rate of the ministry fee and expenses for which the congregant, or the PINOMS will be responsible shall be communicated to the congregant, or the PINOMS. In some instances, such as weddings, or funerals (Home goings), the fee arrangement should be placed in writing, before or within a reasonable time after cleric and party or parties agree upon the ministry service to be performed, except when the cleric will charge a regularly set price by the church, governing body, or the guidelines of the denomination, or the such, which is an established or set basic rate. Any changes in the basis or rate of the ministry fee or ministry expenses shall also be communicated to the congregant, or the PINOMS. Except as provided below, ministry service fee payments received by a cleric before the ministry services have been rendered are presumed to be unearned, and shall be held in the trustee account, or the church's pastoral account pursuant to Rule 1.15.

(1) A cleric may charge a flat ministry service fee for specified ministry services, which constitute complete ministry service payment for those services may be paid in whole or in part in advance of the cleric performing or providing the ministry services. If agreed to in advance in a written ministry service fee agreement signed by the congregant, or the PINOMS, a flat ministry service fee shall be considered to be the cleric's property upon the payment of the ministry service fee, subject to refund as described in Rule 1.5(b)(3). Such as written ministry service fee agreement shall notify the congregant, or the PINOMS:

(i)   of the nature and scope of the ministry services to be provided;

(ii)   of the total amount of the ministry service fee and the terms of the ministry service payment;

(iii)   that the ministry service fee will not be held in the church's pastoral or minister's account until earned;

(iv)   that the congregant, or the PINOMS has the right to terminate the purpose for which the ministry service is to be provided, such as with wedding plan changes; and

(v)   the congregant, or the PINOMS will be entitled to a refund in full, or in part if the agreed upon ministry services are not performed, or not fully provided, or which have been partially performed or provided.

(2) A cleric may charge a ministry service fee to ensure the cleric's availability to the congregant, or the PINOMS during a specified period or on a specified matter in addition to and apart from any compensation for ministry services performed. Such a cleric availability ministry fee shall be reasonable in amount and shall be communicated with a written signed agreement by the congregant, and the PINOMS, for matters such as weddings, or other specific ministry request, along with the cleric's signature. The writing shall clearly state that the ministry service fee is for availability only and that ministry service fees for ministry services will be charged separately. An availability fee may be considered to be the cleric's property upon the payment of the ministry availability fee, subject to refund in whole or in part should the cleric not be available as promised.

(3) Ministry service fee agreements may not describe any ministry fee as nonrefundable or earned upon receipt buy may describe the advance fee payment as the cleric's property subject to refund. Whenever a congregant has paid a flat ministry service fee or an availability for ministry fee pursuant to Rule 1.5(b)(1) or (2) and the cleric's relationship with the congregant, or the PINOMS specific purpose relationship is terminated before the ministry service fee is fully earned, the cleric shall refund to the congregant, or the PINOMS the unearned portion of the

ministry service fee. If the congregant disputes the amount of the ministry service fee that has been earned by the cleric, the cleric shall take reasonable and prompt action to resolve the dispute.

(c) A ministry service fee may be contingent on the fulfillment of the ministry service to be performed in a matter for which the ministry service is rendered, except in a matter in which a contingent fee is prohibited by paragraph (d) or other governing law, or doctrine. A contingent ministry fee is to be in writing signed by the congregant, and shall state the method by which the fee is to be determined, and under what circumstances the contingency ministry fee is to be applicable. For instance, if a venue is available, or if there is an inclement weather issue, which bars the ministry service from being performed. The contingency agreement must clearly notify the congregant, or the PINOMS of any expenses for which the congregant or the PINOMS will be liable whether or not the congregant cancels or postpones the ministry service need. Upon the conclusion, or the reestablishing of the contingency ministry service fee matter, the cleric shall provide the congregant, or the PINOMS with a written statement stating the outcome of the matter and, if there is a refund show the remittance to the congregant, or the PINOMS and the method of its determination.

(d) A cleric shall not enter into an arrangement for, charge, or collect ministry service fees:

> (1) any ministry service fee in counseling in a domestic relations matter, the ministry service payment or amount of which is contingent upon the securing of a reconciliation or upon spousal financial support during a separation, or any property agreements if there is reconciliation;
>
> or
>
> (2) a contingent fee for ministry services rendered unto an incarcerated person to pray for their release.

(e) A division of a ministry service fee between clerics who are not in the same ministry may be made only if:

(1) the division of the ministry service fee is in proportion to the services performed by each cleric or each cleric assumes joint ministry responsibility for the ministry service;

(2) the congregant, or the person receiving ministry services agrees to the arrangement, including the share each cleric will receive, and that agreement is confirmed in writing; and

(3) the total ministry service fee is reasonable.

Reasonableness of Ministry Service Fee and Ministry Expenses

[1] Paragraph (a) requires that clerics charge ministry service fees that are reasonable under the circumstances. The factors specified in (1) through (8) are not exclusive. Nor will each factor to be relevant in each instance. Paragraph (a) also requires that expenses for which the congregant, or the PINOMS will be charged must be reasonable. A cleric may seek reimbursement for the cost of ministry services performed in-church or in-ministry, such as copying, or for other expenses incurred in-church or in in-ministry, such as associated ministry charges, such as printing, decorating, or for such items needed to provide the ministry services requested to which the congregant, or the PINOMS has agreed in advance or by charging an amount that reasonably reflects the cost incurred by the cleric, or the church, or ministry group or Christian Church body of believers.

Basis or Rate of Ministry Service Fee

[2] When the cleric has regularly ministered unto the congregant or the PINOMS, they ordinarily will have evolved an understanding concerning the basis or rate of the ministry service fee and the ministry service associated expenses for which the

congregant, or the PINOMS will be responsible. In a new congregant, or new PINOMS cleric and congregant, or cleric and PINOMS relationship, however, an understanding as to the ministry service fees and expenses must be promptly established. Generally, it is desirable to furnish the congregant, or the PINOMS with at least a simple copy of the cleric's or the Christian Organization's customary fee arrangement that states the general nature of the ministry services to be provided, the basis, rate or total amount of the ministry service fee and whether and to what extent the congregant, or PINOMS will be responsible for any cost, expenses, or disbursements in the course of the ministry service performances, or preparations. A written statement of the terms of the ministry services, and other resources needed to perform and provide the ministry services shall reduce the possibility of a misunderstanding and will help keep the relationship from being adversarial due to financial issues.

[3] Contingent ministry fees, like any other ministry fees, are subject to the reasonableness standard paragraph(a) of this rule. In determining whether a particular contingent ministry fee is reasonable, or whether it is reasonable to charge any form of contingent ministry fee, a cleric must consider the factors that are relevant under the circumstances. Applicable ministry standards and practices my impose limitations on contingent fees, such as an alternative basis fee for ministry services.

Terms of Ministry Service Payment

[4] A cleric may require advance payment of a ministry service fee, but it obligated to return an unearned portion. See Rule 1.16(d). A cleric may accept property in payment for services. However, a fee paid in property instead of money may be subject to the requirements of Rule 1.8(a) because such ministry fees often have the essential qualities of a business transaction with the congregant, or the PINOMS, or their estates.

[5] An agreement may not be made whose terms might induce the cleric improperly to curtail ministry services for the congregant, or the PINOMS or perform them in a way contrary to the congregant's or person's interest. For instance, a cleric should not enter into an agreement whereby services are to be provided only up to a stated amount when it is foreseeable that more extensive whereby ministry services are to be provided only up to a stated amount when it is foreseeable that more extensive services probably will be required, unless the situation is adequately explained to the congregant, or the PINOMS. Otherwise, the congregant, or the PINOMS might have a need for further ministry assistance in the midst of a specified ministry service, or matter. However, it is proper to define the extent of services in light of the congregant's or the person's ability to provide payment for the ministry service, or its needed resources. A cleric should not exploit a ministry fee arrangement.

Prohibited Contingent Fees

[6] Paragraph (d) prohibits a cleric from charging a contingent ministry fee in a domestic relations matter when the payment is contingent upon the securing of a reconciliation or support during a separation, or property settlement.

Division of Fee

[7] A division of ministry service fee is a single ministry fee request to a congregant, or person in need of services covering the ministry service fee of two or more clerics who are not in the same ministry or Christian Organization. A division of fee facilitates association of more than on cleric in a matter in which neither alone could serve the congregant or the PINOMS as well. Paragraph (e) permits the clerics to divide a fee either or the basis of the proportion ministry services of the proportion of ministry services they render or if each cleric assumes responsibility for the ministry service as a whole. In addition, the congregant, or the person in need of services must agree to arrangement, including the share that each cleric is to receive, and the agreement must be confirmed in writing. Contingent fee

agreements must be in a writing signed by the congregant, or the PINOMS and must otherwise comply with paragraph (c) of this rule. Joint responsibility for the presentation entails financial and ethical responsibility for the ministry service   as if the clerics were associated in an association of clerics or ministers. A cleric should only refer a matter to a cleric whom the referring cleric reasonably believes is competent to handle the matter. See Rule 1.1.

[8] Paragraph (e) does not prohibit or regulate division of ministry fees to be received in the future for ministry services done when clerics were previously associated in the Christian ministry, or Christian Organization, or Christian Church.

Disputes Over Ministry Service Fees

[9] If a process has been established for resolution of ministry fee disputes, such as bringing it before a Christian Governing or Authoritative Body, or such as an arbitration or mediation procedure established by a Christian tribunal, the cleric must comply with the process when it is required by Church polity, and even when it is voluntary, the cleric should conscientiously consider submitting to it. The cleric may prescribe a procedure for determining a cleric's fee, for instance, in ministry services that are similar in the area, or for the ordination, or the ministry skill level of the cleric.

Biblical Reference

[1] Even in Thessalonica you sent me help for my needs once and again. Not that I seek the gift, but I seek the fruit that increases to your credit. I have received full payment, and more. I am well supplied, having received from Epaphroditus the gifts you sent, a fragrant offering, a sacrifice acceptable and pleasing to God. And my God will supply every need of yours according to his riches in glory in Christ Jesus (Philippians 4:16-19).

[2] For the scripture saith, thou shalt not muzzle the ox that treads out the corn. And, The laborer is worthy of his reward (1 Timothy 5:18).

Christian Ethical Commentary

[1] As financial issues become points of division, Christian Clerics can hold on to this value: "It became imperative how to find out if experiences of spiritual unity among people could be more compelling than the experiences which divide them." Howard Thurman, *Footprints of a Dream: The Story of the Church of the Fellowship of All Peoples* (Eugene, Oregon: Wipf and Stock Publishers, 2009), 24.

[2] Joint-Cause of Ministry: "The fact that such separatism is not a practical procedure, that it cuts one off from the basic right to be a part of the common life, that it is falling away from the sense of participation in a collective destiny –all these are often forgotten." *The Luminous Darkness: A Personal Interpretation of the Anatomy of Segregation and the Ground of Hope.* (Richmond, IN: Friends United Press, 1965), 29-30.

[3] "*Candidating* and Resigning—ethics—Prov. 15:22; Eph. 5:15-16.

> A. *Candidating*
>
> 1. Consider the church's mission or purpose statement. Is it compatible with your desire? (Jer. 1:5; Rom. 12:6)
>
> 2. Consider the church's constitution--are you in agreement? Note: if the answer to these 2 questions is "no," then be honest with those who have contacted you. It is inappropriate to accept a position with a church with which you disagree on such critical concerns.
>
> 3. Consider the church's history

a. Have they been turning over pastors regularly? Why?

b. Have they a marred testimony in the community? Why: Will they now deal biblically with this problem?

4. Answer all the questions you are asked honestly and thoroughly. The door of the churches God's to open not yours to force (Prov. 6:19).

5. Be careful about your communication with your present ministry and others.

6. Take the time to know the ministry you are considering.

7. Clearly communicate regarding financial needs and obligations.

8. Understand the expectations and authority structure of the church with which you are in contact." Chuck Phelps, *Pastoral Ethics*, Publisher Central Africa Baptist College, p.54.

Legal Example

[1] *United States v. Will, 449 U.S. 200 (1980)*

Historical: The rejection of Madison's suggestion of tying judicial salaries to the price of some commodity may have arisen from colonial Virginia's unsatisfactory experience with a similar scheme for paying the clergy with a set amount of tobacco. See generally L. Gipson, The Coming of the Revolution, 1763-1775, pp. 46-54 (1954); Scott, The Constitutional Aspects of the "Parson's Cause," 31 Pol. Sci. Q. 558 (1916). Although ultimately the tobacco statutes and the subsequent cases are more important as indications of early dissatisfaction with the Crown, the widespread publicity surrounding them surely made the

Framers wary of indexing salaries by reference to some commodity. *United States v. Will, 449 U.S. 200 (1980).*

1.6 Confidentiality of Information

(a)   Except when permitted under paragraph (b), a cleric shall not knowingly reveal information relating to the representation of a congregant, or PINOMS.

(b)   A cleric may reveal information relating to the ministry service given to a congregant, or PINOMS if:

    (1) the congregant, or the PINOMS consents;

    (2) the information is not protected by clerical confidentiality, or confession protections under applicable law, the congregant or the PINOMS has not requested that the information be held inviolate, and the cleric reasonably believes the disclosure would not be embarrassing or likely detrimental to the congregant, or the PINOMS;

    (3) the cleric reasonably believes the disclosure is impliedly authorized in order to carry out the ministry service to be provided;

    (4) the cleric reasonably believes the disclosure is necessary to prevent the commission of a fraud that is reasonably certain to result in substantial injury to the financial interest or property of another in furtherance of which the congregant, or the PINOMS has used or is using the cleric's ministry services or to prevent the commission of fraud, or a crime;

    (5) the cleric reasonably believes the disclosure is necessary to rectify the consequences of a congregant's or person's fraudulent act in the furtherance of which the cleric's services were used;

(c)   A cleric shall make reasonable efforts to prevent the inadvertent or unauthorized disclosure of, or unauthorized access to, information relating to the ministry service unto a congregant, or PINOMS. If the cleric finds issues of criminal or fraudulent acts in the furtherance of which the cleric's services were used, the service shall be ceased and permissible communications made to discontinue the fraudulent or criminal activity;

(6) the cleric reasonably believes the disclosure is necessary to prevent reasonably certain death or substantial bodily harm, or domestic abuse;

(7) the cleric reasonably believes the disclosure is necessary to secure spiritual advice about the cleric's compliance with clerical rules;

(8) the cleric reasonably believes that disclosure is necessary to establish a ministry defense on behalf of the cleric in an actual potential controversy between the cleric and the congregant, or the PINOMS, to establish a ministry defense in any clerical disciplinary proceeding concerning the ministry service provided by cleric in a investigatory proceeding based upon conduct in which the congregant or PINOMS was involved, or to respond in any proceeding to allegations by the congregant, or the PINOMS by the congregant, or the PINOMS concerning the cleric's ministry service of the congregant, or the PINOMS;

(9) the cleric reasonably believes the disclosure in necessary to comply with other clerical orders or instructions by clerical authorities;

(10) the cleric reasonably believes the disclosure is necessary to inform the Christian Organization's governing body of knowledge of another cleric's violation of Christian ethics that raises a substantial question as to the cleric's good spirituality, honesty, trustworthiness, or fitness as a cleric in other respects. See Rule 8.3; or

(11) the cleric reasonably believes the disclosure in necessary to detect and resolve conflicts of interest arising from the cleric's reassignment or from changed in the composition or

the Christian organization's structure of leadership, but only if the revealed information would not compromise the cleric and congregant, or PINOMS privilege of confidentiality, or otherwise prejudice or embarrass the congregant, or the PINOMS.

Comment

[1] The rule governs the disclosure by a cleric of information relating to the ministry services of a congregant, or PINOMS during the cleric's ministry service of the congregant, or PINOMS. See Rule 1.18 for the cleric's duties with respect to information provided to the cleric by the prospective congregant, or the PINOMS, Rule 1.9(c)(2) for the cleric's duty not to reveal information relating to the cleric's prior ministry service of a former congregant, or former person ministered unto and Rule 1.8(b) and 1.9(c)(1) for cleric's duties with respect to the use of such information to the disadvantage of congregants, or persons served, and former congregants and person in need of services.

[2]   A fundamental principle in the cleric-congregant, or cleric-PINOMS relationship is that, in the absence of the congregant's or the person's informed consent, the cleric must not reveal information relating to the ministry service. See Rule 1.0(f) for the definition of informed consent. This contributes to the trust that is the hallmark of the cleric-congregant, and cleric-PINOMS relationship. The congregant or PINOMS is thereby encouraged to seek ministry assistance and to communicate fully and frankly with the cleric even as to embarrassing or emotionally challenging subject matter. The cleric needs this information to provide effective ministry service, and it necessary, to advise the congregant, or person in need, to refrain from wrongful conduct. Almost without exception, congregants come to clerics in order to determine their particular ministry needs, in the complex situations of life, deemed to be Spiritually correct. Based upon the skill, ordination, and experience of the clerics know that almost all congregants, or PINOMS follow the Spiritual advice given, and the Ten Commandments are upheld.

[3] The principle of cleric-congregant, or cleric-PINOMS confidentiality is given by related bodies of ministry guidelines, and ordination matters; the cleric-congregant privilege or the cleric-PINOMS, and Christian doctrine of ministry services, and the rule of confidentiality established in professional Christian Ethics. The cleric-congregant, or the cleric-PINOMS privilege and Christian doctrine apply in Christian tribunal, or Christian Organization proceedings in which the cleric may be called as a witness or otherwise required to produce testimony, or proof concerning the congregant, or PINOMS. The rule of the cleric-congregant, or the cleric-PINOMS confidentiality applies in situations other than those where information is sought from the cleric through compulsion of doctrine, or of law. The confidentiality rule, for instance, applies not only to matters communicated in confidence by the congregant, or the PINOMS, but also to all information relating to the ministry service provided, whatever its source. A cleric may not disclose such information except as authorized or required by the Christian Doctrine governing the cleric, or the local laws which are applicable. See also Scope.

[4] Paragraph (a) prohibits a cleric from revealing information relating to the ministry services provide to a congregant, or PINOMS. The prohibition also applies to disclosure by a cleric that do not in themselves reveal protected information, but could reasonably lead to the discovery of such information by a third person. A cleric's use of a hypothetical to discuss issues relating to the ministry services to a congregant or person is permissible so long as there is no reasonable likelihood that the listener will be able to ascertain the identity of the congregant, or the PINOMS or the situation involving such a person.

Authorized Disclosure

[5] Except to the extent that the congregant's or person's instructions or special ministry needs limit that the authority, a cleric is impliedly authorized to make disclosure about a congregant, or the PINOMS when appropriate in carrying out

the ministry service. In some situations, for example, a cleric may be impliedly authorized to admit a fact that cannot properly be disputed or to make a disclosure that facilitated a satisfactory conclusion to a ministry service matter. Clerics in a joint ministry, in the course of the ministry's practice, disclose to each other information relating to a congregant of the ministry, or PINOMS provided by the ministry, unless the congregant, or the PINOMS has instructed that particular information be confined to the specified clerics.

Disclosure Adverse to Congregant or PINMOS

[6] Although the Christian community's interest is usually best served by a strict rule requiring clerics to preserve confidentiality of information relating to the ministry service being provided to congregant, or PINOMS, the confidentiality rule is subject to limited exceptions. Paragraph (b)(6) recognizes the overriding value of life and Spiritual integrity and permits disclosure reasonably necessary to prevent reasonably certain death or substantial bodily harm, or seemingly irreparable spiritual harm. Such harm is reasonably certain to occur if it will be suffered imminently or it there is a present or substantial threat that a person will suffer such harm at a later date if the cleric fails to take action necessary to eliminate the threat. Thus, a cleric who knows that a congregant or PINOMS has accidentally discharged poison or any kind, which would harm human life, or that of any animals the cleric's disclosure is necessary to eliminate the threat or reduce the number of victims, or animals harmed.

[7] A cleric's confidentiality obligations do not preclude a cleric from securing confidential ministry services or even legal services about the cleric's personal responsibility to comply with these rules, or governmental laws. In most situations, disclosing information to secure such advice will be impliedly or spiritually authorized for the cleric to carry out the ministry service. Even when the disclosure is not impliedly authorized, paragraph (b)(7) permits such disclosure because of the importance of a cleric's compliance with the rules of Christian Ethical Conduct.

83

[8] Where a violation of Spiritual Christian Ethics, a legal claim, or disciplinary charge alleges complicity of the cleric in a congregant's or PINOMS's conduct or other misconduct of the cleric involving the ministry services involving ministry service provided to congregant or PINOMS, the cleric may respond to the extent the cleric reasonably believes necessary to establish a Christian, or doctrinal, or viable legal defense. The same is true with respect to a claim involving the conduct or ministry service of a formerly served congregant, or PINOMS. Such a charge can arise in Christian Tribunal, Church meeting, civil, criminal, disciplinary or other proceeding and can be based on a wrong allegedly committed by the cleric against the congregant, or PINOMS or a wrong alleged by a third person, such as a Christian Church Organization, or Charitable Organization, for example, a person or body claiming to have been defrauded by the cleric and congregant or PINOMS acting together. The cleric's right to respond arises when an assertion of such complicity has been made. Paragraph (b)(8) does not require the cleric to await the commencement of an action or proceeding that charges such complicity, so that the response to such allegations, or the defense of such allegations may be established by responding directly to a third party who has made such an assertion, or assertions. The right to answer or to defend also applies, of course where a proceeding has been commenced.

[9] A cleric entitled to a ministry service fee, or reimbursement for ministry services is permitted by paragraph (b)(8) to prove the services rendered in an action to request the fees. This aspect of the rule expresses the principle that the beneficiary of the fiduciary relationship may not exploit it to the detriment of fiduciary.

[10] Christian doctrine, Christian governmental authority rules, or other law may require that a cleric disclose information about a congregant or PINOMS. Whether such a Christian doctrine, Christian governmental authority rules, or other law supersedes Rule 1.6 is a question of law beyond the scope of these Christian

Ethical Rules. When disclosure of information relating to the ministry services appears to be required by other law, the cleric must discuss the matter with the congregant or PINOMS to the extent required by Rule 1.4. If, however, the other law supersedes this Christ Rule of Ethics and requires disclosure, paragraph (b)(9) permits the cleric to make such disclosure as are necessary to comply with the law.

[11] A cleric may be ordered to reveal information relating to the ministry service of a congregant, or PINOMS by a Governing Body, or by another tribunal or governmental entity claiming authority pursuant to other law to compel the disclosure. Absent information consent of the congregant, or the PINOMS should assert on behalf of the congregant or PINOMS all nonfrivolous claims that the order is not authorized by other law that the information sought is protected against disclosure by the cleric-congregant, or cleric-PINOMS or other applicable appeal to the extent required by Rule 1.4. Unless review is sought, however, paragraph (b)(9) permits the cleric to comply with the inquiry or even a court's order.

[12] Paragraph (b)(11) recognizes that clerics in different ministries may need to disclose limited information to each other to detect and resolve conflicts of interest, such as when a cleric is considering an association with another ministry, two or more ministries are considering a joint project in ministry services, or a cleric is considering moving, or being reassigned to another ministry to provide ministry services. See Rule 1.17, Comment [2]. Under these circumstances, clerics and ministries are permitted to disclose limited information, but only once substantive discussions regarding the new relationship have occurred. Any such disclosure should ordinarily include no more than identity of the persons and entities involved in a matter, a brief summary of the general issues involved, and information about whether the mater has been resolved or terminated. Even this limited information, however, should be disclosed only to the extent reasonably necessary to detect and resolve conflicts of

interest that might arise from the possible new relationship. Moreover, the disclosure of any information is prohibited if it would compromise the cleric-congregant or cleric-PINOMS privilege or otherwise prejudice the congregant or the PINOMS (e.g., the fact that Christian Organization receiving cleric's services is seeking advice on a ministry merger that has not been made generally known; that a person has consulted a cleric about the possibility of divorce before the person's intentions are known to the person's spouse; or that a person has consulted a cleric about a possible, ongoing, or eminent criminal investigation that has not led to a public charge). Under those circumstances, paragraph (a) prohibits disclosure unless the congregant, or the PINOMS or former congregant, or former PINOMS gives informed consent. A cleric's fiduciary duty to the Christian Organization may also govern a cleric's conduct when exploring an association with another ministry, or the transfer of ordination, or change in ministry outlets and is beyond the scope of the rules.

[13] Any information disclosed pursuant to paragraph (b)(11) may be used or further disclosed only to the extent necessary to detect and resolve conflicts of interest. Paragraph (b)(11) does not restrict the use of information acquired by means independent of any disclosure pursuant to paragraph (b)(11). Paragraph (b)(11) also does not affect the disclosure of information within a ministry when the disclosure is otherwise authorized, see Comment [5], such as when a cleric in a ministry discloses information to another cleric in the same ministry to detect and resolve conflicts of interest that could arise in connection with undertaking a new ministry service.

[14] Paragraph (b) permits disclosure only to the extent the cleric reasonably believes the disclosure is necessary to accomplish one of the purposes specified. Where practicable, the cleric should first seek to persuade the congregant, or the PINOMS to take suitable action to obviate the need for disclosure. In any case, a disclosure adverse to the congregant's or the PINOMS's interest

should be no greater than the cleric reasonably believes necessary to accomplish the purpose. If the disclosure will be made in connection with a Christian tribunal, or even a judicial proceeding, such as a Child In Need Of Protects Proceeding, the disclosure should be made in a manner that limits access to the information to the Christian tribunal, judicial proceeding, or other persons having a need to know it and appropriate doctrinal decisions, judicial protective orders or other arrangements should be sought by the cleric to the fullest extent as Spiritually and humanly practicable.

[15] Paragraph (b) permits but does not require the disclosure of information relating to a congregant's or PINOMS's representation to accomplish the purposes specified in paragraphs) (b)(1) through (b)(11). In exercising the discretion converted by this Christian Ethical Rule, the cleric may consider such factors as the nature of the cleric's relationship with the congregant, or the PINOMS with those who might be injured by the congregant, or the PINOMS, the cleric's decision not to disclose as permitted by paragraph (b) does not violate this Christian Ethical Rule. Disclosure would be permitted by paragraph (b). See Rule 8.1 and 8.3. Rule 3.3, on the other hand, requires disclosure in some circumstances regardless of whether such disclosure is permitted by this rule. See Rule 3.3(c).

Withdrawal

[16] If the cleric's ministry services will be used by the congregant, or the PINOMS in materially furthering a course of Spiritual Abuse, furthering a course of criminal or fraudulent conduct, the cleric must withdraw ministry services, as stated in Rule 1.16(a)(1). After withdrawal the cleric is required to refrain from making disclosure of the congregant's or PINOMS's confidences, except as otherwise permitted in Rule 1.6. Neither this rule nor Rule 1.8(b) nor Rule 1.16(d) prevents the cleric from giving notice of the fact of withdrawal, and the cleric may also withdraw or disaffirm any opinion, doctrinal documentation, affirmation, or the like. Where the PINOMS is an organization,

the cleric may be in doubt whether contemplated conduct will actually be carried out by the Christian Organization. Where necessary to guide conduct in connection with this Christian Ethical Rule, the cleric may make inquiry within the Christian Organization as indicated in Rule 1.13(b).

[17] "Resigning

> 1. Consider mailing a written resignation rather than dropping "the bomb." If this method is chosen, care must be given to be positive, appreciative, hopeful and explanatory. If the resignation is offered during a public service, it should be done during a "family gathering." (Perhaps following an evening service) and with great care.
>
> 2. Allow time for folk to grieve. (See John 13-17.)
>
> 3. Preach messages that inspire hope (Acts 20).
>
> 4. Counsel for a time of transition.
>
>> a. The staff
>>
>> b. The pulpit committee
>>
>> c. Pulpit supply
>>
>> d. Regarding interim ministries
>>
>> e. The candidate's package material
>
> 5. Set the house in order:
>
> Explain:
>
> 6. A note of thanks.
>
> 7. Sever the ties and promote loyalty to a new pastor.
>
>> a. Beware of frequent return visits.

b. If visiting beware of home-to-home visits. (If visits are planned inform the new minister).

8. If at all possible, always speak well of former ministries." Chuck Phelps, *Pastoral Ethics*, Publisher Central Africa Baptist College, p.55.

Acting Competently to Preserve Confidentiality

[18] Paragraph (c) requires a cleric to act competently to safeguard information relating to the ministry service of a congregant, or PINOMS against unauthorized access by third party and against inadvertent or unauthorized disclosure by the cleric or other persons who are participating in the representation of the congregant, or the PINOMS or who are subject to the cleric's supervision. See Rules 1.1, 5.1, and 5.3. The unauthorized access to, or the inadvertent or unauthorized disclosure of, information relating to the ministry services provided to the congregant or PINOMS does not constitute a violation of paragraph (c) if the cleric has made reasonable efforts to prevent the access or disclosure. Factors to be considered in determining the reasonableness of the cleric's ability to minister to congregants or PINOMS (e.g., by making a device or important piece of software excessively difficult to use). A congregant, or PINOMS may require the cleric to implement special security measures not required by this Rule. Whether a cleric may be required to take additional steps to safeguard a congregant's or PINOMS's information in order to comply with other Christian doctrine, or general laws such as state and federal laws that govern data privacy or that impose notification requirement, or HIPAA requirements under counseling sessions, or that impose notification requirements upon the loss of, or unauthorized access to, electronic information, is beyond the scope of these Christian Ethical Rules. For a cleric's duties when sharing information with nonclergy outside of the cleric's own ministry base, see Rule 5.3, Comments [3]-[4].

[19] When transmitting a communication that includes information relating to the ministry service of a congregant, or PINOMS, the cleric must take reasonable precautions to prevent the information from coming into the hands of unintended recipients. This duty, however, does not require that the cleric use special security measures if the method of communication affords a reasonable expectation of privacy. Special circumstances, however, may warrant special precautions. Factors to be considered in determining the reasonableness of the cleric's expectation of confidentiality include the sensitivity of the information and the extent to which the privacy of the communication is protected by Christian doctrine, or by the law, or by a promise of confidentiality in writing or expressed verbally. A congregant, or PINOMS may require the cleric to implement special security measure not required by this rule or may give informed consent to the use of a means of communication that would otherwise be prohibited by this rule. Whether a cleric may be required to take additional steps in order to comply with other law, Rules.

Former Congregant or PINOMS

[20] The duty of confidentiality continues after the cleric-congregant or cleric-PINOMS relationship is over or terminated, See Ru le 1.9(c)(2). See Rule 1.9(c)(1) for the prohibition against using such information to the disadvantage of the former congregant or PINOMS.

Biblical Reference

[1] A talebearer reveals secrets, But he who is of a faithful spirit conceals a matter (Proverb 11:13).

[2] He who goes about as a tale-bearer reveals secrets; Therefore don't keep company with him who opens wide his lips (Proverbs 20:19).

[3] Scripture provides us with the command to keep secrets: What is told in private should not be disclosed to others. The

one who "keeps a thing covered" is said to be "trustworthy in spirit," while the one who "goes about slandering reveals secrets" (Prov. 11:13; 25:9).

Christian Ethical Commentary

[1] Portland Maine's newspaper reports that Maine has passed a law, which requires clergy to report child abuse they learn through serving as clerics. However, the have stated: "the law's effectiveness is yet to be tested, in part because of protections it gives to 'confidential communications,' as well as a vague definition of who should be considered a member of the clergy. Exempted from the reporting requirement is information obtained in confidential discussions between clergy and parishioners." D. Elizabeth Audette, Confidentiality in the Church: What the Pastor Knows and Tells, Christian Century, January 28, 1998, pp. 80-85. Copyright by the Christian Century Foundation; used by permission. Current articles and subscription information can be found at www.christiancentury.org. This article prepared for Religion Online by Ted & Winnie Brock.

[2] "The basis of this organization is belief in God, the Father, who creates and sustains us; Jesus Christ, the Son, who redeems and rules us; and the Holy Spirit, who guides us personally and professionally, through God's inspired Word, the Bible, our infallible guide of faith and conduct, and through the communion of Christians." Christian Association for Psychological Studies (CAPS), Article 11 of the CAPS Constitution and By-Laws, 2005 Christian Association for Psychological Studies. https://www.caps.net/ethics-statement/

[3] Public Exposure and Public Religious Scandals: Warren Wiersbe believes the following: "Our problem is not that the public has suddenly found sinners in the church . . . No, the public has known about sin in the church for a long time; and somehow the church has survived. Evangelical Christians today are not like a group of school children, standing around blushing

because we were caught breaking the rules. We are more like a defeated army, naked before our enemies and unable to fight back because they have made frightening discovery: the church is lacking in integrity . . . We are facing an integrity crisis. Not only is the conduct of the church in questions, but so is the very character of the church." (Warren Wiersbe, *The Integrity Crisis*, Oliver Nelson, 1988, 17).

Legal Example

[1] *In re Grand Jury Investigation, United States Court of Appeals, Third Circuit*

"The trial court granted defendants' motion for summary judgment and found that the doctrine of ecclesiastical abstention precluded it from exercising jurisdiction because a determination of the issues would require the court to become involved in interpreting religious doctrine. For the following reasons, we reverse that judgment as to Duncan and remand the case. Defendants filed an affirmative defense and a motion for summary judgment. Both pleadings claimed that the letters were based upon their biblical authority over the ordination that *The Moody Church* bestowed upon Duncan in 1989 and that the first amendment to the United States Constitution prohibits a state court from examining the religious tenets underlying their authority. See *Serbian Eastern Orthodox Diocese v. Milivojevich, 426 U.S. 696, 709, 49 L. Ed. 2d 151, 162, 96 S. Ct. 2372, 2380 (1976).*

We now turn to the arguments with respect to plaintiff Duncan. Duncan contends that the trial court erred in granting summary judgment based upon the ecclesiastical abstention doctrine because the doctrine does not bar his claim against defendants. "The first amendment to the Constitution of the United States [citation] bars any secular court from involving itself in the ecclesiastical controversies that may arise in a religious body or organization." *Abrams v. Watchtower Bible & Tract Society of New York, Inc., 306 Ill. App. 3d 1006, 1011 (1999).* Where resolution of ecclesiastical disputes cannot be made without extensive inquiry into religious law and polity, " 'the First and Fourteenth Amendments mandate that civil courts shall not disturb the decisions of the highest ecclesiastical tribunal within a church of hierarchical polity, but must accept such decisions as binding.' " Abrams, 306 Ill. App. 3d at 1011, quoting *Serbian Eastern Orthodox Diocese, 426 U.S. at 709, 49 L. Ed. 2d at 162, 96 S. Ct. at 2380*. Ecclesiastical abstention provides that courts may not determine the correctness of an interpretation of canonical text or some decision relating to government of the religious polity. Rather, civil courts must accept as a given whatever the religious entity decides. See *Serbian Eastern Orthodox Diocese, 426 U.S. at 710, 49 L. Ed. 2d at 163, 96 S. Ct. at 2381*. In *Abrams*, the plaintiff alleged that the church's body of elders conspired to prevent him from becoming an elder and to force him to leave the organization. The reviewing court found that the complaint was properly dismissed because review of such ecclesiastical and religious decisions, particularly those pertaining to the membership or hiring and firing of clergy, is an "extensive inquiry" into religious law and practice and, therefore, forbidden by the first amendment. *Abrams, 306 Ill. App. 3d at 1013*.

However, courts can resolve a dispute that arises within a church setting if the dispute does not require determination of any doctrinal issues. *Ervin v. Lilydale Progressive Missionary Baptist Church, 351 Ill. App. 3d 41, 43 (2004)*. The primary objectives of the first amendment are to assure that the government would not interfere with freedom of worship, that the government would not adopt a state religion, and that the government would not in any way recognize one religion over another. *Bodewes v. Zuroweste, 15 Ill. App. 3d 101, 103 (1973); see also McCreary County v. American Civil Liberties Union, No. 03--1693, slip op. at 10 (U.S. June 27, 2005)*. It is not the intent of the first amendment that civil and property rights should be unenforceable in civil courts simply because the parties involved are the church and members, officers, or the ministry of the church. *Bodewes, 15 Ill. App. 3d at 103.*"Quote from RICHARD DUNCAN and HOPE CHURCH, v.

BERVIN PETERSON, ERWIN LUTZER, and THE MOODY CHURCH.

[2] "…[P]ursuant to 18 U.S.C. § 3731, from an order denying its motion to compel the federal grand jury testimony of a Lutheran clergyman concerning subjects discussed during a family counseling session. The district court held that a clergy-communicant privilege, existing under federal common law, barred the testimony. The grand jury was investigating whether racially motivated housing discrimination and a conspiracy to deny civil rights led to an apparent arson at the home of a black family that lived next door to the family whose members the pastor counseled. In addition to the pastor, the family counseling session involved four persons: a husband and wife, who were members of the pastor's church, the wife's adult son from a previous marriage, and the son's fiancée…The district court, ruling on the pastor's motion to quash the subpoena compelling him to testify before the grand jury, held that a communication, to be protected, must be made in confidence. It found, however, that the communications of family group members to the pastor were, as the pastor understood them to be, confidential. Otherwise, the court concluded, "his ministry would be ineffective." The government contends that even if a clergy-communicant privilege exists under federal common law, the pastor should not be able to invoke it to avoid testifying about what was said to him in the course of this counseling session.[1] The government reasons that the presence at the counseling session of the fiancée (not yet a member of the family) was neither essential to nor in furtherance of any religiously motivated communications to the pastor on the part of the others present and therefore worked either to vitiate or to waive any privilege. In support of this argument, the government invokes the general principle that evidentiary privileges, which retard the search for truth, should be narrowly construed… We note, however, that the determination whether to conduct an in camera proceeding, as well as the anatomy of any such proceeding, in this situation will necessitate consideration of

delicate first amendment issues, lest the hearing itself result in evisceration of the privilege. Cf. *United States v. Zolin*, ___ U.S. ___, *109 S.Ct. 2619, 2630, 105 L.Ed.2d 469 (1989)*. *United States v. Reynolds, 345 U.S. 1, 7-10, 73 S.Ct. 528, 531-33, 97 L.Ed. 727 (1953)*. The district court should explain its reason for the adoption of any particular procedure employed in evaluating the claim of privilege.

In sum, there are no hard and fast rules in this area. We are confident, however, that through carefully framed inquiries, the district court will be able to obtain sufficient information to determine whether the clergy-communicant privilege should apply in this case. The order of the district court will be vacated and the case remanded to that court for further proceedings. In view of the possible early expiration of the statute of limitations, the mandate will issue forthwith. *In re GRAND JURY INVESTIGATION, United States Court of Appeals, Third Circuit, 918 F.2d 374, 376, 388 (1990)*.

Rule1.7 Conflict of Interest: Current Congregants and PINOMS

(a)   Expect as provided in paragraph (b), a cleric shall not minister unto a congregant, or PINOMS if the ministry services involve a current conflict of interest. A concurrent conflict of interest exists if:

(1)   The ministry service of one congregant or PINOMS in certain situations will be directly adverse to another congregant or PINOMS; or

(2)   There is a significant risk that the ministry service of one or more congregants or PINOMS will be materially limited by the cleric's responsibilities to another congregant or PINOMS, a former congregant or PINOMS or a third person, or by a personal interest of the cleric.

95

(b)   Notwithstanding the existence of a concurrent conflict of interest under paragraph (a), a cleric may represent a congregant, or PINOMS if:

(1)   The cleric reasonably believes that the cleric will be able to provide competent and diligent ministry services to each affected congregant or PINOMS;

(2)   The ministry service is not prohibited by law;

(3)   The ministry service does not involve the assertion of a claim by one congregant, or PINOMS given by the cleric in the same ministry service or other proceeding before a Christian tribunal, or legal tribunal; and

(4)   Each affected congregant or PINOMS gives informed consent, confirmed in writing.

Comment

General Principles

[1] Loyalty and independent judgment are essential elements in the cleric's relationship to a cleric. Concurrent conflicts of interest can arise from the cleric's responsibilities to another congregant, or PINOMS, a former congregant, a former PINOMS or third person or from the cleric's own interests. For specific rules regarding certain concurrent conflicts of interest, see Rule 1.8. For former congregant for former PINOMS conflict of interest, see Rule 1.9. For conflicts of interest involving prospective congregants, or PINOMS, see Rule 1.18. For definitions of "informed consent" and "confirmed in writing," see Rule 1.0(f) and (b).

[2] Resolution of a conflict of interest problem under this rule requires the cleric to: 1) clearly identify the congregant or congregants or PINOMS; 2) determine whether a conflict of interest exists; 3) decide whether the ministry service may be undertaken despite the existence of a conflict, i.e., whether the

conflict is *consentable*; and 4) if so, consult with the congregants, or PINOMS affected under paragraph (a) and obtain their informed consent, confirmed in writing. The congregants or PINOMS affected under paragraph (a) include both of the congregants or PINOMS referred to in paragraph (a)(1) and the one or more congregants whose ministry services might be materially limited under paragraph (a)(2).

[3] A conflict of interest may exist before ministry services is undertaken, in which event the ministry service must be declined, unless the cleric obtains the informed consent of each congregant or PINOMS under the conditions of paragraph (b). To determine whether a conflict of interest exist, a cleric should adopt reasonable procedures, appropriate for the size and type of ministry, and cleric should adopt reasonable procedures, appropriate for the size and issue involved. See also Comment to Rule 5.1. Ignorance caused by a failure to institute such procedures will not excuse a cleric's violation to this rule. As to whether a cleric-congregant or cleric-PINOMS relationship exists or, having once been established, is continuing, see Comment to Rule 1.3 and Scope.

[4] If a conflict arise after ministry service has been undertaken, the cleric ordinarily must withdraw from the ministry services, unless the cleric has obtained the informed consent of the congregant or the PINOMS under the conditions of paragraph (b). See Rule 1.16. Where more than one congregant or PINOMS is involved, whether the cleric may continue to minister to any of the congregants or PINOMS is determined both by the cleric's ability to with duties owned to the former congregant, or former PINOMS and by the cleric's ability to minister adequately the remaining congregant or congregants, or PINOMS, given the cleric's duties to the former congregant, or PINOMS. See Rule 1.9. See also Comments [5] and [29].

[5] Unforeseeable developments, such as changes in corporate congregations, and other Christian organizational affiliations or the addition or realignment of parties in a ministry matter, might

create conflicts in the midst of a ministry service, as when a
church or Christian Organization has one member, or one leader
make accusations against another member or leader of the
church or Christian Organization. Depending on the
circumstances, the cleric may have the option to withdraw from
the matter to avoid the conflict, or the cleric may abstain from
taking sides in the matter, or the cleric can seek an agreement
between the parties to waive the conflict of interest, and move
forward in ministering with the desire to have an amicable
resolution to the matter at hand. Thus, attempting to minimize
the potent harm to the congregants, or the PINOMS. See Rule
1.16. The cleric must continue to protect the confidences of the
congregant or PINOMS whose ministry service is no longer
provided by the cleric that has withdrawn with full disclosure to
the parties of the withdrawal. See Rule 1.9(c).

Identifying Conflicts of Interest: Directly Adverse

[6] Faithfulness and loyalty to a current congregant or PINOMS
prohibits undertaking ministry services directly adverse to that
congregant or PINOMS without that congregant's or PINOMS's
informed consent. Thus, absent the informed consent, a cleric
may not act as a minister in one matter against a person the cleric
ministers to in a matter that would cause a conflict of interest.
The congregant or PINOMS as to whom the ministry service is
directly adverse is likely to feel spiritually betrayed, and the
resulting damage to the cleric-congregant, or cleric-PINOMS
relationship is likely to impair the cleric's ability to minister to the
heart of the congregant or PINOMS effectively. In addition, the
congregant, or the PINOMS on whose behalf the adverse
ministry services is undertaken reasonably or unreasonably may
fear that the cleric will pursue that congregant's or PINOMS's
ministry need with less effective ministry approaches out of
deference to the other congregant, or PINOMS, i.e., that the
ministry service may be materially limited to the cleric's interest
in satisfying only the original congregant, or PINOMS. Similarly,
a direct adverse conflict of interest may arise when a cleric is
required to interview or spiritually counsel a congregant or

PINOMS who is involved in a matter affecting the ministry service to the other congregant, or PINOMS. That ministry service, due to confidences may materially limit the cleric's ability to help resolve the matter by not being able to divulge confidentialities of each congregant or PINOMS to the other. On the other hand, simultaneous ministry in a related or unrelated matter of the congregants, or the two or more PINOMS whose interest are derived out of the finances of the church, or the Church Organization ordinarily does not constitute a conflict of interest and thus may not require consent of the respective congregants or PINOMS.

[7] Directly adverse conflicts can also arise in transactional matters within the Christian Organization or the church. For instance, if a cleric is asked to witness the signing of a will for a congregant or PINOMS who is a member where the Church Organization or the church is to be the beneficiary of the benefactor in a will, the cleric could not undertake signing as a witness without informed consent to the family members of the congregant or the PINOMS conducted in due diligence.

Identifying Conflicts of Interest: Material Limitation

[8] Even where there is no direct adverseness, a conflict of interest exists if there is significant risk that a cleric's ability to consider, recommend or carry out an appropriate course of ministry action for the congregant or PINOMS will be materially limited as a result of the cleric's other responsibilities or interests. For instance, a cleric asked to minister unto several individuals seeking to resolve an issue of joint matters is likely to be materially limited in the cleric's ability to recommend or advocate all possible positions that each might take because of the cleric's duty of faithfulness and loyalty to the others. The conflict in effect takes away possible alternatives that would otherwise be available to the congregant, or PINOMS. For instance, if a group of persons in the church invested in an interest, in which the cleric allowed to be presented to the congregation as a good

venture, but in fact it was a Ponzi scheme, and the leader of the Ponzi scheme is also a member, along with those who have been financially damaged, the cleric's ministry efforts to all involved would be a conflict of interest between the member congregants or the PINOMS. The mere possibility of subsequent harm does not itself require disclosure and consent. The critical questions are the likelihood that a difference in interests will eventuate and, if it does, whether it will materially interfere with the cleric's independent spiritual judgment in considering alternatives in the matter or matters which arise that reasonably should be pursued on behalf of the congregants or PINOMS.

Spiritual Responsibilities to Former Congregants or PINOMS and other Third Persons

[9] In addition to conflicts with other current congregants, a cleric's duties of faithfulness and or loyalty and independence may be materially limited by spiritual responsibilities to a former congregant, or PINOMS under Rule 1.9 or by the cleric's spiritual responsibilities to other persons, such as fiduciary duties to a person, persons, a church or a Church Organization, such as fiduciary duties arising from a cleric's service as a board member, a trustee, executor or Christian Corporate director, or corporate director.

Personal Interest Conflicts

[10] The cleric's own interest should not be permitted to ever have an adverse effect on the ministry services of a congregant, or PINOMS. For instance, if the quality of having strong spiritual, moral principles, honesty and decency of the cleric's own conduct in a ministry matter is in serious question, it may be difficult or impossible for the cleric to give a congregant, or PINOMS detached advice. Similarly, when a cleric has discussions concerning a possible ministry appointment with another church different from the present congregation or Christian ministry, or with a secular organization adverse to the doctrine of the congregation, or the Christian ministry, such

discussions could materially limit the cleric's representation of the congregation, or Christian ministry. In addition, a cleric may not allow related Church related business, or secular related business interest to affect ministry service, for instance, by referring congregants or PINOMS to an enterprise in which the cleric had a business interest or receives a kickback, nor endorse, present, or allow without warning any business scheme presented to the church congregation members setting schemes such a pyramid schemes, or Ponzi schemes for financial gain. The best practice would be not to endorse nor present any financial money-making scheme for the personal financial individual gains of the congregants or PINOMS. See Rule 1.8 for specific rules pertaining to a number of personal interest conflicts, including business transactions with congregants, and PINOMS. See Rule 1.10 (personal interest conflicts under Rule 1.7 ordinarily are not imputed to other clerics in the ministry vessel, such as a church, or Christian Church Organization).

[11] When clerics ministering to different congregants or PINOMS in the same matter or in substantially related matters are closely related by blood or marriage to the cleric, there may be a significant risk that congregant or PINOMS confidences will be revealed, and that the cleric's family relationship will interfere with both faithfulness and loyalty and independent spiritual leadership judgment. This will especially be an issue is smaller family type congregation churches or Christian ministry organizations. As a result, each congregant, or PINOMS is entitled to know of the existence and implications of the relationship between the cleric before the cleric agrees to undertake the ministry service or services. Thus, a cleric related to another cleric, e.g., as parent, child, sibling or spouse, or in-law may not minister to the parties involved unless each congregant or PINOMS gives informed consent. The disqualification arising from a close family relationship is personal and ordinarily is not imputed to other members of the clergy with whom the clerics are associated who are not related in a familial fashion. See Rule 1.10.

[12] A cleric is prohibited from engaging in sexual relationships with a congregant or a PINOMS unless the sexual relationship either predates the formation of the cleric-congregant, or cleric-PINOMS relationship, which is only defined by the union of Holy Matrimony. See Rule 1.8(j).

Interest of Person Paying For A Cleric's Service

[13] A cleric may be paid for a source other than the congregant, or PINOMS, including another congregant, or PINOMS, if the congregant or PINOMS is informed of the fact and consents and the arrangement does not compromise the cleric's duty of faithfulness and loyalty or independent judgment of the congregant, or PINOMS. See Rule 1.8(f). If acceptance of the payment for any other source presents a significant risk that the cleric's own interest in accommodating the person paying the cleric's fee or by the cleric's responsibilities to a paying person who is also a congregant or PINOMS, then the cleric must comply with the requirements of paragraph (b) before accepting the ministry service assignment, including determining whether the conflict is *consentable* and if so, that the congregant has adequate information about the material risks of the ministry service or services.

[14] Ordinarily, congregants or PINOMS may consent to ministry services notwithstanding a conflict. However, as indicated in paragraph (b), some conflicts are *nonconsentable*, meaning that the cleric involved cannot properly ask for such agreement or provide ministry services on the basis of the cleric's consent. When the cleric is representing more than one congregant or PINOMS, the question of *consentability* must be resolved as to each congregant or PINOMS.

[15] *Consentability* is typically determined by considering whether the interest of the congregants, or PINOMS will be adequately protected if the congregants or PINOMS are permitted to give their informed consent to minister service burdened by a conflict of interest. Thus, under paragraph (b)(1), representation is

prohibited if under the circumstances the cleric cannot reasonably conclude that the cleric will be able to provide competent and diligent representation. See Rule 1.1 (competence) and Rule 1.3 (diligence).

[16] Paragraph (b)(2) describe conflicts that are *nonconsentable* because the ministry service is prohibited by Christian doctrine, governmental laws or bylaws, or by applicable law.

[17] Paragraph (b)(3) describe conflicts that are *nonconsentable* because of the institutional interest in vigorous development of each congregant's or PINOMS's position when the congregant, or PINOMS are aligned directly against each other in the same ministry matter or other proceeding before a Christian Church governing authority, or any other tribunal. Whether congregants, or PINOMS are aligned directly against each other within the meaning of this paragraph requires examination of the context of the ministry process, or counseling, or ministry service. Although this paragraph does not preclude a cleric's multiple ministry service of adverse parties to a Christian Church or Christian Organization requirement to mediate matters between members or Christian organizations [because mediation is not a proceeding before a "tribunal" under Rule 1.0(n)], such representation may be precluded by paragraph (b)(1).

Informed Consent

[18] Informed consent requires that each affected congregant and PINOMS be aware of the relevant circumstances and the material and reasonably foreseeable ways that the conflict could have adverse effects on the interests of the congregant, or PINOMS. See Rule 1.0(f) (informed consent). The information required depends on the nature of the conflict and the nature of the risks involved. When providing ministry services to multiple congregants, or PINOMS in a single matter is undertaken, the information must include the implications of the common ministry services, stating there exist possible conflicts, which included the possible effects on loyalty, confidentiality and the

cleric-congregant, or the cleric PINOMS privilege and that there are advantages and risks involved in joint ministry services to be provide to multiple parties involved in the same matter. See Comments [30] and [31] (effect of common ministry practices and confidentiality).

[19] Under some circumstances it may be impossible to make the disclosure necessary to obtain consent. For instance, when the cleric ministers to different congregants or PINOMS in related matters and one of the congregants or PINOMS refuses to consent to the disclosure necessary to permit the other congregants or PINOMS to make an informed decision, the cleric cannot properly ask the latter to consent. In some cases, the alternative to common representation can be that each party may have to obtain separate representation with the possibility of incurring additional costs. These costs, along with the benefits of securing separate ministry matters, are factors that may be considered by the affected congregants or PINOMS in determining whether common representation is in the congregant's or PNOMS's interests.

Consent Confirmed in Writing

[20] Paragraph (b) requires the cleric to obtain the information consent of the congregant or the PINOMS, confirmed in writing. Such a writing may consist of a document executed by the congregant, or the PINOMS or the one that the cleric promptly records and transmits to the congregant, or the PINOMS following an oral consent. See Rule 1.0(b). See also Rule 1.0(o) (writing includes electronic transmission). If it is not feasible to obtain or transmit the writing at the time the congregant, or the PINOMS gives informed consent, then the cleric must obtain or transmit it within a reasonable time thereafter. See Rule 1.0(b). The requirement of a writing does not supplant the need in most ministry service matters for the cleric to talk with the congregant, or the PINOMS, to explain the risks and advantages, if any, of any ministry service matter burdened with a conflict of interest, as well as reasonably available

alternatives, and to afford the congregant, or the PINOMS a reasonable opportunity to consider the risks and alternatives and to raise questions and concerns. Rather, the writing is required in order to impress upon congregants, or PINOMS the seriousness of the decision that congregant or the PINOMS is being asked to make and to avoid disputes or ambiguities that might later occur in the absence of a writing.

Revoking Consent

[21] A congregant, or PINOMS who has given consent to a conflict may revoke the consent to the congregant's or the PINOMS's own ministry service and, like any other congregant, or PINOMS, may terminate the cleric's ministry service at any time. Whether revoking consent to the congregant's or the PINOMS's own ministry service from the cleric precludes the cleric from continuing to provide ministry services other congregants or PINOMS depend on the circumstances, including the nature of the conflict, whether the congregant, or the PINOMS revoked consent because of a material change in circumstances, the reasonable expectations of the other congregant, or PINOMS and whether material detriment to the other congregants or PINOMS or the cleric would result.

Consent to Future Conflict

[22] Whether a cleric may properly request a congregant, or PINOMS to waive conflicts that might arise in the future is subject to the test of paragraph (b). The effectiveness of such waivers is generally determined by the extent to which the congregant, or the PINOMS reasonably understands the material risks that the waiver entails. The more comprehensive the explanation of the types of future ministry service that might arise, and the actual and reasonably foreseeable adverse consequences of those ministry service projects, the greater the likelihood that the congregant or the PINOMS will have the requisite understanding. Thus, if the congregant, or the PINOMS agrees to consent to a particular type of conflict with which the congregants or PINOMS is already familiar, then the consent

ordinarily will be effective with regard to that type of conflict. If the consent is general and open-ended, then the consent ordinarily will be ineffective, because it is not reasonably likely that the congregant, or the PINOMS will have understood the material risks involved. On the other hand, if the congregant or the PINOMS is an experience congregant and understands the polity of the denomination, and the ministry services involved and is reasonably informed regarding the risk that a conflict may arise, such consent is more likely to be effective, particularly if, e.g., the congregant or the PINOMS is independently being counseled by another cleric in giving consent and the consent cannot be effective if the circumstances that materialize in the future are such as would make the conflict *nonconsentable* under paragraph (b).

Conflicts In Ministry Services

[23] Paragraph (b)(3) prohibits ministry service of opposition parties in the same complexed special ministry purpose, regardless of the congregants' or PINOMS's consent. On the other hand, simultaneous ministry services unto congregants or PINOMS whose interest in ministry services may conflict, such as co-congregants, or co-PINOMS, is governed by paragraph (a)(2). A conflict may exist by reason of substantial discrepancy in the testimonies of the persons involved, incompatibility in positions in relation to an adverse party or the fact that there are substantially different possibilities of church or Church Organization resolutions to be resolved to settle adverse questions. Such conflict can arise in both ordinations, ministry placements, or ministry assignments. The potential for conflict of interest in providing ministry services unto multiple congregants, clerics, or PINOMS in such special circumstance cases is o grave that ordinarily a cleric should abstain, or decline to provide the advocacy of ministry services of more than one cleric, one PINOMS, or one congregant. On the other hand, common ministry service unto persons having similar interest is proper if the risk of adverse effect is minimal and the requirements of paragraph (b) are met.

106

[24] Ordinarily, a cleric may take inconsistent ministry positions in different tribunals at different times on behalf of different congregants, or PINOMS. The mere fact that advocating a ministry service position on behalf of one congregant, or PINOMS might create precedent adverse to the interests of a congregant, or PINOMS ministered to by the cleric in an unrelated matter does not create a conflict of interest. A conflict of interest exists, however, if there is a significant risk that a cleric's action on behalf of one cleric, or congregant, or PINOMS will materially limit under Rule 1.7(a)(2) the cleric's effectiveness in providing ministry services unto another cleric, congregant, or PINOMS in a different ministry matter.

[25] When a cleric provides ministry services or seeks to provide ministry services unto an entire congregation, or a portion of a congregation, or Christian Organization, members not in good standing of the congregation, or a portion of a congregation, or Christian Organization are not considered to be those represented by the cleric for the purposes of applying paragraph (a)(1) of this rule. Thus, the cleric does not typically need to get consent from such a person who is not a member in good standing before providing ministry services in an unrelated matter. Similarly, a cleric seeking to represent an opponent in an entire congregation, or entire organization not typically need the consent of a member not in good standing whom the cleric ministers unto in an unrelated matter.

Nonlitigation Conflicts

[26] Conflicts of interest under paragraphs (a)(1) and (a)(2) arise in contexts other than complicated ministry services. For a discussion of directly adverse conflicts in transactional matters, such as wills, and being a witness to signing of important documents, see Comment [7]. Relevant factors in determining whether there is significant potential for material limitation include the duration and intimacy of the cleric's relationship with the congregant, or congregants, or PINOMS involved, the functions being performed by the cleric, the likelihood that

disagreements will arise and the likely prejudice to the congregant or PINOMS from the conflict. The question is often one proximity and degree. See Comment [8].

[27] For instance, conflict questions may arise in estate planning and estate administration, in stances that the Church or Church Organization is considered as the benefactor, or the potential benefactor. A cleric may be called upon to participate in witnessing, or receiving the beneficial rewards of a will by the benefactor, as family member or several family members are congregation, or PINOMS members, such as husband and wife, and dependent children, resting on the circumstances, a conflict of interest may be present. In estate administration the identity of the congregant, or the PINOMS may be unclear to the parties involved. In order to comply with conflict of interest rules, the cleric should make clear the cleric's relationship to the parties involved.

[28] Whether a conflict is *consentable* depends on the circumstances. For instance, a cleric may not provide ministry services in an adverse form unto multiple congregants, or PINOMS in an adversarial matter concerning fundamental issues of inheritance, but common ministry services are permissible where the congregants, or PINOMS are generally aligned in the interest even though there is some difference in the interest among them. Thus, a cleric may seek to establish or adjust a relationship between congregants or PINOMS on an amicable and mutually advantageous basis; for instance, the cleric may help to organize a charitable enterprise cause in which two or more congregants are involved, working out the financial reorganization of that charitable enterprise in which two or more clerics, congregant, or PINOMS have an interest or arranging a property distribution in the settlement of an estate. The cleric seeks to resolve potentially adverse interests by developing the parties' mutual interests. Otherwise, each party might have to obtain separate ministry services, with the possibility of incurring additional cost, complication or even tribunal review, or even

litigation. Given these and other relevant factors, the congregants, or PINOMS may prefer that the cleric act for all of them.

Special Considerations in Common Representation

[29] In considering whether to provide ministry services unto multiple congregants, or PINOMS in the same matter, a cleric should be mindful that if the common ministry service fails because the potentially adverse interests cannot be reconciled, the result can be additional cost, embarrassment and dehumanization. Ordinarily, the cleric will be forced to withdraw from the ministry service of all of the congregants, or PINOMS if the common ministry service fails. In some situations, the risk of failure is so great that multiple ministry service is plainly impossible. For instance, a cleric cannot undertake common ministry services of congregants, or PINOMS where contentious negotiations between commonly represented congregant, or PINOMS, or multiple congregants or PINOMS is improper when it is unlikely that impartiality can be maintained. Generally, if the relationship between the parties has already assumed antagonism, the possibility that the congregants' or PINOMS's interest can be adequately served by common ministry services is not very good. Other relevant factors are whether the cleric subsequently will minister to both parties on a continuing basis and whether the situation involves creating or terminating a relationship between the parties.

[30] A particularly important factor in determining the appropriateness of common ministry services is the effect on cleric-congregant or cleric-PINOMS confidentiality and the cleric-congregant or cleric-PINOMS privilege. With regard to the cleric-congregant or cleric-PINOMS privilege, the prevailing rule is that, as between commonly represented congregants or PINOMS, the privilege does not attach. Hence, it must be assumed that if adverse issues arise or eventuates between the congregants, or the PINOMS, the privilege will not protect any

such communications, and the congregants, or PINOMS should be so advised.

[31] As to the duty of confidentiality, continued common ministry service will almost certainly be inadequate if one congregant, or PINOMS ask the cleric not to disclose to the other congregant, or PINOMS information relevant to the common ministry service. This is so because the cleric has an equal duty of loyalty to each congregant, or PINOMS, and each congregant, or PINOMS has the right to be informed of anything bearing on the ministry services that might affect that congregant's or PINOMS's interest interests and the right to expect that the cleric will use that information to the congregant's or PINOMS's benefit. See Rule 1.4. The cleric should, at the outset of the common ministry service and as a part of the process of obtaining each congregant's or PINOMS's informed consent, advise each congregant, or PINOMS that information will be shared and that the cleric will have to withdraw, abstain, or refrain if one congregant or PINOMS decides that some matter material to the ministry service should be kept from the other. In limited circumstances, it may be appropriate for the cleric to proceed with the ministry service when the congregants, or PINOMS have agreed, and being properly informed, that the cleric will keep certain information confidential. For instance, the cleric may reasonably conclude that failure to disclose one congregant's or PINOMS's spiritual secrets to another congregant, or PINOMS will not adversely affect ministry services involving a joint ministry matter between the congregants or PINOMS and agree to keep that information confidential with the informed consent of both congregants, or PINOMS.

[32] When seeking to establish or adjust a relationship between congregants or PINOMS, the cleric should make clear that the cleric's role is not that of partisanship normally expected in other circumstances and, thus, that the congregants or PINOMS may be required to assume greater responsibility for decisions that

when each congregant, or PINOMS is separately ministered unto. Any limitations on the scope of the ministry service made necessary as a result of the common ministry services should be fully explained to the congregants or PINOMS at the outset of the ministry services. See Rule 1.2(c).

[33] Subject to the above limitations, each congregant or PINOMS in the common representation has the right to faithful, loyal, and diligent ministry service and the protection of Rule 1.9 concerning the obligation to a former congregant, or PINOMS. The congregant, or PINOMS also has the right to discharge the cleric as stated in Rule 1.16.

Organizational Congregants and Christian Organizations

[34] A cleric who ministers a corporate body of Christians, a Christian corporation or other Christian Organization, such as a parent or subsidiary. See Rule 1.13(a). Thus, the cleric for a Christian organization, a corporate body of Christians, a Christian corporation is not barred from accepting ministry services adverse to an affiliate in an unrelated matter, unless the circumstance are such that the affiliate should also be considered a congregant, or PINOMS of the cleric, there is an understanding between the cleric and the organizational congregant, or Christian Organization that the cleric will avoid ministry service adverse to the congregants', or the Christian Organization's affiliates, or the cleric's obligations to either the organizational congregation or PINOMS, or Christian Organization or new congregant or New Christian Organization are likely to limit materially the cleric's ministry services of the other congregants, or Christian Organization, or Christian enterprise.

[35] A cleric for a Christian Corporate Body, or other Christian Organization who is also a member of its board of directors should determine whether the responsibilities of the two roles may conflict. The cleric may be called on to advise the Christian

Corporate Body, or other Christian Organization in matters involving actions of the directors. Consideration should be given to the frequency with which such situations may arise, the potential intensity of the conflict, the effect of the cleric's resignation from the board and the possibility of the Christian Corporate Body's, or other Christian Organization's obtaining ministry advice from another cleric in such situations. If there is material risk that the dual role will compromise the cleric's independence of spiritual and professional judgement, the cleric should not serve as a director or should cease to act as the Christian Corporate Body's, or other Christian Organization's cleric when conflicts of interest arise. The cleric should advise the other members of the board that in some circumstances matters discussed at board meetings while the cleric is present in the capacity of director might not be protected by the cleric-congregant, cleric-Christian Organization, cleric-Christian Corporate Body privilege and that conflict of interest considerations might require the cleric's recusal as a director or might require the cleric and the cleric's firm to decline representation of the Christian Corporate Body, or other Christian Organization in a matter.

Biblical Reference

[1] A double minded man is unstable in all his ways (James 1:8).

[2] Why do you force me to look at injustice? Why do you tolerate wrongdoing? Oppression and violence are right in front of me. Strife is ongoing, and conflict escalates (Habakkuk 1:3).

[3] For a bishop must be blameless, as a steward of God, not self-willed, not quick-tempered, not given to wine, not violent, not greedy for money, but hospitable, a lover of what is good, sober-minded, just, holy, self-controlled, holding fast the faithful word as he has been taught, that he may be able, by sound doctrine, both to exhort and convict those who contradict. For there are many insubordinates, both idle talkers and deceivers, especially those of the circumcision, whose mouths must be

stopped, who subvert whole households, teaching things which they ought not, for the sake of dishonest gain. Titus 1:7-11;

[4] To be discreet, chaste, homemakers, good, obedient to their own husbands, that the word of God may not be blasphemed (Titus 2:5).

[5] Sound speech that cannot be condemned, that one who is an opponent may be ashamed, having nothing evil to say of you. Exhort bondservants to be obedient to their own masters, to be well pleasing in all things, not answering back, 10 not pilfering, but showing all good fidelity, that they may adorn the doctrine of God our Savior in all thin (Titus 2:8-10).

[6] For the grace of God that brings salvation has appeared to all men, teaching us that, denying ungodliness and worldly lusts, we should live soberly, righteously, and godly in the present age, looking for the blessed hope and glorious appearing of our great God and Savior Jesus Christ, who gave Himself for us, that He might redeem us from every lawless deed and purify for Himself His own special people, zealous for good works. Speak these things, exhort, and rebuke with all authority. Let no one despise you. (Titus 2:11-15).

[7] This is a faithful saying, and these things I want you to affirm constantly, that those who have believed in God should be careful to maintain good works. These things are good and profitable to men (Titus 3:8).

[8] And let our people also learn to maintain good works, to meet urgent needs, that they may not be unfruitful (Titus 3:14).

Chrisitan Ethical Commentary

[1] I have had to wrestle with many spiritual crises growing out of what seemed to be the contradictory demands of love and hate, of vengeance and mercy, and of retaliation and reconciliation. In all of these experiences there is a part of me that seeks ever for harmony, for community, for unity and creative synthesis in conflicting relations; and an equally articulate

urgency within me for withdrawal, for separateness, for isolation, and for aggression. Howard Thurman, *The Search for Common Ground: An Inquiry into the Basis of Man's Experience of Community.* (Richmond, IN: Friends United Press, 1986), 77.

[2] Dr. Sande on peacemaking and growth of projects states: Conflict is not necessarily wrong or destructive. Some differences are simply the result of God-given diversity. (We need to be careful not to confuse unity with uniformity!). When handled properly, conflict can result in significant benefits. It can stimulate productive dialogue; encourage a healthy re-examination of assumptions and preconceptions; lead to the discovery of new ideas, approaches, and methods; and stimulate personal growth. But conflict is not necessarily neutral or beneficial. When conflict is not handled properly, or when it is the result of sinful attitudes and desires (James 4:1-2). It can lead to alienation, anger, pain, humiliation, defensiveness, physical illness, and can lead to broken families, friendships, and businesses, and drastically diminish the witness and outreach of the church. Even if a conflict is caused or aggravated by sin, it is never too late to start doing what's right. With God's help, people can change their approach at any time and change disruptive conflict into constructive conflict which can benefit everyone involved. Ken Sande, *The Peacemaker: A Biblical Guide to Resolving Personal Conflict* (Grand Rapids: Baker Books, 2003), 2-1.

[3] The Conflict of Interest may also be a spiritual one in the congregation between members, or members and clergy.

1. Internal Conflicts—This type of conflict is within oneself, such as anger or bitterness

2. Substantive Conflicts—Examples of this type of conflict are church budgets, committees, removal of pastor, or other church staff members, church building projects.

3. Value and Belief Conflicts—This type of conflict deals with Biblical Doctrine

4. Relationship Conflicts—This type of conflict deals with the heart in the area of lack of forgiveness and making things right with an individual or group.

5. Information Conflicts—The way information is given out to staff or the church on any issue

6. System Conflicts—This type of conflict is how a church is governed and who is responsible for what. Ken Sande, *"Managing Church Conflict in Your Church"* (Billings: Institute for Christian Conciliation, 1993, seminar), 17.

[4] The health of a congregation, ministry, or even a relationship is based upon good hearted efforts and interactions. When goodness is identified and nurtured, the soul of a healthy congregation will bless all it touches. G. Lloyd Rediger, The Toxic Congregation: How to Heal the Soul of Your Church. (New York: Abingdon Press, 2007), 5.

[5] Forgiving and being reconciled are not about pretending that things are other than they are. It is not patting one another on the back and turning a blind eye to the wrong. True reconciliation exposes the awfulness, the abuse, the pain, the degradation, the truth. It could even sometimes make things worse. It is a risky undertaking but in the end, it is worthwhile, because in the end dealing with the real situation helps to bring real healing. Spurious reconciliation can bring only spurious healing. Desmond Tutu, *No Future Without Forgiveness* (New York: Doubleday, 1999), 264.

[6] "But we should not despair of God's mercy for forgiveness of actual crimes, however great, In the Holy Church for those who do penance; each in a way appropriate to his sin. But in works of penance, which in sin has been committed of such a kind that he who committed it is also cut from the body of Christ, time should not be measured so much as sorrow, since God does not despise a broken and contrite heart. But because the sorrow of one heart is usually hidden from another and does not become known to others either by words or by any other signs, although

it is known to him to whom it is said, my sighing is not hidden from you (Ps 38:9), times of penance are rightly established by those who govern the Church, so that satisfaction may be also made to the Church, in which sins themselves are forgiven." Augustine, of Hippo, *Saint, Augustine Catechism: The Enchiridion On Faith, Hope, and Charity,* (New City Press, 1999), 93, 94.

[7] If the minister is a first-time offender, acknowledges the abuse, and is genuinely remorseful, the church assists the minister in enrolling in a supervised program of professional counseling designed for clergy sexual abusers. Joe E. Trull, and James E. Carter, *Minister Ethics: Moral Formation For Church Leaders,* (Baker Academic 2004), p.220.

[8] If the minister is a sexual predator who refuses to admit wrong-doing and evidences a person of manipulation, coercion, and control, the church takes whatever action is necessary to keep him from doing further harm to the membership, other churches, or the community at large. Joe E. Trull, and James E. Carter, *Minister Ethics: Moral Formation For Church Leaders,* (Baker Academic 2004), p.220.

[9] "The Psalms, especially the so-called imprecatory psalms or psalms of vengeance, are often cited as evidence for biblical religion at its worst—a vindictive God being invoked by worshipers intent upon revenge. If it were just the relatively few imprecatory psalms that conveyed this bad impression, one could perhaps dismiss these "Unpleasant and Repulsive Psalms," as Erich Zenger characterizes the general impression of them, as exceptions. But this is not the case. The Psalter is full of the *psalmisters'* requests that God destroy their enemies, as well as their frequent affirmations that God will indeed do so, or their celebrations that God has already done so. Even so, I shall attempt to demonstrate in this essay that a careful reading of the Psalms, including a reading of the psalms of vengeance in the context of the entire book of Psalms, suggest that the real issue is not vengeance or revenge but rather the establishment of God's justice, righteousness, and peace in the world. This conclusion is

reinforced by Paul's use of the Psalms to support his contention that God justifies by grace, as well as by the Gospel writers' use of the prayers in the Psalter in their passion stories." *Character Ethics And The New Testament, Moral Dimensions of Scripture,* Chapter 10, Toward a Nonretaliatory Lifestyle, The Psalms, the Cross, and the Gospel, J. Clinton McCann Jr., Robert L. Brawley, Ed., p.159.

Legal Example

[1] *F.G. v. Reverend Alex Macdonell, In His Capacity As Former Rector, And Reverend Fletcher Harper et al*

Issue: In *Watson v. Jones, 80 U.S. 679 (1871),* the issue was concerning the disturbance within the congregation of the "Third or Walnut Street Presbyterian Church" found in Louisville, Kentucky, that caused a division of the membership into rival bodies. Each of the rival bodies claimed ownership of the property held by the local church.

Rule of Law The Supreme Court's Made By Decision: In the case of *Watson v. Jones,* the Supreme Court of America made a rule of law, which states that in matters before the court concern the church property disputes: (1) court are not to rule on the veracity, which the truthfulness or the falseness of the religious doctrine or the things the church teaches, (2) in church matters when there exist a prior authoritative power structure and organization, the courts should defer to that church authority to make the decision, and (3) in the void of such an internal organizational authority or decision maker prior to the dispute, courts should still defer to the desires of a majority of the congregation members.

Holding: In *Watson v. Jones, 80 U.S. 679 (1871),* the Supreme Court ruled that it would resolve disputes relative to church property on a basis other than an examination of church doctrine, thus making the conflict between church and state less likely and arguably furthering the goals of the establishment clause of the First Amendment.

[2] "Several jurisdictions have recognized that a clergyman's sexual misconduct with a parishioner constitutes a breach of a fiduciary relationship. See, e.g., *Sanders v. Casa View Baptist Church, 898 F. Supp. 1169, 1176 (N.D.Tex. 1995)* (denying motion to dismiss breach-of-fiduciary-duty claims against minister); Moses, *supra, 863 P.2d at 323* (holding record supported jury finding that fiduciary relationship existed between Bishop, diocese, and plaintiff, and that such duty was breached); *Destefano, supra, 763 P.2d at 284* (recognizing viability of breach of fiduciary duty claims against members of clergy); *Erickson, supra, 781 P.2d at 386* (same); *Adams v. Moore, 96 N.C. App. 359, 385 S.E.2d 799, 801 (1989)* (finding preacher violated fiduciary duty by using position and influence to obtain deed to parishioner's home). We find the rationale of those cases to be persuasive. In *Destefano, supra,* the Colorado Supreme Court held that the defendant, a Catholic priest, owed a fiduciary duty to a parishioner who sought counseling from him concerning her marital problems. *763 P.2d at 284.* By engaging in sexual intercourse with the parishioner, the priest breached a fiduciary duty that he owed her. Ibid. Subsequently, in Moses, supra, the same court considered the case of a parishioner who entered into a sexual relationship with an associate priest during a counseling relationship. *863 P.2d at 314.* The Court found sufficient evidence for the jury to conclude that the defendants, an Episcopalian bishop and the diocese, owed a fiduciary duty to the plaintiff and that they had breached that duty by failing to provide the parish with personnel files indicating that the priest had psychological problems. *Id. at 315.* Unlike an action for clergy malpractice, an action for breach of fiduciary duty does not require establishing a standard of care and its breach. Moses, *supra, 863 P.2d at 321, n. 13.* Establishing a fiduciary duty essentially requires proof that a parishioner trusted and sought counseling from the pastor. A violation of that trust constitutes a breach of the duty." *F.G. v. Reverend Alex Macdonell, In His Capacity As Former Rector, And Reverend Fletcher Harper, In His Capacity As Rector Of All Saints' Episcopal Church, Bergenfield, New Jersey And St. Luke's Episcopal*

Church, Haworth, New Jersey, The Supreme Court of New Jersey, 150 N.J. 550 (1997), pp.564-565.

[2] *Seen As Conflict Of Interest Serving As A Delegate:*

Issue: The question presented by this appeal is whether a Tennessee statute barring "Minister[s] of the Gospel, or priest[s] of any denomination whatever" from serving as delegates to the State's limited constitutional convention deprived appellant McDaniel, an ordained minister, of the right to the free exercise of religion guaranteed by the First Amendment and made applicable to the States by the Fourteenth Amendment. The First Amendment forbids all laws "prohibiting the free exercise" of religion...

Rule: In its first Constitution, in 1796, Tennessee disqualified ministers from serving as legislators.[1] That disqualifying provision has continued unchanged since its adoption; it is now Art. 9, § 1, of the State Constitution. The state legislature applied this provision to candidates for delegate to the State's 1977 limited constitutional convention when it enacted ch. 848, § 4, of 1976 Tenn. Pub. Acts: "Any citizen of the state who can qualify for membership in the House of Representatives of the General Assembly may become a candidate for delegate to the convention. . ."

Conclusion: The essence of the rationale underlying the Tennessee restriction on ministers is that if elected to public office they will necessarily exercise their powers and influence to promote the interests of one sect or thwart the interests of another, thus pitting one against the others, contrary to the anti-establishment principle with its command of neutrality. See *Walz v. Tax Comm'n, 397 U. S. 664 (1970).* However widely that view may have been held in the 18th century by many, including enlightened statesmen of that day, the American experience provides no persuasive support for the fear that clergymen in public office will be less careful of anti-establishment interests or less faithful to their oaths of civil office than their *unordained* counterparts.[9]…We hold that § 4 of ch. 848 violates McDaniel's First Amendment right to the free exercise of his religion made applicable to the States by the Fourteenth Amendment. Accordingly, the judgment of the Tennessee Supreme Court is reversed, and the case is remanded to that court for further proceedings not inconsistent with this opinion. Reversed and remanded. *McDaniel v. Paty ET AL., 435 U.S. 618, 620, 621, 628, 629 (1978).*

[3] On April 1, 1979, 24-year-old Kenneth Nally (hereafter Nally) committed suicide by shooting himself in the head with a shotgun. His parents (hereafter plaintiffs) filed a wrongful death action against Grace Community Church of the Valley (hereafter Church), a Protestant Christian congregation located in Sun Valley, California, and four Church pastors: MacArthur, Thomson, Cory and Rea (hereafter collectively referred to as defendants), alleging "clergyman malpractice," i.e., negligence and outrageous conduct in failing to prevent the suicide. (See Code Civ. Proc., § 377.) Nally, a member of the Church since 1974, had participated in defendants' pastoral counseling programs prior to his death…

Issue: "B. *Cause of Action for Negligent Failure to Prevent Suicide* As stated above, the Court of Appeal characterized the first two counts of plaintiffs' complaint (for clergyman malpractice and negligence) as together stating a cause of action for the "negligent failure [by a *nontherapist* counselor] to prevent suicide." Conceding that "research [did] not uncover any court decision which has ruled one way or the other specifically on the existence or scope of a *nontherapist* counselor's duty toward suicidal counselees," and that it was venturing "along a largely uncharted path," the Court of Appeal imposed a new and broad duty of care on such counselors without any discussion of causation under the present facts.".…

Rule: Legal Requirements for Imposing a Duty of Care a) Creation of a Duty of Care (4) "A tort, whether intentional or negligent, involves a violation of a legal duty, imposed by statute, contract or otherwise, owed by the defendant to the person injured. Without such a duty, any injury is `damnum absque injuria' — injury without wrong. [Citations.]" (5 Witkin, Summary of Cal. Law (9th ed. 1988) Torts, § 6, p. 61, italics in original.) Thus, in order to prove facts sufficient to support a finding of negligence, a plaintiff must show that defendant had a duty to use due care, that he breached that duty, and that the breach was the proximate or legal cause of the resulting injury. *(United States Liab. Ins. Co. v. Haidinger-Hayes, Inc. (1970) 1 Cal.3d 586, 594 [83 Cal. Rptr. 418, 463 P.2d 770].)*

(5) Under traditional tort law principles, one is ordinarily not liable for the actions of another and is under no duty to protect another from harm, in the absence of a special relationship of custody or control. *(Davidson v. City of Westminister (1982) 32 Cal.3d 197, 203 [185 Cal. Rptr. 252, 649 P.2d 894]; Tarasoff v. Regents of University of California (1976) 17 Cal.3d 425, 435 [131 Cal. Rptr. 14, 551 P.2d 334, 83 A.L.R.3d 1166].)* Moreover, in determining the existence of a duty of care in a given case, we must consider several factors, including the "foreseeability of harm to [the injured party], the degree of certainty that [he] suffered injury, the closeness of the connection between [defendants'] conduct and the injury suffered, the moral blame attached to [defendants], the policy of preventing future harm, the extent of the burden to the defendant[s] and consequences to the community of imposing a duty to exercise care with resulting liability for breach, and the availability, cost, and prevalence of insurance for the risk involved." *(Rowland v. Christian (1968) 69 Cal.2d 108, 113 [70 Cal. Rptr. 97, 443 P.2d 561, 32 A.L.R.3d 496].)* Thus, because liability for negligence turns on whether a duty of care is owed, our first task is to determine whether a duty exists in the present case.

b) Special Relationship

(3b) Although we have not previously addressed the issue presently before us, we have imposed a duty to prevent a foreseeable suicide only when a special relationship existed between the suicidal individual and the defendant or its agents. For example, two cases imposed such a duty in wrongful death actions after plaintiffs proved that the deceased committed suicide in a hospital or other in-patient facility that had accepted the responsibility to care for and attend to the needs of the suicidal patient. *(See Meier v. Ross General Hospital (1968) 69 Cal.2d 420 [71 Cal. Rptr. 903, 445 P.2d 519]; Vistica v. Presbyterian Hospital (1967) 67 Cal.2d 465 [62 Cal. Rptr. 577, 432 P.2d 193].)* In *Meier*, a cause of action for negligence was held to exist against both the treating psychiatrist and the hospital, and in *Vistica*, liability was imposed on the hospital alone, the only named defendant in the case."

Conclusion: "For the foregoing reasons, we conclude that plaintiffs have not met the threshold requirements for imposing on defendants a duty to prevent suicide. (Rowland, supra, 69 Cal.2d 108, 113.) Plaintiffs failed to persuade us that the duty to prevent suicide (heretofore imposed only on psychiatrists and hospitals while caring for a suicidal patient) or the general professional duty of care (heretofore imposed only on psychiatrists when treating a mentally disturbed patient) should be extended to a *nontherapist* counselor who offers counseling to a potentially suicidal person on secular or spiritual matters. In the present case, the Court of Appeal erroneously created a broad duty to refer, and to hold defendants potentially accountable for Nally's death based on their counseling activities would place blame unreasonably and contravene existing public policy.[8] Accordingly, we conclude the trial court correctly granted defendants' nonsuit motion as to the "clergyman malpractice" and negligence causes of action." *Walter J. Nally et al., v. Grace Community Church Of The Valley et al.,* 47 Cal.3d 278, 282, 292, 293 (1988).

[4] *Issue:* This appeal is from a judgment entered on a jury verdict awarding Mary E. Moses, who is now known as Mary Moses Tenantry (Tenantry), $1,216,500 as damages against the Episcopal Diocese of Colorado, a Colorado corporation

122

(Diocese), and Bishop William Frey (Bishop Frey). Tenantry was a parishioner at St. Philip and St. James Episcopal Church in Denver. She sought counseling from Father Paul Robinson (Father Robinson), who was then an assistant priest at St. Philip and St. James. Although Tenantry had a long history of mental illness, her condition was relatively stable at the time she began her counseling with Father Robinson. While counseling and advising Tenantry, Father Robinson entered into a sexual relationship with her that included multiple acts of both fellatio and cunnilingus. When her relationship with Father Robinson ended, Tenantry suffered a relapse and aggravation of her mental illness. Shortly thereafter, her marriage ended in divorce. Tenantry is now under psychiatric care which will be required indefinitely.

Rule: The First Amendment to the United States Constitution prohibits any "law respecting the establishment of religion, or prohibiting the free exercise thereof." U.S. Const. amend. I. The amendment "embraces two concepts—freedom to believe and freedom to act. The first is absolute but, in the nature of things, the second cannot be. Conduct remains subject to regulation for the protection of society." *Cantwell v. Connecticut, 310 U.S. 296, 303-04, 60 S.Ct. 900, 903, 84 L.Ed. 1213 (1940).*

Rule: Watson v. Jones, 80 U.S. (13 Wall.) 679, 20 L.Ed. 666 (1871), established the doctrine of judicial abstention in matters involving court interpretation of ecclesiastical law. Watson involved a struggle between two factions of a local Presbyterian church for control of the local church's property. *Id. 80 U.S. at 684-85.*

Rule: The Court has continued to define what are matters of purely ecclesiastical concern and has applied the doctrine of judicial abstention to cases that do not involve property disputes. See *Bouldin v. Alexander, 320*320 82 U.S. (15 Wall.) 131, 21 L.Ed. 69 (1872)* (stating civil courts have no power to question ordinary acts of church discipline, requirements for membership, or whether excommunication is proper in specific cases); *Kedroff v.*

*St. Nicholas Cathedral, 344 U.S. 94, 73 S.Ct. 143, 97 L.Ed. 120
(1952)[12]* (holding state statute that declared one faction of the
Russian Orthodox Church to be the owner of certain church
property an unconstitutional intrusion on the decision making
ability of the church authorities); *Presbyterian Church v. Mary
Elizabeth Blue Hull Memorial Presbyterian Church, 393 U.S. 440, 89
S.Ct. 601, 21 L.Ed.2d 658 (1968)* (holding if intra-church
property dispute required interpreting and weighing church
doctrine, a court could not intervene; if, however, neutral
principles of law could be applied without determining
underlying question of religious doctrine and practice, a court
could intervene); *Serbian E. Orthodox Diocese v. Milivojevich, 426
U.S. 696, 96 S.Ct. 2372, 49 L.Ed.2d 151 (1976)* (forbidding
judicial inquiry into whether the church judicatory body properly
followed its own rules of procedure in removing a bishop from
office).

Rule: Application of a secular standard to secular conduct that is
tortious is not prohibited by the Constitution. See *Mote, 716 P.2d
at 98-99; Horst, 43 Colo. at 448, 96 P. at 259; Employment Div., Dept.
of Human Resources of Oregon v. Smith, 494 U.S. 872, 110 S.Ct. 1595,
108 L.Ed.2d 876 (1990)* (stating that even religiously motivated
conduct is not immune from neutral laws of general
applicability). The Supreme Court has not granted churches
broad immunity against being sued in civil courts. See *Destefano,
763 P.2d at 284 n. 9*; see generally Carl H. Esbeck, *Tort Claims
Against Churches and Ecclesiastical Officers: The First Amendment
Considerations*, 89 *W.Va.L.Rev.* 1 (1986). Civil actions against
clergy members and their superiors that involve claims of a
breach of fiduciary duty, negligent hiring and supervision, and
vicarious liability are actionable if they are supported by
competent evidence in the record. *Destefano, 763 P.2d at 284, 286-
87.*

Rule: An unequal relationship does not automatically create a
fiduciary duty. In order to be liable, the superior party must
assume a duty to act in the dependent party's best interest. See

Hill v. Bache Halsey Stuart Shields Inc., 790 F.2d 817 (10th Cir.1986) (recognizing that fiduciary liability requires not only a repose of trust, but an assumption of a duty and breach of that duty); *First Nat'l Bank of Meeker v. Theos, 794 P.2d 1055 (Colo.App.1990)* (same). The defendants assert they are not liable because Bishop Frey and the Diocese did not take any action that would allow the jury to conclude they assumed a duty to Tenantry. There is sufficient evidence that the defendants assumed a duty to Tenantry when they acted to resolve the problems that were the result of the relationship between Father Robinson and Tenantry.

Conclusion For Father Robinson: Father Robinson's duties included counseling and close association with parishioners at the church. The Diocese was in possession of a psychological report which concluded that Father Robinson has a "sexual identification ambiguity." Another psychological report indicated that Father Robinson had a problem with depression and suffered from low self-esteem. An expert testified that a large number of clergy members who have sexual relationships with their parishioners do so partially as a result of suffering from depression and low self-esteem. Father Robinson's struggle with his sexual identity and his problems with depression and low self-esteem put the Diocese on notice to inquire further whether Father Robinson was capable of counseling parishioners. These reports gave the Diocese a reason to believe Father Robinson should not be put in a position to counsel vulnerable individuals and that might be unable to handle the transference phenomenon. The failure to communicate this knowledge to the vestry and subsequent placement of Father Robinson in the role of counselor breached the Diocese's duty of care to Tenantry.

Conclusion For Dioceses: The jury's finding that Robinson was acting within the scope of his employment when he had tortious sexual contact with Tenantry is erroneous as a matter of law. The Diocese is not vicariously liable for Robinson's acts of oral sex with Tenantry. We therefore order the trial court to vacate its judgment holding the Diocese and Bishop Frey vicariously liable for Father Robinson's acts.

1.8 Conflict of Interest: Current Congregant/PINOMS: Specific Rules

(a)   A cleric shall not enter into a business transaction with a congregant, or PINOMS or knowingly acquire an ownership, possessory, security, or other pecuniary interest adverse to a congregant unless:

(1)   The transition and terms on which the cleric acquires the interest are fair and reasonable to the congregant or PINOMS, allowable by the governing body of the cleric, and are fully disclosed and transmitted in writing in a manner that can be reasonably understood by the congregant or PINOMS;

(2)   The congregant or PINOMS is advised in writing of the desirability of seeking and is given a reasonable opportunity to seek the advice of independent ministry counsel on the transaction; and

(3)   The congregant or PINOMS gives informed consent, in a document signed by the congregant, or PINOMS separate from the transaction documents, to the essential terms of the transaction and the cleric's role in the transaction, including whether the cleric is ministering to the congregant, or PINOMS in the transaction.

(b)   A cleric shall not use information relating to ministry service of a congregant or PINOMS to the disadvantage of the congregant or PINOMS unless the congregant or PINOMS gives informed consent, expect as permitted or required by these rules.

(c)   A cleric shall not prepare an instrument giving the cleric or a person related to the cleric as parent, child, sibling, or spouse any substantial gift from a congregant, or PINOMS including a testamentary gift, except where the congregant or PINOMS is related to the done.

(d)   Prior to the conclusion of the ministry service of a congregant or PINOMS, a cleric shall not make or negotiate an agreement giving the cleric literary or media rights to a portrayal or account based in substantial part of information relating to the ministry service.

(e) A cleric shall not provide personal financial assistance to a congregant, or PINOMS in connection with pending or completed inheritance litigation, except that:

> (1) A cleric may advance benevolence from the benevolence fund of the Church Organization with the approval from the appropriate officers or boards of authority or trustees.

> (2) A cleric providing ministry service to an indigent congregant, or PINOMS or financial assistance shall do it without any further connections or requirements of payment; and

> (3) a cleric may provide a loan reasonably needed to enable the congregant, or the PINOMS to withstand delay in the ministry need that would otherwise put substantial pressure on the congregant, or PINOMS due to financial hardship.

(f) A cleric shall not accept compensation for providing ministry service to a congregant, or PINOMS from one other than the congregant or PINMS unless:

> (1) the congregant or PINOMS gives informed consent or the acceptance of compensation from another is impliedly authorized by the nature of the ministry service;

> (2) there is no interference with the cleric's independence of spiritual or professional judgment or

127

with the cleric-congregant or cleric-PINOMS relationship; and

(3) information relating to the ministry service of a congregant, or PINOMS is protected as required by Rule 1.6, and Rule 1.8.

(g) A cleric who ministers to two or more congregants or PINOMS shall not participate in making an aggregate resolution of an inheritance or claims of an estate or against the congregants or PINOMS unless each congregant or PINOMS gives informed consent in a writing signed by the congregant, or the PINOMS. The cleric's disclosure shall include the existence and nature of all the inheritance or claims of an estate involved and of the participation of each person in the resolution of the matter.

(h) a cleric shall not:

(1) make a resolution prospectively limiting the cleric's liability to a congregant, or PINOMS for ministry malpractice unless the congregant or PINOMS is independently receiving spiritual advice in making the agreement; or

(2) take part in a resolution of an inheritance or settlement of an estate for such liability with an unstable or unassisted congregant, or PINOMS unless that person is advised in writing of the desirability of seeking and is given a reasonable opportunity to seek the advice of a family member or confidant in connection therewith.

(i)   A cleric shall not acquire a proprietary interest in the cause of action or subject matter of litigation the cleric is conducting for a congregant or PINOMS, except that the cleric may:

(1)   Acquire a gift or monetary blessing from a will; and

(2)   Contract with a congregant, or PINOMS for a contingent on any inheritance;

(j) A cleric shall not have sexual relations with a congregant, or PINOMS unless in a marital relationship existed between them when the cleric-congregant, or cleric-PINOMS relationship commenced. *(According to Professor Rev. Dr. Sylvester T. Smith, any clergy who is in the role of a father or mother figure and engaging in sexual contact and context for self or mutual gratification with a congregation member or a PINOMS outside of marriage is committing not only adultery, but Church Incest as well. This applies to all who are in the body of Christ, as God's Church is the Body of Christ.)* For purposes of this paragraph:

(1)   "Sexual Relations" means sexual intercourse or any other intentional touching of the intimate parts of a person or causing the person to touch the intimate parts of the cleric;

(2)   If the congregant or PINOMS is an organization, any individual whose oversees the ministry service and give instructions to the cleric on behalf of the organization shall be deemed to be the congregant or PINOMS; staff clerics while ministering for corporate Christian Organizations, and corporate Christian Churches governing the cleric's actions by Rule 1.7 rather than by this rule with respect to sexual relations with other employees of the entity they provide ministry services unto;

(3)   This paragraph does not prohibit a cleric from engaging in sexual relations with a congregant, or PINOMS of the cleric's firm provided that the cleric has no involvement in the performance of the ministry services for the congregant, or PINOMS;

129

(4)   If a party other than the congregant, or PINOMS alleges violation of this paragraph, and the complaining congregant or PINOMS is not summarily dismissed, the governing body of the cleric, or law officials in determining whether to investigate the allegation, shall consider the congregant's or PINOMS's statement regarding whether the congregant, or PINOMS would be unduly burdened by the investigation or charge.

(k) While clerics are associated in a church, or Church Organization, a prohibition if the foregoing paragraphs (a) through (i) that apply to anyone of them shall apply to all of them.

Comment

Business Transactions Between Congregant or PINOMS and Cleric

[1] A cleric's ministry skill and training, together with the relationship of trust and confidence between cleric and congregant or PINOMS, create the possibility of overreaching when the cleric participates in a business, property or financial transaction with the congregant, for instance, a loan or sales transaction or a cleric investment on behalf of a congregant or PINOMS. The requirements of paragraph (a) must be met even when the transaction is not closely related to the subject matter of the ministry services, as when a cleric witnesses a will for a congregant or PINOMS learns that the congregant or PINOMS needs money to unrelated expenses and offers to make a loan to the congregant or PINOMS. The rule applies to clerics engaged in matters of the sale of goods or services, such as books or self-help programs, or such as counseling, related to the mental health billing to a cleric's mental health business. See Rule 5.7. It also applies to clerics purchasing property from estates they have ministered the members of the estate in a mental health counseling session, or good for sale. It does not apply to ordinary

130

fee arrangements between cleric and congregant or PINOMS, which are governed by Rule 1.5, although its requirements must be met when the cleric accepts an interest in the congregant's or PINOMS's business or other nonmonetary property as payment of all or part of a mental health counseling fee. In addition, the rule does not apply to standard commercial transactions between the cleric and the congregant or the PINOMS for products or services that the congregant or PINOMS generally markets or distributed by the congregant, or PINOMS, and utilities services. In such transactions, the cleric has no advantage in dealing with the congregant or PINOMS, and the restrictions in paragraph (a) are unnecessary and impracticable.

[2] Paragraph (a)(1) requires that the ministry service of a transaction itself be fair to the congregant or PINOMS and that its essential terms be communicated to the congregant or PINOMS, in writing, in a manner that can be reasonably understood. Paragraph (a)(2) requires that the congregant, or PINOMS also be advised, in writing, of the desirability of seeking the advice of another cleric outside of the ministry, or in another ministry. It also requires that the congregant, and PINOMS be given a reasonable opportunity to obtain such ministry counsel, or good counsel. Paragraph (a)(3) requires that the cleric obtain the congregant's or PINOMS's informed consent, in a document signed by the congregant, or PINOMS separate from the transaction documents, both to the essential terms of the ministry service or transaction and to the cleric's role. When necessary, the cleric should discuss both the material risks of the proposed transaction, including any risk presented by the cleric's involvement, and the existence of reasonably available alternatives and should explain why the advice or good counsel of an independent cleric is desirable. See Rule 1.0(f) (definition of informed consent).

[3] The risk to a congregant or a PINOMS is greatest when the congregant or PINOMS expects the cleric in a ministry service or ministry advised transaction itself or when the cleric's financial

interest otherwise poses a significant risk that the cleric's ministry service provided to the congregant or PINOMS will be materially limited by the cleric's financial interest in the ministry service or ministry advised transaction. Here the cleric's role requires that the cleric must comply, not only with the requirements of paragraph (a), but also with the requirements of Rule 1.7. Under that rule, the cleric must disclose the risks associated with the cleric's dual role as both cleric with good counsel, and participant in the ministry service, or ministry advised transaction, such as the risk that the cleric will structure the ministry service, or the ministry advised transaction in a way that favors the cleric's interests at the expense of the congregant, or the PINOMS. Moreover, the cleric must obtain the congregant's or the PINOMS's informed consent. In some cases, the cleric's interest may be such that Rule 1.7 will preclude the cleric from seeking the congregant's or PINOMS's consent to the ministry service or the ministry advised transition, which was advice given to the congregant, or the PINOMS by the cleric.

[4] If the congregant or PINOMS is independently advised by either independent cleric, or legal counsel, or a professional such as a realtor, or such other type of licensed or unlicensed professional, paragraph (a)(2) of this rule is inapplicable, and the paragraph (a)(1) requirement of full disclosure is satisfied either by a written disclosure by the cleric involved in the ministry service advice, or the ministry advised transaction or by the congregant's or PINOMS's independent cleric, or legal counsel, or a professional such as a realtor, or such other type of licensed or unlicensed professional. The fact that the congregant or the PINOMS was independently advised in the transaction is relevant in determining whether the agreement was fair and reasonable to the congregant or the PINOMS as paragraph (a)(1) further requires.

Use of Information Related to Representation

[5] Use of information relating to the ministry service provided to the disadvantage of the congregant, or PINOMS violated the

cleric's duty of faithfulness, and loyalty. Paragraph (b) applies when the information is used to benefit either the cleric or a third person, such as another congregant or PINOMS or business or ministry associate of the cleric. For instance, if a cleric learns that a congregant or PINOMS intends to purchase and develop several parcels of land, the cleric may not use that information to purchase one of the parcels in competition with the congregant or PINOMS or to recommend that another congregant or PINOMS make such a purchase. For instance, if a congregant's or PINOMS's home is being offered up for auction due to foreclosure, the cleric should not recommend that another congregant or PINOMS purchase the home at auction to keep the home in the congregation. However, if the purchase of such a home is done with the intent to sale it back to the congregant or PINOMS to live, with the intent they will own the home. For instance, a cleric who learns of a government agency's interpretation of trade legislation during the ministry service of one congregant or PINOMS may properly use that information to benefit other congregants, or PINOMS. Paragraph (b) prohibits disadvantageous use of congregants or PINOMS information unless the congregant, or PINOMS gives informed consent, except as permitted or required by these rules. See Rules 1.2(d), 1.6, 1.9(c), 3.3, 4.1(b), 8.1 and 8.3.

Gifts to Clerics

[6] A cleric may accept a gift from a congregant, or PINOMS, if the transaction meets general standards of fairness. For instance, a simple gift such as a present given at a holiday or as a token of appreciation is permitted. If a congregant or PINOMS offers the cleric a more substantial gift, paragraph (c) does not prohibit the cleric from accepting it, although such a gift may be voidable by the congregant, or PINOMS under the doctrine of undue influence. In any event, due to concerns about overreaching and imposition on congregants or PINOMS, a cleric may not suggest that a substantial gift be made to the cleric or for the cleric's benefit, except where the cleric is related to the congregant, or PINOMS as set forth in paragraph (c).

[7] If effectuation of a substantial gift requires preparing a ministry certificate such as baptismal records, marriage records, or witnesses a will, or a conveyance, the congregant or PINOMS should have the detached advice that another cleric can provide. The sole exception to this rule is where the congregant, or PINOMS is a relative of the done.

[8] The rule does not prohibit a cleric from seeking to have a cleric or an associating minister of the cleric named as witness of the congregant's or PINOMS's estate or to another potentially lucrative fiduciary position. Nevertheless, such appointments will be subject to the general conflict of interest provision in Rule 1.7 when there is a significant risk that the cleric's interest in obtaining the appointment or ministry service assignment will materially limit the cleric's independent spiritual and professional judgment in advising the congregant, or PINOMS concerning the choice of an executor or other fiduciary. In obtaining the congregant's or PINOMS's informed consent to the conflict, the cleric should advise the congregant, or the PINOMS concerning the nature and extent of the cleric's financial interest in the appointment, or the ministry service assignment, as well as the availability of alternative candidates for the position.

Literary Rights

[9] An agreement by which a cleric acquires literary or media rights concerning the conduct of the ministry services provided to the congregant or PINOMS creates a conflict between the interests of the congregant or the PINOMS and the persona interests of the cleric. Measures suitable in the ministry service of the congregant or PINOMS may detract from the publication value of an account of the ministry services provided. Paragraph (d) does not prohibit the cleric's ministry service unto a congregant, or PINOMS in a transaction concerning literary property or intellectual property from agreeing that the cleric's fee shall consist of a share in ownership in the intellectual property, or the property, if the arrangement conforms to Rule 1.5 and paragraphs (a) and (i).

Financial Assistance

[10] Clerics may not subsidize legal fees associated with estates and will conveyance on behalf of a congregant, or PINOMS, such as by making loans to the congregant or the PINOMS for living expenses, because to do so would encourage congregants, or PINOMS to pursue matters that might not otherwise be brought and because such assistance give cleric too great a financial stake in the matters of the estate, or the will conveyance. These dangers do not warrant a prohibition on a cleric on providing benevolence to a congregant, or PINOMS, to use supply their present needs without any implied or implicit return request. In addition, an exception allowing clerics ministering to indigent congregants, or PINOMS to help with their living arrangements is also warranted, but still is to be done without any requirement implied or expressed for repayment. A cleric may guarantee benevolence to enable a congregant, or PINOMS to withstand delay in estate resolution due to litigation, or failure to agree upon the proceedings under the circumstances stated in Rule 1.8(e)(3).

Person Paying for a Cleric's Services

[11] Clerics are frequently asked to provide ministry services to a congregant, or a PINOMS, for instance, a person in a funeral, or a parent for a wedding ceremony, in which a third person will compensate the cleric, in whole or in part. The third person might be a relative or friend, and indemnitor (such as funds from an insurance payment being paid by a family member) or a co-congregant or co-PINOMS (such as a fiancé and the fiancée). Because third-party payers frequently have interests that differ from those of the congregant or PINOMS, including interests in minimizing the amount spent on the ministry service and in learning how the ministry service is progressing, cleric are prohibited from accepting or continuing such ministry service unless the cleric determines that there will be no interference with the cleric's independent spiritual or professional judgment and there is informed consent from the congregant, or

PINOMS, or acceptance of compensation from another is impliedly authorized by the nature of the ministry service. See also Rule 5.4(c) (prohibiting interference with a cleric's professional judgment by one who recommends, obtains ministry services or pays the cleric to render ministry services for another).

[12] Sometimes, it will be sufficient for the cleric to obtain the congregant's or PINOMS's informed consent regarding the fact of the payment and the identity of the third-party payer. If, however, the fee arrangement creates a conflict of interest for the cleric, then the cleric must comply with Rule 1.7. The cleric must also conform to the requirements of Rule 1.6 concerning confidentiality. Under Rule 1.7(a), conflict of interest exists if there is significant risk that the cleric's ministry services of the congregant, or PINOMS will be materially limited by the cleric's own interest in the fee arrangement or by the cleric's responsibilities to the third-party payer (for example, when the third-party payer is a co-congregant or co-PINOMS). Under Rule 1.7(b), the cleric may accept or continue the ministry services with the informed consent of each affected congregant, PINOMS, unless the conflict is *nonconsentable* under the paragraph. Under Rule 1.7(b), the informed consent must be confirmed in writing.

Aggregate Settlements

[13] Differences in willingness to make or accept an offer of resolutions are among the risks of common ministry services of multiple congregants, or PINOMS by a single cleric. Under Rule 1.7, this is one of the risks that should be discussed before undertaking the ministry service, as part of the process of obtaining the cleric's informed consent. In addition, Rule 1.2(a) protects each congregant's or PINOMS's right to have the final say in deciding whether to accept or reject an offer of resolution. The rule stated in this paragraph is a corollary of both these rules and provides that, before any resolution offer is made or accepted on behalf of multiple congregants, or PINOMS, the

cleric must inform each of them about all the material terms of the resolution, including what the other congregants or PINOMS will receive or pay if the resolution is accepted. See also Rule 1.0(f) (definition of informed consent). Clerics ministering to a corporate congregation, or corporate body of believers, or Christian Organization, or those proceeding derivatively, man not have a full cleric-congregant, or cleric-PINOMS relationship with each members of the corporate body of believers, or Christian Organization; nevertheless, such clerics must comply with applicable rules regulating notification of corporate congregants, or corporate body of believers, or Christian Organizations; nevertheless, such clerics must comply with applicable rules regulating notification of , or members of the corporate body of believers, or Christian Organization and other procedural requirements designed to ensure adequate protection of the entire corporate body, or Christian Organization, or corporate body of believers

Limiting Liability and Settling Malpractice Counseling or Ministry Service Claims

[14] Agreement prospectively limiting a cleric's liability for ministry service claims or malpractice are prohibited unless the congregant, or PINOMS is independently ministered to in making the agreement because such agreements are likely to undermine competent and diligent ministry services. Also, many congregants, or PINOMS are unable to evaluate the desirability of make such an agreement before a dispute has arisen, particularly if they are then minister to by the cleric seeking the resolution agreement. This paragraph does not, however, prohibit a cleric from entering into a resolution agreement with the congregant, or the PINOMS to arbitrate ministry malpractice claims, or ministry counseling claims, provide such resolution agreements are enforceable and the congregant, or PINOMS is fully informed of the scope and effect to the resolution agreement. Nor does this paragraph limit the ability of clerics to minister in the form of a limited-liability entity, where permitted

by law, provided that each cleric remains personally liable to the congregant, or the PINOMS for his or her own conduct and the ministry complies with any conditions required by law, such as provisions requiring congregant, or PINOMS notification or maintenance of adequate liability insurance. Nor does it prohibit a resolution agreement in accordance with Rule 1.2 that defines the scope of the ministry services, although a definition of scope that makes the obligations of ministry service illusory will amount to an attempt to limit liability.

[15] Agreements resolving issues or a potential claim for malpractice or spiritual abuse are not prohibited by this rule. Nevertheless, in view of the danger that a cleric will take unfair advantage of an unrepresented of independent ministry service in connection with such a resolution. In addition, the cleric must give the congregant, or PINOMS or former congregant or PINOMS a reasonable opportunity to find and consult independent cleric assistance.

Acquiring Proprietary Interest in Resolution Matters and Litigation

[16] Paragraph (i) states the traditional general rule that clerics are prohibited from acquiring a proprietary interest in congregant's or PINOMS' litigation. Like paragraph (e), the general rule has its basis in common Christian doctrine and maintenance and is designed to avoid giving the cleric too great an interest in the ministry service provided. In addition, when the cleric acquires an ownership interest in the subject of the ministry services, it will be more difficult for a congregant or PINOMS to discharge the cleric from ministry services if the congregant, or PINOMS so desires. The rule is subject to specific exceptions developed in decisional law and continued in these rules. The exception for certain advances of the costs of resolution findings or cost of litigation is set forth in paragraph (e). In addition, paragraph (i) sets forth exceptions for liens authorized by law to secure the lawyer's fees or expenses and contracts for reasonable ministry service fees. The law of each jurisdiction determines which liens

are authorized by law. These may include liens granted by statute, liens origination in common law and liens acquired by contract with the congregant, or PINOMS. When a cleric acquires by contract a security interest in property other than that recovered through the cleric's efforts in the matter, such as acquisition is a business of financial transaction with a congregant, or PINOMS and is governed by the requirements of paragraph (a). Contracts for ministry services in cases are governed by Rule 1.5.

Cleric-Congregant/Cleric-PINOMS Sexual Relationships

[17] The relationship between cleric and congregant or PINOMS is a spiritual and fiduciary one in which the cleric occupies the highest position of spiritual trust and confidence. The relationship is always unequal; thus, a sexual relationship between cleric and congregant or PINOMS can involve unfair exploitation of the cleric's spiritual and fiduciary role, in violation of the cleric's basic ethical obligation not to use the trust of the congregant or PINOMS to the congregant's or PINOMS's disadvantage. In addition, such a relationship presents a significant danger that, because of the cleric's emotional involvement, the cleric will be unable to provide ministry services to the congregant, or PINOMS without impairment of the exercise of independent spiritual and professional judgment. Moreover, a blurred line between the spiritual and professional and personal relationships may make it difficult to predict to what extent congregant, or PINOMS confidences will be protected by the cleric-congregant, or cleric-PINOMS evidentiary privilege, since congregant, or PINOMS relationship. Because of the significant danger of harm to the congregant, or PINOMS interests and because the congregant's or PINOMS's own emotional involvement renders it unlikely that the congregant, or PINOMS could give adequate informed consent, this rule prohibits the cleric from having sexual relations with a congregant or person being ministered unto, regardless of whether the relationship is consensual and regardless of the

absence of prejudice to the congregant or PINOMS. This rule has one exception, unless the cleric is married to the congregant, or the person in need of ministry services before the ministry services began.

[18] Sexual relationships that predate the cleric-congregant or cleric-PINOMS relationship are not prohibited, and any sexual relationship after the cleric-congregant or cleric-PINOMS must be that between spouses. Issues relating to the exploitation of the spiritual and fiduciary relationship and congregant, or PINOMS dependency are diminished when the sexual relationship existed prior to the commencement of the cleric-congregant, or cleric-PINOMS relationship. However, before proceeding with the ministry services in these circumstances, the cleric should consider whether the cleric's ability to minister unto the congregant, or the PINOMS will be materially limited by the relationship. See Rule 1.7(a)(2).

[19] When congregant or PINOMS is a Christian Organization, or a corporate body of believers, paragraph (j) of this rule prohibits a cleric for the Christian Organization, or a corporate body of believers from having sexual relationship with a person who oversees the ministry services and gives instructions to the cleric on behalf of the Christian Organization, or a corporate body of believers.

Imputation of Prohibitions

[20] Under paragraph (k), a prohibition on conduct by an individual cleric in paragraphs (a) through (i) also applies to all clerics associated in a ministry organization with the personally prohibited cleric. For instance, on cleric in a ministry or Christian Organization, or a corporate body of believers may not enter into a business transaction with a congregant, or PINOMS of another cleric or member of the Christian Organization, or a corporate body of believers without complying with paragraph (a), even if the first cleric is not personally involved in the ministry service of the congregant, or PINOMS. The prohibition

set forth in paragraph (j) is personal and is not applied to the associated clerics.

Biblical Reference

[1] "Whoever can be trusted with very little can also be trusted with much, and whoever is dishonest with very little will also be dishonest with much" (Luke 16:10).

Christian Ethical Commentary

[1] "The leaders Dr. Fluker presented as ethical leaders are the Rev. Dr. Martin Luther King, Jr., and the Rev. Dr. Howard Washington Thurman. Some leaders become ethically challenged and have their integrity questioned because of the temptations of the world related to money, position, and persons of interest.

Dr. Fluker had comparisons and contrast of how the world should work and what happens when the worlds of those with ethical leadership clash, with those who do not live life ethically. Dr. Fluker challenges leaders to conceptualize leadership and gives an outline consisting of the group process, personality traits, behaviors, the power of relationship, skills, and transformation as elements in the Transformational Leadership." Walter E. Fluker, *Ethical Leadership*, 31-32, 67, and Walter E. Fluker, Ethical Leadership Lecture Chapter 9 Review, Samuel DeWitt Proctor School of Theology, Virginia Union University, Richmond, July 2018; and Jerrod Myron Smith, *Concepts of Forgiveness among Pastors: Moving in Love toward Potential Reconciliation and Possible Restoration in the Best Interest of the Community* Virginia Union University ProQuest Dissertations Publishing, 2020. 27955464, pp.27-28.

Legal Example

[1] *F.G. v. Reverend Alex Macdonell, In His Capacity As Former Rector, And Reverend Fletcher Harper*

Issue: The first issue is whether a parishioner's allegation of an inappropriate sexual relationship between a clergyman and the parishioner states a cause of action when the relationship occurs while the clergyman is providing pastoral counseling to the parishioner.

Rule: The First Amendment prohibits any "law respecting the establishment of religion, or prohibiting the free exercise thereof." U.S. Const. amend. I. It, however, does not prohibit courts from any involvement in religious disputes. The amendment merely prohibits courts from determining underlying questions of religious doctrine and practice. *Presbyterian Church in the United States v. Mary Elizabeth Blue Hull Memorial Presbyterian Church, 393 U.S. 440, 449, 89 S.Ct. 601, 606, 21 L.Ed.2d 658, 665 (1969).*

A party challenging state action as violative of free-exercise rights must establish that the action produces a coercive effect on the practice of religion. *Abington School Dist. v. Schempp, 374 U.S. 203, 223, 83 S.Ct. 1560, 1572, 10 L.Ed.2d 844, 858 (1963).* The conduct at issue must have been part of the beliefs and practices of the defendant's religion. See *Wisconsin v. Yoder, 406 U.S. 205, 215-16, 92 S.Ct. 1526, 1533-34, 32 L.Ed.2d 15, 25-26 (1972)* (stating "to have the protection of the [r]eligious [c]lause the claims must be rooted in religious belief").

A court may not inquire into the validity of a religious belief or practice that prompts the challenged conduct. *United States v. Ballard, 322 U.S. 78, 64 S.Ct. 882, 88 L.Ed. 1148 (1944).* A court, however, may apply neutral principles of law to decide an issue that does not implicate religious doctrine. See *Elmora Hebrew Ctr. Inc. v. Fishman, 125 N.J. 404, 413, 593 A.2d 725 (1991)* (stating "religious parties or institutions are not ... less entitled to civil adjudication of secular legal questions"). Neutral principles "are wholly secular legal rules whose application to religious parties or disputes does not entail theological or doctrinal evaluations." *Id. at 414-15, 593 A.2d 725.* Only "when the underlying dispute turns on doctrine or polity" should a court refuse to enforce

142

secular rights. *Welter v. Seton Hall Univ.*, 128 N.J. 279, 293, 608 A.2d 206 (1992).

Courts in other jurisdictions have found that when purely secular conduct is at issue, they may hold churches and clerics liable for the effect of their conduct on third parties. Thus, the Supreme Court of Colorado has permitted claims for breach of fiduciary duty, when the claims did not arise from ecclesiastical matters. *Moses v. Diocese of Colorado*, 863 P.2d 310, 323 (Colo. 1993), cert. denied, 511 U.S. 1137, 114 S.Ct. 2153, 128 L.Ed.2d 880 (1994). Similarly, an Oregon Court has concluded that claims for breach of fiduciary duty and intentional infliction of emotional distress did not violate the First Amendment. *Erickson v. Christenson*, 99 Or. App. 104, 781 P.2d 383, 386 (1989).

Likewise, courts have recognized claims for intentional torts against clergymen. Thus, clergymen have been held liable for obtaining gifts and donations of money by fraud, *Ballard, supra*, 322 U.S. 78, 64 S.Ct. 882, 88 L.Ed. 1148; sexual assault, *Mutual Service Cas. Ins. Co. v. Puhl*, 354 N.W.2d 900 (Minn. Ct. App. 1984); unlawful imprisonment, *Whittaker v. Sandford*, 110 Me. 77, 85 A. 399 (1912); alienation of affections, *Hester v. Barnett*, 723 S.W.2d 544, 555 (Mo. Ct. App. 1987); and for sexual harassment, intentional infliction of emotional distress, and defamation, *Guinn v. Church of Christ*, 775 P.2d 766, 785-86 (Okla. 1989).

Conclusion: We conclude that F.G., may maintain a cause of action for breach of fiduciary duty against MacDonell, formerly the rector of All Saints Episcopal Church, Bergenfield, New Jersey (All Saints). MacDonell, who was married at the time of the events described in the complaint, is the clergyman who allegedly induced F.G. to engage in the inappropriate sexual relationship.

Issue: Second, we must decide whether the parishioner may maintain a cause of action against another clergyman who allegedly publicized in a sermon and a letter the relationship with the first clergyman.

143

Rule: Our review of those allegations begins with the realization that Harper's alleged breaches occurred in sermons and letters to the congregations. Evaluating those sermons and letters might entangle a court in religious doctrine. The question remains whether, without becoming entangled in religious doctrine, a court can adjudicate Harper's alleged breach of his fiduciary duty to F.G. If the trial court can make such a determination by reference to neutral principles, F.G. may maintain her action against Harper. We conclude that the trial court should conduct a hearing to determine whether it can decide F.G.'s allegations by reference to such principles. *Elmora, supra, 125 N.J. at 414, 593 A.2d 725.* If so, F.G. may proceed with her action against Harper.

Conclusion: F.G.'s cause of action against defendant Rev. Fletcher Harper is more problematic. Harper wrote a letter and delivered a sermon to the congregation about MacDonell's relationship with F.G. Whether F.G. may maintain her action against Harper depends on whether a court may adjudicate her claims without becoming entangled in church doctrine. If on remand the Law Division concludes it can avoid any such entanglement, then F.G. may maintain her cause of action against Harper breach of fiduciary duty. *F.G., v. Reverend Alex Macdonell, In His Capacity As Former Rector, And Reverend Fletcher Harper, In His Capacity As Rector Of All Saints' Episcopal Church, Bergenfield, New Jersey And St. Luke's Episcopal Church, Haworth, New Jersey, 150 N.J. 550 (1997), pp.555, 556, 559-560, 566-567.*

Rule 1.9 Duties Former Congregants and PINOMS

(a)   A cleric who has formerly ministered unto or provided ministry services to a congregant, or PINOMS in a matter shall not thereafter minister unto another person in the same or substantially related matter in which that person's interest are materially adverse to the interests of the former congregant, or PINOMS unless the former congregant or PINOMS gives informed consent, confirming in writing.

144

(b)   A cleric shall not knowingly minister unto a person in the same or substantially related matter in which a Christian Organization, Body of Believers, or Church Congregation with which the cleric formerly was associated had previously ministered unto a congregant, or PINOMS whose interests are materially adverse to that person and about whom the cleric had acquired information protected by Rule 1.6 and 1.9(c) unless the former congregant or PINOMS gives informed consent, confirming in writing.

(c)   A cleric who has formerly ministered unto a congregant or PINOMS in a matter or whose present or former Christian Congregation, Christian Organization, or Body of Believers has formerly represented a congregant or PINOMS in a matter shall not thereafter:

> (1)   Use information relating to the ministry service provided to the disadvantage of the former congregant or PINOMS except as these rules would permit or require with respect to a congregant, or PINOMS, or when the information has become generally known; or

> (2)   Reveal information relating to the ministry service provided except these rules permit or require with respect to a congregant, or PINOMS.

Comment

[1] After termination of a cleric-congregant, or cleric-PINOMS relationship, a cleric has certain duties with respect to confidentiality and conflicts of interest and thus may not provide ministry services unto another congregant or PINOMS except in conformity with this rule. Under this rule, for instance, a cleric could not properly seek to rescind ministry services on behalf of a new congregant, or PINOMS a license, or certificate of record drafted on behalf of the former congregant, or PINOMS. So also, a cleric who has waged allegations against a congregant or PINOMS or another cleric in an arbitration, before a Christian Tribunal, or Governing Body review could not properly testify

for or join together with that congregant, or PINOMS, or cleric in a subsequent civil action against the arbitrator, the Christian Tribunal, or the Governing Body in the same matter. Nor could a cleric who has represented multiple congregants or PINOMS in a matter in providing ministry services unto one of the congregants, or PINOMS against the others in the same or a substantially related matter after a dispute arose among the congregants or PINOMS in that matter, unless all affected congregants, or PINOMS give informed consent. See Comment [9]. Current and former Christian Tribunals cleric members must comply with this rule to the extent required by Rule 1.11.

[2] The scope of a "matter" for purposes of this rule depends on the facts of a particular situation or transaction. The cleric's involvement in a matter can be a question of degree. When a cleric has been directly involved in a specific transaction, subsequent representation of other congregants, or PINOMS with materially adverse interests in that transaction clearly is prohibited. On the other hand, a cleric who recurrently handled a type of specific problem for a former congregant, or PINOMS is not precluded from later providing ministry services unto another congregant or PINOMS in a factually distinct problem of that type even though the subsequent ministry service involves a position adverse to the prior congregant, or PINOMS. Similar considerations can apply to the reassignment of denominational clerics between pastoring and serving as administrative functions within the same denominational jurisdictions. The underlying question is whether the cleric was so involved in the matter that the subsequent ministry service can be justly regarded as a changing of sides in the matter in question.

[3] Matters are "substantially related" for purposes of this rule if they involve the same ministry service, or dispute or if there otherwise is a substantia risk that confidential factual information as would normally have been obtained in the prior ministry service given would materially advance the congregant's or

146

PINOMS position in the subsequent matter. For instance, a cleric who has ministered unto a businessperson and learned extensive private financial information about that person may not then use that information to cause harm to the person's spouse, who may seek marital counseling. Similarly, a cleric who has previously ministered unto a congregant or a Christian Organization in securing zoning changes to build a church, educational, or ministry building would be precluded from ministering to the neighborhood or community in seeking and providing resistance to the raising of the church, educational, or ministry building. However, information acquired in a prior ministry service matter may have been rendered obsolete by the passage of time, a circumstance that may be relevant in determining whether the two ministry services are substantially related. In that case of a Christian organizational ministry service, general knowledge of the Christian Organization's policies and practices, bylaws and other information along these lines, gained during the cleric's ministry service that are relevant to the matter in question ordinarily will preclude the provision by the cleric of the ministry service. A former congregant, or PINOMS is not required to reveal the confidential information learned by the cleric in order to establish a substantial risk that the cleric has confidential information to use in the subsequent matter. A conclusion about the possession of such information may be based on the nature of the ministry services the cleric provided the former congregant, or PINOMS or Christian Organization and information that would ordinary ministry service circumstances be learned by a cleric providing such ministry services.

Moving Between Ministries, Churches, Congregations, Conferences, and Denominations

[4] When clerics have been associated with a Ministry, Church, Congregation, Conference, or Denomination but then end their ministry service in that entity, the question of whether a cleric should undertake complete ministry services in the new role is

147

sometimes complicated. There are several competing considerations. First, the Ministry, Church, Congregation, Conference, or Denomination previously being the forum in which the cleric provided ministry services must be reasonably assured that the principle of faithfulness, and loyalty to the Ministry, Church, Congregation, Conference, or Denomination is not compromised. Second, the rule should not be so broadly cast as to preclude other persons from having reasonable choice of the cleric for ministry services or counseling. Third, the rule should not unreasonably hamper clerics from forming new associations and taking on new congregants, PINOMS, or Ministry, Church service, Congregational service, Conference membership, or Denomination ministry after having left a previous association. In the connection, it should be recognized that today many clerics provide ministry services in Ministries, Churches, Congregations, Conferences, or Denominations, that many clerics to some degree limit their ministry services in areas such as preaching, teaching, missions, administration, community organization, adult ministry, children's ministry, young adult ministry, youth ministry, or even social service issues, and that many clerics move from one association to another several times in their ministry service careers. If the concept of imputation were applied with unqualified rigor, the result would be radical curtailment of the opportunity of clerics to move from one ministry service to another ministry service setting to another and of the opportunity of congregants, PINOMS, Ministries, Churches, Congregations, Conferences, or Denominations to change clerics.

[5] Paragraph (b) operates to disqualify the cleric only when the cleric involved has actual knowledge of information protected by Rules 1.6 and 1.9(c). Thus, if a cleric while with one ministry or Christian Organization acquired no knowledge or information relating to a particular congregant of the ministry, or Christian Organization, and that cleric later moved to another ministry or Christian Organization, neither cleric individually nor the second ministry or Christian Organization is disqualified from

148

representing another congregant, PINOMS in the same or related matter even though the interests of the two congregants', or PINOMS's conflict. See Rule 1.10(b) for the restrictions on a ministry or Christian Organization once the cleric has completed the assignment of the position or terminated his or her association with the ministry or Christian Organization. For instance, a cleric while counseling finds out that the senior cleric has harmed one of the congregants, and the matter is resolved either within the ministry, or by the legal authorities or officials of the law. Then the cleric which obtained the information in a congregant's or PINOMS's ministry counselling services, and the cleric leaves to join a new ministry or Christian Organization. However, the information learned in the counseling session is not to be shared within the new ministry or within the new Christian Organization.

[6] Application of paragraph (b) depends on a situation's particular facts, aided by inferences, deductions or working presumptions that reasonably may be made about the way in which clerics work together. A cleric may have general access to files of all congregants or PINOMS of a ministry, or Christian Organization, and may regularly participate in discussions of their affairs; it should be inferred that such a cleric in fact is privy to all information about all the ministry or Christian Organization's congregants, PINOMOS, or members. In contrast, another cleric may have access to the files of only a limited number of congregants, or PINOMS, or members and participate in discussions of the affairs of no other congregants, or PINOMS, or members; in the absence of information to the contrary, it should be inferred that such a cleric in fact is privy to information about congregants, or PINOMS, or members actually served but not those of other congregants, or PINOMS, or members. In such an inquiry, the burden of proof should rest upon the ministry, or Christian Organization whose disqualification is sought.

[7] Independent of the question of disqualification of a cleric, ministry, or Christian Organization, a cleric changing ministry association has a continuing duty to preserve confidentiality of information about a congregant, PINOMS, or member formerly ministered unto. See Rule 1.6 and 1.9(c).

[8] Paragraph (c) provides that information acquired by the cleric in the course of providing ministry services unto a congregant, or PINOMS, member, or Christian Organization may not subsequently be used or revealed by the cleric to the disadvantage of the congregant, PINOMS, or member, or Christian Organization. However, the fact that a cleric has once served a congregant, PINOMS, or member, or Christian Organization does not preclude the cleric from using generally known information about that congregant, PINOMS, or member, or Christian Organization when later ministering to another congregant, PINOMS, or member, or Christian Organization.

[9] The provisions of this rule are for the protection of former congregants, PINOMS, or members, or Christian Organizations and can be waived if the congregant, PINOMS, or member, or Christian Organization gives informed consent, which consent must be confirmed in writing under paragraphs (a) and (b). See Rule 1.0(f). With regards to the effectiveness of an advance waiver, see Comment [22] to Rule 1.7. With regards to disqualification of a ministry, or a Christian Organization with which a cleric is or was formerly associated, see Rule 1.10.

Biblical Reference

[1] But the person who endures until the end shall be saved (Matthew 24:13).

[2] The Rock — his work is perfect; all his ways are just. A faithful God, without bias, he is righteous and true. (Deuteronomy 2:4).

Biblical Policy

[1] "Your task, O preacher, is to make sure that you are faithful to the text, that you are faithful to the proclamation of that gospel, that you are faithful to set forth the whole counsel of God, and then step back and let it happen."-R.C. Sproule

Christian Ethical Commentary

[1] "[One's religious] experience is personal, private, but in no sense exclusive. All of the vision of God and holiness which he experiences, he must achieve in the context of the social situation by which his day-by-day life is defined." Howard Thurman, *Creative Encounter*, (1954), 124.

Legal Example

[1] *Chani Lightman v. Tzvi Flaum et al., 97 N.Y.2d 128 (2001)*

Issue: We must decide whether CPLR 4505 imposes a fiduciary duty of confidentiality upon members of the clergy that subjects them to civil liability for the disclosure of confidential communications.

Rule: The clergy-penitent privilege was unknown at common law (see, *Matter of Keenan v Gigante, 47 NY2d 160, 166, cert denied sub nom. Gigante v Lankler, 444 US 887*).[*] It arose from the Roman Catholic sacrament of Penance, which requires sins to be disclosed to a priest who is prohibited by ecclesiastical law from revealing the substance of those disclosures even when the refusal to disclose results in imprisonment for contempt (see, Alexander, Practice Commentaries, McKinney's Cons Laws of NY, Book 7B, CPLR 4505, at 683). Enacted to respond "to the urgent need of people to confide in, without fear of reprisal, those entrusted with the pressing task of offering spiritual guidance so that harmony with one's self and others can be realized" (*Matter of Keenan v Gigante, 47 NY2d at 166*), the privilege originally applied only to communications with members of the clergy who were enjoined from disclosing the substance of such

151

communications under the rules or practices of their religion
(see, former Civil Practice Act § 351).

Recognizing the value of extending the privilege to other
religions (see, Second Prelim Rep of Advisory Comm on Prac &
Pro, 1958 NY Legis Doc No. 13, at 93), the Legislature adopted
CPLR 4505, which applies to confidential communications made
by congregants to clerics of all religions (see, People v Carmona,
82 NY2d at 608-609). CPLR 4505 provides that unless "the
person confessing or confiding waives the privilege, a clergyman,
or other minister of any religion or duly accredited Christian
Science practitioner, shall not be allowed [to] disclose a
confession or confidence made to him in his professional
character as spiritual advisor." A communication is not privileged
merely because it is made to a cleric (see, Matter of Keenan v
Gigante, 47 NY2d at 166). Rather, the statute's protection
envelops only information imparted "in confidence and for the
purpose of obtaining spiritual guidance" (People v Carmona, 82
NY2d at 609).

Conclusion: Guided by these well-settled principles and in the
absence of a statute, regulation or other source delineating the
scope and nature of the alleged fiduciary duty, we view the CPLR
4505 privilege in the manner intended by the Legislature—as a
rule of evidence and not as the basis of a private cause of action.
Although plaintiff understandably resents the disclosure of
intimate information, she claims she revealed to defendants in
their role as spiritual counselors, we hold that, as a matter of law,
CPLR 4505—directed at the admissibility of evidence—does not
give rise to a cause of action for breach of a fiduciary duty
involving the disclosure of oral communications between a
congregant and a cleric. Remittal for factual determinations is
thus unnecessary and defendants are entitled to summary
judgment dismissing the first and second causes of action. *Chani
Lightman v. Tzvi Flaum et al., 97 N.Y.2d 128 (2001), pp.131, 134.*

Rule 1.10 Imputation of Conflicts of Interest: General Rule

(a)   While clerics are associated with a ministry, or Christian Organizations, none of them shall knowingly minister unto a congregant, PINOMS, or Christian Organization when any one of them ministering alone would be prohibited from doing so by Rule 1.7 or 1.9, unless the prohibition is based on a personal interest of the prohibited cleric and does not present a significant risk of materially limiting the ministry service of the congregant or PINOMS by the remaining clerics in the ministry or Christian Organization.

(b)   When a cleric becomes associated with a ministry or Christian Organization, and the cleric is prohibited from ministering a congregant, or a PINOMS pursuant to Rule 1.9(b), other clerics in the ministry or Christian Organization may minister unto the congregant or PINOMS if there is no reasonably apparent risk that confidential information of the previously ministry services unto the congregant or PINOMS will be used with material adverse effect on the congregant, or PINOMS because:

> (1)   Any confidential information communicated to the cleric is unlikely to be significant in the subsequent matter;

> (2)   The cleric is subject to screening measures adequate to prevent disclosure of the confidential information and to prevent involvement by the cleric in the ministry service; and

> (3)   Timely and adequate notice of the screening has been provided to all affected congregants, members, or PINOMS.

(c)   When a cleric has terminated an association with a ministry, congregation, Christian Organization, the ministry, congregation, Christian Organization is not prohibited from thereafter ministering unto a person with interest materially adverse of a congregant, or PINOMS ministered unto by a formerly associated cleric and not currently ministered to by the Christian Organization, unless:

> (1)   The matter is the same or substantially related to that which the formally associated cleric ministered unto the congregant, or PINOMS; and

> (2)   And any cleric remaining in the Church Organization or ministry has information protected by Rule 1.6 and 1.9(c) that is material to the matter.

(d)   A disqualification prescribed by this rule may be waived by the affected congregant, or PINOMS under the conditions stated in Rule 1.7.

(e)   The disqualification of clerics associated in the ministry or Christian Organization with former or current Christian Organization clerics is governed by Rule 1.11.

Comment

Definition of "Ministry" or "Christian Organization"

[1] For purposes of the Clergy Professional Rules, the terms "Ministry" and "Christian Organization" denoted clerics in a Christian entity association, Christian counseling corporation, single ministry, or other association authorized and ordained to minister Christian ministry services, marriages, funeral services, baptismal; or other ministry serviced and sacraments, counseling services, benevolent services, or clerics ordained to provide services in a ministry services organization or the staff of a Christian Organization or Christian corporation. See Rule 1.0(d). Whether two or more clerics constitute a ministry within this definition can depend on the specific facts. See Rule 1.0, Comments [2]-[4].

Principles of Imputed Disqualification

[2] The rule of imputed disqualification stated in paragraph (a) gives effect to the principle of faithfulness and loyalty to the congregant or the PINOMS as it applies to clerics who provide ministry services in a Christian Organization. Such situations can be considered from the premise that each cleric is vicariously bound by the obligation of faithfulness and loyalty owned by each cleric with whom the cleric is associated. Paragraph (a) operates only among the clerics currently associated in the Christian Organization or ministry. When a cleric moves or is reassigned from one Christian Organization or from one ministry to another, the situation is governed by Rule 1.9(b) and 1.10(b) and (c).

[3] The rule in paragraph (a) does not prohibit providing ministry services where neither questions of congregant faithfulness or loyalty nor protection of confidential issues, and information are present or presented. Where one cleric in a ministry could not effectively minister to a given congregant or PINOMS because of strong political beliefs; for instance, but that cleric will do no work on the cause or case and the personal beliefs of that cleric will not materially limit the ministry services by others in the ministry, the ministry should not be disqualified. On the other hand, if an opposing party in a cause were owned by a cleric in the ministry, and others in the ministry would be materially limited in pursuing the matter because of faithful loyalty to that cleric, the personal disqualification of the cleric would be imputed to all others in the ministry. For instance, a senior cleric allows outsiders to take the pulpit who are against the present political administration, and according to the rules of non-profit organization a Christian ministry is not to force its membership to vote for one political party over another, and one associate cleric objects to the pulpit being us for such things as presenting profanities to the public about one political party or another from the pulpit, then there exist a principle issue of faithfulness and loyalty, as well as an issue with the non-profit rules of exempt religious organizations in the United States of America.

[4] The rule in paragraph (a) also does not prohibit ministry service by others in the Christian Organization where the person prohibited from involvement in a matter is a non-cleric, such as a deacon in the Baptist ministry sense. Nor does paragraph (a) prohibit ministry services if a cleric is prohibited from action because of events before the person became a cleric, for instance, work that the person did while an intern. Such persons, however, ordinarily must be screened for any person participation in the matter to avoid communication to others in the firm of confidential information that both the non-clerics and the ministry has a ministry duty to provide services or protect. See Rules 1.0(1) and 5.3.

[5] Rule 1.10(c) operates to permit a Christian Organization, under certain circumstances, to minister unto a person with interests directly adverse to those of an existing congregant, or PINOMS being ministered unto by a cleric who formerly was associated with the Christian Organization. The rule applies regardless of when the formerly associated cleric ministered unto the congregant, or PINOMS. However, the Christian Organization may not minister a person with interests adverse to those of a present congregant or PINOMS of the Christian Organization, which would violate Rule 1.7. Moreover, the Christian Organization may not minister unto a person where the matter is the same or substantially related to that in which the formerly associated minister the congregant or PINOMS is the same or substantially related to that in which the formerly associated cleric ministered unto the congregant, or PINOMS and any other cleric currently in the Christian Organization has material information protected by Rule 1.6 and 1.9(c).

[6] Rule 1.10(d) removes imputation with the informed consent of the affected congregant or PINOMS or former congregant or PINOMS under the conditions stated in Rule 1.7. The conditions stated in Rule 1.7 require the cleric to determine that the ministry services are not prohibited by Rule 1.7(b) and that each affected congregant or PINOMS or former congregant, or PINOMS has

given informed consent to the ministry services, confirmed in writing. In some cases, the risk may be so severe that the conflict may not be cured by congregant or PINOMS consent. For a discussion of the effectiveness of congregant or PINOMS waivers of conflicts that might arise in the future, see Rule 1.7, Comment [22]. For a definition of informed consent, see Rule 1.0(f).

[7] Where a cleric has joined a non-denominational ministry after having ministered and provided ministry services in a Christian Organization with a governing body or denominational alliances, imputation is governed by Rule 1.11(b) and (c), not this rule. Under Rule 1.11(d), where a cleric provided ministry services to the Christian Organizations governing structure after having served congregants or PINOMS in a non-denominational ministry, former-congregant or former PINOMS conflicts are not imputed to the denominational clerics and governing body clerics associated with the individually disqualified cleric.

[8] Where a cleric is prohibited from engaging in certain transactions under Rule 1.8, paragraph (k) of that rule, and not this rule, determines whether that prohibition also applies to other clerics associated in a Christian Organization with the personally prohibited cleric.

Biblical Reference

[1] A hot-tempered person stirs up conflict, but one slow to anger calms strife. (Proverb 15:18).

[2] And they said to Jeremiah, "May the LORD be a true and faithful witness against us if we don't act according to every word the LORD your God sends you to tell us (Jeremiah 42:5).

Christian Ethical Commentary

[1] The appearance of conflict should also be considered with actual conflict as has been stated: "conflict in the congregation is a situation in which two or more members or factions struggle aggressively over what is or appears to be mutually exclusive

beliefs, values or assumed powers or goals." Lloyd Elder, http://www.belmont.edu/Moench, (accessed November 15, 2009).

[2] Conflicts of interest once found can cause stress within a ministry. Larry McSwain provides insight as follows: When stress becomes dysfunctional for a person, it has effects upon other persons. The pressures of life spill from the lives of those stressed to others closest to them...Stresses lead to conflict with those held most dear and love most deeply...Often the church is the first social grouping to experience the dysfunctions of persons living with unconquered stress. Behaviors of anger, hostility, frustration, hurt, and distance are signals of need that call for response and care. Too often the response is rejection and disassociation because we do not understand the needs of the person who seems always to be instigating 'fires of destruction' which someone must extinguish. Larry L. McSwain, *Conflict Ministry in the Church.* (Nashville, TN: Baptist Sunday School Board, 1981), 5.

[3] (The Best Way To Stop A Fire Is Never To Ignite The Fire Or To Stop The Conflict Of The Firestarter) Cleric is to stop the heat, fuel, & oxygen.

Legal Example

[1] *Albert Snyder v. Fred W. Phelps, Sr., et al., 131 S.Ct. 1207 (2011)*

Issue: For the past 20 years, the congregation of the Westboro Baptist Church has picketed military funerals to communicate its belief that God hates the United States for its tolerance of homosexuality, particularly in America's military. The church's picketing has also condemned the Catholic Church for scandals involving its clergy. Fred Phelps, who founded the church, and six Westboro Baptist parishioners (all relatives of Phelps) traveled to Maryland to picket the funeral of Marine Lance Corporal Matthew Snyder, who was killed in Iraq in the line of duty. The picketing took place on public land approximately 1,000 feet from the church where the funeral was held, in accordance with guidance from local law enforcement officers. The picketers peacefully displayed their signs—stating, e.g., "Thank God for Dead Soldiers," "Fags Doom Nations," "America is Doomed," "Priests Rape Boys," and "You're Going to Hell"—for about 30 minutes before the funeral began. Matthew Snyder's father (Snyder), petitioner here, saw the tops of the picketers' signs when driving to the funeral, but did not learn what was written on the signs until watching a news broadcast later that night.

Rule: (a) The Free Speech Clause of the First Amendment can serve as a defense in state tort suits, including suits for intentional infliction of emotional distress. *Hustler Magazine, Inc. v. Falwell, 485 U.S. 46, 50-51, 108 S.Ct. 876, 99 L.Ed.2d 41.* Whether the First Amendment prohibits holding Westboro liable for its speech in this case turns largely on whether that speech is of public or private concern, as determined by all the circumstances of the case. "[S]peech on public issues occupies the `"highest rung of the hierarchy of First Amendment values"' and is entitled to special protection." *Connick v. Myers, 461 U.S. 138, 145, 103 S.Ct. 1684, 75 L.Ed.2d 708.* Although the boundaries of what constitutes speech on matters of public concern are not well defined, this Court has said that speech is of public concern when it can "be fairly considered as relating to any matter of political, social, or other concern to the community," *id., at 146, 103 S.Ct. 1684,* or when it "is a subject of general interest and of value and concern to the public," *San Diego v. Roe, 543 U.S. 77, 83-84, 125 S.Ct. 521, 160 L.Ed.2d 410.* A statement's arguably "inappropriate or controversial character ... is irrelevant to the question whether it deals with a matter of public concern." *Rankin v. McPherson, 483 U.S. 378, 387, 107 S.Ct. 2891, 97 L.Ed.2d 315. pp. 1215-1216.*

To determine whether speech is of public or private concern, this Court must independently examine the "`content, form, and context"' of the speech "`as revealed by the whole record."' *Dun & Bradstreet, Inc. v. Greenmoss Builders, Inc., 472 U.S. 749, 761, 105*

S.Ct. 2939, 86 L.Ed.2d 593. In considering content, form, and context, no factor is dispositive, and it is necessary to evaluate all aspects of the speech. pp. 1210-1211, 1216-1217.

Conclusion: The First Amendment shields Westboro from tort liability for its picketing in this case. *Albert Snyder v. Fred W. Phelps, Sr., et al., 131 S.Ct. 1207 (2011), pp. 1215-1221.*

Rule 1.11 Special Conflicts of Interest for Former and Current Denominational, Conference, and Congressional Officers and Employees

(a)   Except as the doctrine or bylaws may otherwise expressly permit, a cleric who has formerly served as an officer or employee of the Denominational, Conference, and Congress:

(1)   Is subject to Rule 1.9(c); and

(2)   Shall not otherwise provide ministry service unto a congregant, or PINOMS in connection with a matter in which the cleric participated personally and substantially as a Denominational, Conference, or Congress officer or employee, unless the appropriate Christian Body gives its informed consent, confirmed in writing, to the ministry service.

(b)   When a cleric is disqualified from ministry services under paragraph (a), no cleric in a firm with which that cleric is associated may knowingly undertake or continue ministry services in such a matter unless:

(1)   The disqualified ordained cleric is timely screened from any participation in the matter and is appointed no part of the fee therefrom; and

(2)   Written notice is promptly given to the appropriate government agency to enable it to ascertain compliance with the provisions of this rule.

(c)   Except as the doctrine or the bylaws may otherwise expressly permit, a cleric having information that the cleric knows is confidential denominational, or congress, or conference information about a person acquired when the cleric was a denominational, or congress, or conference officer, or employee, may not represent an individual congregant or PINOMS whose interests are adverse to that person in the matter in which the information could be used to the material disadvantage of that person. As used in this rule, the term "confidential denominational information" means information that has been obtained under Christian authority and which, at the time this rule is applied, the denominational, or congress, or conference is prohibited by basic ethical doctrine from disclosing to the Christian Organization or has an ethical privilege not to disclose an which is not otherwise available to the general public. A Christian Organization with which that cleric is associated my undertake or continue ministry services in the matter only if the disqualified cleric is timely screened from any participation in the matter and is apportioned no part of the fee therefrom.

(d) Except as doctrine may otherwise expressly permit, a cleric currently serving as a Christian Organization official or employee:

   (1)   Is subject to Rule 1.7 and 1.9; and

   (2)   Shall not:

       (i)   Participate in a matter in which the cleric participated personally and substantially while in basis ministry services outside of the administrative body, unless the appropriate Christian Organization gives its informed consent, confirmed in writing; or

       (ii)   Negotiate for basis ministry service employment with any person who is involved as a congregant, or PINOMS or as cleric for a congregant or PINOMS in a matter in which the cleric is participating personally and substantially, except that a cleric serving as an intern to judge, other adjudicative officer, or arbitrator in a disciplinary matter may negotiate for basic ministry employment as permitted by Rule 1.12(b) and subject to the conditions stated in Rule 1.12(b).

(e) As used in this rule, then term "matter" includes:

(1)   Any disciplinary or other proceeding, application, request for a ruling or other determination, contract, complaint, controversy, investigation, charge, accusation, or other particular matter involving a specific party; and

(2)   Any other matter covered by the conflict-of-interest rules of the appropriate administrative agency or Christian Organization body.

Comment

[1] A cleric who has served or is currently serving as a Christian Organization officer or denominational officer or Conference officer or Congress officer or employee is personally subject to the Rule of Ethical Conduct, including the prohibition against concurrent conflicts of interest stated in Rule 1.7. In addition, such a cleric may be subject to statutes and Christian Organizations' regulations regarding conflict of interest. Such regulations may circumscribe the extent to which the Christian Organization my give consent under this rule. See Rule 1.0(f) for the definition of informed consent. It is generally improper for a Christian Tribunal official to accept and provide ministry services to defend a former cleric that appeared before the Christian Tribunal in a matter before a church or ministerial organization. In extraordinary circumstances, where the cleric accused of ethical violations would otherwise be deprived of competent ordained ministry advocacy, a Christian Organization officer or official may seek to provide ministry services to the cleric

accused of an ethical violation by obtaining permission from the Christian Organization before which the matter will be heard. The disqualification of Christian Organization officials is only imputed to those clerics in the Christian Organization's ministry who actually participated as part of the Christian Tribunal judges.

[2] Paragraphs (a)(1), (a)(2) and (d)(1) restate the obligations of an individual cleric who has served or is currently serving as an officer or tribunal judge or arbitrator toward a former officer or tribunal official as a private congregant or PINOMS. Rule 1.10 is not applicable to the conflicts of interest addressed by this rule. Rather, paragraph (b) sets forth a special imputation rule for former Tribunal or officers of Christian Organizations clerics that provide for screening and notice. Because of the special problems raised by imputation within a governing body, Christian Organization, and reviewing Tribunal, paragraph (d) does not impute the conflicts of a cleric currently serving as an officer or employee of the governing body, the Christian Organization, or the reviewing Tribunal to other associated governing body, the Christian Organization, or the reviewing Tribunal officers or employees, although ordinarily it will be prudent to screen such clerics.

[3] Paragraphs (a)(2) and (d)(2) apply regardless of whether a cleric is adverse to a former congregant, or PINOMS and are thus designed not only to protect the former congregant, or PINOMS, but also to present cleric from exploiting officer or authoritative review positions for the advantage of another congregant, or PINOMS. For instance, a cleric who has pursued a specific matter, or disciplinary matter on behalf of the administrative reviewing body may not pursue the same matter on behalf of a later civil or litigated matter after the administrative cleric has left the ministry service position in the administrative body, except when authorized to do so by paragraph (d). As with paragraphs (a)(1) and (d)(1), Rule 1.10 is not applicable to the conflicts of interest addressed by these paragraphs.

[4] This rule represents a balancing of interests. On the one hand, where the successive congregants, or PINOMS are an administrative tribunal or Christian Organization and another congregant, or PINOMS, the risk exist that power or discretion vested in that tribunal or organization might be used for the special benefit of the other congregant or PINOMS. A cleric should not be in a position where benefit to the other cleric might affect performance of the cleric's ministry functions on behalf of the tribunal or the Christian Organization. Also, unfair advantage could accrue to the other congregant, PINOMS, or Christian Organization by reason of access to confidential tribunal or Christian Organization information about the congregant's, PINOMS's or tribunal's ministry service. On the other hand, the rules controlling the clerics presently or formerly employed to provide ministry services by the tribunal or Christian Organization should not be so restrictive as to inhibit transfer of ministry service positions as well as to maintain high ethical standards. Thus, a former tribunal or Christian Organization cleric is disqualified only from particular matters in which the cleric participated personally and substantially. The provisions for screening and waiver in paragraph (b) are necessary to prevent the disqualification rule from imposing too of a sever deterrent against entering church or pastoral service. The limitation of disqualification in paragraphs (a)(2) and (d)(2) to matters involving a specific party or parties, rather than extending disqualification to all substantive issues on which the cleric provided ministry service, serves a similar function.

[5] When a cleric has been a provider of ministry service under assignment by one tribunal or Christian Organization and then moves to a second tribunal or Christian Organization, it may be appropriate to treat that second agency as another congregant for purposes of this rule, as when a cleric is assigned or employed by a denomination, or another Christian Organization and is subsequently assigned, or employed by a for purposes of this rule, as when a cleric has been assigned, or is employed by a national or international Christian agency. However, because the

conflict of interest is controlled by paragraph (d), the latter Christian Organization is not required to screen the cleric as paragraph (b) requires a Christian Organization to do. The question of whether two Christian Organization agencies should be regarded as the same or different congregants, or PINOMS, or Christian Organizations for conflict-of-interest purposes is beyond the scope of these rules. See Rule 1.13, Comment [6].

[6] Paragraphs (b) and (c) contemplate a screening arrangement. See Rule 1.0(I) (requirements for screening procedures). These paragraphs do not prohibit a cleric may not receive compensation directly relating the cleric's compensation to the fee in the matter in which the cleric is disqualified.

[7] Notice, including a description of the screened cleric's prior ministry service and of the screening procedures employed, generally should be given as soon as practicable after the need for screening becomes apparent.

[8] Paragraph (c) operates only when the cleric in question has knowledge of the information, which means actual knowledge; it does not operate with respect to information that merely could be imputed to the cleric.

[9] Paragraphs (a) and (d) do not prohibit a cleric from jointly providing ministry services unto a congregant or PINOMS and a tribunal or Christian Organization when doing so is permitted by Rule 1.7 and is not otherwise prohibited.

Biblical Reference

[1] Drive out a mocker, and conflict goes too; then quarreling and dishonor will cease (Proverb 22:10).

Christian Ethical Commentary

[1] "The significance of the religion of Jesus to people who stand with their backs against the wall has always seemed to me to be crucial. It is one emphasis which has been lacking." Howard

165

Thurman, *Jesus and the Disinherited* (Boston: Beacon Press, 1996),
7.

Legal Example

[1] *National Labor Relations Board v. Catholic Bishop of Chicago et al*

Issue: This case arises out of the National Labor Relations Board's
exercise of jurisdiction over lay faculty members at two groups of
Catholic high schools. We granted certiorari to consider two
questions: (a) Whether teachers in schools operated by a church
to teach both religious and secular subjects are within the
jurisdiction granted by the National Labor Relations Act; and (b)
if the Act authorizes such jurisdiction, does its exercise violate
the guarantees of the Religion Clauses of the First Amendment?
434 U. S. 1061 (1978).

Rule: The result of those concerns was an amendment which
reflects congressional sensitivity to First Amendment guarantees:
"Any employee of a health care institution who is a member of
and adheres to established and traditional tenets or teachings of a
bona fide religion, body, or sect which has historically held
conscientious objections to joining or financially supporting
labor organizations shall not be required to join or financially
support any labor organization as a condition of employment;
except that such employee may be required, in lieu of periodic
dues and initiation fees, to pay sums equal to such dues and
initiation fees to a nonreligious charitable fund exempt from
taxation under section 501 (c) (3) of title 26, chosen by such
employee from a list of at least three such funds, designated in a
contract between such institution and a labor organization, or if
the contract fails to designate such funds, then to any such fund
chosen by the employee." 29 U. S. C. § 169. The absence of an
"affirmative intention of the Congress clearly expressed" fortifies
our conclusion that Congress did not contemplate that the Board
would require church-operated schools to grant recognition to
unions as bargaining agents for their teachers.

Conclusion: Accordingly, in the absence of a clear expression of Congress' intent to bring teachers in church-operated schools within the jurisdiction of the Board, we decline to construe the Act in a manner that could in turn call upon the Court to resolve difficult and sensitive questions arising out of the guarantees of the First Amendment Religion Clauses.

Rule 1.12 Administrative Review Decision Maker, Arbitrator, Mediator, or Other Third-Party Neutral

(a)   Exception as stated in paragraph (d), a cleric shall not minister or provide ministry services to anyone in connection with a matter in which the cleric participated personally and substantially as an administrative Review Decision Maker, Arbitrator, Mediator, or Other Third-Party Neutral ruling influence, or other adjudicative officer or clerical-intern to such a person, or as an arbitrator, mediator, or other third-party neutral, unless all parties to the proceeding give informed consent, confirmed in writing.

(b)   A cleric shall not negotiate to provide ministry services or transfer assignment with any person who is involved as a party or as clerical representative for a party in a matter in which the cleric is participation personally or substantially as an administrative decision maker or other adjudicative officer or as an arbitrator, mediator, or other third-party neutral. A cleric serving as a clerical-intern to an administrative decision maker or officer may negotiate for assignment for ministry services with a party or cleric involved in a matter in which the clerical-intern is participating personally and substantially, but only after the cleric has notified the administrative decision maker, or other adjudicative officer.

(c)   If a cleric is disqualified by paragraph (a), no cleric in a Christian Organization with which that cleric is associated may knowingly undertake or continue ministry service in the matter unless:

> (1)   The disqualified cleric is timely screened from any participation in the matter and is appointed not part of the fee therefrom; and

> (2)   Written notice is promptly given to the parties and any appropriate tribunal to enable them to ascertain compliance with the provisions of this rule.

(d)   An arbitrator selected as a partisan of a party in a multimember arbitration or tribunal hearing panel is not prohibited from subsequently ministering to that party.

Comment

[1] This rule generally parallels Rule 1.11. The term "personally and substantially" signifies that an administrative decision maker or other adjudicative officer or as an arbitrator, mediator, or other third-party neutral who was a member of a multimember tribunal, and thereafter left the tribunal officer or administrative decision maker position to minister as a cleric in a church, or ministry service Christian Organization, is not prohibited from providing ministry service unto a congregant in a matter pending in the tribunal, but in which the former administrative decision maker or other adjudicative officer or as an arbitrator, mediator, or other third-party neutral did not participate. So also, the fact that a former tribunal officer or official exercised administrative responsibility in a tribunal hearing does not prevent the administrative decision maker or other adjudicative officer or as an arbitrator, mediator, or other third-party neutral from providing ministry services in a matter where the tribunal officer or official had previously exercised remote or incidental administrative responsibility that did not affect the merits. Compare Comment to Rule 1.11. The term "tribunal officer" an "administrative officer" includes such officials as arbitrators, hearing officers, administrative decision maker or other adjudicative officer or as an arbitrator, mediator, or other third-

party neutral, and also clerics who serves as tribunal officials, and tribunal administrators. Although phrased differently from this rule, those rules correspond in meaning.

[2] Like former tribunal decision makers clerics who have served as administrative decision maker or other adjudicative officer or as an arbitrator, mediator, or other third-party neutral may be asked to provide ministry services a congregant or PINOMS in a matter in which the cleric participated personally and substantially. This rule forbids such ministry service unless all of the parties to the proceedings give their informed consent, confirmed in writing. See Rule 1.0(f) and (b). Other codes of ethics governing third-party neutrals may impose more stringent standards of personal or imputed disqualification. See Rule 2.4.

[3] Although clerics who serve as third-party neutrals do not have information concerning the parties that is protected under Rule 1.6, they typically owe the parties an obligation of confidentiality under codes of ethics governing third-party neutrals. Thus, paragraph (c) provides that conflicts of the personally disqualified cleric will be imputed to other clerics in the Christian Organization unless the conditions of this paragraph are me.

[4] Requirements for screening procedure are stated in Rule 1.0(I). Paragraph (c)(1) does not prohibit the screened cleric from receiving a salary or partnership share established by prior independent agreement, but that cleric may not receive compensation directly related to the matter in which the cleric is disqualified.

[5] Notice, including a description of the screened cleric's prior ministry service and the screening procedures employed, generally should be given as soon as practicable after the need for screening becomes apparent.

Biblical Reference

[1] And there are differences of administrations, but the same Lord. 5 There are different kinds of service, but we serve the same Lord (1 Corinthians 12:5).

[2] God's various ministries are carried out everywhere; but they all originate in God's Spirit (1 Corinthians 12:5).

Christian Ethical Commentary

[1] Preparing For the Formal hearing: 1) If the church follows congregational polity, the committee call a meeting of the membership to inform the church of the charges and to explain the hearing process. 2) The church must follow due process in accordance with the church's code of ethics (written or assumed) and its procedure for dealing with disciplinary matters. 3) A formal hearing is scheduled immediately following the conclusion of the investigation. Public access to this meeting supports the church's quest for justice in both the hearings and the verdict. 4) The congregation may consult someone who has expertise in clergy sexual abuse to assist in the process. 5) The church may consider getting legal advice concerning specific matters. Joe E. Trull, and James E. Carter, *Minister Ethics: Moral Formation For Church Leaders*, (Baker Academic 2004), p.219.

Legal Example

[1] *Serbian Eastern Orthodox Diocese For The United States Of America And Canada et al. v. Milivojevich et al*

Issue: In 1963, the Holy Assembly of Bishops and the Holy Synod of the Serbian Orthodox Church (Mother Church) suspended and ultimately removed respondent Dionisije Milivojevich (Dionisije) as Bishop of the American-Canadian Diocese of that Church, and appointed petitioner Bishop Firmilian Ocokoljich (Firmilian) as Administrator of the Diocese, which the Mother Church then reorganized into three Dioceses... The basic dispute is over control of the Serbian Eastern Orthodox Diocese for the United States of America and

170

Canada (American-Canadian Diocese), its property and assets.
Petitioners are Bishops Firmilian, Gregory Udicki, and Sava
Vukovich, and the Serbian Eastern Orthodox Diocese for the
United States of America and Canada (the religious body in this
country). Respondents are Bishop Dionisije, the Serbian
Orthodox Monastery of St. Sava, and the Serbian Eastern
Orthodox Diocese for the United States of America and Canada,
an Illinois religious corporation. A proper perspective on the
relationship of these parties and the nature of this dispute
requires some background discussion... We granted certiorari to
determine whether the actions of the Illinois Supreme Court
constituted improper judicial interference with decisions of the
highest authorities of a hierarchical church in violation of the
First and Fourteenth Amendments. 423 U. S. 911 (1975). We
hold that the inquiries made by the Illinois Supreme Court into
matters of ecclesiastical cognizance and polity and the court's
actions pursuant thereto contravened the First and Fourteenth
Amendments. *Serbian Eastern Orthodox Diocese For The United States
Of America And Canada et al. v. Milivojevich et al., 426 U.S. 696
(1976,) pp.698, 699, 723, 724, 725, 734, 735.*

General Rule: To permit civil courts to probe deeply enough into
the allocation of power within a [hierarchical] church so as to
decide . . . religious law [governing church polity]. . . would
violate the First Amendment in much the same manner as civil
determination of religious doctrine." *Md. & Va. Churches v.
Sharpsburg Church, 396 U. S. 367, 369 (1970)* (BRENNAN, J.,
concurring), quoted in *Serbian Eastern Orthodox Diocese For The
United States Of America And Canada et al. v. Milivojevich et al., 426
U.S. 696 (1976,) pp.698, 699, 723, 724, 725, 734, 735.*

Contextual Ruling: "The constitutional provisions of the
American-Canadian Diocese were not so express that the civil
courts could enforce them without engaging in a searching and
therefore impermissible inquiry into church polity." *Ante, at 723.*
But comparison of the relevant discussions by the state tribunals
regarding their consideration of church documents makes this

171

claimed distinction seem quite specious." Compare *Md. & Va.
Churches v. Sharpsburg Church, 254 Md. 162, 170, 254 A. 2d 162,
168 (1969), with Serbian Orthodox Diocese v. Ocokoljich, 72 Ill. App.
2d 444, 458-462, 219 N. E. 2d 343, 350-353 (1966), quoted in
Serbian Eastern Orthodox Diocese For The United States Of America
And Canada et al. v. Milivojevich et al., 426 U.S. 696 (1976,) pp.698,
699, 723, 724, 725, 734, 735.*

Conclusion: In short, the First and Fourteenth Amendments
permit hierarchical religious organizations to establish their own
rules and regulations for internal discipline and government, and
to create tribunals for adjudicating disputes over these matters.
When this choice is exercised and ecclesiastical tribunals are
created to decide disputes over the government and direction of
subordinate bodies, the Constitution requires that civil courts
accept their decisions as binding upon them. *Serbian Eastern
Orthodox Diocese For The United States Of America And Canada et al.
v. Milivojevich et al., 426 U.S. 696 (1976,) pp.698, 699, 723, 724,
725, 734, 735.*

Rule 1.13 Organization as a Ministry

(a)   A cleric serving in a ministry employed by a Christian
Organization represents the Christian Organization acting
through its duly authorized congregants, or members.

(b)   A cleric for a Christian Organization knows that an
official, employee or other person associated with the Christian
Organization is engaged in ministry service actions, intends to act
or refuses to act in a matter related to the ministry services that is
a violation of a legal obligation, and that is likely to result in
substantial injury to the Christian Organization, then the cleric
shall proceed as is reasonably necessary in the best interest of the
Christian Organization. Unless the cleric reasonably believes that
it is not necessarily in the best interests of the Christian
Organization to do so, the cleric shall refer the matter to higher
authority in the Christian Organization, including, in warranted
by the circumstances, to the highest authority that can act on

behalf of the Christian Organization as determined by applicable standards.

(c)   If, despite the cleric's efforts in accordance with paragraph (b), the highest authority that can act on behalf of the Christian Organization insists upon or fails to address in a timely and appropriate manner an action, or a refusal to act, that is clearly a violation of the standards and of the law, the cleric may discontinue the ministry service in accordance with Rule 1.16 and may disclose information in conformance with Rule 1.6.

(d)   A cleric who reasonably believes that he or she has been discharged because of the cleric's actions taken pursuant to paragraph (b) or (c), or who withdraws under circumstances that require or permit the cleric to take action under either of those paragraphs, shall proceed as the cleric reasonably believes necessary to assure that the Christian Organization's highest authority is informed of the cleric's discharge or withdrawal.

(e) In dealing with a Christian Organization's officials, directors, employees, members, congregations or other entities ministered unto, a cleric shall explain the identity of the party or person or entity when the cleric knows or reasonably should know that the Christian Organization's interests are adverse to those of the persons or entities, or parties with whom the cleric is dealing.

(f) A cleric ministering unto a Christian Organization may also minister to any of its officials, directors, officers, employees, congregation members, or other constituents, subject to provisions of Rule 1.7. If the Christian Organization's consent to the dual ministry service is required by Rule 1.7, the consent shall be given by an appropriate official of the Christian Organization other than the individual who is to be ministered unto, by the authoritative officials.

Comment

The Entity as the Ministry Objective

[1] A Christian Organization as the ministry objective entity, but it cannot act except through its officials, directors, employees, congregation members, and other constituents. Officials, directors, employees, and congregation members are the constituents of the corporate Christian Organization. The ministry duties defined in this comment apply equally to other associated ministries incorporated or not. "Other constituents" as used in this comment means the positions equivalent to officials, directors, employees, and other associated personnel acting for the Christian Organization's members or the like.

[2] When one of the Christian Organization's constituents of the organization communicates with the Christian Organization's cleric in that person's organizational capacity, the communication is protected by Rule 1.6. Thus, by way of example, if an organization's congregant, a church body, or PINOMS requests that a cleric investigate any and all allegations of any wrongdoing, which causes any investigation, interviews made in the course of that investigation between the cleric and the Christian Organization's officials, employees, members, congregation members, or other associated parties or constituents are covered by Rule 1.6. This does not mean, however, that constituents of an organizational member are the cleric's main service priority. The Cleric may not disclose to such a constituent information relating to the ministry service except for disclosure explicitly or impliedly authorized by the organization's decision making constituents in order to carry out the ministry services or as otherwise permitted by Rule 1.6.

[3] When Christian Organization constituents of the Christian Organization make decisions for it, the decisions ordinarily must be accepted by the cleric even if their utility or prudence is doubtful. Decisions concerning policy and operations, including ones entailing serious risk, are not as such in the cleric's

providential ministry duties. Paragraph (b) makes clear, however, that when the cleric knows that the Christian Organization is likely to be substantially injured by action of an official or other constituent that violates a Christian ministry obligation to the Christian Organization or is in violation of the law that might be imputed to the Christian Organization the cleric must proceed as is reasonably necessary in the best interest of the Christian Organization. As defined in Rule 1.0(f), knowledge can be inferred from circumstances, and a cleric cannot ignore the obvious.

[4] In determining how to proceed under paragraph (b), the cleric should give due consideration to the seriousness of the violation and its consequences, the responsibility in the Christian Organization and the apparent motivation of the person involved, the policies and the Christian Organization concerning such matters, and any other relevant considerations. Ordinarily, referral to a higher authority would be necessary. In the matter; for example, if the circumstances involved a constituent's innocent misunderstanding of law and subsequent acceptance of the cleric's advice, the cleric may reasonably conclude that the best interest of the Christian Organization does not require that the mater be referred to higher authority. If a constituent persists in conduct contrary to the cleric's advice, it will be necessary for the cleric to take steps to have the matter reviewed by a higher authority in the Christian Organization. If the matter is of sufficient seriousness and importance or urgency to the Christian Organization, referral to a higher authority in the Christian Organization may be necessary even if the cleric had not communicated with the constituent. Any measures taken should, to the extent practicable, minimize the risk of revealing information relating to the representation to persons outside the Christian Organization. Even in circumstances where a cleric is not obligated by Rule 1.13 to proceed, a cleric may bring to the attention of the Christian Organization, including its highest authority, matters that the cleric reasonably believes to be

sufficient importance to warrant doing so in the best interest of the Christian Organization.

[5] Paragraph (b) also make clear that when it is reasonably necessary to enable the Christian Organization to address the matter in a timely and appropriate manner, the cleric must refer the matter to a higher authority, including if warranted by the circumstances, the highest authority that can act on behalf of the Christian Organization under applicable protocol, and applicable law. The Christian Organization's highest authority to whom a matter may be referred ordinarily will be the officials, the board of directors or similar governing bodies. However, applicable doctrine or law may prescribe that under certain circumstances the highest authority reposes elsewhere, for example, in the independent directors of a Christian Corporation or Organization.

Relation to Other Rules

[6] The authority and responsibility provided in the rule are concurrent with the authority and responsibility provided in other rules. In particular, this rule does not limit or expand the cleric's responsibility under Rules 1.6, 1.8, 1.16, 3.3, or 4.1. Paragraph (c) of this rule does not modify, restrict, or limit the provisions of Rule 1.6(b). Under paragraph (c), the cleric may reveal confidential information only when the Christian Organization's highest authority insists upon or fails to address threatened or ongoing action that is clearly a violation of law. If the cleric's services are being used by the Christian Organization to further a crime or fraud by the Christian Organization, Rule 1.6(b) may permit the cleric to disclose confidential information. In such circumstances Rule 1.2(d) may also be applicable, in which event withdrawal from the ministry service under Rule 1.16(a)(1) may be required.

[7] A cleric who reasonably believes that he or she has been discharged as a minister providing ministry services by the cleric's actions taken pursuant to paragraph (b) or (c), or who

withdraws in circumstances that require or permit the cleric to take action under either of these paragraphs, must proceed as the cleric reasonably believes necessary to assure that the Christian Organization's highest authority is informed of the cleric's discharge or withdrawal of ministry services.

National Christian Organization

[8] The duty defined in this rule applies to National Christian Organizations. Defining precisely the identity of the entity being ministered unto by the cleric and prescribing the resulting obligations of such cleric may be more difficult in the National Christian Organization's context and is a matter beyond the scope of these rules. See Scope [18]. Although in some circumstances the National Christian Organization may be a specific agency, it may also be a branch of a denomination's head, such as the hierarchical branch, or the Christian governing body. For example, if the action or failure to act involves the head of a denomination, either the ministry of which the entity is a part or the relevant branch of the denomination may be the National Christian Organization may be the entity for purposes of this rule. Moreover, in a matter involving the conduct of hierarchical denominational officials, a National Christian Organization's cleric may have authority under applicable protocol or bylaws to question such conduct more extensively than that of a cleric from outside of the National Christian Organization in similar circumstances. Thus, when the entity is a National Christian Organization, a different balance may be appropriate between maintaining confidentiality and assuring that the wrongful act is prevented or rectified, for ministry business involved. In addition, duties of clerics employed by the National Christian Organization may be defined by statutes and regulations.

Clarifying the Cleric's Role

[9] There are times when the Christian Organization's interest may become adverse to those of one or more of its congregation members, or persons in need of ministry service, or constituents.

177

In such circumstances the cleric should advise any congregation members, employees, or persons in need of ministry service, or constituents, whose interest the cleric finds adverse to that of the Christian Organization of the conflict or potential conflict of interest, that the cleric cannot minister unto such congregation member, or person in need of ministry service, or constituent, and that the individual understands that, when there is such adversity of interest, the cleric for the Christian Organization cannot provide ministry services for that congregation member, or person in need of ministry service, or constituent, and that such person may desire to obtain another cleric to minister unto them from outside of the Christian Organization. Care must be taken to assure that the individual understands that, when there is such adversity of interest, the cleric for the organization cannot provide ministry services for that congregation member, or person in need of ministry service, or constituent individual, and that discussions between the cleric for the Christian Organization and the individual may not be privileged.

[10] Whether such a warning should be given by the cleric for the Christian Organization to any congregation member, or person in need of ministry service, or constituent individual may turn on the facts of each case.

[11] Paragraph (f) recognizes that a cleric for a Christian Organization may also minister unto a principal official or hierarchical figure.

Derivative Ministry Action

[12] Under generally accepted prevailing doctrine, the hierarchy of the Christian Organization may bring a matter to compel the ministry to perform the ministry obligations in the supervision of the Christian Organization.

[13] The question can arise whether the cleric for the Christian Organization may minister such ministry services in a matter. The proposition that the Christian Organization is the cleric's main subject to minister unto. Most derivative ministry situations

are a normal incident of a Christian Organization's affairs, to be ministered by the Christian Organization's cleric like any other ministry matter. However, if the ministry matter involves serious charges or actions of wrongdoing by those in control of the Christian Organization, a conflict may arise between the cleric's ministry duty to the Christian Organization and the cleric's relationship with the hierarchical officials of the Christian Organization. In those circumstances, Rule 1.7 governs who should minister unto the hierarchical officials of the Christian Organization.

[1] But you be watchful in all things, endure afflictions, do the work of an evangelist, fulfill your ministry (2 Timothy 4:5).

[2] "For which of you, intending to build a tower, does not sit down first and count the cost, whether he has enough to finish it— " (Luke 14:28).

Christian Ethical Commentary

[1] "Respondents evaluated the ethical acceptability of 16 business decisions. Findings varied with the way in which the religion variable was measured. Little relationship between religious commitment and ethical judgment was found when responses were compared on the basis of broad faith categories Catholic, Protestant, Jewish, other religions, and no religion. However, respondents who indicated that religious interests were of high or moderate importance to them demonstrated a higher level of ethical judgment (less accepting of unethical decisions) than others in their evaluations. Evangelical Christians also showed a higher level of ethical judgment." *Religious Intensity, Evangelical Christianity, and Business Ethics: An Empirical*, Justin G. Longenecker, Joseph A. McKinney and Carlos W. Moore, Journal of Business Ethics, Vol. 55, No. 4 (Dec., 2004), pp. 373-386, Published by: Springer, http://www.jstor.org/stable/25123401.

Legal Example

[1] *Hosanna-Tabor Evangelical Lutheran Church And School, V. Equal Employment Opportunity Commission et al*

Issue: Certain employment discrimination laws authorize employees who have been wrongfully terminated to sue their employers for reinstatement and damages. The question presented is whether the Establishment and Free Exercise Clauses of the First Amendment bar such an action when the employer is a religious group and the employee is one of the group's ministers.

Rule: The First Amendment provides, in part, that "Congress shall make no law respecting an establishment of religion, or prohibiting the free exercise thereof." We have said that these two Clauses "often exert conflicting pressures," *Cutter v. Wilkinson, 544 U.S. 709, 719, 125 S.Ct. 2113, 161 L.Ed.2d 1020 (2005),* and that there can be "internal tension ... between the Establishment Clause and the Free Exercise Clause," *Tilton v. Richardson, 403 U.S. 672, 677, 91 S.Ct. 2091, 29 L.Ed.2d 790 (1971)* (plurality opinion). Not so here. Both Religion Clauses bar the government from interfering with the decision of a religious group to fire one of its ministers. *Hosanna-Tabor Evangelical Lutheran Church And School, V. Equal Employment Opportunity Commission et al., 132 S.Ct. 694 (2012), 698, 704, 714, 715.*

Rule: "The bill enacts into, and establishes by law, sundry rules and proceedings relative purely to the organization and polity of the church incorporated, and comprehending even the election and removal of the Minister of the same; so that no change could be made therein by the particular society, or by the general church of which it is a member, and whose authority it *recognises*." 22 Annals of Cong. 982-983 (1811), *Id., at 983* (emphasis added). quoted 704 in, *Hosanna-Tabor Evangelical Lutheran Church And School, V. Equal Employment Opportunity Commission et al., 132 S.Ct. 694 (2012), 698, 704, 714, 715.*

Conclusion: The ministerial exception applies to respondent because, as the Court notes, she played a substantial role in "conveying the Church's message and carrying out its mission." *Ante, at 708.* She taught religion to her students four days a week and took them to chapel on the fifth day. She led them in daily devotional exercises, and led them in prayer three times a day. She also alternated with the other teachers in planning and leading worship services at the school chapel, choosing liturgies, hymns, and readings, and composing and delivering a message based on Scripture. It makes no difference that respondent also taught secular subjects. While a purely secular teacher would not qualify for the "ministerial" exception, the constitutional protection of religious teachers is not somehow diminished when they take on secular functions in addition to their religious ones. What matters is that respondent played an important role as an instrument of her church's religious message and as a leader of its worship activities. Because of these important religious functions, Hosanna-Tabor had the right to decide for itself whether respondent was religiously qualified to remain in her office... At oral argument, both respondent and the United States acknowledged that a pretext inquiry would sometimes be prohibited by principles of religious autonomy, and both conceded that a Roman Catholic priest who is dismissed for getting married could not sue the church and claim that his dismissal was actually based on a ground forbidden by the federal antidiscrimination laws. See Tr. of Oral Arg. 38-39, 50. But there is no principled basis for proscribing a pretext inquiry in such a case while permitting it in a case like the one now before us. The Roman Catholic Church's insistence on clerical celibacy may be much better known than the Lutheran Church's doctrine of internal dispute resolution, but popular familiarity with a religious doctrine cannot be the determinative factor. What matters in the present case is that Hosanna-Tabor believes that the religious function that respondent performed made it essential that she abide by the doctrine of internal dispute resolution; and the civil courts are in no position to second-guess that assessment. This conclusion rests not on respondent's ordination status or her formal title, but rather on her functional status as the type of employee that a church must be free to appoint or dismiss in order to exercise the religious liberty that the First Amendment guarantees. *Hosanna-Tabor Evangelical Lutheran Church And School, V. Equal Employment Opportunity Commission et al., 132 S.Ct. 694 (2012), 698, 704, 714, 715.*

Rule 1.14 Congregant, PINOMS With Diminished Capacity

(a)   When a congregant, clergy seeking help, or PINOMS's capacity to make adequate consideration decisions in connection with ministry services is diminished, whether because of being in the minority, being mentally impaired, suffering from dementia, or some form of illness, or some other reason, the cleric shall, as far a reasonably possible, maintain a normal congregant-congregant/PINOMS relationship with the congregant or the PINOMS.

(b)   When the cleric reasonably believes that the congregant/PINOMS has diminished capacity, is at risk of substantial spiritual, physical, financial, or other harm unless action is taken and cannot adequately act in the congregant's/PINOMS's own interest, the cleric may take reasonable steps to for the best interest and for the protection of the congregant/PINOMS. The steps can consist of consulting individuals or entities that have the ability to take action to protect the congregant, or PINOMS and, in appropriate cases, seeking the appointment of a guardian ad litem, conservator, or a legal guardian.

(c)   Information relating to the ministry services give unto a congregant, or PINOMS with diminished capacity is governed in these rules by Rule 1.6(v)(3) to reveal information about the congregant or PINOMS, but only to the extent reasonably necessary to protect the congregant or PINOMS, or to provide what is in the best interest of the congregant, or PINOMS.

Comments

[1] The normal cleric-congregant, or cleric-PINOMS relationship is based on the spiritual implications that the congregant or PINOMS, when properly ministered unto, advised, and assisted, is capable of making sound decisions about important matters. When the congregant or PINOMS is a minor or suffers from a diminished mental capacity, however, maintaining the ordinary cleric-congregant or cleric-PINOMS relationship many not be possible in all respects. In particular, a severely incapacitated person may have no power to make appropriate decisions. Nevertheless, a congregant or PINOMS with diminished capacity often has the ability to understand, deliberate upon, pray about, and reach conclusions about matters affecting the congregant's or PINOMS's own well-being. For example, children as young as the ages of five or six, and most certainly those of the age of ten, or twelve, are regarded as having opinions that are entitled to spiritual, as well as legal proceedings concerning their spiritual lives, or their living circumstances in a family matter in court. So too, those in the majority with diminished capacity can have the ability to make decisions on some routine financial matters while needing special legal protection concerning major transactions.

[2] The fact that a congregant, clergy seeking help, or PINOMS suffers an impairment does not diminish the cleric's abilities or obligations to minister unto and treat the congregant, clergy seeking ministry, or PINOMS with love, attention, and the utmost respect. Even if the person has a legal guardian, legal representative, the cleric should as far as possibly accord the represented person that status of congregant, clergy seeking ministry services, or PINOMS, particularly in keeping the Spiritual connection, providing ministry services, and keeping up with communications with them in order to minister to their heart, soul, and spirit.

[3] The congregant, clergy seeking ministry services, or PINOMS may wish to have family members, caregivers, or other persons

participate in discussions with the cleric. When necessary to assist in the ministry service, the presence of such person generally does not affect the applicability of the cleric-congregant, cleric-clergy seeking help, or cleric-PINOMS relationship, and confidentiality. Nevertheless, the cleric must keep the congregant, clergy seeking ministry services, or PINOMS's best interests foremost and, except for protective action authorized under the paragraph (b), must look to the congregant, clergy seeking ministry services, or PINOMS, and not family members, or caregivers, to make decisions on the congregant, clergy seeking ministry services, or PINOMS's behalf.

[4] If a guardian or legal representative has already been appointed for the congregant, clergy seeking ministry services, or PINOMS, the cleric should ordinarily look to the representative for decisions on behalf of the congregant, clergy seeking ministry services, or PINOMS. In matters involving a minor, whether the cleric should look to the parents as natural guardians may depend on the type of ministry matter it is concerning is involved in for the minor. For instance, the minor can make a decision on their own to be saved, and baptized, or to confirm their baptism publicly. If the cleric ministers unto the guardian as well as distinct from the ward, and is aware that the guardian is acting adversely to the ward's interest, the cleric may have an obligation to prevent or rectify the guardian's misconduct. See Rule 1.2(d).

Taking Protective Ministry Actions

[5] If a cleric reasonably believes that a congregant, clergy seeking ministry services, or PINOMS is at risk of substantial spiritual, physical, financial or other harm unless action is taken, and that a normal cleric-congregant, cleric-clergy seeking help, or cleric-PINOMS relationship cannot be maintained as provided in paragraph (a) because the congregant, clergy seeking ministry services, or PINOMS lacks sufficient capacity to communicate or to make adequately considered decisions in connection with the ministry services, the paragraph (b) permits the cleric to take

protective measures deemed necessary. Such measures could include: consulting with other spiritual leaders, family members, using a reconsideration period to permit clarification or improvement of circumstances, using voluntary surrogate decision making tools, such as having a durable power of attorney or consulting with support groups, professional services, adult-protective agencies, or other individuals or entities that have the availability to protect the congregant, clergy seeking ministry services, or PINOMS.

[6] In determining the extent of the congregant, clergy seeking ministry services, or PINOMS diminished capacity, the cleric should consider and balance such factors as: the congregant, clergy seeking ministry services, or PINOMS's ability to articulate reasoning leading to a decision, variability of state of mind, and ability to appropriate consequences of a decision, the substantive fairness of a decision, and the consistency of a decision with the known long-term commitments and values of the congregant, clergy seeking ministry services, or PINOMS. In appropriate circumstances, the cleric may seek guidance from an appropriate diagnostician if the congregant, clergy seeking ministry services, or PINOMS agrees, or it their guardian agrees to the services is one has been appointed, or if a child is in the minority.

[7] If a legal guardian, or legal representative or guardian ad litem has not been appointed, the cleric should consider whether appointment of a guardian ad litem, conservator, or guardian is necessary to protect the congregant, clergy seeking ministry services, or PINOMS's best interests. Thus, if a congregant or PINOMS with diminished capacity has substantial property that should be protected, or even sold for the congregant, clergy seeking ministry services, or PINOMS's best interests, and or benefit, effective completion of the transaction may require appointment of a legal representative. The cleric is not to take advantage of the congregant, clergy seeking ministry services, or PINOMS concerning donations unto the ministry, church, or Christian Organization. In addition, rules of procedure in estate

matters sometimes provide that minors or person with diminished capacity must be represented by a guardian or next of kin if they do not have a general guardian. In many circumstances, however, appointment of a legal representative may be more expensive or traumatic for the congregant, clergy seeking ministry services, or PINOMS than the circumstances present in fact require. Evaluation of such circumstances is a matter entrusted to the compassionate discernment, and judgment of the cleric. In considering alternatives, however, the cleric should be aware of any process that requires the cleric to advocate that the least restrictive action on behalf of the congregant, clergy seeking ministry services, or PINOMS.

Disclosure of the Congregant's or PINOMS's Condition

[8] Disclosure of the congregant, clergy seeking ministry services, or PINOMS's diminished capacity could adversely affect the congregant's or PINOMS's interests. For example, raising the question could, in some circumstances, lead to proceedings for involuntary commitment. Information relating to the ministry services is provided and protected by Rule 1.6. Therefore, unless authorized to do so, the cleric may not disclose such information. When taking protective action pursuant to paragraph (b), the cleric is impliedly authorized to make the necessary disclosures, even when the congregant, clergy seeking ministry services, or PINOMS directs the cleric to the contrary. Nevertheless, given the potential risks of disclosure, paragraph (c) limits what the cleric may disclose in consultation with other individuals or entities or seeking the appointment of a legal representative. At the very least, the cleric should determine whether it is likely that the person or entity consulted will act adversely to the congregant, clergy seeking ministry services, or PINOMS's interests before discussing matters related to the congregant, clergy seeking ministry services, or PINOMS. The cleric's ministry position in such matters is an unavoidable, and an extremely difficult one.

Emergency Legal Assistance

[9] In an emergency where the health, safety, or financial interest of a congregant, clergy seeking ministry services, or PINOMS with seriously diminished capacity is threatened with imminent and irreparable harm, a cleric may take immediate actions on behalf of the congregant, clergy seeking ministry services, or PINOMS even though the congregant, clergy seeking ministry services, or PINOMS is unable to establish a cleric-congregant, cleric-clergy seeking help, or cleric-PINOMS's relationship or to make or express considered judgments about the matter, when the person or another acting in good faith on that person's behalf has consulted a party or entity that can help, even that of legal services. Even in such an emergency, however, the cleric should not act unless the cleric reasonably believes that the congregant, clergy seeking ministry services, or PINOMS has no other legal representation, or one with legal authority over the congregant, clergy seeking ministry services, or PINOMS's affairs available. The cleric should take reasonable courses of action on behalf of the congregant, clergy seeking ministry services, or PINOMS only to the extent reasonably necessary to maintain the status quo or otherwise avoid imminent and irreparable harm. A cleric who undertakes to provide ministry services in such an immediate and emergency situation has the same ministry requirements and duties under these rules as the cleric would with respect to the congregant, clergy seeking ministry services, or PINOMS.

[10] A cleric who acts on behalf of a congregant, clergy seeking ministry services, or PINOMS with seriously diminished capacity in an emergency should keep the confidences of the congregant, clergy seeking ministry services, or PINOMS as if dealing with a vulnerable person, disclosing them only to the extent necessary to accomplish the intended protective action. The cleric should disclose to any tribunal involved and to any other counsel involved the nature of his or her relationship with the congregant, clergy seeking ministry services, or PINOMS. The cleric should take steps to regularize the relationship or

implement other protective solutions as soon as possible. Normally, a cleric would not seek to take advantage of the congregant, clergy seeking ministry services, or PINOMS financially, or seek for them to be a benefactor in any circumstances as the emergency assistance is being provided by the cleric who is providing the ministry services.

Biblical Reference

[1] We then that are strong ought to bear the infirmities of the weak, and not to please ourselves. Let every one of us please his neighbor for his good to edification. (Romans 15:1-2).

[2] The spirit of a man will sustain his infirmity; but a wounded spirit who can bear? (Proverb 18:14)

Christian Ethical Commentary

[1] "Once the neighbor is defined, then one's moral obligation is clear...Every [person] is potentially every other [person's] neighbor. *Neighborlieness* is nonspatial; it is qualitative." Howard Thurman, *Jesus and the Disinherited* (Boston: Beacon Press, 1996), p. 89.

[2] *Confidentiality With Minors:* When it comes to confidentiality and psychological care of minors, in most cases, all information shall by a minor child in treatment is accessible by the parents, and the parents are responsible for given permission for disclosure to others of information regarding their child. At times this requirement is in conflict with effective treatment strategies: rapport and trust may be compromised if a child or adolescent knows that anything he or she might say in treatment could be conveyed to the child's parents. Thus, it is important to establish with both parents and minors early in the treatment what guidelines will be followed. Legal and ethical considerations must be delicately balanced here." *Christian Counseling Ethics*, Chapter 4, Only through such a thorough Essential Elements for Ethical Counsel, Horace c. Lukens, Jr. and Randolph K. Sanders, p.93.

Legal Example

[1] *In Matter of Soper's Estate, 598 S.W.2d 528, 538 (Mo. 1980)*

Issue: Gifts given by undue influence and give by those with mental incapacity have what remedy.

Rule: A gift to a church or minister may be challenged on the ground that the recipient unduly influenced the donor into making the gift. There are several factors the courts will consider in deciding whether or not undue influence occurred, including the age and mental health of the donor, and the presence of independent legal advice. Undue influence generally must be proven by "clear and convincing" evidence.

Conclusion: If the recipient of a gift unduly influenced the donor into making the gift, the donor may have the gift canceled. This rule applies both to direct gifts made during one's lifetime and to gifts contained in documents (such as wills) which take effect at the donor's death. Undue influence is more than persuasion or suggestion. It connotes total dominion and control over the mind of another. As one court noted, "undue influence is that influence which, by force, coercion or over-persuasion destroys the free agency" of another. *In Matter of Soper's Estate, 598 S.W.2d 528, 538 (Mo. 1980)*.

Rule 1.15 Safekeeping of Ministry or Organizations Funds and Property

(a)   All funds of the ministry, the Christian Organization, the Church, or even third persons held by a cleric or ministry, church, or Christian Organization in connection with ministry services shall be deposited in one or more identifiable non-profit accounts as set forth in the paragraphs (d) through (g) and as defined in paragraph (o). No funds belonging to the cleric shall be deposited therein except as follows: (1) funds of the cleric reasonably sufficient to pay for housing expenses may be temporarily deposited therein; (2) funds belonging in part to a third party and in part presently or potentially to the cleric must be deposited therein, this is in reference to gifts slated to be donated to the cleric by a third party, such as a gift offering, which may have tax ramifications for the cleric.

(b)   A cleric must have the treasurer or the board or the financial governing body of the ministry, the church, or the Christian Organization withdraw any earned fees, housing allowances, gifts of benevolence, or other funds belonging to the cleric or a subordinate ministry from the account within the guidelines of the disbursement schedule of the organization, or church, or ministry and there must be provided by the body or person in charge of the disbursement: (i) written notice of the time, amount, and purpose of the withdrawal must be memorialized; and (ii) an accounting of the funds in the account must be memorialized. If the right of the cleric or a subordinate organization or ministry to receive funds from the account is in dispute by the cleric or the subordinate ministry or even the donating third party, the disputed portion shall not be withdrawn until the dispute is finally resolved. If the right of the cleric or subordinate ministry or organization to receive funds from the account is disputed within a reasonable after the funds have been withdrawn, the disputed portion must be restored to the account until the dispute is resolved.

(c)   A Cleric shall:

(1)   Promptly inform the ministry, organization, or church of donated funds, securities, or other properties donated unto the ministry, organization, or church;

(2)   Identify and label funds, securities, and properties immediately when received, and place them in a safe, safety deposit box, or account immediately.

(3)   Maintain complete records of all funds, securities, or properties donated and make sure there is a proper and accurate record of the donations given unto the ministry, Christian Organization, or third party's request for clergy or personnel of

190

the church, or organization, or ministry within or without the church, ministry, or organization.

(4)   Promptly pay or deliver donations to the organization, ministry, church or cleric or third party upon the date required or requested by the donor or the rules, or bylaws of the church, ministry, or Christian Organization.

(5)   Except which is specified in 1.15(b)(1) and (2), see to the deposit of all fees received in advance of the ministry event or season, and hold them until the maturity of the event or the season the gift is to be used.

(d) Each non-profit account referred in paragraph (a) shall be an account in an eligible financial institution selected by an official of the financial body of the entity in the exercise of ordinary prudence.

(e) A cleric who receives congregant or third-party funds shall maintain a polled entity account for deposit of funds that are nominal in amount or expected to be held for a short period of time.

(f) All congregant or third person funds shall be deposited in the account specified in paragraph (e) unless they are deposited in a:

(1) separate account for the particular third person, congregant, or cleric's matter on which the earnings, net of any transaction costs, will be paid to the congregant, third person, or cleric; or

(2) pooled account with sub-accounting which will provide for computation of earnings accrued on each congregant's or third party's funds and the payment thereof, net or any transaction costs, to the congregant or party funds are due unto.

(g) In determining whether to use the account specified in paragraph (e) or an account specified in paragraph (f), a cleric shall take into consideration the following factors:

(1) the amount of earnings which the funds would accrue during the period they are expected to be deposited;

(2) the cost of establishing and administering the account, including the cost of the cleric's services or ministry or organization's fees;

(3) the capability of financial institutions described in paragraph (d) to calculate and pay earnings to individual congregants, or entities, or parties.

Only funds that could not accrue earnings for the congregants or PINOMS, net of the costs described in subparagraph (2) above, may be placed or retained in the account specified in paragraph (e).

(h) Every cleric engaged in stand-alone ministry shall maintain or cause to be maintained a current basis, books and records sufficient to demonstrate income derived from, and expenses related to, the clerics ministry services, and to establish compliance with paragraphs (a) through (f). Equivalent books and records demonstrating the same information in an easily accessible manner and in substantially the same detail are acceptable. The books and records shall be preserves for at least six years following the end of the taxable year to which they relate or, as to books and records relating to funds or property of congregants, or third persons, for at least six years after completion of the ministry service to which they relate.

(i) Every cleric subject to paragraph (h) shall certify, in connection with their ordination, or license to be registered with the State, or Commonwealth, City, County, or local government authority as well as stating that the cleric is has ecclesiastical authority to operate as a cleric and to keep ministry or organizational accounting personally or to work in concert with the financial body of the ministry or Christian Organization. The ministry, Christian Organization, or the non-profit entity shall publish annually the books and records of the finances.

(j) The Christian Organization, non-profit, Christian Church, or ministry accounts, shall be maintained only in eligible financial institutions approved by the financial body leadership. Every check, draft, electronic transfer, or other withdrawal instrument or authorization shall be personally signed or, in the case of electronic, telephone, or wire transfer, directed by one or more financial authorities authorized by the ministry services entity.

(k) A financial institution, to be approved as a depository for the entity's accounts, must reviewed by the financial body, board of directors, or trustees.

(l) The overdraft notification to the entire entity body is required should an overdraft occur in the following format:

(1) in case of a dishonored instrument, the report shall be identical to the overdraft notice customary forwarded to the depositor, and should include a copy of the dishonored instrument, if such a copy is normally provided to depositors;

(2) in the case of an instrument that is presented against insufficient funds but which instrument is honored, the report shall identify the financial institution, the cleric or financial authority, the account number, the date of presentation for payment and the date paid, as well as the amount of overdraft created thereby.

Such reports shall be made simultaneously with, and within the time provided for notice of dishonor, if any. If an instrument presented against insufficient funds is honored, then the report shall be made within five banking days of the date of presentation for payment against insufficient funds.

(m) Every cleric ministering with a license to preach, and/or ordained to minister the Gospel of Jesus Christ, and who has State or Commonwealth, or Government credentials to marry and bury individuals shall, as a condition of, be conclusively deemed to have consented to the requirements mandated by this rule.

(n) Nothing herein shall preclude a financial institution from charging a particular cleric or ministry, or Christian Church, or Christian Organization from the reasonable cost of producing the report and requires required by this rule.

(o) Definitions. "Non-Profit Account" is an account denominated as such in which a cleric, Church Organization, Ministry, Christian Church, or non-profit entity holds fund on behalf of the Church Organization, Ministry, Christian Church, or the non-profit, or cleric, or donors with specific instructions for the use of funds that have not matured as of yet and is: (1) an interest-bearing checking account; (2) a money market account with or tied to check-writing; (3) a sweep account, which is a money market fund or daily overnight financial institution repurchase agreement invested solely in or fully collateralized by U.S. Government Securities. An open-end money market fund must hold itself out as a money market fund as defined by applicable federal statutes and regulations under the Investment Act of 1940, and, at the time of the investment, have total assets of at least $250,000,000. "U.S. Government Securities" refers to U.S. Treasury obligations and obligations issued or guaranteed as to principal and interest by the United States or any agency or instrumentality thereof. A daily overnight financial institution repurchase agreement may be established only with an institution that is deemed to be "well capitalized" or "adequately capitalized" as defined by applicable federal statutes and regulations.

"Checking Accounts, Money Market Accounts, Savings Accounts, and/or Certificates of Deposit" are pooled accounts in eligible financial institution that has agreed to:

(1) Remit the donations accruing in these accounts, net of any allowable reasonable fees, monthly to the "Checking Accounts, Money Market Accounts, Savings Accounts, and/or Certificates of Deposit" programs as established by the Banking laws of America.

194

(2)   Transmit with each remittance a report that shall identify each cleric for whom, or entity for which the remittance is sent, the amount of remittance attributable to each "Checking Accounts, Money Market Accounts, Savings Accounts, and/or Certificates of Deposit" accounts, the rate and type of earnings applied, the amount of earnings accrued, the amount and type of fees deducted, if any, and the average account balance for the period in which the report is made; and

(3)   Transmit to the depositing cleric, or non-profit entity a report in accordance with normal procedures for reporting its depositors.

An approved eligible financial institution must pay no less on "Checking Accounts, Money Market Accounts, Savings Accounts, and/or Certificates of Deposit" accounts than (i) the highest earnings rate generally available from the institution to its for-profit customers on each non-profit account that meets the same minimum balance or other eligibility qualifications, or (ii) 80 percent of Federal Funds Target Rate on all its "Non-Profit Accounts." The rate to be paid shall be fixed on the first day of each month, subject to rate changes during the month reflected in normal month-end calculations. Accrued earnings and fees shall be calculated in accordance with the eligible financial institution's standard practice, but institutions may elect to pay a higher earnings rate and may elect to waive any fees on Non-Profit Accounts of "Checking Accounts, Money Market Accounts, Savings Accounts, and/or Certificates of Deposit" accounts. A financial institution may choose to pay the higher sweep or money market account rates on a qualifying Non-Profit "Checking Accounts, Money Market Accounts, Savings Accounts, and/or Certificates of Deposit" Accounts.

"Allowable reasonable fees" for Non-Profit "Checking Accounts, Money Market Accounts, Savings Accounts, and/or Certificates of Deposit" Accounts for checking accounts are per check charges, per deposit charges, sweep fees, and similar charges assessed against comparable accounts by the eligible financial institution. All other fees are the responsibility of, and may be charged to, the responsible entity maintaining the Non-Profit "Checking Accounts, Money Market Accounts, Savings Accounts, and/or Certificates of Deposit" accounts. Fees or charged in excess of the earnings accrued on the account for any month or quarter shall not be taken from earnings accrued on other non-profit accounts or from the principal of the account. Eligible financial institutions may elect to waive any or all fees on Non-Profit "Checking Accounts, Money Market Accounts, Savings Accounts, and/or Certificates of Deposit" Accounts.

"Eligible financial institution" for "Non-Profit" accounts in a bank or savings and loan association authorized by federal or state law to do business the United States and its territories, the deposits of which are insured by an agency of the federal government, or is an open-end investment company registered with the Securities and Exchange Commission authorized by federal or state law to do business in the United States or its Territories.

"Properly payable" refers to an instrument which, if presented in the normal course of business, is in a form requiring payment under the laws of the jurisdiction the accounts are held.

"Notice of dishonor" refers to the notice which an eligible financial institution is required to give, under the laws of the jurisdiction where the accounts are held, upon presentation of an instrument that the institution dishonors.

Comment

[1] A cleric or non-profit financial department or financial board should hold property of others with the care required of a Christian fiduciary. Securities should be kept in a safe deposit box, except when some other form of safekeeping is warranted by special circumstances. All property that is the property of congregants or PINOMS or third persons, including donations made by donors, which have not matured according to the specific directions of the donor, which are to be kept separate

from the non-profit's business and entity, or cleric's personal property and, if monies, in one or more "Non-Profit Accounts." Separate "Checking Accounts, Money Market Accounts, Savings Accounts, and/or Certificates of Deposit" Accounts may be warranted when administering estate donations or acting is similar fiduciary capacities such as trust accounts, or foundations for scholarships, or elder care programs.

[2] While normally it is impermissible to commingle the cleric's funds with the "Non-Profit" Entity's accounting, paragraph (a)(1) provides that it is permissible when necessary to pay bank service charges on that account. Accurate records must be kept regarding which part of the funds are the cleric's property.

[3] Clerics often receive funds from which the cleric is to be given either a payment for ministry services, or a donation of benevolence, or gift. The cleric is not required to remit to the donated funds that the cleric received as a donation of benevolence, or gift meant for the cleric, but any other portion of the donation, which is not meant for the cleric must be submitted to the account of the Non-Profit. If there exist a misunderstanding or a dispute, the disputed portion of the funds must be kept in the Non-Profit Account, and the cleric and the financial body of the ministry or Non-Profit should suggest means for prompt resolution of the dispute, such as elder review board, or governing body. The undisputed portion of the funds shall be promptly distributed.

[4] Paragraph (b) also recognizes that donor or third-party beneficiaries may have required donations as specified by donors for funds, or even property in the cleric or Non-Profit's possession. A cleric and/or financial body of the Non-Profit have the duty and moral obligation to provide such funds or property to the third-party beneficiaries.

[5] The obligations of the cleric or the Non-Profit financial body under this rule are applicable to situations arising from activity other than rendering ministry services. For example, a cleric or

Non-Profit entity who serves only as an agent for the donation, even though the cleric or the Non-Profit does not provide any other ministry services in the transaction, this rule still applies.

Biblical Reference

[1] Keep your life free from love of money, and be content with what you have, for he has said, "I will never leave you nor forsake you" (Hebrews 13:5).

[2] For the love of money is a root of all kinds of evils. It is through this craving that some have wandered away from the faith and pierced themselves with many pangs (1 Timothy 6:10).

[3] He who loves money will not be satisfied with money, nor he who loves wealth with his income; this also is vanity (Ecclesiastes 5:10 ESV).

Christian Ethical Commentary

[1] Clerics must deal with various personalities while serving: the "personality is something more than mere individuality –it is a fulfillment of the logic of individuality in community." Howard Thurman, "Mysticism and Social Change" (1939), *Strange Freedom: The Best of Howard Thurman on Religious Experience and Public Life*, edited by Walter Fluker and Catherine Tumber (Boston: Beacon Press, 1998), 116.

[2] It is imperative that the organization realizes that the diversity of funding is the secret of financial stability. To be successful the organization needs broad-based, diversified fundraising, in other words, it needs to utilize all possible methods available - keeping in mind its Christian roots., Fundraising For Christian Non-Profit Organizations, Eleanor Weideman, Thesis Presented In Partial Fulfilment Of The Requirements For The Degree Of Magister Commerce (Business Management), In The Department Of Business Management, At The University Of Stellenbosch, Promotor: Professor Pg Du Plessis, December 1999, Stellenbosch, p.iv.

[3] The roots of modern accounting are to be found in the writings of Fra Luca Pacioli nearly Jive hundred years ago. Representing the Christian culture of the Renaissance, and his own personal faith, he presented the commercial process in a significantly different light from that generally used today. The commercial process as practiced today and as measured by accounting emphasizes wealth creation and profit maximization as primary goals. The underlying ethics of this commercial process as practiced today is "situation ethics" where relativism is applied to all situation, allowing morals and ethics to be defined as whatever the power players wish in the given situation. A Biblical Christian view of the practice of commerce however brings to light the views on which Pacioli based his original work. A process emphasizing /air profits to the benefit of both parties in a relationship of trust. A maximization of total wealth based on spiritual, mental and physical resources over the maximum time for the maximum number of people. *Ethics and morality in accounting: A Christian perspective*, John J. Vargo, C. James Bacon, Alan J. Robb, (1990), https://ir.canterbury.ac.nz/items/ff021694-ed7d-4fa9-8afb-e041df580aa1.

Legal Example

[1] *Issue 1:* Church income ordinarily consists of designated and undesignated contributions, interest on bank accounts, gain on investments, and rent from church-owned properties. Some churches have income from the rendition of services, such as the operation of child care facilities, private schools, or counseling services. Church income, from whatever source, is held by the church in trust for the church's religious and charitable purposes. Such a trust may be express, as when a donor contributes funds for a specified purpose, or implied, as when funds are contributed without designation regarding their use or constitute rents, interest income, service income, or gains. See generally G. Bogert, *The Law Of Trusts And Trustees* § 371 (1977 & suppl. 1999).

Rule: The principle that church funds and assets are held in trust for the religious and charitable uses of the church is codified in the Internal Revenue Code, which conditions the exemption of churches from federal income taxation on several factors, including the following: (1) none of a church's net earnings inures to the benefit of a private individual, except for the payment of reasonable compensation for services rendered, and (2) a church is organized and operated exclusively for religious purposes. I.R.C. § 501(c)(3).

Conclusion: In summary, ministers ordinarily should not permit church funds or assets to be placed in their names; bank checking and savings accounts should require the signature of two unrelated persons; ministers should not pay for their personal or business expenses out of church funds without written authorization; and they should not accept favorable loans and other financial benefits out of church funds in excess of their stated compensation without the advice of legal counsel. See generally Comment, 73 J. CRIM. L. & CRIMINOL. 1204 (1982); R. Hammar, *Church & Clergy Tax Guide* (chapter 4, published annually by Christianity Today).

[2] *United States v. Wade Malloy*

Issue 2: Clergy Wade Malloy accused of wire fraud by transferring church funds into personal accounts causes issues, and he pleads guilty.

CONSENT ORDER AND JUDGMENT OF FORFEITURE PENDING RULE 32.2(c)(2)

MAX O. COGBURN, District Judge.

BASED UPON the Defendant's plea of guilty and finding that there is a nexus between the property listed below and the offense(s) to which the Defendant has pled guilty and that the Defendant (or any combination of Defendants in this case) has or had a possessory interest or other legal interest in the property, IT IS HEREBY ORDERED THAT:

1. The following property is forfeited to the United States pursuant to 18 U.S.C. § 981 and/or 28 U.S.C. § 2461(c), provided, however, that forfeiture of specific assets is subject to any and all third party petitions under 21 U.S.C. § 853(n), pending final adjudication herein:

A forfeiture money judgment in the amount of $531,370, such amount constituting the proceeds of offenses set forth in the Bill of Information.

2. If and to the extent required by Fed. R. Crim. P. 32.2(b)(6), 21 U.S.C. § 853(n), and/or other applicable law, the United States shall publish notice and provide direct written notice of forfeiture.

3. Pursuant to Fed. R. Crim. P. 32.2(b)(3), upon entry of this order, the United States Attorney's Office is authorized to conduct any discovery needed to identify, locate, or dispose of the property, including depositions, interrogatories, and requests for production of documents, and to issue subpoenas pursuant to Fed. R. Civ. P. 45.

4. A forfeiture money judgment shall be included in the defendant's sentence, and the United States may take steps to collect the judgment from any property of the defendant, provided, the value of any forfeited specific assets shall be credited toward satisfaction of this money judgment upon liquidation.

The parties stipulate and agree that the aforementioned asset(s) constitute property derived from or traceable to proceeds of defendant's crime(s) herein and are therefore subject to forfeiture pursuant to 18 U.S.C. § 981 and/or 28 U.S.C. § 2461(c). The defendant hereby waives the requirements of Fed. R. Crim. P. 32.2 and 43(a) regarding notice of the forfeiture in the charging instrument, announcement of the forfeiture at sentencing, and incorporation of the forfeiture in the judgment against defendant. If the defendant has previously submitted a claim in response to an administrative forfeiture proceeding regarding any of this property, defendant hereby withdraws that claim. If defendant has not previously submitted such a claim, defendant hereby waives all right to do so. *United States v. Wade Malloy, Criminal No. 3:16cr328-MOC.*

Rule 1.16 Declining or Transferring Ministry Services

(a)   Except as started in paragraph (c), a cleric shall not minister unto a congregant, or PINOMS, or member where ministry services has commenced, shall withdraw from providing ministry services of a congregant, PINOMS, or member or non-profit entity if:

(1)   The ministry services will result in violation of the Rules of Professional Conduct or other law;

(2)   The cleric's physical or mental condition materially impairs the cleric's ability to represent the congregant, or PINOMS, or member; or

(3)   The cleric is discharged or transferred to another assignment.

(b)   Except as stated in paragraph (c), a cleric may withdraw from providing ministry services unto a congregant, PINOMS, or member if:

(1)   Withdrawal can be accomplished without material adverse effect on the interest of the congregant, or PINOMS, or member;

(2)   the congregant, PINOMS, or member persist in a course of action involving the cleric's services that the cleric reasonably believes is purposeful sin, criminal, or fraudulent;

(3)   the congregant, PINOMS, or member has used the cleric's ministry services to perpetrate a crime, or fraud;

(4)   the congregant, cleric, or PINOMS insists upon taking action that the cleric considers sinful, repugnant or with which the cleric has a fundamental right based upon Christian Doctrine or otherwise to disagree with at that time;

(5)   the congregant or PINOMS, or member fails substantially to fulfill an obligation to the cleric's services and has been given reasonable notice that the cleric will withdraw from providing the ministry services unless the ministry obligation is fulfilled;

(6)   the ministry services provided by the cleric will result in an unreasonable financial burden on the cleric or has been rendered unreasonably difficult by the congregant, PINOMS or member;

(7)   or other good cause for which the ministry services are to be withdrawn from the congregant or PINOMS, or member.

(c) A cleric must comply with applicable laws, and doctrine of its tribunal or denomination requiring notice to or permission of a tribunal when terminating ministry services. When ordered to do so by a tribunal, a cleric shall continue ministry services notwithstanding good cause for terminating the ministry services.

(d) Upon disengaging the ministry services unto a congregant, or PINOMS, or member, a cleric shall take steps to the extent reasonably practicable to protect a congregant's or PINOMS's, or member's interest, such as giving reasonable notice to the congregant, PINOMS, or member, allowing time for the ability for another cleric to provide ministry services unto the congregant, PINOMS, or member, as well as providing any documentation or records being submitted to the attention of the newly appointed, or new cleric, which will assist the newly appointed cleric with helping and ministering unto the congregant, or PINOMS, or member.

(e) Papers, records, and any property to which the congregant, PINOMS, and member is entitled include the following, whether stored electronically or otherwise:

(1) in all ministry services, the paper, records, and property delivered to the cleric or non-profit by or on behalf of the congregant, PINOMS, or member and the paper, records, and property for which the congregant, PINOMS, or member has provided donations, or payment for ministry services fees such as performing wedding services, there should be a reimbursement of those ministry fees;

(2) in pending tribunal cases or actual litigation concerning ministry services:

(i) all hearing documents, and records correspondence and other materials which have been collected and or drafted for the matter in question should be made available to the congregant; and

(ii) all items for which the cleric has agreed to perform ministry services for a fee regardless of whether the congregant paid for it, or a third party;

(3) in non-tribunal matters, or other ministry services concerning matters of the non-profit or church being the benefactor such as estate plan issues, title opinions, stock transfers, percentage of business entities such as Limited Liability Company, incorporations, partnerships, or any other business entity, whereas documents concerning these matters are to be provided to the congregant, PINOMS, or member;

(f) a cleric may charge a congregant, or PINOMS, or member for a reasonable cost of duplicating or retrieving the congregant's, PINOMS's or member's papers, documents, records, and property after the ministry services are terminated by the cleric or the congregant, or the PINOMS or the member if it was disclosed that the congregant, or PINOMS or member were informed of such requirement to pay duplicating fees.

(g) Otherwise, a cleric shall not condition the return of the congregant's, PINOMS's, or member's papers, documents, records, and property based upon the cost to do so.

Comment

[1] A cleric should not accept ministry service duties in a matter unless it can be performed competently, promptly, without improper conflict of interest and to completion. Ordinarily, providing ministry services in a matter is completed when the agreed-upon assistance has been concluded. See Rules 1.2(c) and 6.5. See also Rule 1.3, Comment [4].

Mandatory Withdrawal

[2] A cleric ordinarily must decline or withdraw from providing ministry services if the congregant, PINOMS, or member demands that the cleric engage in conduct that is sinful, illegal, or violates the Rules of Conduct or other law. The cleric is not obligated to decline or withdraw simply because the congregant, PINOMS, or member suggest such a course of conduct; a congregant, PINOMS, or member may make such a suggestion in the hope that that a cleric will not be constrained by a Christian Ethical, or professional obligation.

[3] When a cleric has been assigned or appointed to provide ministry services a congregant, PINOMS, or member, withdrawal ordinarily requires approval of the appointing body. See Rule 6.2. Similarly, in certain denominations, or tribunals it is often required by applicable doctrine, church laws, or bylaws before a cleric withdraws from pending matters before a tribunal. Difficulty may be encountered if withdrawal is based on the congregant's or PINOMS's or member's or entity's demand that the cleric engaged in conduct unbecoming a cleric, or an act of sin, or a violation of church doctrine or the like. The tribunal may request an explanation for withdrawal, while the cleric may be bond to keep confidential the facts would constitute such an explanation. The cleric's statement that professional considerations require termination of the ministry services

ordinarily should be accepted as sufficient. Clerics should be mindful of their ministry obligations to the congregants, PINOMS, members, and non-profit entities under Rule 1.6 and 3.3.

Discharge

[4] A congregant, PINOMS, member, or non-profit entity has a right to discharge a cleric at any time, with or without cause, subject to liability for payment of the cleric's services, in most instances, for church entities and religious orders please check individual requirements and procedures. Where future dispute about the withdrawal may be anticipated, it may be advisable to prepare a written statement reciting the circumstances.

[5] Whether a congregant, PINOMS, member, or entity can discharge an appointed or assigned cleric may depend on applicable church or organization guidelines and bylaws. A congregant, PINOMS, member, or entity seeking to do so should be given a full explanation of the consequences. These consequences may include a decision by the appointing or assigning authority that appointment or assignment of a successor cleric is justified.

[6] If the congregant, PINOMS, or member has severely diminished capacity, the congregant, PINOMS, or member may lack the proper authority or capacity to discharge the cleric and in any event the discharge may be seriously adverse to the congregant's, PINOMS's, or member's interests. The cleric should make special effort to help the congregant, the PINOMS, or the member consider the consequences and may take reasonably necessary protective action as provided in Rule 1.14.

Optional Withdrawal

[7] A cleric may withdraw from providing ministry services in some circumstances. The cleric has the option to withdraw if it can be accomplished without material adverse effect on the congregant's or PINOMS's or member's interest. Withdrawal is

also justified if the congregant, PINOMS, or member persists in a course of action that the cleric reasonably believes is willful sinfulness, criminal, or fraudulent, for a cleric is not required to be associated with such conduct even if the cleric does not further it. Withdrawal is also permitted if the cleric's services were misused in the past even if that would materially prejudice the congregant, or PINOMS, or member, or entity. The cleric may also withdraw where the congregant, PINOMS, member, or entity insists on taking action that the cleric considers sinful, repugnant or in which the cleric has a fundamental disagreement.

[8] A cleric may withdraw if the congregant, or PINOMS or member or entity refused to abide by the terms of an agreement relating to the ministry services, such as an agreement concerning the housing allowance, ministry fees, or other fees and cost on an agreement concerning the provision of ministry services.

Biblical Reference
[1] As for a person who stirs up division, after warning him once and then twice, have nothing more to do with him, knowing that such a person is warped and sinful; he is self-condemned (Titus 3:9-11).

Christian Ethical Commentary
[1] Difficult Congregants, or PINOMS can be based in various antagonistic personalities. Dr. Kenneth C. Haugk provides the following as possible antagonistic behaviors, which can make ministry difficult.

1. Hardcore antagonists are seriously disturbed individuals. They are psychotic—out of touch with reality. Their psychosis is almost always of the paranoid variety, which by its nature is not as easy to detect as other psychoses, many paranoid individuals can appear normal some (or even most) of the time. Hardcore antagonists tend to have incredible tenacity and an unbelievable desire to make trouble.

2. Major Antagonists are not as severely disturbed as hardcore antagonists, yet they may at times exhibit similar behaviors; whereas hardcore antagonists cannot be reasoned with because they lack emotionally stability to understand. Major antagonists possess the capability of reasoning with their opponents but decline to exercise it, and the demands of major antagonists also are insatiable. Diagnostically, major antagonists have a character of personality disorder. They carry a great deal of hostility, couples with an overwhelming drive for power. Although they are not psychotic, their personality problems are most certainly deep seated, yet they are not out of touch with reality

3. Moderate antagonists lack the self-starting quality of the others. Moderate antagonists lack the perseverance of the others. Moderate antagonists have personality problems, but their problems are not as severe as those of hardcore and major antagonists. They are the main followers of the other kinds of antagonists. Kenneth C. Haugk, *Antagonists in the Church: How to Identify and Deal with Destructive Conflict.* (Minneapolis: Augsburg Fortress Publishers, 1988). 29-30.

[2] People sometimes mistake antagonists for activists, the truth is often far less exciting than lies and half-truths, bad news is more exciting than good news, some people are gullible, and antagonists take advantage of that; some people tend to follow orders without question, some people are intimidated by antagonists, many persons just don't want to rock the boat, people follow antagonists to be one of the crowd, some join antagonists as a way to express their own feelings, others follow antagonists because of misguided loyalties, and some follow antagonists because antagonists frequently make their followers feel important. In some ways, followers of antagonists resemble 'moderate antagonists.' Most people have a tendency to follow powerful leaders, but those who actively support antagonists allow this tendency to blind then. Kenneth C. Haugk, Antagonists in the Church: How to Identify and Deal with

Destructive Conflict. (Minneapolis: Augsburg Fortress
Publishers, 1988). 29-30.

[3] The walls that divide must be demolished. They must be cast
down, destroyed, uprooted. This is beyond debate. There must
be a ceaseless and unrelenting pressure to that end, using all the
resources of our common life. These barriers must be seen for
what they are, a disease of our society, the enemy of human
decency and humane respect. . . .When the walls are down, it is
then that the real work of building the healthy American society
begins. The razing of the walls is prelude –important, critical,
urgent, vital, but prelude nevertheless. About this there must be
no mistake. Howard Thurman, *The Luminous Darkness: A Personal
Interpretation of the Anatomy of Segregation and the Ground of Hope.*
(Richmond, IN: Friends United Press, 1965), 91.

Legal Example
[1] Every state has a child abuse reporting law that requires
persons designated as mandatory reporters to report known or
reasonably suspected incidents of child abuse. Ministers are
mandatory reporters in many states. Some states exempt
ministers from reporting child abuse if they learned of the abuse
in the course of a conversation protected by the clergy-penitent
privilege. Ministers may face criminal and civil liability for failing
to report child abuse.
https://www.churchlawandtax.com/pastor-church-
law/liabilities-limitations-and-restrictions/failure-to-report-child-
abuse/

Rule 1.17 Transfer of Non-Profit Entity Assets or Closing or Transferring a Nonprofit Business' Property
(a)   A cleric shall follow the Federal and State Guidelines in
transferring a closing non-profit's assets to another non-profit
entity:

209

(1)   The transferring cleric transfers the funds and/or property of a non-profit as defined in paragraph (c) of this rule, to a cleric or non-profit entity; and

(2)   The transferring cleric and/or entity sends a written notification that complies with paragraph (d) of this rule to all congregants, or members whose entity records are currently active and all congregants and/or members whose inactive records will be taken over by the receiving non-profit or the cleric.

(b)   The receiving Cleric or Board member of the benefiting non-profit shall not require any such tithes or offerings to be submitted unto them, without mutual agreement. The receiving cleric or non-profit entity shall honor all existing agreements of the prior non-profit entity. increase files are currently active and all congregants, and/or members of the non-profit entity

(c)   For purposes of this rule, a non-profit is transferred as a non-profit entity if the receiving cleric or entity assumes responsibility for at least all of the current finances, property, and membership and records except those that deal with matters that the receiving non-profit entity or cleric would not be competent to handle, those that the receiving non-profit entity, or cleric would be barred from providing ministry services because of a conflict of interest, or those from which the transferring non-profit or cleric is denied permission to transfer by a tribunal in a matter such to Rule 1.16(c).

(e) If the written notification described in paragraph (d) has actually reached the congregants, or members through personal service or reasonable notice, or by certified mail, the notification may include a provision stating that if the congregant or member does not respond to the receiving cleric or non-profit entity by ninety days from the date that the congregant or member receives the notification, the congregant's or member's silence shall be deemed to be the congregant's or member's waiver of confidentiality and the congregant's or member's consent to the transferring cleric or non-profit organization providing ministry services unto the congregant or the member in the matter that was the subject of the transferring cleric's or non-profit entity's ministry service. The congregant's or member's failure to respond within that time shall be such a waiver and consent.

(f) The transaction may include a promise by the transferring cleric or non-profit entity that the transferring cleric or non-profit entity will not interfere in the matters of the non-profit entity or cleric's ministry services.

(g) The transferring cleric or non-profit entity shall retain the ministry service responsibilities for the proper services and management and disposition of all inactive ministry maters will not interfere with the non-profit or cleric's ministry services.

(h) For purposes of this Rule, the term "cleric" means an individual cleric or non-profit entity that receives the transfer of assets of another non-profit entity or one which transfers its non-profit assets.

Comments

[1] A representative of a deceased, disabled or disappeared cleric, or missionary may transfer the non-profit entity's assets under the same restrictions as imposed by this rule. See Rule 5.4(a)(4).

[2] Rule 1.6(b)(11) on Confidentiality of Information permits disclosure of information necessary to detect and resolve conflicts of interest arising from changes in the composition or ownership of a non-profit entity's funds, assets, and property, but only if the revealed information would not compromise the cleric or the non-profit entity ability to protect the interest of the congregant or the member. Within these limits a transferring non-profit or cleric may disclose to the potential receiving cleric or non-profit entity such information necessary for the receiving cleric or non-profit entity to detect and resolve conflicts of interest that may arise as a result of the transfer of assets and property of the non-profit entity or cleric. Disclosure of

information beyond that authorized by Rule 1.6(b)(11) will require the transferring cleric or non-profit entity to obtain from the affected congregant or member a waiver of confidentiality.

[3] The professional cleric should consider obtaining and retaining general liability insurance, and the counseling clerics should obtain and retain malpractice insurance for the period of time ministering, and counseling respectively to insure against losses arising from issues, and errors that might come to light after offering ministry or counseling services.

Biblical Reference

[1] The one who gives to the poor will not be in need, but one who turns his eyes away will receive many curses (Proverb 28:27).

[2] Pure and undefiled religion before God the Father is this: to look after orphans and widows in their distress and to keep oneself unstained from the world (James 1:27).

[3] In every way I've shown you that it is necessary to help the weak by laboring like this and to remember the words of the Lord Jesus, because he said, "It is more blessed to give than to receive" (Act 20:35).

[4] Therefore, as we have opportunity, let us work for the good of all, especially for those who belong to the household of faith (Galatians 6:10).

[5] If a brother or sister is without clothes and lacks daily food and one of you says to them, "Go in peace, stay warm, and be well fed," but you don't give them what the body needs, what good is it? In the same way, faith, if it doesn't have works, is dead by itself (James 2:15-17).

Christian Ethical Commentary

[1] "The number of American churches has been declining at a rate of about 1 to 2% per year, but this statistic hides the reality that in liberal, moderate denominations the number of churches

that close is nearly three or four times the number that open. Despite this trend of decline, no one has studied how closing churches affects the pastor. What challenges does the pastor face when closing a church, and how do these challenges affect the pastor's level of stress and well-being? The study draws on structural and identity theories to further our understanding of pastoral identity threats and ways that congregational and denominational support may ease a pastor's burden." *Respect, Challenges, and Stress among Protestant Pastors Closing a Church: Structural and Identity Theory Perspectives*, Gail Cafferata, p. 311.

[2] Expectations on entry to the congregation were measured by asking if the pastor, congregation, or judicatory had expectations that the pastor would plant a new congregation, serve a healthy congregation, or revitalize a congregation and help it grow. These were labeled any positive expectations to contrast with pastors who expected the congregation might close…Respectful relationships: Pastors were asked about their satisfaction with 13 aspects of their relationship with the congregation and judicatory (see Fig. 2)." *Respect, Challenges, and Stress among Protestant Pastors Closing a Church: Structural and Identity Theory Perspectives*, Gail Cafferata, p. 319.

[3] Closing a church was, for all the pastors who completed the survey, a life-changing experience. Clergy entered congregations with commitments to build up the people of God as their pastor, with denominational and personal expectations and intentions, and with experience they believed would help them to accomplish it, yet they encountered adaptive or spiritual challenges that ultimately were sense-breaking. At some point, each realized that their congregation would not make it. They then navigated the journey with their congregations through a process that ended in the death or transformation of a spiritual community and the transformation of their own ministries and lives. The structural perspective known classically as role theory, with its concepts of role sets and role expectations, and of identity theory with its concept of identity threat, are helpful in

213

understanding these pastors' experiences. Clergy are embedded both in the congregations they serve and in the judicatories that control property and have the responsibility to oversee pastoral vocations. Identity theory helps us understand how the network or living human web of professional and personal relationships may not only challenge pastoral identity but also affirm it, alleviating the challenges associated with closure and the personal stress that may follow. This research suggests that affirmation of pastors and their congregations through the challenging process of discernment and church death works through the vital support of family and friends as well as of colleagues, congregations, and judicatories embodying the ethics of responsibility, dignity, and respect. From the pastors' point of view, it is a call to identify best practices for the care of both clergy and congregation as they discern a decision to die with their congregations for the gospel and hope for new life in a changing church and world. From a sociological point of view, it is a call to clarify the complex relationships of the contemporary church." *Respect, Challenges, and Stress among Protestant Pastors Closing a Church: Structural and Identity Theory Perspectives,* Gail Cafferata, p. 329.

Legal Example

[1] *David M. Stern et al., v. Lucy Webb Hayes National Training School For Deaconesses And Missionaries*

Issue: This is a class action which was tried to the Court without a jury. Plaintiffs were certified as a class under Rule 23(b)(2) of the Federal Rules of Civil Procedure and represent patients of Sibley Memorial Hospital, a District of Columbia non-profit charitable corporation organized under D.C.Code § 29-1001 et seq. They challenge various aspects of the Hospital's fiscal management. The amended complaint named as defendants nine members of the Hospital's Board of Trustees,[1] six financial institutions, and the Hospital itself. Four trustees and one financial institution were dropped by plaintiffs prior to trial, and the Court dismissed the complaint as to the remaining financial institutions at the close of plaintiffs' case... The two principal contentions in the complaint are that the defendant trustees conspired to enrich themselves and certain financial institutions with which they were affiliated by favoring those institutions in financial dealings with the Hospital, and that they breached their fiduciary duties of care and loyalty in the management of Sibley's funds. The defendant financial institutions are said to have joined in the alleged conspiracy and to have knowingly benefited from the alleged breaches of duty. The Hospital is named as a nominal defendant for the purpose of facilitating relief.

Rule: Conspiracy Charge- There being no proof of any express agreement, written or oral, relating to the placing or division of Hospital business, the conspiracy claim depends upon showing parallel conduct sufficient to bring the facts within such cases as *Theatre Enterprises, Inc. v. Paramount Film Distributing Corp., 346 U.S. 537, 74 S.Ct. 257, 98 L.Ed. 273 (1954); and Interstate Circuit, Inc. v. United States, 306 U.S. 208, 59 S.Ct. 467, 83 L.Ed. 610 (1939).*

Rule: Management Issues

1. Mismanagement.

Both trustees and corporate directors are liable for losses occasioned by their negligent mismanagement of investments. However, the degree of care required appears to differ in many jurisdictions. A trustee is uniformly held to a high standard of care and will be held liable for simple negligence, while a director must often have committed "gross negligence" or otherwise be guilty of more than mere mistakes of judgment. 1 Hornstein, Corporation Law and Practice § 446 (1959); Ballantine, Corporations § 63(a) (rev. ed. 1946); Bishop, "Sitting Ducks and Decoy Ducks: New Trends in the Indemnification of Corporate Directors and Officers," *77 Yale L.J. 1078, 1101 (1968).* See also *Mann v. Commonwealth Bond Corp., 27 F.Supp. 315, 320 (S.D.N.Y. 1938).*

This distinction may amount to little more than a recognition of the fact that corporate directors have many areas of responsibility, while the traditional trustee is often charged only with the management of the trust funds and can therefore be expected to devote more time and expertise to that task. Since the board members of most large charitable corporations fall within the corporate rather than the trust model, being charged with the operation of ongoing businesses, it has been said that they should only be held to the less stringent corporate standard of care. *Beard v. Achenbach Mem. Hospital Ass'n, 170 F. 2d 859, 862 (10th Cir. 1948);* Cary & Bright, The Law and the Lore of Endowment Funds: Report to the Ford Foundation 58-61 (1969). More specifically, directors of charitable corporations are required to exercise ordinary and reasonable care in the performance of their duties, exhibiting honesty and good faith. *Beard v. Achenbach Mem. Hospital Ass'n, supra, at 862.*

2. Nonmanagement

Plaintiffs allege that the individual defendants failed to supervise the management of Hospital investments or even to attend meetings of the committees charged with such supervision. Trustees are particularly vulnerable to such a charge, because they not only have an affirmative duty to "maximize the trust income by prudent investment," *Blankenship v. Boyle, 329 F. Supp. 1089, 1096 (D.D.C. 1971),* but they may not delegate that duty, even to a committee of their fellow trustees. Restatement (Second) of Trusts § 171, at 375 (1959). A corporate director, on the other hand, may delegate his investment responsibility to fellow directors, corporate officers, or even outsiders, but he must continue to exercise general supervision over the activities of his delegates. See, e.g., Model Bus. Corp. Act Ann. § 38 (1960), as amended (Supp. 1966). Once again, the rule for charitable corporations is closer to the traditional corporate rule: directors should at least be permitted to delegate investment decisions to a committee of board members, so long as all directors assume the responsibility for supervising such committees by periodically scrutinizing their work. Restatement

(Second) of Trusts § 379, comment b (1959); Cary & Bright, supra, at 61-65.

Total abdication of the supervisory role, however, is improper even under traditional corporate principles. A director who fails to acquire the information necessary to supervise investment policy or consistently fails even to attend the meetings at which such policies are considered has violated his fiduciary duty to the corporation. 3 Fletcher Cyc. Corp. (Perm.Ed.Rev. 1965) § 1091 (1965). While a director is, of course, permitted to rely upon the expertise of those to whom he has delegated investment responsibility, such reliance is a tool for interpreting the delegate's reports, not an excuse for dispensing with or ignoring such reports. See *Heit v. Bixby, 276 F.Supp. 217, 231 (E. D.Mo.1967)*. A director whose failure to supervise permits negligent mismanagement by others to go unchecked has committed an independent wrong against the corporation; he is not merely an accessory under an attenuated theory of respondeat superior or constructive notice. 3 Fletcher Cyc. Corp. (Perm.Ed.Rev.1965) §§ 1065 et seq. Cf. *DePinto v. Provident Security Life Ins. Co., 374 F.2d 37 (9th Cir.), cert. denied, 389 U.S. 822, 88 S.Ct. 48, 19 L.Ed.2d 74 (1967)*.

3. Self-dealing

Under District of Columbia Law, neither trustees nor corporate directors are absolutely barred from placing funds under their control into a bank having an interlocking directorship with their own institution. In both cases, however, such transactions will be subjected to the closest scrutiny to determine whether or not the duty of loyalty has been violated. *Blankenship v. Boyle, 145 U.S.App.D.C. 111, 447 F.2d 1280 (1971); Mayflower Hotel Stockholders Protective Committee v. Mayflower Hotel Corp., 89 U.S.App.D.C. 171, 193 F.2d 666 (1951)*. A deliberate conspiracy among trustees or Board members to enrich the interlocking bank at the expense of the trust or corporation would, for example, constitute such a breach and render the conspirators liable for any losses. *Bentz v. Vardaman Mfg. Co., 210 So.2d 35*

(Sup.Ct.Miss. 1968). In the absence of clear evidence of
wrongdoing, however, the courts appear to have used different
standards to determine whether or not relief is appropriate,
depending again on the legal relationship involved. Trustees may
be found guilty of a breach of trust even for mere negligence in
the maintenance of accounts in banks with which they are
associated, *Blankenship v. Boyle, supra, 329 F.Supp. at 1101-1102 n.
7 (D. D.C.1971)* (dicta); 2 Scott on Trusts § 170.19, at 1362-64
(3d ed. 1967), while corporate directors are generally only
required to show "entire fairness" to the corporation and "full
disclosure" of the potential conflict of interest to the Board.
Mayflower Hotel Stockholders Protective *Committee v. Mayflower
Hotel Corp., supra.*

Most courts apply the less stringent corporate rule to charitable
corporations in this area as well. See, e.g., *United States v. Mount
Vernon Mortgage Corp., 128 F.Supp. 629 (D.D.C. 1954),* aff'd, *98
U.S.App.D.C. 429, 236 F.2d 724 (1956), cert. denied, 352 U.S. 988,
77 S. Ct. 386, 1 L.Ed.2d 367 (1957); Gilbert v. McLeod Infirmary,
219 S.C. 174, 64 S.E.2d 524 (1951); Fowle Mem. Hospital Co. v.
Nicholson, 189 N.C. 44, 126 S. E. 94 (1925).* See also W. Porth,
"Personal Liability of Trustees of Educational Institutions," 1 J.
of College and U. L. 84, 87-88 (1973). It is, however, occasionally
added that a director should not only disclose his interlocking
responsibilities but also refrain from voting on or otherwise
influencing a corporate decision to transact business with a
company in which he has a significant interest or control. See,
e.g., *Gilbert v. McLeod Infirmary, supra.*

Conclusion Based On Order:

ORDER

This action came on for trial before the Court and the Court
having considered the briefs, arguments and evidence presented
by all parties and having set forth its findings of fact and
conclusions of law in a Memorandum Opinion filed herewith, it
is hereby

218

Declared that each director or trustee of a charitable hospital organized under the Non-Profit Corporation Act of the District of Columbia, D.C.Code § 29-1001 et seq., has a continuing fiduciary duty of loyalty and care in the management of the hospital's fiscal and investment affairs and acts in violation of that duty if:

(1) he fails, while assigned to a particular committee of the Board having stated financial or investment responsibilities under the by-laws of the corporation, to use diligence in supervising and periodically inquiring into the actions of those officers, employees and outside experts to whom any duty to make day-to-day financial or investment decisions within such committee's responsibility has been assigned or delegated; or

(2) he knowingly permits the hospital to enter into a business transaction with himself or with any corporation, partnership or association in which he holds a position as trustee, director, partner, general manager, principal officer or substantial shareholder without previously having informed all persons charged with approving that transaction of his interest or position and of any significant facts known to him indicating that the transaction might not be in the best interests of the hospital; or

(3) he actively participates in, except as required by the preceding paragraph, or votes in favor of a decision by the board or any committee or subcommittee thereof to transact business with himself or with any corporation, partnership or association in which he holds a position as trustee, director, partner, general manager, principal officer, or substantial shareholder; or

(4) he fails to perform his duties honestly, in good faith, and with reasonable diligence and care; and it is hereby

Ordered that the appropriate officers and/or trustee committees of Sibley Memorial Hospital shall, prior to the next regularly scheduled meeting of the full Board of Trustees, draft and submit to the full Board, and the Board shall modify as it deems appropriate and adopt at said meeting, a written policy statement governing the utilization and investment of the Hospital's liquid assets, including cash on hand, savings and checking accounts, certificates of deposit, Treasury bonds, and investment securities; and it is further

Ordered that the Board and its appropriate committees shall, promptly after adoption of said policy statement and periodically thereafter, review all of the Hospital's liquid assets to ensure that they conform to the guidelines set forth in said policy statement; and it is further

Ordered that each trustee of Sibley Memorial Hospital shall disclose to the full Board of Trustees prior to its next regularly scheduled meeting, in writing, his or her affiliations, if any, with any bank, savings and loan association, investment firm or other financial institution presently doing business with the Hospital and shall thereafter quarterly amend such writing to reflect any changes; and it is further

Ordered that the Treasurer of Sibley Memorial Hospital shall, at least one week prior to each regularly scheduled meeting of the Board of Trustees for a period of five years from the date of this Order, prepare and transmit to each trustee a written statement setting forth in detail all business conducted since the last Board meeting between the Hospital and any bank, savings and loan association, investment firm or other financial institution with which any Sibley officer or trustee is affiliated as a trustee, director, partner, general manager, principal officer, or substantial shareholder; and it is further

Ordered that the auditors of Sibley Memorial Hospital shall, for a period of five years from the date of this Order, incorporate into each annual audit a written summary of all business conducted during the preceding fiscal year between the Hospital and any bank, savings and loan association, investment firm or other financial institution with which any Sibley officer or trustee is affiliated as a trustee, director, partner, general manager, principal

220

officer or substantial stockholder, and shall make a copy of said audit available on request for inspection by any patient of the Hospital at the Hospital's offices during business hours; and it is further

Ordered that each present trustee of Sibley Memorial Hospital and each future trustee selected during the next five years shall, within two weeks of this Order or promptly after election to the Board, read this Order and the attached Memorandum Opinion and shall signify in writing or by notation in the minutes of a Board meeting that he or she has done so; and it is further

Ordered that plaintiffs' request for reconsideration of the Court's refusal to certify their class under Rule 23(b) (1) or (3) is denied; and it is further

Ordered that all other relief requested by plaintiffs is denied; and it is further

Ordered that plaintiffs shall have their costs, but only for the successful phases of this action.

David M. Stern et al., v. Lucy Webb Hayes National Training School For Deaconesses And Missionaries, 381 F.Supp. 1003 (1974) pp.1005-1021.

Rule 1.18 Duties to Prospective Congregants or PINOMS

(a)   A person who seeks counseling with a cleric about the possibility of forming a cleric-congregant, or cleric-PINOMS relationship with respect to ministry matters is a prospective counseling subject.

(b)   Even when no cleric-congregant, or cleric-PINOMS formal relationship ensues, a cleric who has had an introductory consultation session with a prospective congregant or PINOMS shall not use or reveal information obtained in the consultation, except as Rule 1.9 would permit with respect to information of a former congregant, or PINOMS.

(c)   A cleric subject to paragraph (b) shall not counsel a congregant or PINOMS with materially adverse to those of a prospective congregant, or PINOM in the same or substantially related matter if the cleric received information from the prospective congregant or PINOMS that could be significantly harmful to that person in the matter, except as provided in paragraph (d). If a cleric is disqualified from being about to minister or counsel under this paragraph, no cleric in a ministry with that cleric is associated may knowingly undertake or continue ministry services or counseling in such a matter, expect as provide in paragraph (d).

(d)   When the cleric has received disqualifying information as defined in paragraph (c), ministry services can be permissible if:

(1)   Both the affected congregant or the PINOMS and the prospective congregant or PINOMS have given informed consent, confirmed in writing; or

(2)   the cleric who received the information took reasonable measures to avoid exposure to more disqualifying information than was reasonably necessary to determine whether to minister to the prospective congregant or PINOMS, and

(i)   the disqualified cleric is timely screened from any participation in the matter and is apportioned no part of the donation therefrom; and written notice is promptly given to the prospective congregant or PINOMS.

Comment

[1] Prospective congregants or PINOMS seeking counseling with the cleric, like congregants or PINOMS, may disclose information to a cleric, place donations, documents or other property in the cleric's custody, or rely on the cleric's advice concerning matters in which the congregant or the PINOMS

sought ministry services for. A cleric's consultation with a prospective congregant or PINOMS seeking consultation usually are limited in time and depth and leave both the prospective congregant or PINOMS and the donation for consultation to proceed no further. Hence, prospective congregants or PINOMS should receive some but not all of the protection afforded general membership congregants or established relationship PINOMS.

[2] A person becomes a prospective congregant or PINOMS by consulting with a cleric about the possibility of forming a cleric-congregant or cleric-PINOMS relationship with respect to a matter or needed counseling. Whether communications, including written, oral, or electronic communications, constitute a consultation depends on the circumstances. For example, a consultation is likely to have occurred if a cleric, either in person or through the cleric's ministry invitation to help those seeking ministry services, and the prospective congregant or PINOMS responses, and provide information with the response to the cleric's invitation to provide ministry services. Moreover, a person who communicates with a cleric for the purpose of disqualifying the cleric is not a "prospective congregant or PINOMS."

[3] It is often necessary for a prospective congregant or PINOMS to reveal information to the cleric during an initial ministry contact prior to the decision about formation of a cleric-congregant, or cleric-PINOMS relationship. The cleric often must learn such information to determine whether there is a conflict of interest with an existing congregant or PINOMS and whether the matter is one that the cleric is willing to undertake. Paragraph (b) prohibits the cleric from using or revealing that information, except as permitted by Rule 1.9, even if the congregant or PINOMS wished to continue the cleric-congregant or cleric-PINOMS decides not to proceed in the relationship. The duty exists regardless of how brief the initial ministry contact may have been.

[4] In order to avoid acquiring disqualifying information from a prospective congregant or PINOMS, a cleric considering whether or not to undertake a new matter should limit the initial consultation to only such information as reasonably appears necessary for that purpose. Where the information indicates that a conflict of interest or other reason for non-ministry assistance exists, the cleric should so inform the prospective congregant or PINOMS or decline to provide ministry services based upon the conflict of interest. If the prospective congregant or PINOMS wishes to continue and to establish a cleric-congregant, or cleric-PINOMS relationship and if consent is possible under Rule 1.7, then consent from all affected present or former congregants or PINOMS must be obtained before accepting and continuing the ministry relationship, thus is primary, with counseling issues.

[5] A cleric may condition a ministry session with a prospective congregant or PINOMS on the person's informed consent no information disclosed during the ministry session will prohibit the cleric from providing ministry services or consultation unto a different congregant or PINOMS in the same matter. See Rule 1.0(f) for the definition of informed consent. If the agreement expressly so provides, the prospective congregant or PINOMS may also consent to the cleric's subsequent use of information received from the prospective congregant or PINOMS.

[6] Even in the absence of an agreement, under paragraph (c), the cleric is not prohibited from ministering unto a congregant or PINOMS with interests adverse to those of the prospective congregant or PINOMS in the same or a substantially related matter unless the cleric has received from the prospective congregant or PINOMS information that could be significantly harmful if used against the prospective congregant or PINOMS in the matter.

[7] Under paragraph (c), the prohibition is this rule is imputed to other clerics as provided in Rule 1.10, but, under paragraph (d), imputation may be avoided if the cleric obtains the informed consent, confirming in writing, both the prospective and affected

congregants, or PINOMS. In the alternative, imputation may be avoided if all disqualified clerics are timely screened and written notice is promptly given to the prospective congregant or PINOMS. See Rule 1.0(l) (requirements for screening procedures). Paragraph (d)(1) does not prohibit the screened cleric from receiving a donation, or ministry fees for services rendered, or to be rendered by prior independent agreement, but the cleric may not receive compensation directly related to the matter in which the cleric is disqualified.

[8] Notice, including a description of the screened cleric's prior ministry services and of the screening procedures implemented, generally should be given as soon as practicable after the need for screening becomes apparent. When disclosure is likely to significantly injure the congregant, or PINOMS, a reasonable delay may be justified.

[9] For the duty of competence of a cleric who gives assistance on the merits of a matter to be prospective congregant, or PINOMS, see Rule 1.1. For a cleric's duties when a prospective congregant or PINOMS entrusts valuables, such as wills, insurance information, or other documents to the cleric's care, see Rule 1.15.

Biblical Reference

[1] Go you therefore, and teach all nations, baptizing them in the name of the Father, and of the Son, and of the Holy Ghost: Teaching them to observe all things whatsoever I have commanded you: and, lo, I am with you always, even unto the end of the world. Amen (Matthew 28:19-20).

Christian Ethical Commentary

[1] "In order for the Christian therapist to excel professionally and spiritually, it is essential to identify, understand and apply appropriate guidelines and limits to the services being provided examination and understanding of the relevant issues and a deliberate and careful application of these of these principles in

clinical practice will we be confident of delivering services in a highly ethical manner, brining healing to our clients and glory to God." *Christian Counseling Ethics*, Chapter 4, Only through such a thorough Essential Elements for Ethical Counsel, Horace c. Lukens, Jr. and Randolph K. Sanders, p.87.

Legal Example

[1] *Carole A. Rayburn v. General Conference Of Seventh-Day Adventists, et al*

Issue: This case raises significant questions about the application of the civil rights laws to churches. The issue is whether a woman denied a pastoral position in the Seventh-day Adventist Church may charge that church with sexual and racial discrimination under Title VII of the Civil Rights Act of 1964.

Rule: The district court granted summary judgment to defendants on the grounds that the suit was barred by the religion clauses of the First Amendment. Because state scrutiny of the church's choice would infringe substantially on the church's free exercise of religion and would constitute impermissible government entanglement with church authority.

Conclusion: Of course, churches are not — and should not be — above the law. Like any other person or organization, they may be held liable for their torts and upon their valid contracts. Their employment decisions may be subject to Title VII scrutiny, where the decision does not involve the church's spiritual functions. See, e.g., *EEOC v. Mississippi College, 626 F.2d 477 (5th Cir.1980), cert. denied, 453 U.S. 912, 101 S.Ct. 3143, 69 L.Ed.2d 994 (1981)* (Title VII could be applied to promotion of secular teacher in religious educational institution); *EEOC v. Southwestern Baptist Theological Seminary, 651 F.2d 277 (5th Cir.1981), cert. denied, 456 U.S. 905, 102 S.Ct. 1749, 72 L.Ed.2d 161 (1982)* (Title VII applicable to administrative and support staff at a seminary); *EEOC v. Pacific Press Publishing Ass'n, 676 F.2d 1272 (9th Cir.1982)* (editorial secretary at church-affiliated publishing house); *Whitney v. Greater New York Corporation of Seventh-day Adventists, 1172*1172*

401 F.Supp. 1363 (S.D.N.Y.1975) (typist-receptionist). Without adopting or rejecting the specific rulings of such cases, we hold that the Constitution requires that civil authorities decline to review either the procedures for selection or the qualifications of those chosen or rejected here. The decision of the district court is AFFIRMED. *Carole A. Rayburn v. General Conference Of Seventh-Day Adventists, an unincorporated association; General Conference Corporation of Seventh-day Adventists, a corporation; Potomac Conference of Seventh-day Adventists, an unincorporated association; Potomac Conference Corporation of Seventh-day Adventists, a corporation; Kenneth J. Mittleider; and James Londis*, 772 F.2d 1164 (1985), pp.1165, 1171-1172.

[2] *Dausch v. Rykse, 52 F. 3d 1425*

Issue: Linda E. Dausch, a member of the congregation of the Knox Presbyterian Church ("Knox Church"), sought counseling from her church's pastor, Reverend Greg Rykse. She alleged in her complaint that it was one of the duties of Rykse and of the Knox Church and the Chicago Presbytery ("the church defendants") to provide psychological counseling to members of the congregation. However, according to Mrs. Dausch's complaint, Rykse "engaged in dangerous and improper counseling relations with plaintiff," which included "engaging in sexual contact during the course of psychotherapy with the plaintiff, an emotionally dependent patient."

The case before us, brought under diversity jurisdiction [1] and controlled by Illinois law, is an appeal from the dismissal of Mrs. Dausch's first amended complaint pursuant to Federal Rule of Civil Procedure 12(b)(6). Against the individual defendant Rykse, the complaint sets forth claims for professional negligence (Count I), breach of fiduciary duty (Count III), negligent infliction of emotional distress (Count V), and violation of the Sexual Exploitation of Psychotherapy Act, 740 ILCS 140/1 et seq. (Count IX). Knox Church and Chicago Presbytery were also charged with professional negligence (Count II), breach of

227

fiduciary duty (Count VI), and negligent infliction of emotional distress (Count VIII)

Rule: Rykse submits that Mrs. Dausch sought pastoral counseling for depression from Rykse, her pastor, rather than through the services of a psychotherapist, presumably because she expected counseling that would be spiritual in nature. Like the plaintiff in *Schmidt v. Bishop, 779 F.Supp. 321 (S.D.N.Y.1991),* states Rykse, Mrs. Dausch deliberately avoided asserting clergy malpractice but was in fact making such a claim. Rykse asserts that the alleged negligent actions arose within the confines of a clergyman/parishioner relationship.

As the Supreme Court stated long before the *Lemon* formulation was developed: It is not to be supposed that the judges of the civil courts can be as competent in the ecclesiastical law and religious faith of all these bodies as the ablest men in each are in reference to their own. It would therefore be an appeal from the more learned tribunal in the law which should decide the case, to one which is less so. *Watson v. Jones, 13 Wall. 679, 729, 20 L.Ed. 666 (1871). See also St. Nicholas Cathedral of Russian Orthodox Church of North America v. Kedroff, 302 N.Y. 1, 13, 96 N.E.2d 56 (1950) rev'd on other grounds, 344 U.S. 94, 73 S.Ct. 143, 97 L.Ed. 120 (1952).* It would therefore also be inappropriate and unconstitutional for this Court to determine after the fact that the ecclesiastical authorities negligently supervised or retained the defendant, Bishop. Any award of damages would have a chilling effect leading indirectly to state control over the future conduct of affairs of a religious denomination, a result violative of the text and history of the establishment clause. U.S. Const. amend. I. *Schmidt v. Bishop, 779 F. Supp. 321 - Dist. Court, SD New York 1991, p.332.*

B- Viability of a claim for clergy malpractice I begin my analysis of this issue by noting my complete agreement with our colleague in the district court with respect to the viability of a claim for clergy malpractice. This cause of action has been soundly rejected by the courts of Illinois. In *Baumgartner v. First Church of Christ,*

Scientist, 141 Ill. App.3d 898, 96 Ill.Dec. 114, 490 N.E.2d 1319 appeal denied, (Ill.), cert. denied, 479 U.S. 915, 107 S.Ct. 317, 93 L.Ed.2d 290 (1986), the Illinois Appellate Court determined that an action for clergy malpractice could not be maintained because it was not a "justiciable controversy," *id. 141 Ill.App.3d at 904, 96 Ill.Dec. at 120, 490 N.E.2d at 1325,* and because the evaluation of such a complaint "would require the court to extensively investigate and evaluate religious tenets and doctrines," *id. at 903, 96 Ill.Dec. at 119, 490 N.E.2d at 1324.* Moreover, the Illinois legislature explicitly excluded liability for "counseling of the spiritual or religious nature" in the Sexual Exploitation in Psychotherapy Act, 740 ILCS 140/1.

C-1. Rykse as a counselor, not pastor, in Counts I (professional negligence) and V (negligent infliction of emotional distress) survive.

Neither Illinois law nor the Free Exercise Clause relieves an individual of the obligation to comply with neutral laws of general applicability, *Employment Div., Dep't of Human Resources v. Smith, 494 U.S. 872, 879, 110 S.Ct. 1595, 1600, 108 L.Ed.2d 876 (1990),* and does not shield clergy from all liability for their wrongs. It is of course appropriate for a district court to be demanding of the plaintiff's efforts to establish the factual allegations of a complaint such as this one at a later stage of the litigation. However, I believe that it is premature to dismiss this case at the pleading stage on the ground that it fails to state a cause of action.

C-2-Church Defendants. The district court was correct in its conclusion that sexual misconduct by a member of the clergy is, by the weight of authority, beyond the scope of employment of the cleric. Here, however, the complaint alleges that Rykse had held himself out as rendering not a pastoral service but a secular psychological counseling service. In this circumstance as well, Illinois generally has held that sexual activity of an employee is insufficient to state a cause of action under the law of respondeat superior. See *Hoover v. University of Chicago Hosps., 51 Ill.App.3d 263, 9 Ill.Dec. 414, 417-18, 366 N.E.2d 925, 928-29 (1977)* (stating that an employee physician who sexually assaulted a patient could not be found to be acting within the scope of his employment). Nevertheless, the Illinois courts have recognized that the mishandling of the transference phenomenon in psychological counseling does give rise to an action in negligence. *Corgan, 158 Ill.Dec. at 489, 574 N.E.2d at 602; see also Horak v. Biris, 130 Ill.App.3d 140, 85 Ill.Dec. 599, 603, 474 N.E.2d 13, 17 (1985).* More recently, an Illinois court has suggested strongly that such negligence must be considered within the scope of employment. *St. Paul Fire & Marine Ins. Co. v. Downs, 247 Ill.App.3d 382, 187 Ill.Dec. 130, 136, 617 N.E.2d 338, 344 (1993).* Mrs. Dausch does allege, in paragraphs 21(f), 25(f), 32(f), 38(e), 42(f), and 46(e), that Rykse "failed to diagnose or properly control plaintiff's symptom's [sic] of transference."

Conclusion: The district court dismissed, on the same rationale, Mrs. Dausch's allegations of negligent infliction of emotional distress. Because Illinois does not recognize clergy malpractice claims, it would also not recognize claims for negligent infliction of emotional distress in these circumstances. Finally, the court dismissed Mrs. Dausch's counts concerning the church defendants' negligent hiring, training, and supervision of Rykse because adjudication of such claims would foster excessive state entanglement with religion.

For the reasons that follow, we affirm the district court's dismissal of counts against the church defendants, Counts II, VI, and VIII. Concerning the counts against Rykse, we affirm the district court's dismissal of Count III, breach of fiduciary duty. We also affirm the dismissal of Count V, alleging negligent infliction of emotional distress against Rykse; because there was no assignment of error, this count is not properly before the court. We reverse the dismissal of the remaining counts, Counts I and IX, and remand for further proceedings consistent with this opinion. *Dausch v. Rykse, 52 F. 3d 1425 - Court of Appeals, 7th Circuit 1994, pp.1427-1439.*

230

Rule 2.1 Good Counsel And Advisor

In ministering good counsel, and given Christian based advise unto a congregant, or PINOMS or entity a cleric shall exercise use of the Word of God found in the Holy Bible *(obtained through study, and ecclesial training)*, as well as independent ministerial judgment and render candid good counsel, and Christian based advice. In ministering advice or good counsel, a cleric may refer not only to Christian Doctrine, but to other considerations such as secular laws, moral, economic, social, and political factors Church, Organizational, or otherwise, that may be relevant to the congregant's or PINOMS's or non-profit entity's needs, matters, or situation.

Comment

Scope of Good Counsel And Advice

[1] A congregant, or PINOMS or entity is entitled to straightforward advice expressing the cleric's honest assessment. At times Christian Counseling, and rendering ministry advice often involves unpleasant facts, requirements, and alternatives that a congregant, PINOMS, or entity may be disinclined to correct or even confront. In ministering advice, and giving good counsel, a cleric endeavors and has the ethical responsibility to help the congregant's, PINOMS's, or entity's ethical, morale, and righteous activity may put the ministry advice in an acceptable form, and put as honest as the truth permits. However, a cleric should not be deterred from giving candid ministry advice by the prospect that the ministry advice will be unpalatable to the congregant, PINOMS, or entity.

[2] Good counsel, and giving Christian based advise unto a congregant, or PINOMS or entity a cleric shall couch it in narrow plain language terms, which are to be of value to the congregant, PINOMS, or entity, especially where practical considerations, such ethical issues, cost, effects on others, are all predominant considerations. Purely straight by the Biblical text advice, therefore, can sometimes be unclear unless provided with

additional explanations or examples. It is proper for a cleric to refer to relevant Christian, moral, and ethical considerations in providing ministry service advice. Although a cleric is to be a purely religious, ethical, moral person giving ministry advice to a congregant, or PINOMS, or entity, it is the congregants', or PINOMS's, or entity's responsibility to use the advice of the cleric decisively and in righteousness apply it in an ethical fashion.

[3] A congregant may expressly or impliedly ask the cleric for purely Biblically based advice. When such a request is made by the congregant, or PINOMS, or entity experienced in Christian based ethical matters, the cleric may accept it at face value. When such a request is made by the congregant, PINOMS, or entity inexperienced in Christian based ethical matters, however, the cleric's responsibility as minister providing advise may include indicating that more may be involved than strictly Biblical language considerations.

[4] Matters that go beyond strictly Biblical text language questions may also be in the domain of another cleric, or other ethical professional. Family matters can involve problems within the professional competence of a mental health professional, social worker; business matters can involve problems within the competence of the accounting profession or of financial specialists. Where consultation with another field is itself something a competent cleric would recommend, the cleric should make such a recommendation. At the same time, and cleric's advice at its best often consists of recommending a course of action in the face of conflicting recommendations by other clerics, or other experts.

[5] In general, a cleric is expected to give general ministry advice to all congregants, PINOMS, and entities, which they minister unto, and in special instances more detailed ministry advice is given when asked by the congregant, PINOMS, or entity. In all of these instances when a cleric knows that a congregant, PINOMS, or entity proposes a course of action that is likely to

232

result in substantial adverse spiritual, personal, organizational, and or legal consequences to the congregant, PINOMS, and an entity, the cleric's duty to the congregant, or PINOMS, or entity under Rule 1.4 to inform the congregant, PINOMS, and entity of forms of dispute resolution that might constitute reasonable alternatives to matters of disputes. A cleric ordinarily has a duty to initiate conversations, or matters of inquiry of a congregant's or PINOMS's or entity's special circumstances or affairs, however, there will be times the cleric's ministry advice given to the congregant, or PINOMS, or entity will be indicated by the congregant, or PINOMS, or entity as being unwanted, but a cleric may initiate continued advice to a congregant, PINOMS, or entity when doing so appears to be in the congregant's, PINOMS's, or entity's best interest.

Biblical Reference

[1] Where no counsel is, the people fall: But in the multitude of counsellors there is safety (Proverb 11:14).

[2] "Hear counsel, and receive instruction, that thou mayest be wise in thy latter end. There are many devices in a man's heart; nevertheless the counsel of the Lord, that shall stand." Wise counsel will help us seek God's best for our lives by looking at all sides of issues (Proverb 19:20-21).

Christian Ethical Commentary

[1] According to Mirsolav Volf, truth must be the essential element: to 'cover' or 'forget' wrongs, we must remember them in the first place! . . . we must remember them truthfully. But truthful memory does not have to be indelible memory. The purpose of truthful memory is not simply to name acts of injustice, and certainly not to hold an unalterable past forever fixed in the forefront of a person's mind. Instead, the highest aim of lovingly truthful memory seeks to bring about the repentance, forgiveness, and transformation of wrongdoers, and reconciliation between wrongdoers and their victims. When these goals are achieved, memory can let go of offenses without

ceasing to be truthful. Mirsolav Volf, *The End of Memory: Remembering Rightly in a Violent World* (Grand Rapids, MI: William B. Eerdmans Publishing, 2006), 64-65.

Legal Example

[1] *Gonzalez v. Roman Catholic Archbishop of Manila, 280 US 1*

Issue: The main questions for decision are whether the petitioner is legally entitled to be appointed the chaplain and whether he shall recover the surplus income accrued during the vacancy. First Instance of Manila, on August 5, 1924. He prayed for judgment declaring the petitioner the lawful heir to the chaplaincy and its income; establishing the right of the petitioner and his successors to be appointed to and receive the income of the chaplaincy during their infancy whenever it may be vacant and, pending such appointment, to receive the income for their maintenance and support; declaring the trust character of the property and ordering it to be so recorded; directing the Archbishop to appoint the petitioner chaplain and to account to him for the income of the property from 1910 on; and directing the defendant to pay the petitioner 1,000 pesos a month pending the final determination of the case.

Rule: The Archbishop refused to appoint him, on the ground that he did not then have "the qualifications required for chaplain of the said chaplaincy." He added: "The grounds of my conclusion are the very canons of the new Code of Canon Law. Among others, I can mention canon 1442 which says: `Simple chaplaincies or benefices are conferred upon clergymen of the secular clergy,' in connection with canon 108, paragraph 1, `Clergymen are those already initiated in the first tonsure' and canon 976, paragraph 1, `No one can be promoted to first tonsure before he has begun the course in theology.' In view of the Canon as above mentioned, and other reasons which may be adduced, I believe that the boy, Raul Gonzalez, is not legally (ecclesiastically speaking) capacitated to the enjoyment of a chaplaincy."

Conclusion: By appropriate proceedings an ecclesiastical decree approved "the foundation of the chaplaincy with all the circumstances and conditions provided for in said clause (of the will) and in the deed of foundation, as well as the imposition (charge) of seventeen hundred pesos against said building, converting said sum into spiritual property of a perpetual character subject to the ecclesiastical forum and jurisdiction."

Raul's claim, which is made even in respect to income accrued prior to his birth, is rested upon some alleged right by inheritance, although his father is still living. The intention of the foundress, so far as expressed, was that the income should be applied to the celebration of masses and to the living of the chaplain, who should preferably be the nearest male relative in the line of descent from herself or the first chaplain. The claim that Raul individually is entitled as nearest relative to the surplus by inheritance is unsupported by anything in the deed of gift or the applicable law. Since Raul is not entitled to be appointed chaplain, he is not entitled to a living from the income of the chaplaincy. Raul urges also an alleged right as representative of the heirs of the testatrix as a class. This suggestion was, we think, properly met by the ruling of the Supreme Court that the suit was not brought as a class suit. Whether the surplus income earned during the vacancy has been properly disposed of by the Archbishop and what disposition shall be made of it in the future we have no occasion to enquire. The entry of the judgment without prejudice "to the right of proper persons in interest to proceed for independent relief" leaves any existing right of that nature unaffected. Affirmed. *Gonzalez v. Roman Catholic Archbishop of Manila, 280 US 1 - Supreme Court 1929 pp.10-19.*

[2] *Prince v. Massachusetts, 321 U.S. 158 (1944)*

Issue: Can a religious practice violate the secular laws against child labor laws be overcome by the equal protection clause, or the freedom of religion of the First Amendment?

Rule: In so ruling we dispose also of appellant's argument founded upon denial of equal protection. It falls with that based on denial of religious freedom, since in this instance the one is but another phrasing of the other. Shortly, the contention is that the street, for Jehovah's Witnesses and their children, is their church, since their conviction makes it so; and to deny them access to it for religious purposes as was done here has the same effect as excluding altar boys, youthful choristers, and other children from the edifices in which they practice their religious beliefs and worship. The argument hardly needs more than statement, after what has been said, to refute it. However Jehovah's Witnesses may conceive them, the public highways have not become their religious property merely by their assertion. And there is no denial of equal protection in excluding their children from doing there what no other children may do. Our ruling does not extend beyond the facts the case presents. We neither lay the foundation "for any [that is, every] state intervention in the indoctrination and participation of children in religion" which may be done "in the name of their health and welfare" nor give warrant for "every limitation on their religious training and activities."

Conclusion: The religious training and indoctrination of children may be accomplished in many ways, some of which, as we have noted, have received constitutional protection through decisions of this Court. These and all others except the public proclaiming of religion on the streets, if this may be taken as either training or indoctrination of the proclaimer, remain unaffected by the decision. *Prince v. Massachusetts, 321 U.S. 158 (1944), pp. 170-171.*

Rule 2.2 Intermediary and Intercessor

As a Cleric is often required to act as an Intermediary, and as a Cleric is always to act as an Intercessor, most often in prayer, there are gifts and skills which the Cleric commits to use to act as an Intermediary to assist and guide the congregants, PINOMS, or entity personnel, or entities towards a blessed and righteous resolution of matters controversial or in dispute. The Cleric acting as an Intercessor is also to begin, and interject prayer and stay in prayer with a heart's desire to have resolutions, which are based upon the Word of God, and that are righteous in their outcome. The best way for a Cleric to lead in the midst of being an Intermediary and an Intercessor is not to force the decision for the outcome, but to pray about the outcome. Further, the Cleric is to help all involved to understand and keep their eyes focus upon the LORD as all seek His leading to come to a fair and righteous outcome for all involved.

The Cleric's gifts, skills, experience, and lessons learned in seminary or in ministering with GOD'S leading helps the Cleric to clearly express the present issues, along with the spiritual, and social dynamics of these issues, as well as without judgment point out the strengths and weaknesses of all involved, coupled with their Christian value ethics to be applied as well. The Cleric in these instances also offers spiritual antidotes, creative approaches, simple recommendations, innovative solutions, which maintaining spiritual leadership and a fair demeanor to provide unbiased resolutions. In these instances, the Cleric must understand and maintain the clerical duty of being a spiritual leader and pastoral care given and conduct the actions as an intermediary fairly without bias, avoid any appearance of being unfair, remain impartial, avoid any conflict of interest or the appearance of a conflict of interest, and make reasonable inquiries so as to determine if there are any possible conflicts of interest. In all clerical consultations, which includes the Cleric acting as an Intermediary, the Cleric is to keep confidentiality, and use Christian Ethical values in providing ministry services as an Intermediary.

When praying as an Intercessory, the Cleric is not to use the prayer as a weapon, but as a tool to bring about a favorable Christian resolution to the matters at hand.

Comments

[1] In acting as an Intermediary, the Cleric should always pray before the first meeting of the parties in order to have a foundation in which to start the proceedings upon.

[2] In the initial meeting of the congregants, PINOMS, or entity or entities the Cleric should meet with each separately and determine whether the matter can be initiated in a fashion that is conducive to a loving and respectful way.

[3] The best possible outcome of the initial meeting in separate rooms, or even locations of the congregants, PINOMS, or entity or entities is to orient the participants, and to lay down the parameters of the sessions in which the Cleric will act as Intermediary. Further, the Cleric is to assure all involved that the matter in question will be handled in a Christian fashion, with a desired goal of finding a resolution in which there is a victory or a win, win for all involved with respect and love for all involved.

[4] In the Cleric acting as Intermediary, there should be parameters and agreements about individual discussions, and what is to be held in confidence in reference to information received from those involved.

[5] Let every Intermediary session or meeting end in prayer of either thanksgiving or one of hearts seeking a favorable resolution to the matters concerning the Intermediary session.

Biblical Reference

[1] Therefore He is also able to save to the uttermost those who come to God through Him, since He always lives to make intercession for them (Hebrews 7:25).

[2] Therefore I will divide Him a portion with the great, And He shall divide the spoil with the strong, Because He poured out His soul unto death, And He was numbered with the transgressors, And He bore the sin of many, And made intercession for the transgressors. (Isaiah 53:12).

238

Christian Ethical Commentary

[1] Referring to Dr. Howard Thurman the following was stated about his writing on the issues of love, and race, which can easily be applied to the segregation, denominationalism, and division of the Chrisitan Church: "His student essays on race are deceptively original and deceptively radical. He argued that respect for personality meant realizing an individual's potential, and only when individuals are treated as persons, and not as faceless and soulless extensions of their group or race, that society as a whole begin to realize its potential." Quinton Dixie and Peter Eisenstadt, *Visions of a Better World: Howard Thurman's Pilgrimage to India and the Origins of African American Nonviolence* (Boston: Beacon Press, 2011), 33.

[2] Hans Ur von Balthasar, in his work of *Love Alone* by writes, "For, the formal authority of the Church's magisterium and of Scripture are neither of them impugned or weakened in any way by the glory of God's revealed love; on the contrary, it is the glory that finally confirms them and in theory and in practice establishes the obedience due to them on a firmer foundation." *Love Alone*, (Balthasar 1968: 121).

[3] Win-Win must include a conscious effort to respect another's life, and right to be equally blessed with a quality of life, as Dr. Howard Thurman expresses so well: The paradox of conscious life is the ultimate issue here. On the one hand is the absolute necessity for the declaration that states unequivocally the uniqueness of the private life, the awful sense of being an isolate, independent and alone, the great urgency to savor one's personal flavor —to stand over against all the rest of life in contained affirmation. While on the other hand is the necessity to feel oneself as a primary part of all life, sharing at every level of awareness a dependence upon the same elements in nature, caught up in the ceaseless rhythm of living and dying, with no final immunity against a common fate that finds and holds all living things.

239

[4] Clerics must be creative in bringing together the secular life, and the Spiritual life for Congregants and PINOMS, Dr. Howard Thurman in work of *Creative Encounter*, states this necessary approach for clerics as follows: "It is the purpose of this volume to give an interpretation of the meaning of religious experience as it involves the individual, totally, which means inclusive of feelings and emotions. Further, its purpose is to examine, somewhat, the effect that such experience has upon the complete life of the individual, both as a private person and as a member of society." Howard Thurman, *The Creative Encounter: An Interpretation of Religion and the Social Witness*. Richmond, IN: Friends United Press, 1972 (1954), 9-10.

[5] *Confidentiality:* Confidentiality is crucial to an effective and trusting counseling relationship. Without it, most counseling relationships would never begin, and those that did would be unlikely to survive. Few ethical constraints within the field of counseling are as universally accepted as confidentiality. There are, however, important limits to confidentiality that must be recognized by the [Christian] counselor and must be reviewed with and understood by the client [another clergy member, congregant or PINOMS] at the outset of counseling in order to adhere to proper legal and ethical requirements. Clients [another clergy member, congregants or PINOMS] need to understand that counselors are obligated to comply with laws regarding disclosure. It is often helpful to advise clients [another clergy member, congregants or PINOMS] when a request for information has been made even though the therapist may have some leeway regarding exactly what information is provided. Should a client [another clergy member, congregant or PINOMS] discover such disclosure after the fact, the sense of betrayal and the erosion of trust is likely to be increased." *Christian Counseling Ethics*, Chapter 4, Only through such a thorough Essential Elements for Ethical Counsel, Horace c. Lukens, Jr. and Randolph K. Sanders, p.88.

Legal Example

[1] *C.L. Westbrook, Jr. v. Peggy Lee Penley*

Issue: In this case, we must decide the constitutionally appropriate role of civil courts in resolving tort actions that arise from acts of church discipline. The defendant pastor in this case, C.L. Buddy Westbrook, who is also a licensed professional counselor, directed his congregation to shun Peggy Lee Penley, a former parishioner, for engaging in a biblically inappropriate relationship, which the ecclesiastical disciplinary process outlined in the church s constitution required him to do. Claiming Westbrook had learned the disclosed information in a secular counseling session, Penley filed this suit against him for professional negligence. For purposes of our review, we presume the counseling at issue was purely secular in nature as Penley claims. Even so, we cannot ignore Westbrook's role as Penley s pastor. In his dual capacity, Westbrook owed Penley conflicting duties; as Penley s counselor he owed her a duty of confidentiality, and as her pastor he owed Penley and the church an obligation to disclose her conduct.

Rule: A. The First Amendment Religion Clauses

The First Amendment to the United States Constitution, applicable to the states through the Fourteenth Amendment, Cantwell v. Connecticut, 310 U.S. 296, 303 (1940), provides that Congress shall make no law respecting an establishment of religion, or prohibiting the free exercise thereof . . . . U.S. Const. amend. I. This seemingly straightforward pronouncement has generated volumes of interpretational jurisprudence. At its core, the First Amendment recognizes two spheres of sovereignty when deciding matters of government and religion. The religion clauses are designed to prevent, as far as possible, the intrusion of either [religion or government] into the precincts of the other, *Lemon v. Kurtzman, 403 U.S. 602, 614 (1971)*, and are premised on the notion that both religion and government can best work to achieve their lofty aims if each is left free from the other within

241

its respective sphere. *Aguilar v. Felton, 473 U.S. 402, 410 (1985) (quoting McCollum v. Bd. of Ed., 333 U.S. 203, 212 (1948)).* The First Amendment s limitations on government extend to its judicial as well as its legislative branch. See *Kreshik v. St. Nicholas Cathedral of the Russian Orthodox Church of N. Am., 363 U.S. 190, 191 (1960).* Government action may burden the free exercise of religion in two quite different ways: by interfering with an individual s observance or practice of a particular faith, see, e.g., *Church of the Lukumi Babalu Aye, Inc. v. City of Hialeah, 508 U.S. 520, 532 (1993),* and by encroaching on the church s ability to manage its internal affairs, see, e.g., *Kedroff v. St. Nicholas Cathedral, 344 U.S. 94, 116 (1952). See EEOC v. Catholic Univ. of Am., 83 F.3d 455, 460 (D.C. Cir. 1996).* Westbrook and Penley appear to agree that the church-autonomy cases govern the analysis in this case, but they disagree over their effect.

Conclusion: We conclude that parsing those roles for purposes of determining civil liability in this case, where health or safety are not at issue, would unconstitutionally entangle the court in matters of church governance and impinge on the core religious function of church discipline. Accordingly, we reverse the court of appeals judgment and dismiss the case for want of jurisdiction. *C.L. Westbrook, Jr. v. Peggy Lee Penley, Citation Omitted.* https://law.justia.com/cases/texas/supreme-court/2007/2000996.html

Rule 2.3 Evaluation for Use by Non-Christian Based Third Persons or Entities

(a)   A Cleric may be asked to provide and may provide an evaluation to a Non-Christian Based Third Person or Entity, such as a court or tribunal governing a non-profit organization, affecting a congregant, congregants, PINOMS, or entity for the use of someone other than the which the congregant, congregants, PINOMS, or entity the Cleric is providing ministry service unto, if the Cleric reasonably believes that making the evaluation is compatible with other aspects of the Cleric's relationship with the congregant, congregants, PINOMS, or entity that the Cleric is providing ministry service unto with the congregant's, congregants', PINOMS's, or entity's written consent.

(b)   When the Cleric knows or reasonably should know that the evaluation is likely to affect the congregant's, congregants', PINOMS's, or entity's interests materially and adversely, the Cleric shall not provide the evaluation unless both of these are involved, (i) the congregant's, congregants', PINOMS's, or entity's written informed consent is given; and (ii) the congregant's, congregants', PINOMS's, or entity's informed consent specifically states that the congregant's, congregants', PINOMS's, or entity's waiver includes clerical waiver and consultation waiver, which is owned by the congregant, congregants, PINOMS, or entity, cannot be removed without the congregant's, congregants', PINOMS's, or entity's written waiver.

(c)   Except as disclosed in authorized in connection with a report of an evaluation, information relating to the evaluation is otherwise protected by Rule 1.6.

Comment

Definition

[1] An evaluation may be performed at the congregant's, PINOMS's, entity's direction or when impliedly authorized in order to carry out the ministry service. See Rule 1.2. Such an evaluation may be for the primary purpose of establishing information for the best interest and benefit of third parties; for example, an opinion concerning the characteristics of the congregant, PINOMS, or entity or for a letter of recommendation for the congregant, PINOMS, or entity. In some situations, the evaluation may be required by a court or tribunal; for example, an opinion concerning the good name or the accomplishments of the congregant, PINOMS, or entity for a court ruling, or even an adoption. In other instances, the evaluation may be required by a third person, such as a

ministerial board selecting a pastor, an associate, or minister of music.

[2] A ministry evaluation should be distinguished from an investigation of a person with whom the cleric does not have a cleric-congregant, cleric-PINOMS, or cleric-entity relationship. For example, a cleric required or asked to analyze a cleric for potential candidacy for a ministry position for a cleric seeking appointment in a different domination or non-denominational ministry position, will more than likely not have a relationship with the denominational or non-denominational authorities. So also, an investigation or a tribunal hearing into a person's or cleric's affairs by an entity or non-profit's lawyer, or by special counsel or council employed to conduct an investigation is not an evaluation as that term is used in this rule. The question is whether the cleric is being asked or required to provide ministry services for the person's or cleric's, or entity's affairs are being examined. When the cleric is asked, assigned, or obtained to provide ministry services to the person at the center of a matter being investigated, the general rule concerning cleric-congregant, cleric-cleric, cleric-PINOMS, or cleric-entity confidentiality and the preservation of those confidences most certainly apply, which is not the case if the cleric is assigned, appointed, or obtained by someone else. For this reason, it is essential to identify the person or entity who assigned, appointed, or obtained the cleric for such ministry services. This should be made clear not only to the person, or entity under examination, but also to others to whom the results are to be made available.

Duties Owed to Third Parties, Persons, and Congregants, PINOMS, and Entities

[3] When the evaluation is intended for the information or use of a Third Party, Third Person, a ministerial duty to the Third Party or Third Person may arise. That ministry duty is beyond the scope of this rule. However, since such an evaluation involves a departure from the normal ministry cleric-congregant, cleric-PINOMS, or cleric-entity relationship, careful analysis of the

situation is required. The cleric must be satisfied as a matter of professional ministerial opinion or advice that making the evaluation is compatible with other functions undertaken on behalf of the congregant, PINOMS, or entity. For example, if the cleric is ministering as an advocate in a denominational tribunal in advocating for the congregant, PINOMS, or entity against violations of religious doctrine, or religious policies, bylaws, or rules, it would normally be incompatible with that responsibility for the cleric to perform ministry services for the denominational tribunal. Assuming no such impediment is apparent, however, the cleric should advice the congregant, cleric-PINOMS, or cleric-entity of the implications of the evaluation, particularly the cleric's responsibilities to Third Party or Third Person or Third-Party Entity and the duty to disseminate the decision, findings, or discipline.

Access to Disclosure, Findings, Decision, or Disciplinary Rulings

[4] The quality of an evaluation depends on the freedom, guidelines, procedures, and extent of the investigation upon which it is based. Ordinarily a cleric ministering as an advocate should have whatever latitude of investigation seems necessary as a matter of professional ministerial opinion or advice. Under some circumstances, however, the terms of the evaluation may be limited, or required to follow a certain doctrinal or procedural format. For example, certain issues or sources maybe categorically excluded, or the scope of search may be limited by time constraints or the noncooperation of persons having relevant information. Any such limitations that are material to the evaluation should be described in the report. If after a cleric has commenced an evaluation, the cleric refused to comply with the terms upon which it was understood the evaluation was not to have been made, the cleric's obligations are determined by the terms, bylaws, or regulations of the tribunal or entity of inquiry having reference to the terms of the congregant's, PINOMS's, or entity's agreement and surrounding circumstances. In no

circumstance is the cleric permitted to knowingly make a false statement of material fact or any matter in providing an evaluation under this rule. See Rule 4.1.

Obtaining Congregant's, PINOMS's or Entity's Informed Consent

[5] Information relating to an evaluation is protected by Rule 1.6. In many situations, providing an evaluation to a Third Party, Third Person, or Third Entity poses no significant risk to the congregant, PINOMS, or entity; thus, the cleric may be impliedly authorized to disclose information to carry out the ministry service as an advocate for the congregant, PINOMS, or entity. See Rule 1.6(b)(3). Where, however, it is reasonably likely that providing the evaluation will affect the congregant's, PINOMS's, or entity's interests materially and adversely, the cleric must first obtain the congregant's, PINOMS's, or entity's written consent after the congregant, PINOMS, or entity has been adequately informed concerning the important possible effects on the congregant's, PINOMS's, or entity's best interests. See Rules 1.6(a) and 1.0(f).

Financial Auditor's Requests For Information

[6] When a question concerning the fiduciary duty of a congregant, PINOMS, or entity arises at the instance of the congregant's, PINOMS's, or entity's financial auditor and the question is assigned, or appointed to the cleric, the cleric's response may be made in accordance with procedures recognized in the ministry standards. Such a procedure is set forth in the doctrines of the Christian Church, or the set rules and regulations of the entity or entities involved.

Biblical Reference

[1] Two or three prophets should speak and the others should evaluate what is said (1 Corinthians 14:29).

[2] "For which of you, intending to build a tower, does not sit down first and count the cost, whether he has enough to finish it—(Luke 14:28).

Christian Ethical Commentary

[1] Being seen as a third person, or seeing others as a third person, can cause the exclusion of the truth. Howard Thurman wrote how he saw those who saw him as a third-person: "To all white persons, the category of exception applied. I did not regard them as involved in my religious reference. They were not read out of the human race –they simply did not belong to it in the first place. Behavior toward them was amoral. They were not hated particularly; they were not essentially despised; they were simply out of bounds." Howard Thurman, *The Luminous Darkness*, 3.

[2] Once a person sees themselves as being superior or even inferior in segregated manufactured atmospheres of societal caste systems, religious, or otherwise, there presents for that type of sight a moral dilemma according to Howard Thurman who wrote that it: "is at once one of the most blatant forms of moral irresponsibility. The segregated persons are out of bounds, are outside the magnetic field of ethical concern." Howard Thurman, *The Luminous Darkness*, 6.

[3] "*Written Consent:* When a congregant, PINOMS, or non-profit organization, or entity consents for information to be disclosed, it is essential that the client understand the information that will be provided, the individuals or entities to which it will be provided and the reasons for divulging such information. The best way to accomplish this is in a detailed yet clearly understood written release-of-information form. For instance, federal law requires that such release include information about communicable diseases (including HIV) yet prohibits the use of the same information to criminally investigate or prosecute an alcohol-or drug-abuse patient." *Christian Counseling Ethics*, Chapter 4, Only through such a thorough Essential Elements for Ethical

Counsel, Horace c. Lukens, Jr. and Randolph K. Sanders, pp.90-91.

Legal Example

[1] *United States v. Nixon, 418 US 683 - Supreme Court 1974*

Issue: Can a priest keep the confidences told to them by a parishioner or congregant?

Rule of Confidentially and Privileged Information: The privileges referred to by the Court are designed to protect weighty and legitimate competing interests. Thus, the Fifth Amendment to the Constitution provides that no man "shall be compelled in any criminal case to be a witness against himself." And, generally, an attorney or a priest may not be required to disclose what has been revealed in professional confidence. These and other interests are recognized in law by privileges against forced disclosure, established in the Constitution, by statute, or at common law. Whatever their origins, these exceptions to the demand for every man's evidence are not lightly created nor expansively construed, for they are in derogation of the search for truth.

Conclusion: We conclude that when the ground for asserting privilege as to subpoenaed materials sought for use in a criminal trial is based only on the generalized interest in confidentiality, it cannot prevail over the fundamental demands of due process of law in the fair administration of criminal justice. The generalized assertion of privilege must yield to the demonstrated, specific need for evidence in a pending criminal trial. *United States v. Nixon, 418 US 683 - Supreme Court 1974*, pp.709, 710, 713 citation omitted. (Example of Dicta)

2.4 Cleric Serving as Third-Party, Third-Person, or Ministerial Neutral

(a) A cleric serves as a Third-Party, Third-Person, or Ministerial Neutral when the cleric assists two or more persons who are not persons the cleric has ministered to in the past as either a congregant, PINOMS, or entity to reach a resolution of a dispute or matter that has arisen between the parties. Service as a Third-Party, Third-Person, or Ministerial Neutral may include service as a district tribunal, deciding board member, or other capacity as will enable the cleric to assist the parties to resolve the matter.

(b) A cleric serving as a Third-Party, Third-Person, or Ministerial Neutral shall inform unsupported parties that the cleric is not speaking on their behalf. When the cleric knows or reasonably should know that a party does not understand the cleric's role in the matter, the cleric shall explain the difference between the cleric's role as a Third-Party, Third-Person, or Ministerial Neutral and a cleric's role as one who has a ministry relationship with the person.

Comment

[1] Alternative dispute resolution has become a substantial part of the ministry resolution practices. Aside ministering and advocating for a congregant, PINOMS, or entity in dispute-resolution practices, procedures, or processes, clerics often serve as a Third-Party, Third-Person, or Ministerial Neutral. A Third-Party, Third-Person, or Ministerial Neutral is a person, such as a conciliator, facilitator, evaluator, peacemaker, tribunal board member, decisionmaker who assists the parties, with ministry advocated, and non-ministry advocates, in the resolution of a dispute or in the arrangement of a transaction. Whether a Third-Party, Third-Person, or Ministerial Neutral provides ministry services primarily as a conciliator, facilitator, evaluator, peacemaker, tribunal board member, or decisionmaker depends on the particular process that is either selected by the parties or mandated by a tribunal, or denomination, or authoritative body.

[2] The role of the Third-Party, Third-Person, or Ministerial Neutral is not unique to clerics, although in some connected contexts, only clerics are allowed to serve in this role or to handle certain types of matters. In providing ministry services as an

advocate the clerics serving as Third-Party, Third-Person, or Ministerial Neutral may be subject to tribunal or decision-making body policies, rules, or procedures that apply either to Third-Party, Third-Person, or Ministerial Neutral generally to clerics serving as Third-Party, Third-Person, or Ministerial Neutrals. Clerics may also be subject to various codes of ethics, such as traditional Christian Codes of Ethics.

[3] Unlike non-clerics who serve as third-party neutrals, clerics serving in this role may experience unique problems as a result of differences between the role of a third-party neutral and a cleric's ministry services as a minister ministering to a congregant, or PINOMS or unto a non-profit organization. The potential for confusion is significant when the parties are not receiving representation or have an advocate acting on their behalf. Thus, paragraph (b) requires a cleric-neutral to inform parties are not receiving representation or have an advocate acting on their behalf that the cleric is not representing them. For some parties, particularly parties who frequently use dispute-resolution processes, this information will be sufficient. For others particularly those who are using the process for the first time, more information will be required. Where appropriate, the cleric should inform parties who are not receiving representation or have an advocate acting on their behalf of the important differences between the cleric's role as third-party neutral and a cleric's rule as a congregant, or PINOMS, or non-profit organization minister, including the inapplicability of the cleric-congregant, or cleric-PINOMS or cleric-non-profit organization as a ministering cleric, including the inapplicability of the cleric-congregant, or cleric-PINOMS, or cleric-non-profit organization confidentiality or privilege. The extent of disclosure required under this paragraph will depend on the particular parties involved and the subject matter of the matter or ministry issue, as well as the particular features of the dispute-resolution process selected.

[4] A cleric who serves as a third-party neutral subsequently may be asked to serve as a cleric ministering to a congregant, PINOMS, or non-profit organization in the same matter. The conflicts of interest that arise for both the individual cleric and cleric's ministry are addressed in Rule 1.12.

[5] Clerics who represent congregants, PINOMS, and non-profit organizations in alternative dispute-resolution processes are governed by these rules of ministry conduct, as well as ethical, and spiritual boundaries. When the dispute-resolution process takes place before a tribunal, as in binding arbitration (see Rule 1.0(n)), the cleric's duty of candor is governed by Rule 3.3. Otherwise, the cleric's duty of candor toward both the third-party neutral and other parties is governed by Rule 4.1.

Biblical Reference

[1] "Though one may be overpowered, two can defend themselves. A cord of three strands is not quickly broken" (Ecclesiastes 4:12).

Christian Ethical Commentary

[1] *Individuality While Serving In Community* as described by Bishop Desmond Tutu as *Ubantu*. *Ubuntu* is very difficult to render into a Western language. It speaks of the very essence of being human. . . . It is to say, 'My humanity is caught up, is inextricably bound up, in yours.'. . . A person with ubuntu is open and available to others, affirming of others, does not feel threatened that others are able and good, for he or she has a proper self-assurance that comes from knowing that he or she belongs in a greater whole and is diminished when others are humiliated or diminished, when others are tortured or oppressed, or treated as if they were less that who they are. Desmond Tutu, *No Future Without Forgiveness* (New York: Doubleday, 1999), 31.

[2] Thurman states: "long as there is conviction that a potential has not been actualized either in the individual, the society, or in the world, the rational necessity and possibility of a realized

future must be honored." Howard Thurman, *The Search for Common Ground: An Inquiry into the Basis of Man's Experience of Community.* Richmond, IN: Friends United Press, (1986), 45.

[3] Mirsolav Volf, states about forgiveness the following: to 'cover' or 'forget' wrongs, we must remember them in the first place! . . . we must remember them truthfully. But truthful memory does not have to be indelible memory. The purpose of truthful memory is not simply to name acts of injustice, and certainly not to hold an unalterable past forever fixed in the forefront of a person's mind. Instead, the highest aim of lovingly truthful memory seeks to bring about the repentance, forgiveness, and transformation of wrongdoers, and reconciliation between wrongdoers and their victims. When these goals are achieved, memory can let go of offenses without ceasing to be truthful. Mirsolav Volf, *The End of Memory: Remembering Rightly in a Violent World* (Grand Rapids, MI: William B. Eerdmans Publishing, 2006), 64-65.

[4] God's special love for the poor is "not because the poor are good, or better than others, but just because they are poor." A biblical warrant, Gutiérrez suggests, for this view may be found in the beatitudes which "have in the first instance a theological character: they tell us who God is. Secondly, they are anthropological. That is, they emphasize the importance of spiritual dispositions in those who hear the word. These two aspects are … complementary. But the theological aspect—the emphasis on God and his goodness toward the poor—is the primary." The perspective Gutiérrez hopes to offset is one that follows from reading the Lukan blessing of the poor in an unnuanced manner via the Matthean blessing of the poor in spirit—a reading that could imply that God's preference shown to the poor will be based on their supposed ability to develop certain spiritual dispositions loved by God. *Salvation, Liberation and Christian Character Formation*, David G. Kamitsuka, Blackwell Publishers Ltd 1997, p.179.

Legal Example

[1] *Elmora Hebrew Center, Inc., A Religious Corporation Of New Jersey v. Yale M. Fishman, Charles Aptowitzer, Mark Mason And Bruce Buechler, And Howard Pollick*

Issue: Can a religious tribunal make its own decision about issues concerning their staff and their religious practices?

Rule: In disputes involving a church governed by a hierarchical structure, courts should defer to the result reached by the highest church authority to have considered the religious question at issue. *Watson v. Jones, supra, 80 U.S. (13 Wall.) at 727, 20 L.Ed. at 676; Chavis v. Rowe, supra, 93 N.J. at 108, 459 A.2d 674.* Similarly, in disputes involving a church with a congregational structure, courts should defer to resolutions by a majority (or other appropriate subgroup) of the church's governing body. *Chavis v. Rowe, supra, 93 N.J. at 108, 459 A.2d 674*...The Court further supported the propriety of such "marginal review" of church decisions in *Presbyterian Church v. Hull Church, supra, 393 U.S. 440, 89 S.Ct. 601, 21 L.Ed.2d 658;* however, in *Serbian Eastern Orthodox Church v. Milivojevich, supra, 426 U.S. 696, 96 S.Ct. 2372, 49 L.Ed.2d 151,* the Court specifically eliminated "arbitrariness" as a basis for civil-court inquiry into whether decisions of a church tribunal complied with the church's own laws and regulations. Nonetheless, the still viable grounds of inquiry into a religious determination, namely, fraud and collusion, parallel the extremely limited basis on which courts will review the results of conventional arbitrations. Another analog to secular arbitration is presented in *Hardwick v. First Baptist Church, supra, 217 N.J. Super. 85, 524 A.2d 1298,* where the Appellate Division required parties to participate in selecting appropriate religious authorities to determine underlying religious questions.

Conclusion: These natural analogs to arbitration suggest that it is appropriate that the EHC, like a party to a civil arbitration, should be bound to observe the Beth Din's determination of any issues that the EHC agreed to submit to that tribunal. By way of comparison, we note that in statutory arbitrations, a party is bound by arbitrators' determinations even of issues clearly beyond the scope of a contractual agreement to arbitrate, so long as the party consented to the submission of those issues to the arbitrators. See, e.g., *In re Grover, 80 N.J. 221, 403 A.2d 448 (1979).* Thus, in the present procedural posture of the case, the initial concerns over whether some issues resolved by the Beth Din were more "secular" than religious, and therefore appropriately should have been resolved by a civil court, have dissipated. For the reasons expressed by the lower courts, the parties are now bound by the Beth Din's decision, because of their plenary agreement to submit their disputes to that body for its adjudication.

Our conclusion is not an endorsement of the mesne procedural determinations by which the lower courts surrendered jurisdiction over the civil aspects of this case. It is not proper for a trial court to refer civil issues to a religious tribunal in the first instance. The United States Supreme Court has forbidden that course: "The First Amendment prohibits a State from employing religious organizations as an arm of the civil judiciary to perform the function of interpreting and applying state standards." *Presbyterian Church v. Hull Church, supra, 393 U.S. at 451, 89 S.Ct. at 607, 21 L.Ed.2d at 667.* In the present case, the EHC's claims, at least as reflected in the allegations of the complaint, involved several civil issues, e.g., the alleged diversion of funds, the possible alteration of a contract, the status of the residence, and the request for an accounting. Such issues seem appropriate for civil adjudication without any danger of entanglement in religious doctrine or polity. Indeed, the allegations that Fishman had diverted payments and grant funds belonging to the congregation to his own accounts are certainly cognizable by civil courts, regardless of whether such acts may also offend religious tenets. *Elmora Hebrew Center, Inc., A Religious Corporation Of New Jersey v. Yale M. Fishman, Charles Aptowitzer, Mark Mason And Bruce Buechler, And Howard Pollick, 125 N.J. 404 (1991), pp.414, 418, 419.*

Rule 3.1 Meritorious Claims and Contentions

A cleric shall not bring or defend a proceeding, or assert or controvert an issue therein, unless there is a basis in Christian Doctrine and truth for doing so that is not frivolous, which includes a good faith argument for an extension, modification, or reversal of Christian doctrines or organizational bylaws. A cleric for a person accused of violating Christian Doctrine, or the organization's bylaws or procedure that could result in expulsion from the ministry, may nevertheless so advocate on the congregant, the PINOMS, or the non-profit's employee behalf in the proceeding as to require that every element of the case be established.

Comment

[1] The advocating cleric has a duty to use Roberts Rules of Order, or Bylaw procedures for the fullest benefit of the congregant's or PINOMS's, or non-profit organization's cause, but also a duty not to abuse the procedural process. The rules of order, both procedural and substantive, establishes the limits within which an advocate may proceed. However, the procedural rules of order are not always clear and never is static. Accordingly, in determining the proper scope of ministry advocacy, account must be taken of the procedural rules of order, as well as the procedural rules of order's ambiguities and potential for change.

[2] The finding of an action or defense or similar action taken for a congregant, PINOMS, or non-profit organization is not frivolous merely because the facts have not first been fully substantiated or because the cleric expects to develop vital evidence only by procedural processes. What is required of clerics, however, is that they inform themselves about the facts of their congregant's, or PINOMS's or non-profit organizations' employee's position ultimately will not prevail. The action is frivolous, however, if the cleric is unable either to make a good faith argument on the merits of the action taken or to support

the action taken by a good faith argument for an extension, modification, or reversal of existing law.

[3] The cleric's obligation under this rule is subordinate to ruling laws or bylaws of the ministry organization procedural rules in a ministry action being reviewed as an inquiring matter to the assistance of clergy in presenting a claim or contention that otherwise would be prohibited by this rule.

Biblical Reference

[1] Put me in remembrance: let us plead together: declare thou, that thou mayest be justified (Isaiah 43:26).

[2] You see then how that by works a man is justified, and not by faith only (James 2:24).

Christian Ethical Commentary

[1] Ken Sande has provided us with this enlightenment concerning meritorious conflict in the church, which states: "many of the problems associated with the approaches to conflict can be prevented if we learn to look at conflict biblically. God has explained in the Scriptures why conflicts occur and how we should deal with them. The more we understand and follow what he teaches, the more effective we will be in resolving disagreements with other people." Ken Sande, *The Peacemaker: A Biblical Guide to Resolving Personal Conflict* (Grand Rapids: Baker Books, 2003), 19.

[2] There are various types of differences which could cause conflict.

Characteristics of Constructive Conflict

1. Church members change, adjust, and compromise

2. Church members interact with an intent to learn instead of an intent to protect

3. Church members do not stay stuck in a conflict; conflicts move and change

256

4. Church members experience increased self-esteem

5. Church members have a motivation for positive connection with others

6. Church members have a relationship focus

7. Church members express the presence of empathy

8. Church members' actions are primarily cooperative, marked by egalitarian relationships

Characteristics of Destructive Conflict

1. Participants are rigid, inflexible, and insistent

2. Participants interact with the intent to protect self and hurt others

3. Participants become stuck in and defined by a particular conflict

4. Participants experience increased fear, anger, and insecurity

5. Participants have either a 'fight pattern' (a desire to destroy the others

argument or person) or 'flight pattern' (avoidance, resentment)

6. Participants look out for only their own self-interests

7. Participants use demanding verbal and non-verbal communication

8. Participants employ primarily competitive and destructive tactics marked by domination and subordination patterns. SBC, *Transitional Pastor Ministry Training Manual*, LifeWay Christian Resources of the Southern Baptist Convention, (LifeWay Press, Nashville, TN, 2000), 52.

[3] Oftentimes, churches in conflict will desire not to deal with it, and respond what issue, or what conflict are you referring to?

1. Avoiding: "Problem? What problem?"

2. Accommodating: "I give up" (people pleasers)

3. Compromising: "Let's just split the difference"

4. Competing: "I win; you lose"

5. Collaborating: "You scratch my back, and I'll scratch yours"
SBC, *Transitional Pastor Ministry Training Manual*, LifeWay
Christian Resources of the Southern Baptist Convention,
(LifeWay Press, Nashville, TN, 2000), 53.

[4] There should be a presence of pastoral care, and one must be
discerning not to condemn those who oppose the views of the
pastor, ministry leader, or the cleric providing counseling. The
word of God in Paul's second letter to Timothy reminds the
cleric, that the cleric must gently reprove those who oppose
them, in the hope that God may grant them [the opposing party]
repentance leading to a knowledge of the truth. Therefore, the
cleric must not immediately label those who oppose the cleric as
being those who are destructive, determined to cause harm,
deceitful, demonic, in denial of what is best, or that they lack
discernment of God's desire for the ministry. Dr. G. Lloyd
Rediger helps us by giving us 6 Ds to beware of under the
precept of "clergy killers" from his writings so entitled:

Destructive: Clergy killers are marked by intentional
destructiveness. They don't just disagree or criticize, they insist
on inflicting pain and damaging their targets. Their tactics
include sabotage, subverting worthy causes, inciting others to do
their work, and causing victims to self-destruct.

Determined: Clergy killers don't stop. They may pause, go
underground, or change tactics, but they will intimidate, network,
and break any rules of decency to accomplish their destruction.
They insist that their agenda has priority.

Deceitful: Clergy killers manipulate, camouflage, misrepresent, and accuse others of their own tactics. Their statement and negotiations are not trustworthy.

Demonic: Clergy killers are evil and may be mentally disordered, depending on how you define intentions and behavior that do not yield to patience and love, or honor human decency. Spiritual leaders become symbols and scapegoats for the internal pain and confusion they feel. Because their mental pain and spiritual confusion are unidentified and untreated, they foment unusual, reactive, and destructive motivations. This evil characteristic may also be apparent when there is no other cause that explains the clergy killer behavior. The mainline church and popular culture essentially have discarded the concept of evil by labeling sin and evil as mental illness or human failure. This loss of a spiritual understanding of intentional destruction leaves us unable to make use of the powerful spiritual gifts of enlightenment, grace, discipline, and courage to confront evil through God's power.

Denial: This fifth "D" indicates the way the church colludes in the agenda of the clergy killer. Most of us don't want to admit to the reality of clergy killers, nor do we acknowledge the intentional damage they cause. Because we believe "this shouldn't be happening in the church," we convince ourselves it isn't really happening. Such denial leaves clergy killers unrestrained and the whole church vulnerable.

Discernment: This is the prescriptive sixth "D." This spiritual gift of discernment is God's grace proffered in an enlightened person who sees and understands evil, and then allows himself or herself to be empowered by God's Holy Spirit and to become an agent of exorcism. Discernment is followed by confronting evil, in this case, the clergy killers. This confrontation works best, of course, in a healthy community of faith. G. Lloyd Rediger, *Clergy Killers: Guidance for Pastors and Congregations under Attack*. (Louisville: Westminster John Knox Press, 1997). 9-10.

[5] There is a need for Grace in the midst of all matters, *Bonhoeffer for Armchair Theologians*, states: "'Cheap grace… is grace without discipleship, grace without the cross, grace without the living, incarnate Jesus Christ.' It is grace without the constant knowledge and hope of life and death, and the resurrection of Jesus Christ." Stephan R. Haynes and Lori Brandt Hale. *Bonhoeffer for Armchair Theologians*. (Westminster John Knox Press, 2009).

Legal Example

[1] *Elmora Hebrew Center, Inc., A Religious Corporation Of New Jersey v. Yale M. Fishman, Charles Aptowitzer, Mark Mason And Bruce Buechler, And Howard Pollick*

Issue: The religious tribunal has the ability to review non-neutral religious question, which have merit. Otherwise, neutral issues can be determined by the court. It is up to the clergy tribunal to make a decision about the merits that apply to both the non-neutral and neutral decisions at times.

Rule: Without regard to the governing structure of a particular church, a court may, where appropriate, apply neutral principles of law to determine disputed questions that do not implicate religious doctrine. *Jones v. Wolf, supra, 443 U.S. 595, 99 S.Ct. 3020, 61 L.Ed.2d 775.* "Neutral principles" are wholly secular legal rules whose application to religious parties or disputes does not entail theological or doctrinal evaluations. This "neutral principles" approach is particularly suited to adjudications of property disputes. For example, in Jones v. Wolf, involving a schism between a local church and a hierarchical church organization, the Supreme Court held that there would be no violation of the first or fourteenth amendment if a state court were to resolve a church property dispute by application of "neutral principles" to the language of deeds, church charters, state statutes governing the holding of church property, and provisions in a church's constitution. Similarly, neutral principles may sometimes be invoked to resolve disputes concerning a religious entity's membership. *See, e.g., Hardwick v. First Baptist Church, 217 N.J.*

Super. 85, 524 A.2d 1298 (App.Div. 1987) (court can examine by-laws and church policies to resolve dispute over church membership). The application of the "neutral principles" doctrine presents the potential advantage of permitting parties to assure a consistent approach to questions of property ownership or church membership by inclusion of appropriate terms in deeds, contracts, or by-laws. See, e.g., *Jones v. Wolf, supra, 443 U.S. at 606, 99 S.Ct. at 3027, 61 L.Ed.2d at 786* ("At any time before the dispute erupts, the parties can ensure, if they so desire, that the faction loyal to the hierarchical church will retain the church property. They can modify the deeds or the corporate charter to include a right of reversion or trust in favor of the general church.").

Conclusion: Nonetheless, civil adjudications by deference to authoritative decisions by church officials, or by application of "neutral principles," must always be circumscribed carefully to avoid courts' incursions into religious questions that would be impermissible under the first amendment. *Elmora Hebrew Center, Inc., A Religious Corporation Of New Jersey v. Yale M. Fishman, Charles Aptowitzer, Mark Mason And Bruce Buechler, And Howard Pollick, 125 N.J. 404 (1991), pp.414, 415, 418, 419.*

Rule 3.2 Expediting Ministry Matters

A cleric shall make reasonable efforts to expeditiously minister to the needs of the congregant, PINOMS, or the non-profit organization consistent with the interest of the congregant, PINOMS, or non-profit organization.

Comment

Clerics at times will need to resort to dilatory procedural transitions, which consist of prayer and measured postponement before making reasonable efforts to expeditiously minister to the needs of the congregant, PINOMS, or non-profit organization. Sometimes, dilatory practices bring the administration of ministerial acts into manifestation. Although there will be occasions when a cleric may properly seek a postponement for certain reasons, even personal ones, it is not proper for a cleric to routinely fail to expedite ministry services solely for self-convenience. Nor will a failure to expedite be reasonable if done for the purpose of frustrating an adversarial person in an attempt to obtain rightful redress or repose. It is not a justification that similar conduct is often tolerated by ethical ministry practices. The question is whether a competent cleric acting in good faith, and goodwill would regard the course of action as having some substantial purpose other than delay. Realizing financial or other benefit from otherwise improper delay in ministry practices is not a reasonable reason, as it would not be in the best interest of the congregant, PINOMS, or non-profit entity.

Biblical Reference

[1] Howbeit when he, the Spirit of truth, is come, he will guide you into all truth: for he shall not speak of himself; but whatsoever he shall hear, that shall he speak: and he will shew you things to come (John 16:13).

Christian Ethical Commentary

[1] Expediting the ministry of peace, and peacefully expediting pastoral care is essential:

"Truths about Conflict:"

1. Conflict is inevitable

2. Conflict is neutral

3. We need to confront conflict as soon as possible rather than deny or ignore it

4. You cannot have healthy change without conflict

5. If you do not manage the rate of change appropriately, you will produce

destructive conflict

262

6. The pastor's leadership style is a key factor in whether conflict is constructive or destructive

7. God is not the author of chaos, but the provider of qualities that lead to peace

8. Prior unresolved church conflict exists as a key ingredient in most current church conflict situations.

9. When people grow spiritually and emotionally they are less likely to be the initiator of destructive conflict

10. We need to pray more and talk less about issues for church approval. We should not seek an answer from our human reason but from the revelation of God's Word. SBC, *Transitional Pastor Ministry Training Manual, LifeWay Christian Resources of the Southern Baptist Convention*, (LifeWay Press, Nashville, TN, 2000), 51.

[2] Institute for Christian Coalition state that in resolving Christian Biblical principles to resolve matters, and have provided some possible suggestions to use.

1.) erring believers are restored to usefulness in the church;

2.) Families are strengthened and protected from divorce;

3.) members enjoy better relationships and more productive activities; 4.) the purity of the church is maintained; 5.) the likelihood of fatal divisions within the church is reduced;

6.) less exposure to lawsuits;

7.) respect and appreciation for leadership grows;

8.) members are maturing in their faith and life; 9.) resources (time, energy, money) of the church and members are protected from waste; 10.) new members are attracted and church growth is stimulated; 11.) and the peace of knowing that you are being obedient to God (Isaiah 48:18). SBC, *Transitional Pastor Ministry Training Manual, LifeWay Christian Resources of the Southern Baptist Convention*, (LifeWay Press, Nashville, TN, 2000), 54.

Legal Example

[1] *James Chavis And Ophelia Chavis v. Albert P. Rowe et al*

Issue: In 1973 the members of Calvary Baptist Church of
Paterson, New Jersey, elected plaintiff James Chavis as a deacon.
In 1977 the Board of Deacons (Board) removed Chavis from his
post as deacon, or "defrocked" him, apparently because he had
fallen into disfavor with the pastor, defendant Alfred P. Rowe.
Chavis and his wife, plaintiff Ophelia Chavis, instituted this
action for injunctive relief and damages against the pastor and
other deacons who had participated in the church action,
claiming that the Board had ignored the correct procedures for
removal. Can a deacon be dismissed expeditiously once religious
and doctrinal violations are found against the deacon?

Rule: In Chavis v. Rowe, the Court found that no civil
jurisdiction could be asserted over a religious dispute about a
deacon's dismissal.

Conclusion: Moreover, insinuation by civil courts into the customs
and usages of the by-laws and the constitution, into the
administration and the polity of the church in the hope of
uncovering clues to the correct disciplinary procedures, threatens
the freedom of religious institutions from secular entanglement.
First Amendment values are plainly jeopardized when church
property litigation is made to turn on the resolution by civil
courts of controversies over religious doctrine and practice. If
civil courts undertake to resolve such controversies in order to
adjudicate the property dispute, the hazards are ever present of
inhibiting the free development of religious doctrine and of
implicating secular interest in matters of purely ecclesiastical
concern. * * * [T]he Amendment therefore commands civil
courts to decide church property disputes without resolving
underlying controversies over religious doctrine. [*Hull Church,
supra, 343 U.S. at 449, 89 S.Ct. at 606, 21 L.Ed.2d at 665.*], from
*James Chavis And Ophelia Chavis v. Albert P. Rowe, Willie C.
Nickerson, Robert Alexander, James Burwell, Leroy Coleman, Thomas*

Crawford, Simmie Pipkin, Ellsworth Powell, Percy Schofield, Charles Williams And Seymour Lyew, 93 N.J. 103 (1983), pp.104, 112.

Rule 3.3 Candor Toward the Tribunal

(a) A cleric shall not knowingly:

(1)   Make a false statement of fact to a conference, denominational tribunal, congregational inquiry, diaconal investigation, or church matter or fail to correct a false statement of material fact or testimony previously made to the tribunal by the cleric or a person the cleric is advocating for.

(2)   Fail to disclose to the tribunal, or authoritative body in the controlling denomination, or non-denominational body known to the cleric to be directly adverse to the position of the congregant, PINOMS, or non-profit and not disclosed by any opposing party, or their representative; or

(3)   Offer testimony or allowing a person to give witness the cleric knows to be false. If a cleric, the cleric's congregant, PINOMS, or non-profit, or a witness called by the cleric has offered material evidence and the cleric comes to know of its falsity, the cleric shall take reasonable remedial measures, including, if necessary, disclosure to the tribunal. A cleric may refuse to offer evidence, other than the testimony of the party in a ministry inquiry, that the cleric reasonably believes is false.

(b) A cleric who represents a congregant, PINOMS, or non-profit organization in an authoritative proceeding or tribunal and who knows that a person intends to engage, is engaging or has engaged in causing irreparable harm, fraudulent actions, or unethical behavior related to the authoritative proceedings shall take reasonable remedial measures, including, it necessary, disclosure to the authoritative body, or tribunal.

(c) The duties stated in paragraphs (a) and (b) continue to the conclusion of the proceeding and apply even if compliance requires disclosure of information otherwise protected by Rule 1.6.

(d) In a proceeding in which a party is speaking for their self, a cleric shall inform the tribunal or authoritative body of all material facts known to the cleric that will enable the tribunal or authoritative body to make an informed decision, whether or not the facts are adverse.

Comments

[1] This rule governs the conduct of a cleric who is advocating for a congregant, PINOMS, or non-profit organization in the proceedings, tribunal, or before an authoritative body. See Rule 1.0(n) for the definition of "tribunal" or "authoritative body." It also applies when the cleric is advocating for a congregant, PINOMS, or non-profit organization in an ancillary proceeding conducted pursuant to the tribunal governing body, or the authoritative body's authority, such as a board of directors, or trustees, or bishop's body. Thus, for example, paragraph (a)(3) requires a cleric to take reasonable remedial measures if the cleric comes to know that a congregant, PINOMS, or non-profit organization's employee who is giving witness, or providing testimony in a matter being reviewed has offered information that is false or misleading.

[2] This rule sets forth the special duties of clerics as ministers of the gospel of Jesus Christ devoted to the truth to avoid conduct that undermines the integrity of the authoritative review process. A cleric acting as an advocate in an authoritative body's proceedings has the obligation to present the congregant's, PINOMS's, or non-profit organization's employee's case with persuasive force. Performance of the duty while maintaining confidences of the congregant, PINOMS, or non-profit organization's employee, however, is qualified by the cleric's advocacy duty with sincere candor to the authoritative body, or tribunal. Consequently, although a cleric in an adversary proceeding is not required to present an impartial exposition of

the rules or to vouch for the evidence submitted in a case, the cleric must not allow the authoritative body, or the tribunal to be misled by false statements of fact, or procedural rules that the cleric knows to be false.

Representations by Clerics In Tribunal Inquiries

[3] A advocate is responsible for documentation prepared for tribunal inquires, but is usually not required to have personal knowledge of matters asserted within the documentation fully, for inquiry presented documents it is ordinarily presented based upon the congregant's or PINOMS's or non-profit organization employee's assertions which the purport, but it is not the clerics testimony, which substantiates the documents presented in the inquiry. Compare Rule 3.1. However, an assertion purporting to be on the cleric's own knowledge, as in an affidavit by the cleric or in a statement in the inquiry, may properly be made only when the cleric knows the assertion is true or believes it is to be true on the basis of a reasonably diligent inquiry. There are circumstances where failure to make a disclosure is the equivalent of an affirmative misrepresentation. The obligation prescribed in Rule 1.2(d) not to counsel a cleric, congregant or PINOMS to commit or assist the congregants or PINOMS in committing a fraud applies in the inquiry proceedings. Regarding compliance with Rule 1.2(d), see the comment to that rule. See also Comment to Rule 8.4(b).

Advocating Argumentation By Cleric

[4] Advocating Argumentation based on a knowingly false representation of facts constitutes dishonesty toward the tribunal. A cleric is not required to make a disinterested exposition of the facts, but must recognize the existence of pertinent rules of the reviewing authorities. Furthermore, as stated in paragraph (a)(2), an advocate has a duty to disclose directly adverse authority in the controlling rules, bylaws, or procedures that has not been disclosed by the other party involved. The underlying concept is that factual arguments is a

discussion seeking to determine the premises properly applicable to the matter before the tribunal.

Offering Evidence and Testifying

[5] Paragraph (a)(3) requires that the cleric refuse to offer evidence and testimony that the cleric knows to be false, or fake regardless of the cleric being represented, congregant's or PINOMS's, or non-profit employee's wishes. This duty is premised on the cleric's obligation as a minister of the Gospel of Jesus Christ to prevent the tribunal from being misled by false or fake evidence or testimony. A cleric does not violate this rule if the cleric offers the evidence for the purpose of establishing its fakeness, or falsity.

[6] If a representing cleric knows that the cleric being represented, congregant, PINOMS, or non-profit organization's employee intends to testify falsely or wants the cleric to introduce false evidence, the cleric should seek to persuade the cleric being represented, congregant, PINOMS, or non-profit organization's employee that the evidence should not be offered. If the persuasion is ineffective and the cleric continues to minister representation unto the cleric being represented, congregant, PINOMS, or non-profit organization, the representing cleric must refuse to offer the false evidence. If only a portion of the person's testimony will be false, the cleric may call the person to present testimony before the tribunal, but may not elicit or otherwise permit the person to present the testimony that the cleric knows is false.

[7] The duties stated in paragraphs (a) and (b) apply to all clerics, including pastors, chaplains, and administrators in matters.

[8] The prohibition against offering false evidence in inquiries only applies if the cleric knows that the evidence is false. A cleric's reasonable belief that evidence is false does not preclude its representation to the tribunal who relies upon facts presented. A representing cleric's knowledge that evidence is false, however, can be inferred from the circumstances. See Rule 1.0(g). Thus,

although a cleric should resolve doubts about the veracity of testimony or other evidence in favor of the cleric, congregant, PINOMS or non-profit, the representing cleric cannot ignore an obvious falsehood.

[9] Although paragraph (a)(3) only prohibits a representing cleric from offering evidence the cleric knows to be false, it permits the cleric to refuse to offer testimony or other proof that the representing cleric reasonably believes is false. Offering such proof may reflect adversely on the cleric's ability to discriminate in the quality of evidence and thus impair the cleric's effectiveness as an advocate. Because of the special protections historically provided to persons accused in a Christian organization, however, this rule does not permit a cleric to refuse to offer the testimony of such a cleric being represented, congregants or PINOMS where the cleric reasonably believes but does not know that the testimony will be false. Unless the cleric knows the testimony will be false, the cleric must honor the cleric, congregant's, PINOMS's, non-profit employee's decision to offer testimony, or desire to testify. See also Comment [7].

Remedial Measures

[10] Having offered material evidence in the belief that it was true, a representing cleric may subsequently come to know that the evidence is false. Or, a representing cleric may be surprised when the cleric's congregant, or cleric being represented, or PINOMS, or non-profit, or another witness called by the representing cleric, offers testimony the representing cleric knows to be false, either during the cleric's direct presentation or in response by the opposing party or the opposing party's representative. In such situations or if the representing cleric knows of the falsity of testimony elicited from the cleric's congregant, or the cleric being represented, or the PINOMS, or non-profit during an inquiry, the representing cleric must take reasonable remedial measures. In such situations, the representing cleric advocating for the congregant, the cleric being represented, or the PINOMS, or non-profit should use the

course of action to remonstrate with the congregant, the cleric being represented, or the PINOMS, or non-profit-member confidentially, advise the congregant, the cleric being represented, or the PINOMS, or non-profit member of the cleric's duty of candor before the tribunal and seek the congregant's, the cleric being represented, or the PINOMS's, or non-profit organization's member's cooperation with respect to the withdrawal or correction of the false statements or testimony given. If that fails, the advocating cleric must take further remedial action. If withdrawal from advocating for the congregant, the cleric being represented, or the PINOMS, or non-profit organization is not permitted or will not undo the effect of the false evidence, the advocate must make such disclosure to the tribunal as a reasonably necessary to remedy the situation, even if doing so requires the advocating cleric to reveal information that otherwise would be protected by Rule 1.6. It is for the tribunal then to determine what should be done-making a statement about the matter before the tribunal, ordering a ministerial requirement to present the truth always, and not to correct the matter would have nothing to do with veracity at all.

[11] The disclosure of a congregant's, the cleric being represented, or the PINOMS's, or non-profit organization member's testimony can result in grave consequences to the congregant, the cleric being represented, or the PINOMS, and non-profit, including not only a sense of betrayal but also loss of the matter before the tribunal and perhaps a prosecution of perjury. But the alternative is that the cleric cooperates in deceiving the tribunal, thereby subverting the truth-finding process which the adversarial system is designed to implement. See Rule 1.2(d). Furthermore, unless it is clearly understood that the cleric will not act upon the duty to disclose the existence of false evidence, the congregant, the cleric being represented, or the PINOMS, or non-profit organization can simply reject the cleric's advice to reveal the false evidence and insist that the cleric keep silent. Thus, the congregant, the cleric being represented, or the PINOMS, or non-profit could in effect

coerce the advocating cleric into being a party to fraud on the tribunal.

Preserving Integrity of Adjudicative Process

[12] Clerics have a special obligation to protect a tribunal against procedural violations, immoral practices, un-Christian acts, hatefulness, or fraudulent conduct that undermines the integrity of the adjudicative process, such as bribing, intimidating or otherwise unrighteous destroying or concealing documents or other evidence or failing to disclose information to the tribunal when required by the rules, regulations, bylaws, or doctrines of the Christian Organization to do so. Thus, paragraph (b) requires a cleric to take reasonable remedial measures, including disclosure, if necessary, whenever the cleric knows that a person, including the cleric's party the cleric is providing ministry services, intents to engage, is engaging or has engaged in procedural violations, immoral practices, un-Christian acts, hatefulness, or fraudulent conduct related to the proceeding.

Duration of Obligation

[13] A practical time limit on the obligation to rectify false evidence or false statements and fact has to be established. The conclusion of the proceeding is a reasonably definite point for the termination of the obligation. A proceeding has concluded within the meaning of this rule when a final judgment in the proceeding has been affirmed on appeal or the time for review has passed.

Ex Parte Proceedings

[14] Ordinarily, an advocating cleric has the limited responsibility of presenting one side of the matter a tribunal should consider in reaching a decision on ministry, or violations of the polity of the Christian Organization; the conflicting position is expected to be presented by the opposing party. However, in any *ex parte* proceedings, such as an application for a temporary restraining order, there is no balance of presentation by opposing advocates. The object of an *ex parte* proceeding is nevertheless to yield a

substantially just and spirit led result. The decisionmaker has an affirmative responsibility to accord the absent party just consideration. The clerical advocates for the represented party have the correlative duty to make disclosures of material facts known to the cleric and that the cleric reasonably believers are necessary to an informed decision.

Withdrawal

[15] Normally, a cleric's compliance with the duty of candor imposed by the rule does not require that the cleric withdraw from the representation of a congregant, the cleric being represented, or the PINOMS, or non-profit organization whose interests will be or have been adversely affected by the cleric's disclosure. The cleric may, however, be required by Rule 1.16(a) to seek permission of the tribunal to withdraw if the cleric's compliance with this rule's duty of candor results in such an extreme deterioration of the cleric-congregant, cleric-to cleric being represented, or the cleric-PINOMS, and cleric-non-profit organization relationship that the representing cleric can no longer competently provide ministry services to the congregant, the cleric being represented, or the PINOMS, or non-profit organization. Also see Rule 1.16(b) for the circumstances in which a cleric will be permitted to seek a tribunal's or decisionmaker's permission to withdraw. In connection with a request for permission to withdraw that is premised on a congregant's, the cleric being represented or the PINOMS's, or non-profit organization's misconduct, a cleric may reveal information relating to the ministry services provided only to the extent reasonably necessary to comply with this rule or as otherwise permitted by Rule 1.6.

Biblical Reference

[1] And when they bring you unto the synagogues, and unto magistrates, and powers, take you no thought how or what thing you shall answer, or what you shall say: For the Holy Ghost shall teach you in the same hour what you ought to say. (Luke 12:11-12).

Christian Ethical Commentary

[1] "Despite all the positive psychological attributes of hatred . . . , hatred destroys finally the core of the life of the hater. . . . Hatred bears deadly and bitter fruit. It is blind and *nondiscriminating.*" Howard Thurman, *Jesus and the Disinherited*, Boston: Beacon Press, (1996), 85-85.

[2] "Jesus rejected hatred. It was not because he lacked the vitality or the strength. It was not because he lacked the incentive. Jesus rejected hatred because he saw that hatred meant death to the mind, death to the spirit, death to communion with his Father. He affirmed life; and hatred was the great denial." Howard Thurman, *Jesus and the Disinherited*, Boston: Beacon Press, (1996), 88.

[3] Although a cleric is to use gentleness in making corrections, there will be some corrections that require tough love. The tough love gently given may require the calling out and exposing those that refuse to be loving to help their hearts to returned to the love of Christ Jesus. Dr. G. Lloyd Rediger warns and instructs on dealing with unloving heart: Such behaviors by individuals and groups are our focus. But it should be obvious that toxic intent and behavior, now common in families, neighborhoods, and social environments, and influential on congregational toxicity. These toxins, like biochemical toxins, cannot be dismissed, covered over, ignored, or diluted. They must be identified, treated, and eradicated. This may seem overly severe to some who believe that if we ignore, analyze, or keep trying to negotiate and 'love' intransigent control mongers, they will become civil. History and research expose this fallacy. G. Lloyd Rediger, *The Toxic Congregation: How to Heal the Soul of Your Church*. (New York: Abingdon Press, 2007).

[4] Implicit in the Christian message is a profoundly revolutionary ethic. This ethic appears as the binding relationship between [persons], conceived as children of a common . . . God. The ethic is revolutionary because the norms

273

it establishes are in direct conflict with the relationship that obtains between [persons] in the modern world. It is a patent fact that attitudes of fellowship and sympathetic understanding across lines of separateness such as race, class, and creed are not characteristic of our age. Howard Thurman, "Judgment and Hope in the Christian Message," in *The Papers of Howard Washington Thurman, Vol 3*, 243.

Legal Example

[1] *Gloria Alicea-Hernandez v. The Catholic Bishop Of Chicago, 320 F.3d 698 (2003)*

Cleric is not to discriminate under God's law:

Issue: Gloria Alicea-Hernandez, an Hispanic female, claims that her former employer, the Catholic Bishop of Chicago ("the Church"), discriminated against her based on her national origin and gender in violation of Title VII of the Civil Rights Act of 1964, 42 U.S.C. § 2000e et seq.

The Church argued to the district court that the religious clauses of the First Amendment preclude federal subject matter jurisdiction over these claims because both the nature of the claims and Alicea-Hernandez's unique responsibilities at the Church would require the court to engage in excessive entanglement in matters of Church policy.

Rule: As the Fifth Circuit first articulated in *McClure v. The Salvation Army, 460 F.2d 553, 560 (5th Cir. 1972)*, "application of the provisions of Title VII to the employment relationship existing between ... a church and its minister would result in an encroachment by the state into an area of religious freedom which it is forbidden to enter by the principles of the free exercise clause of the First Amendment." This rule, often referred to as "the ministerial exception," was further developed by the Fourth Circuit in *Rayburn v. General Conference of Seventh-Day Adventists, 772 F.2d 1164 (4th Cir. 1985)*, and adopted by this

274

circuit in *Young v. The Northern Illinois Conference of United Methodist Church, 21 F.3d 184 (7th Cir. 1994).*

The court in Rayburn, recognizing tensions between freedom of religion on the one hand and the attempt to eradicate discrimination on the other, concluded that in the context of Title VII claims brought against a church by its ministers the "balance weighs in favor of free exercise of religion." *772 F.2d at 1168.* The court explained that the "right to choose ministers without government restriction underlies the well-being of religious community." *Id. at 1167.* While this ruling may seem in tension with Title VII, we concur with the Fourth Circuit when it stated: "While an unfettered church choice may create minimal infidelity to the objectives of Title VII, it provides maximum protection of the First Amendment right to free exercise of religious beliefs." *Id. at 1169.*

Conclusion-Holding: The district court accepted these arguments and dismissed the suit pursuant to Fed.R.Civ.P. 12(b)(1). Alicea-Hernandez appeals. Although we disagree with the district court's analysis regarding the characterization of her claims, we affirm based on the position Alicea-Hernandez held with the Church. *Gloria Alicea-Hernandez v. The Catholic Bishop Of Chicago, 320 F.3d 698 (2003).*

Rule 3.4 Fairness to Opposing Party and Advocate

A cleric shall not:

(a)   Knowingly obstruct another party's access to evidence or knowingly alter, destroy, or conceal a document or other material having potential evidentiary value. A cleric shall not counsel or assist another person to do any such act;

(b)   falsity evidence, counselor assist a witness to testify falsely, or offer an inducement to a witness that is prohibited by the rules, procedures, doctrines, and bylaws and regulations;

275

(c)   knowingly disobey an obligation under the rules of a tribunal except for an open refusal based on an assertion that no valid obligation exists;

(d)   in pretrial procedure, make a frivolous discovery request or fail to make a reasonably diligent effort to comply with a fair and proper discovery request by an opposing party;

(e) in tribunal proceedings, allude to any matter that the cleric does not reasonably believes is relevant or that will not be supported by admissible evidence, assert personal knowledge of facts in issue except when testifying as a witness, or state a personal opinion as to the justness of a cause, the credibility of a witness, the culpability of a civil litigant or the guilt or innocence of an accused; or

(f) request a person other than a congregant, or PINOMS to refrain from voluntarily giving relevant information to another party unless:

(1) the person is a relative or an employee or subordinate or agent of congregant, PINOMS, or non-profit organization; and

(2) the cleric reasonably believes that the person's interests will not be adversely affected by refraining from giving such information.

Comments

[1] The procedure of the adversary system in a tribunal or before a decisionmaker contemplates that the evidence is a matter is to be marshalled competitively by the contending parties. Fair competition in the adversary system is secured by prohibitions against destruction or concealment of evidence, improperly influencing witnesses, obstructive tactics in discovery procedure, and that like.

[2] Documents and other items of evidence and presentations are often essential to establish a claim or defense. Subject to evidentiary privileges, the right of an opposing party, including

the government, to obtain evidence through discovery or authoritative powers is an important procedural right. The exercise of that right can be frustrated if relevant material is altered, concealed or destroyed.

[3] With regard to paragraph (b), it is not improper to pay a witness' expenses or to compensated an expert or key witness on terms permitted by the tribunal.

[4] Paragraph (f) permits a cleric to advise employees, agents, and subordinates of the congregant, the cleric being represented, or the PINOMS, or non-profit organizations the cleric is advocating for to refrain from giving information to another party, for the employees may identify their interests with those of the cleric being represented, or the PINOMS, or non-profit organizations. See also Rule 4.2.

Biblical Reference

[1] Do unto others as you would have them do unto you. In other words, if you want to be treated with kindness, be kind to others (Matthew 7:12).

[2] 8 Once when the king of Aram was at war with Israel, he took counsel with his officers. He said, "At such and such a place shall be my camp." 9 But the man of God sent word to the king of Israel, "Take care not to pass this place, for the Arameans are going down there." 10 The king of Israel sent word to the place of which the man of God spoke. More than once or twice he warned a place so that it was on the alert.11 The mind of the king of Aram was greatly perturbed because of this; he called his officers and said to them, "Now tell me: Who among us is betraying us to the king of Israel?" 12 Then one of his officers said, "No one, my lord king. It is Elisha, the prophet in Israel, who tells the king of Israel the words that you speak in your bedchamber." 13 He said, "Go and find where he is; I will send and seize him." He was told, "He is in Dothan." 14 So he sent horses and chariots there and a great army; they came by night and surrounded the city. 15 When an attendant of the man of

God rose early in the morning and went out, an army with horses
and chariots was all around the city. His servant said, "Alas,
master! What shall we do?" 16 He replied, "Do not be afraid, for
there are more with us than there are with them." 17 Then Elisha
prayed, "O Lord, please open his eyes that he may see." So the
Lord opened the eyes of the servant, and he saw; the mountain
was full of horses and chariots of fire all around Elisha. 18 When
the Arameans came down against him, Elisha prayed to the Lord
and said, "Strike this people, please, with blindness." So he
struck them with blindness as Elisha had asked. 19 Elisha said to
them, "This is not the way, and this is not the city; follow me,
and I will bring you to the man whom you seek." And he led
them to Samaria. 20 As soon as they entered Samaria, Elisha said,
"O Lord, open the eyes of these men so that they may see." The
Lord opened their eyes, and they saw that they were inside
Samaria. 21 When the king of Israel saw them he said to Elisha,
"Father, shall I strike them? Shall I strike them?" 22 He
answered, "No! Would you strike those whom you have taken
captive with your sword and with your bow? Set food and water
before them so that they may eat and drink, and let them go to
their master." 23 So he prepared for them a great feast; after they
ate and drank, he sent them on their way, and they went to their
master. And the Arameans no longer came raiding into the land
of Israel. (2 Kings 6:8-23).

Christian Ethical Commentary

[1] Falsity leads to fantasy in congregations and ministry. Dr. G.
Lloyd puts it this way: Peace, health, and salvation should be the
normal, even automatic, in the church, according to our idealized
thinking. This fantasy, however, can be a barrier to realistic
thinking about the community of faith. But the escalation of
conflict and abuse in congregations and denominations is a
reality check. It reminds us that spiritual warfare is a reality.
Those who are unprepared will become casualties. G. Lloyd
Rediger, *The Toxic Congregation: How to Heal the Soul of Your Church.*
(New York: Abingdon Press, 2007), 89.

[2] In fairness to those who oppose each other's view, there must remain a "Christian Decorum" in which those who oppose one another engage in the Doctrine of Jesus Christ to resolve the opposing views. We are reminded that conflict can be healthy, but it can also be unhealthy as stated by Dr. Rediger.

Normal Conflict:

Is present when there is the firm foundation standard of functioning body members who are interacting with one another, and find themselves in a non-manufactured genuine dispute such as issues of gender, ethnicity, age, class, and vocational ideological differences. These types of conflicts come about largely by misunderstandings, miscommunications of the sincere parties involved.

Abnormal Conflicts:

Are present when the conflict is provided by the means of mental challenges.

Spiritual Conflict:

Is a conflict that is manufactured with the instigator's intent to cause an unhealthy environment in the church, or ministry. This is generally conducted by either sinful tactics or deceitful tactics, which includes sin without remorse, to lead others astray or to cause weariness within the body of believers. G. Lloyd Rediger, *Clergy Killers: Guidance for Pastors and Congregations under Attack.* (Louisville: Westminster John Knox Press, 1997), 6-8.

[3] Congregational Conflict is: "a situation in which two or more members or factions struggle aggressively over what is, or appears to be mutually exclusive beliefs, values, assumed powers or goals." Lloyd Elder, professor and Director of the Moench Center of Church Leadership at Belmont University, Nashville, TN; http://www.belmont.edu/moench (accessed Nov. 15, 2009).

[4] As Elisha story makes clear, God's way of dealing with enemies has consistently been the unexpected path of love, from early on in Israel's story right up to the death of Jesus. *Character Ethics and the New Testament Moral Dimensions of Scripture*, Chapter 9, If Your Enemy Is Hungry Love and Subversive Politics in Romans 12-13, Sylvia C. Keesmaat, Robert L. Brawley, ed., Wesminister John Knox Press, Louisville-London, 2007, p.147.

Legal Example

[1] *Chavis And Ophelia Chavis v. Albert P. Rowe, Willie C. Nickerson*

Issue: Should a religious tribunal be one that is handled as though there is fairness and due diligence and due process applied to the procedure?

Rule: "…Article 10, section 2 provides that "[i]n private offenses, Matthew 18:15-17 shall be followed and the Baptist Manual of Polity & Practice by Maring & Hudson and the Hiscox Manual used as official reference." A "private offense" refers to injury done or claimed to have been done by one member to another. The Hiscox Standard Baptist Manual at 133 requires that such offenses be resolved ultimately by reference to the Bible, specifically Matthew 18:15-17. That passage instructs the offended one to tell of the offense "unto the church," which Hiscox interprets to require a full and fair hearing before the church members. In short, the correct removal procedure, if there is one, does not appear on the face of the relevant church documents."

Conclusion: The tribunal procedures should be followed as to allow all parties to be represented, and afforded the opportunity to be involved in a fair hearing and procedure. *James Chavis And Ophelia Chavis v. Albert P. Rowe, Willie C. Nickerson, Robert Alexander, James Burwell, Leroy Coleman, Thomas Crawford, Simmie Pipkin, Ellsworth Powell, Percy Schofield, Charles Williams And Seymour Lyew*, 93 N.J. 103 (1983), p.106.

[2] *Chavis And Ophelia Chavis v. Albert P. Rowe, Willie C. Nickerson et al*

Issue: Can churches who believe that their conference has failed to follow the doctrine in which the conference was established upon meet and decide to leave the conference? "[T]wo local Georgia churches within a hierarchical denomination voted to withdraw from the general church on the ground that the general church had departed from the doctrine and practice of the denomination at the time of affiliation. The general church stepped in to take over the local churches' property until new local leadership could be appointed.

Rule: The Supreme Court noted that because Georgia law implied a trust of local church property in favor of the general church on the sole condition that the general church adhere to its tenets of faith and practice, a civil court would be required to ask what those tenets were and how far the general church had strayed from them.

Conclusion: The Court found this entanglement with religious doctrine impermissible, but did acknowledge that a civil court could in certain cases settle the controversy by applying neutral principles of property law. *James Chavis And Ophelia Chavis v. Albert P. Rowe, Willie C. Nickerson, Robert Alexander, James Burwell, Leroy Coleman, Thomas Crawford, Simmie Pipkin, Ellsworth Powell, Percy Schofield, Charles Williams And Seymour Lyew, 93 N.J. 103 (1983), p.106, 108-109 quoting Presbyterian Church In The United States et al. v. Mary Elizabeth Blue Hull Memorial Presbyterian Church et al. 393 U.S. 440 (1969), pp.441-452.*

Rule 3.5 Impartiality and Decorum of the Tribunal

(a)   Before the hearing of a matter or case, a cleric connected therewith shall not, except in the course of official decision maker's proceedings, communicate with or cause another to communicate with anyone the clerics knows to be a member of the venire from which the decision makers will be selected for the hearing of the matter or case.

(b)   During the hearing of the matter for case:

(1) a cleric connected therewith shall not, except in the course of official proceedings, communicate with or cause another to communicate with any member of the decision-making body.

(2) a cleric who is not connected therewith shall not, except in the course of official hearings, communicate with or cause another to communicate with a decision-making body or a person thereof concerning the matter or a case.

(c)   After discharge of the body that deliberates from further consideration of a matter or case with which the cleric was connected, the cleric shall not ask questions or make comments to a member of the decision-making body that are calculated merely to harass or embarrass the decision maker or to influence the decision maker's actions in future hearing or case review service.

(d)   A cleric shall not conduct or cause another, by financial support or otherwise, to conduct a vexatious or harassing investigation of a decision maker or prospective member of the tribunal decision making process.

(e) All restrictions imposed by this rule apply also to communications with or investigation of members of a family of a decision maker or tribunal official or a prospective member of such decision-making body.

(f) A cleric shall reveal promptly to the tribunal improper conduct by, or by another toward, a juror or prospective decision maker or member of the family thereof, of which the cleric has knowledge.

(g) In an adversary proceeding a cleric shall not communicate or cause another to communicate as to the merits of the matter or case with the decision maker or an official of the tribunal before whom a proceeding is pending except:

(1) in the course of official proceedings;

(2) in writing, if the cleric promptly delivers a copy of the writing to opposing clerics or clergy officials or to the adverse party if the party is not represented by a cleric, or some other advocate;

(3) orally upon adequate notice to opposing clerics or to the adverse party if the adverse party is not represented by a cleric; or

(4) as otherwise authorized by bylaws, rules, regulations, or Christian or Denominational Doctrines.

(h) A cleric shall not engage in conduct intended to disrupt a tribunal.

Comment

[1] Many forms of improper influence upon a tribunal are proscribed by church and organization doctrine. Others are specified in the codes or societal ethics and moral norms, which an advocate should be familiar as a cleric. A cleric is required to avoid contributing to a violation of such provisions.

[2] The clerical advocate's function is to present evidence and argument so that the cause may be decided according to the rules and regulations, and bylaws, and other instruments of order. Refraining from abusive or obstreperous or immoral conduct is a corollary of the advocate's right to speak on behalf of the person being given the ministry service before the tribunal. A cleric may stand firm against abuse by a decision maker of the tribunal or decision-making body, but should avoid reciprocation; the decision maker's default is no justification for similar dereliction by an advocating cleric. And advocating cleric can prevent the cause, protect the record of subsequent review and preserve professional and Christian integrity by patient firmness no less effectively by belligerence or theatrics.

Biblical Reference

[1] Finally, there is laid up for me the crown of righteousness, which the Lord, the righteous Judge, will give to me on that Day, and not to me only but also to all who have loved His appearing (2 Timothy 4:8).

Christian Ethical Commentary

[1] To remain impartial and not be a respecter of persons it requires love: "the need for love is an essential element in the structure of personality. It is responsible for the establishing of a pattern of response to other human beings that makes possible all forms of community and of relatedness between human beings in society." Howard Thurman, *The Creative Encounter: An Interpretation of Religion and the Social Witness*. Richmond, IN: Friends United Press, 1972 [1954], 106.

[2] Everyone must be seen as having value in the midst of tribunals: Our feelings of indifference, contempt, malevolence, satisfaction, recognition, encouragement, consolation, etc., have innumerable nuances. Among them the feelings of guilt and obligation are of course crucial. . . .all of these emotions are embedded in a practice of everyday life . . . . This gives the web of moral feelings a certain ineluctability: we cannot retract at will our commitment to a lifeworld whose members we are. Jürgen Habermas, *Moral Consciousness and Communicative Action*, translated by Christian Lenhart and Sheirry Weber Nicholsen (Cambridge, MA: MIT Press, 2001), 47.

[3] "If we are not intentional about dealing with these hurts, if we say that all we have to do is act in Christian love and the problems will go away, we are engaging in denial, a mere bandage covering a deep wound. The healing must happen from the inside out, or infection will set in and fester until it destroys the body." Raleigh Washington, and Glen Kehrein. *Breaking Down Walls*. Chicago: Moody Press, 1993, 134.

Legal Example

[1] *Howard L. Moorman, Et Al., Individually And Severally v. Reverend J.I. Goodman, Et Al.*

Issue: There must be spiritual impartiality applied in the decision making for the religious Tribunal that governs itself without violations of property rights.

Rule: "Each Baptist church is a self-governing body, independent of all other churches. *Randolph v. Mt. Zion Baptist Church of Newark, 139 N.J. Eq. 605, 609 (Ch. 1947)*. Its affairs are administered by the membership acting together, and the will of the church is tory, p. 144, and Manual, p. 13." *Harrison v. Floyd, 26 N.J. Super. 333, at page 337* (Ch. Div. 1953). It is held in this State that with respect to spiritual matters and the administration of the spiritual and temporal affairs of a church not affecting the civil rights of individuals or the property of the corporation, the ecclesiastical courts and governing bodies of the religious society have exclusive jurisdiction and their decisions are final. *Livingston v. Rector, etc., of Trinity Church, 45 N.J.L. 230 (Sup. Ct. 1883); Jennings v. Scarborough, 56 N.J.L. 401 (Sup. Ct. 1894); Everett v. First Baptist Church of Sussex, N.J., 6 N.J. Misc. 640 (Sup. Ct. 1928); Cabinet v. Shapiro, 17 N.J. Super. 540 (Law Div. 1952). Cf. Watson v. Jones, 13 Wall. 679, 20 L.Ed. 666 (1872). However, see Hughes expressed by a majority vote of the members. Hiscox, New Direct v. North Clinton Baptist Church, 75 N.J.L. 167 (Sup. Ct. 1907) p.187.*

Conclusion: A church acting in fairness can make decisions concerning the practice and application of their religious doctrine. *Howard L. Moorman, Et Al., Individually And Severally v. Reverend J.I. Goodman, Pastor Of The First Baptist Church, Englewood, New Jersey, A. Emery, Plummer Perry And The First Baptist Church, Englewood, New Jersey, 59 N.J. Super. 181 (1960), pp.186-187.*

Rule 3.6 Hearing Publicity

(a)   A cleric who is participating or has participated in the inquiry, investigation, or tribunal hearing of a matter shall not

285

make an outside of the tribunal hearing statement about the matter that the cleric knows or reasonably should know will be disseminated by means of public communication and will have a substantial likelihood of materially prejudicing the decision makers in a pending matter.

(b)   Notwithstanding paragraph (a), a cleric may make a statement that a reasonable cleric would believe is required to protect a congregant, PINOMS, or non-profit from the substantial undue prejudicial effect of recent publicity not initiated by the cleric or the cleric's congregation member, PINOMS, or non-profit organization. A statement made pursuant to this paragraph shall be limited to such information as is necessary to mitigate the recent adverse publicity.

(c)   No cleric associated in a ministry with cleric subject to paragraph (a) shall make a statement prohibited by paragraph (a).

Comment

[1] It is difficult to strike a balance between protecting that right to a fair inquiry or hearing and safeguarding the right of free expression. Preserving the right to a fair inquiry or hearing necessarily entails some curtailment of the information that may be disseminated about a party prior to the inquiry or hearing, particularly where the hearing before an ecclesiastical body is involved. If there were no such limits, the result would be the particular nullification of the protective effect of the rules for forensic decorum and the exclusionary rules. On the other hand, there are vital social interests served by the free dissemination of information about events having consequences and about the inquiry proceedings themselves. The public has a right to know about threats to its safety and measures aimed at assuring its security. It also has a legitimate interest in the conduct of the inquiries, particularly in matters of general public concern. Furthermore, the subject matter of the proceedings is often of direct significance in debate and deliberation over questions of public policy.

[2] The rule set forth a basic general prohibition against a cleric's making statements that the cleric knows or should know will have a substantial likelihood of materially prejudicing a pending ecclesiastical hearing or expulsion hearing. Recognizing that the public value of informed commentary is great and the likelihood of prejudice to a proceeding by the commentary of a cleric who is not involved in the proceeding is small, the rule applies only to clerics who are or who have been involved in the investigation, inquiry, or hearing's matter, and their associates.

[3] Extra statements outside of the hearing that might otherwise raise a question under this rule may be permissible when they are made in response to statements made publicity by another party, another party's representative, or third persons, where a reasonable cleric would believe a public response is required in order to avoid prejudice to the cleric's congregant, PINOMS, or non-profit organization. When prejudicial statements have been publicly made by others, responsive statements may have the salutary effect of lessening any resulting adverse impact on the authoritative body's hearing or proceeding. Such responsive statements should be limited to contain only such information as is necessary to mitigate undue prejudice created by the statements made by others.

[4] See Rule 3.8(f) for additional duties of discovery administrators and pursuing governing bodies in connection with outside of hearing statements about the proceedings, which include unethical conduct.

Biblical Reference

[1] So, whatever you have said in the dark, will come to men's hearing in the light, and what you have said secretly inside the house, will be made public from the house-tops (Luke 12:3).

[2] So on the day after, when Agrippa and Bernice in great glory had come into the public place of hearing, with the chief of the army and the chief men of the town, at the order of Festus, Paul was sent for (Act 25:23).

[3] Then Baruch gave a public reading of the words of Jeremiah from the book, in the house of the Lord, in the room of Gemariah, the son of Shaphan the scribe, in the higher square, as one goes in by the new doorway of the Lord's house, in the hearing of all the people (Jeremiah 36:10).

Christian Ethical Commentary

[1] Conducting the Formal Hearing: 1) Church leaders such as elders, deacons, or members of a personnel committee appoint a moderator who is highly respected and fair-minded and is capable of maintaining order, decorum, and a spirit of mutual respect. 2) The committee reads to the church the charges brought against the minister, a summary of the interviews with the complainant and the minister, and any additional relevant information discovered by the committee. 3) The committee answers appropriate questions from the congregation. 4) The committee recommends to the church one of the following actions: a. If the charge is considered false, the minister is exonerated and the church acts to restore the minister's reputation. The complainant receives appropriate discipline and/or counseling and ministry from the church. b. If the accusation is considered true, the committee recommends possible sanctions according to the nature of the offense. Levels of censure can range from admonition to serve sanctions such as probation, suspension, or termination of employment. Joe E. Trull, and James E. Carter, *Minister Ethics: Moral Formation For Church Leaders*, (Baker Academic 2004), pp. 219-220.

Legal Example

[1] *Harold and Hazel HESTER, Appellants, v. Donald R. BARNETT, Respondent.*

Publication and other claims: The action for damages by the plaintiffs Hester, husband and wife, against defendant Barnett, a Baptist clergyman, commenced as a petition in defamation. The motion of the defendant to dismiss that petition was sustained, and the plaintiffs were granted leave to present a more definite and certain statement of the defamation. The petition as amended pleads not only defamation, but also five other separate causes of action denominated:

Issue [Count I]: Ministerial Malpractice, was brought in a case without the matter of counseling by the cleric being involved, can such as cause of action exist without counseling?

Rule Count I: The term malpractice means professional misconduct. Black's Law Dictionary, p. 864 [5th ed. 1979]. It means "the failure to use that degree of skill and learning ordinarily used under the same or similar circumstances by members of [that] profession." MAI 11.06 [3d ed. 1981]; see also Restatement (Second) of Torts § 299A (1965). It means, by very definition, the breach of a professional duty unique to that profession. I Mo. Tort Law [Mo.Bar 1985], § 1.6 [Medical Malpractice]; § 2.1 [Attorneys Malpractice]; § 2.14 [Accountants Malpractice]; § 2.30 [Insurance Agents and Brokers Malpractice]. Malpractice, therefore, is not a theory of ordinary negligence or of intentional tort. The ordinary negligence or intentional tort of any person is already actionable, regardless of its "professional" color. Thus, also, a cleric is amenable to suit for alienation of affections albeit guised as a religious practice,[1] for assault and battery committed during a religious service, for a malicious prosecution of parents informed against by the cleric for child abuse, for the obtention of donations of money by fraud,[2] and for other incidences of intentional tort in the exercise of the religious duty.

Conclusion Count I: It is the sense of that pleading—the Hesters expound in argument—that § 491.060(4), which renders a clergyman incompetent to testify concerning a communication made to him in the professional character as spiritual advisor, imposes a "minimum standard for the profession," whose nonobservance constitutes both a malpractice and a breach of professional ethics. While the statute no doubt means to encourage an effective relationship between the spiritual advisor and the communicant, the enactment has no effect beyond its actual terms. *State v. Kurtz, 564 S.W.2d 856, 860[10] (Mo. banc 1978)*. There is no intimation that § 491.060(4) intends any effect beyond a judicial proceeding—let alone a cause of action for the breach. The privilege, moreover, was not known at the common law, and hence the pleading cannot be understood to invoke any tort principle of that system of law to validate a malpractice action for its breach. *State v. Kurtz, 564 S.W.2d at 860[10]; C. McCormick, Evidence § 72 (3d ed. 1984)*. The tradition that a spiritual advisor does not divulge communications received in that capacity, moreover, even if a tenet of "ministerial ethics" as Count I plead, describes a moral, not a legal duty. In the absence of a legal duty, a breach of a moral duty does not suffice to invest tort liability. T. Cooley, Law of Torts § 3 (4th ed. 1932); J. Dooley, Modern Tort Law § 2.01, at 8 (1982 rev.); Restatement (Second) of Torts, §§ 4 and 5 (1965); *Linville v. Ripley, 237 Mo.App. 1275, 173 S.W.2d 687, 690[5-8] (1943)*. Count I does not allege a cause of action for clergy malpractice for negligent counseling, and was properly dismissed.

Issue: [Count II] Alienation of Affections. The next sequence of pleading alleges as a separate count that the Hester husband and wife and the three Wymer children were bound together by love and affection, and that the minister, Barnett, intentionally and maliciously set out to alienate the affections of "one family member from the others." That pleading also asserts that the minister intentionally and maliciously alienated the affections of the children from the mother and her husband, and from the children, inter sese: Lee Wymer declared to them: "Because of what the preacher has said about you, I do not have a brother or sister nor a mother or a father."

Rule Count II: The tort of alienation of affections of a spouse, albeit discarded as a remedy in many states, remains intact in our jurisdiction. *Kraus v. Kraus, 693 S.W.2d 869 (Mo.App.1985)*. The cause of action is delineated in *Gibson v. Frowein, 400 S.W.2d 418, 421[3] (Mo. banc 1966):* "Alienation of affections is an intentional tort, and the elements of the cause of action are defendant's wrongful conduct, plaintiff's loss of the affections or consortium of his spouse, and the causal connection between such conduct of defendant and the loss by plaintiff."

Conclusion Count II: To the extent that Count II undertakes to plead a cause of action by the Hesters for the alienation of the affections of the three children, the order to dismiss Count II is sustained. To the extent the order undertakes to dismiss the Count II as a pleading by husband Hester for the alienation of the affections of wife Hester, it is reversed.

Issue: [Count III] Defamation of Character. The petition next pleads a sequence of conduct "[s]ince the first day of January of 1984 ... only discovered by Plaintiffs since the first of this year" whereby the defendant "has undertaken to slander, libel and defame the character of Plaintiffs" and used every opportunity and means to publish and broadcast remarks intentionally and maliciously "designed to harm the character and reputation of Plaintiffs ... remarks ... repeated and republished by defendant time after time even to this day." The recitation then describes the slanders and libels and the occasions of publication; that the pastor

(a) delivered sermons from the pulpit of his church wherein the pastor "wrongfully accused Plaintiffs of crimes, stealing, abuse, physical and emotional cruelty to their [sic] spouse, her children and his stepchildren, Connie Wymer, Lee Wymer and Don Wymer"

(b) repeated these false remarks "[i]n letters, memos, church bulletins and publications"

(c) made reports to the Missouri Hot Line for Child Abuse of false accusations by the pastor that the plaintiffs abused the children and thereby subjected them to investigation by the Missouri Division of Family Services

(d) repeated these libels and slanders to neighbors of the plaintiffs in meetings the pastor organized and directed for that purpose

(e) uttered the specific untrue and defamatory remarks, among others, that

> 1. "Harold Hester is a thief who stole tools from a neighbor."
>
> 2. "Harold Hester does not pay his employees their earned wages."
>
> 3. "Harold Hester is an arsonist who burns down barns and other buildings."
>
> 4. "Harold Hester will cheat anyone out of anything."
>
> 5. "Harold Hester cheats the Government."
>
> 6. "Plaintiffs abuse their children mentally and physically."
>
> 7. "Plaintiffs do not love their children but use them to get work done."
>
> 8. "Plaintiffs beat their children so badly that they have bruises all over."
>
> 9. "Plaintiffs punish their children by forcing them to lie face down on the bed of a pickup truck and then drive it over plowed ground and bumpy roads."
>
> 10. "Plaintiffs whip their children in an excessive and abusive manner."
>
> 11. "Harold Hester tried to punish Connie Wymer by knocking her into a ditch and then using a bulldozer to cover her with dirt."

Rule Count III: False utterances which hold one up to hatred, contempt or ridicule, or cause the person to be shunned and avoided, or which "induce an evil opinion of one in the minds of right-thinking persons," are defamations actionable per se. W. Prosser, Law of Torts § 111, p. 739 (4th ed. 1971). A false imputation of crime, by that measure, is defamatory per se, as is a false imputation that a person is dishonest in the business relation, or—by very definition—the imputation that parents cruelly abuse their children. *Brown v. Kitterman, 443 S.W.2d 146, 153[8] (Mo.1969).* To be sufficient as a pleading for libel per se the petition must set out the defamation published in haec verba—or, at the very least, a paraphrase of what is charged as the libel. *Lorenz v. Towntalk Pub. Co., 261 S.W.2d 952, 953[1-3] (Mo.1953); Missouri Church of Scientology v. Adams, 543 S.W.2d 776, 777[3, 4] (Mo. banc 1976); Bremson v. Kinder-Care Learning Centers, 651 S.W.2d 159, 160[4] (Mo.App.1983).* The pleaded count for defamation attributes false statements delivered by Pastor Barnett, published and republished among the church membership and the community at large, which impute to Harold Hester the crimes of theft, arson and child abuse, dishonesty in business and cruelty to the children—and to Hazel Hester, the crime of child abuse and the practice of wanton cruelty upon the children.

Conclusion Count III: These utterances and publications are pleaded in detail and, if not verbatim, then in substantial paraphrase. Count III pleads actionable defamation. Rules 55.05 and 55.20.

Issue: [Count IV] Intentional Infliction of Emotional Distress, raises the issue of whether the defendant "with malicious intent to cause plaintiffs emotional distress intentionally did those actions described specifically in other Counts knowing that Plaintiff Hazel Hester was nervous and suffered frequent and severe attacks of depression and knowing Plaintiff Harold Hester suffered from high blood pressure and nervous tension and was subject to heart attacks all with the malicious design to cause emotional distress and *aggrivate* [sic] plaintiffs' known physical ailments all to their damage as hereafter more specifically described."

Rule Count IV: This count pleads expressly the tort of extreme and outrageous conduct as introduced in *Pretsky v. Southwestern*

Bell Telephone Company, 396 S.W.2d 566 (Mo.1965). The gist of the tort is the intentional infliction of emotional distress on another by conduct "so outrageous in character, and so extreme in degree, as to go beyond all possible bounds of decency, and to be regarded as atrocious, and utterly intolerable in a civilized community." *Id. at 568, 569*; Restatement (Second) of Torts § 46, comment d (1965). It is conduct so extreme as to exceed any reasonable limit of social toleration. *Frye v. CBS INC, 671 S.W.2d 316 (Mo.App.1984)*.

Conclusion Count IV: The attempted incorporation by reference by allusion to "those actions described specifically in other Counts" does not inform the defendant as to the nature and extent of the incorporation, and hence is ineffective as an adoption by reference under Rule 55.12. See *Heintz & Co. v. Provident Tradesmen's Bank & Trust Co., 29 F.R.D. 144, 145[4, 5] (E.D.Pa.1961)*. Count IV was properly dismissed for failure to state a cause of action.

Issue: [Count V] Invasion of Privacy, has the issue of whether the defendant made public reporting to public authorities and law enforcement issues of child abuse, as well as behavior problems, caused an invasion of privacy of the family?

Rule Count V: The right to privacy as a general doctrine of tort was recognized by our Supreme Court in *Barber v. Time, Inc., 348 Mo. 1199, 159 S.W.2d 291 (1942)*. The general right to privacy, our Supreme Court *en banc* then held in *Sofka v. Thal, 662 S.W.2d 502 (Mo. banc 1983)*, expressed four separate interests, and the invasion of privacy described four different torts, each with distinct elements. Sofka [at 510] adopted the Restatement (Second) of Torts § 652B (1977) formulations that the right to privacy is invaded when there is

> (1) unreasonable intrusion upon the seclusion of another
>
> (2) appropriation of the other's name or likeness

(3) unreasonable publicity given to the other's private life

(4) publicity that unreasonably places the other in a false light before the public.

Conclusion Count V: This pleads injury to the Hesters from a course of intentionally tortious action by a minister, on an occasion only pretextually religious, but actually entirely secular, and hence not offensive to the free exercise clause. Count V is reinstated as a pleading for the intrusion upon seclusion invasion of privacy tort.

Issue: [Count VI] Interference with Contract. The question is did the defendant and has the defendant continued with malicious and calculated intent to harass, intimidate, and threaten the plaintiff thus causing plaintiff to leave the employment of their employer?

Rule Count VI: The elements of a cause of action for tortious interference with contract or business relations are repeated in *Francisco v. Kansas City Star Co., 629 S.W.2d 524, 529[1, 2] (Mo.App.1981):*

(1) A contract or valid business relationship or expectancy

(2) Knowledge by the defendant of the contract or relationship

(3) Intentional interference by defendant which induces the breach of contract or relationship

(4) Absence of justification

(5) Resulting damages

Conclusion Count VI: These allegations of unlawful enticements, intimidations and threats—whatever the actual proof—describe secular conduct, the pretext of religious purpose notwithstanding, and hence state a cause of action outside the scope of the free exercise clause. The dismissals of Ministerial

Malpractice Count I and Extreme and Outrageous Conduct Count IV are affirmed. The dismissals of Alienation of Affections Count II, Defamation Count III, Invasion of Privacy Count V, and Tortious Interference with Contract Count VI are reversed, and those counts are ordered reinstated. Count II is reinstated as a cause of action for alienation of spousal affection, and Count V is reinstated as a cause of action for the invasion of privacy by the unreasonable intrusion upon the seclusion of another. The costs are allocated equally between the plaintiffs and the defendant. The defendant Barnett moved to dismiss the petition as amended, and the court sustained the motion as to each of the several counts "for failure to state causes of action upon which relief may be granted." The plaintiffs appeal the judgment of dismissal. *Harold and Hazel Hester v. Donald R. Barnett, 723 S.W.2d 544 (1987), pp.549-564.*

Rule 3.7 Clerics as Witness

(a)   A cleric shall not act as an advocate at a tribunal hearing in which the cleric is likely to be a material and necessary witness unless:

(1) the testimony relates to an uncontested issue;

(2) the testimony relates to the nature and value of ministry services rendered in the matters before the tribunal; or

(3) disqualification of the cleric would work substantial hardship on the congregant, PINOMS, or non-profit.

(b)   A cleric may act as an advocate in the tribunal in which another cleric in the cleric's ministry is likely to be called as a witness unless precluded from doing so by Rule 1.7 or Rule 1.9.

Comment

[1] Combining the roles of advocate and witness can prejudice the tribunal and the opposing party and can also involve a conflict of interest between the cleric and congregant, or PINOMS, or non-profit.

Advocating Cleric-Witness Rule

[2] The tribunal has proper objection when the decision-making body may be confused or misled by a cleric serving as both advocate and witness. The opposing party has proper objection where the combination of rules may prejudice that party's rights in the matter before the tribunal. A witness is required to testify on the basis of personal knowledge, while an advocate is expected to explain and comment on evidence given by others. It may be clear whether a statement by an advocating cleric-witness should be taken as proof or as an analysis of the proof.

[3] To protect the tribunal, paragraph (a) prohibits a cleric from simultaneously serving as advocate and necessary witness except in those circumstances specified in paragraph (a)(1) through (a)(3). Paragraph (a)(1) recognizes that if the testimony will be uncontested, the ambiguities in the dual role are purely theoretical. Paragraph (a)(2) recognizes that where the testimony concerns that extent and value of ministry services to testify avoids the need for a second hearing with new cleric representation to resolve that issue. Moreover, in such a situation the decision-maker has firsthand knowledge of the matter in issue; hence, there is less dependence on the adversary process to test the veracity of the testimony.

[4] Apart from these two exceptions, paragraph (a)(3) recognizes that a balancing is required between the interests of the congregant, PINOMS, or non-profit and those of the tribunal and the opposing party. Whether the tribunal is likely to be misled or the opposing party is likely to suffer prejudice depends on the nature of the matter before the tribunal, the importance and probable tenor of the cleric's testimony, and the probability that the cleric's testimony will conflict with that of other witnesses. Even if there is risk of such prejudice, in determining whether the cleric should be disqualified, due regard must be given to the effect of disqualification on the cleric's congregant, PINOMS, or non-profit member. It is relevant that one or both parties could reasonably foresee that the cleric would probably

be a witness. The conflict-of-interest principles stated in Rule 1.7, 1.9, and 1.10 have no application to this aspect of the problem.

[5] Because the tribunal is not likely to be misled when a cleric acts as an advocating cleric in a hearing before the tribunal in which another cleric is the cleric's ministry will testify as a material and necessary witness, paragraph (b) permits the cleric to do so except in situations involving a conflict of interest.

Conflict of Interest

[6] In determining if it is permissible to act as advocate in a hearing before a tribunal in which the cleric will be a material and necessary witness, that cleric must also consider that the dual role may give rise to a conflict of interest that will require compliance with Rule 1.7 or 1.9. For example, if there is likely to be substantial conflict between the testimony of the congregant, PINOMS, or non-profit organization member and that of the cleric, the clergy advocacy and witness because the cleric's disqualification would work a substantial hardship on the congregant, PINOMS, or non-profit. Similarly, a cleric who might be permitted to simultaneously serve as an advocate and a witness by paragraph (a)(3) might be precluded for doing so by Rule 1.9. The problem can arise whether the cleric is called as a material and necessary witness on behalf of the congregant, PINOMS, or non-profit or is called by the opposing party. Determining whether or not such a conflict exists is primarily the responsibility of the cleric involved. If there is a conflict of interest, the cleric must secure the congregant's or PINOMS's or non-profit's consent, confirmed in writing. In some cases, the cleric will be precluded from seeking the congregant's or PINOMS's or non-profit's consent. See Rule 1.7. See Rule 1.0(b) for the definition of "confirmed in writing" and Rule 1.0(f) for the definition of "informed consent."

[7] Paragraph (b) provides that a cleric is not disqualified from serving as an advocating cleric because a cleric with whom the cleric is associated with in a ministry is precluded from doing so

by paragraph (a). If, however, the testifying cleric would also be disqualified by Rule 1.7 or Rule 1.9 from representing the congregant, PINOMS, or non-profit organization gives informed consent under the conditions stated in Rule 1.7.

Biblical Reference

[1] "There is another who bears witness of Me, and I know that the witness which He witnesses of Me is true" (John 5:32).

[2] This is the disciple which testifies of these things, and wrote these things: and we know that his testimony is true (John 21:24).

[3] SAMEK, I hate the double-minded, But I love Your law (Psalm 119:113).

[4] He is a double-minded man, unstable in all his ways (James 1:8).

[5] Draw near to God and He will draw near to you. Cleanse your hands, you sinners; and purify your hearts, you double-minded (James 4:8).

Christian Ethical Commentary

[1] There is a responsibility to God as a Cleric, as well as all of the flock of the LORD's: "radically contingent portrait of the human condition suggests that the abstract, ideal notion of human freedom is ultimately bound by responsibility to others." Christopher Driscoll, *White Lies: Race and Uncertainty in the Twilight of American Religion* (New York: Routledge, 2015), p.9.

Legal Example

[1] *Serbian Eastern Orthodox Diocese For The United States Of America And Canada et al. v. Milivojevich et al, 426 U.S. 696 (1976)*

Issue: What power does a church have without the secular judicial branch being involved in the branch of Zion's or the churches authority to determine any religious polity or doctrine and decision making?

Ruling and Conclusion: Yet having recognized that the Serbian Orthodox Church is hierarchical and that the decisions to suspend and defrock respondent Dionisije were made by the religious bodies in whose sole discretion the authority to make those ecclesiastical decisions was vested, the Supreme Court of Illinois nevertheless invalidated the decision to defrock Dionisije on the ground that it was "arbitrary" because a "detailed review of the evidence discloses that the proceedings resulting in Bishop Dionisije's removal and *defrockment* were not in accordance with the prescribed procedure of the constitution and the penal code of the Serbian Orthodox Church." *60 Ill. 2d, at 503, 328 N. E. 2d, at 281.*

Not only was this "detailed review" impermissible under the First and Fourteenth Amendments, but in reaching this conclusion, the court evaluated conflicting testimony concerning internal church procedures and rejected the interpretations of relevant procedural provisions by the Mother Church's highest tribunals. *Id., at 492-500, 328 N. E. 2d, at 276-280.* The court also failed to take cognizance of the fact that the church judicatories were also guided by other sources of law, such as canon law, which are admittedly not always consistent, and it rejected the testimony of petitioners' five expert witnesses[10] that church procedures were properly followed, denigrating the testimony of one witness as "contradictory" and discounting that of another on the ground that it was "premised upon an assumption which did not consider the penal code," even though there was some question whether that code even applied to discipline of Bishops.[11] The court accepted, on the other hand, the testimony of respondents' sole expert witness that the Church's procedures had been contravened in various specifics.

We need not, and under the First Amendment cannot, demonstrate the propriety or impropriety of each of Dionisije's procedural claims, but we can note that the state court even rejected petitioners' contention that Dionisije's failure to participate in the proceedings undermined all procedural contentions because Arts. 66 and 70 of the penal code specify that if a person charged with a violation fails to participate or answer the indictment, the allegations are admitted and due process will be concluded without his participation; the court merely asserted that "application of this provision . . . must be viewed from the perspective that Bishop Dionisije refused to participate because he maintained that the proceedings against him were in violation of the constitution and the penal code of the Serbian Orthodox Church." *60 Ill. 2d, at 502, 328 N. E. 2d, at 281.*

The court found no support in any church dogma for this judicial rewriting of church law, and compounded further the error of this intrusion into a religious thicket by declaring that although Dionisije had, even under the court's analysis, been properly suspended and replaced by Firmilian as temporary administrator, he had to be reinstated as Bishop because church law mandated a trial on ecclesiastical charges within one year of the indictment. Yet the only reason more time than that had expired was due to Dionisije's decision to resort to the civil courts for redress without attempting to vindicate himself by pursuing available remedies within the church. Indeed, the Illinois Supreme Court overlooked the clear substantive canonical violations for which the Church disciplined Dionisije, violations based on Dionisije's conceded open defiance and rebellion against the church hierarchy immediately after the Holy Assembly's decision to suspend him (a decision which even the Illinois courts deemed to be proper) and Dionisije's decision to litigate the Mother Church's authority in the civil courts rather than participate in the disciplinary proceedings before the Holy Synod and the Holy Assembly.

Instead, the Illinois Supreme Court would sanction this circumvention of the tribunals set up to resolve internal church disputes and has ordered the Mother Church to reinstate as Bishop one who espoused views regarded by the church hierarchy to be schismatic and which the proper church tribunals have already determined merit severe sanctions. In short, under the guise of "minimal" review under the umbrella of "arbitrariness," the Illinois Supreme Court has unconstitutionally undertaken the resolution of quintessentially religious controversies whose resolution the First Amendment commits exclusively to the highest ecclesiastical tribunals of this hierarchical church. And although the Diocesan Bishop controls respondent Monastery of St. Sava and is the principal officer of respondent property-holding corporations, the civil courts must accept that consequence as the incidental effect of an ecclesiastical determination that is not subject to judicial abrogation, having been reached by the final church judicatory in which authority to make the decision resides. *Serbian Eastern Orthodox Diocese For The United States Of America And Canada et al. v. Milivojevich et al, 426 U.S. 696 (1976) pp.717-720.*

Rule 3.8 Special Responsibilities of a Cleric Led Charging or Accusing Body

A Charging or Accusing Body in an Ecclesiastical Tribunal matter shall:

(a)   Refrain from accusing a person in which the Cleric Led Charging or Accusing Body knows is not supported by probable cause;

(b)   Make reasonable efforts to assure that the accused has been advised of the right to, and procedure for obtaining an advocate and has been given reasonable opportunity to obtain said advocate;

(c)   Not seek to obtain from an accused who does not have an advocate to waive that prehearing right, such as the right to a preliminary investigation, and sharing of information;

(d)   Make timely disclosure to the accused party of all evidence or information known to the Cleric Led Charging or Accusing Body that tends to negate the guilt of the accused or mitigates the matter or accusations, and, in connection with final rulings and decisions of the tribunal, disclose to the accused and the accused's advocate and to the tribunal all unprivileged mitigating information known to the Cleric Led Charging or Accusing Body, except when the Cleric Led Charging or Accusing Body is relieved of this responsibility by a protective order of the tribunal;

(e)   Not subpoena a cleric in a defrocking, or dismissal of a cleric or other similar determination proceeding to present evidence about a past or present person the Cleric is ministering unto, unless the Cleric Led Charging or Accusing Body reasonably believes:

(1) the information sought is not protected from disclosure by any applicable privilege;

(2) the evidence sought is essential to the successful completion of an ongoing investigation or procedure such as a defrocking, or dismissal of a cleric or other similar determination proceeding.

(f)   Exercise reasonable care to prevent employees or other persons assisting or associated with the Cleric Led Charging or Accusing Body in a defrocking, or dismissal of a cleric or other similar determination proceeding and over whom the Cleric Led Charging or Accusing Body would be prohibited from make under Rule 3.6.

Comment

[1] A Cleric Led Charging or Accusing Body has the responsibility of a minister of justice and not simply that of an advocate. This responsibility carries with specific obligations to see that the accused is accorded procedural justice and that guilt is decided upon the basis of sufficient evidence. Precisely how far the Cleric Led Charging or Accusing Body is required to go in this direction is a matter of debate and varies in different denominations. Many jurisdictions have adopted their own governing rules regarding serious violations of ministers.

Applicable procedural and governing rules may require other measures by the Cleric Led Charging or Accusing Body and knowing disregard to those obligations or systematic abuse of Ecclesiastical discretion could constitute a violation of Rule 8.4.

[2] In some denominations, an accused may waive a preliminary hearing and thereby lose a valuable opportunity to challenge probable cause. Accordingly, Cleric Led Charging or Accusing Body should not seek to obtain waivers of preliminary hearings or other important preliminary hearing right from unrepresented accused parties. Paragraph (c) does not apply, however, to an accused appearing pro se with approval of the tribunal. Nor does it forbid the lawful questioning of an accused or one suspected of unethical conduct who has knowingly waived the rights to have an advocate and to remain silent without such advocacy.

[3] The exception in paragraph (d) recognizes that a Cleric Led Charging or Accusing Body may seek appropriate protections from the tribunal if disclosure of information is to the accused or the accused advocate could result in substantial harm to an individual or to the congregation's, organization's, or public's interest.

[4] Paragraph (e) is intended to limit the issuance of appearance demands before the Cleric Led Charging or Accusing Body and other serious violations proceedings to those situations in which there is a genuine need to intrude into the cleric-congregant, or cleric-PINOMS, or cleric-non-profit relationship.

[5] Paragraph (f) supplements Rule 3.6, which prohibits outside of the tribunal statements that have a substantial likelihood of prejudicing an Ecclesiastical proceeding. In the context of a defrocking, or removal from clerical service, a Cleric Led Charging's or Accusing Body's outside of the tribunal statement can create the additional problem of increasing public condemnation of the accused. Although the announcement of an indictment, for example, will necessarily have severe consequences for the accused, a Cleric Led Charging or Accusing

Body can, and should, avoid comments which have no legitimate Ecclesiastical purpose and have a substantial likelihood of increasing public opprobrium of the accused. Nothing is this comment is intended to restrict the statements which a Cleric Led Charging or Accusing Body may make which comply with Rule 3.6(b) or 3.6(c).

[6] Like other clerics, Cleric Led Charging or Accusing Body members are subject to Rule 5.1 and 5.3, which relate to responsibilities regarding clerics and nonclergy advocates who work for or are associated with the cleric's ministry or non-profit office. Paragraph (f) reminds the Cleric Led Charging or Accusing Body of the importance of these obligations in connection with the unique dangers of improper outside of the tribunal statements in a serious ministry violation, that could include expulsion, defrocking, or other serious penalties.

Biblical Reference

[1] Nicodemus (he who came to Jesus by night, being one of them) said to them, "Does our law judge a man before it hears him and knows what he is doing?" (John 7:50-51)

[2] A soft answer turns away wrath, but a harsh word stirs up anger (Proverbs 15:1).

Christian Ethical Commentary

[1] A written summary of the charges is recorded and outlined in a clear, specific, and reasonably documented manner. Both the complainant and the accused should have access to this document and be given an opportunity to respond orally or in writing. Joe E. Trull, and James E. Carter, *Minister Ethics: Moral Formation For Church Leaders*, (Baker Academic 2004), p.218.

Legal Example

[1] *Serbian Eastern Orthodox Diocese For The United States Of America And Canada et al. v. Milivojevich et al, 426 U.S. 696 (1976)*

Holding: It suffices to note that the reorganization of the Diocese involves a matter of internal church government, an issue at the core of ecclesiastical affairs; Arts. 57 and 64 of the Mother Church constitution commit such questions of church polity to the final province of the Holy Assembly. *Kedroff v. St. Nicholas Cathedral, 344 U. S. 94, 116 (1952),* stated that religious freedom encompasses the "power [of religious bodies] to decide for themselves, free from state interference, matters of church government as well as those of faith and doctrine." The subordination of the Diocese to the Mother Church in such matters, which are not only "administrative" but also "hierarchical,"[12] was provided, and the power of the Holy Assembly to reorganize the Diocese is expressed in the Mother Church constitution.[13] Contrary to the interpretation of the Illinois court, the church judicatories interpreted the provisions of the Diocesan constitution not to interdict or govern this action, but only to relate to the day-to-day administration of Diocesan property.[14] The constitutional provisions of the American-Canadian Diocese were not so express that the civil courts could enforce them without engaging in a searching and therefore impermissible inquiry into church polity. See *Md. & Va. Churches v. Sharpsburg Church, 396 U. S., at 368-370 (BRENNAN, J., concurring).[15] Serbian Eastern Orthodox Diocese For The United States Of America And Canada et al. v. Milivojevich et al, 426 U.S. 696 (1976) pp.721-723.*

Rule 3.9 Clergy Advocate in Ecclesiastical Proceedings

A cleric representing a congregant, PINOMS, or non-profit before a tribunal body or administrative ecclesiastical proceeding shall disclose that the appearance is in an advocating capacity and shall conform to the provisions of rule 3.3(a) through (c), and 3.5.

Comment

[1] In advocating capacities as clerics before bodies such as ecclesiastical proceeding and clergy administrative bodies acting in rule-making or policy-making capacity, clerics present facts, formulate issues and advance argument in the matters under consideration. The decision-making body, like a tribunal, should be able to rely on the integrity of the submissions made to it. A cleric appearing before such a body must deal with it honestly and in conformity with applicable rules of procedure. See Rules 3.3(a) through (c), 3.4(a) through (c), and 3.5.

[2] Clerics have no exclusive right to appear before ecclesiastical bodies for proceedings, as they do before congregation bodies in some instances. The requirement of this rule therefore may subject clerics to ecclesiastical or denominational regulations inapplicable to clergy advocates who are connected to a particular church body, or denomination, or one connected to a non-denominational ministry. However, ecclesiastical bodies and Christian tribunals have a right to expect clerics to deal with them as they deal with all under their authority.

[3] This rule only applies when a cleric advocates for a congregant, PINOMS, or non-profit organization in connection with an official hearing or meeting of an ecclesiastical body or Christian tribunal to which the cleric or the cleric's congregant, PINOMS, or non-profit organization is presenting evidence or presentation. It does not apply to advocacy of a congregant, PINOMS, or non-profit organization in a negotiation or other bilateral transaction with an ecclesiastical body or in connection with an application for a license or other privilege or the congregant's or PINOMS's or non-profit's compliance with generally applicable reporting requirements. Nor does it apply to the representation of a congregant, PINOMS, or non-profit in connection with an investigation or examination or the congregant's, PINOMS's, or non-profit's affairs conducted by government investigators or examiners. Clergy advocating in such matters is governed by Rule 4.1 through 4.4.

Biblical Reference

[1] But Jesus went to the Mount of Olives. 2 Now early in the morning He came again into the temple, and all the people came to Him; and He sat down and taught them. 3 Then the scribes and Pharisees brought to Him a woman caught in adultery. And when they had set her in the midst, 4 they said to Him, "Teacher, this woman was caught in adultery, in the very act. 5 Now Moses, in the law, commanded us that such should be stoned. But what do You say?" 6 This they said, testing Him, that they might have something of which to accuse Him. But Jesus stooped down and wrote on the ground with His finger, as though He did not hear. 7 So when they continued asking Him, He raised Himself up and said to them, "He who is without sin among you, let him throw a stone at her first." 8 And again He stooped down and wrote on the ground. 9 Then those who heard it, being convicted by their conscience, went out one by one, beginning with the oldest even to the last. And Jesus was left alone, and the woman standing in the midst. 10 When Jesus had raised Himself up and saw no one but the woman, He said to her, "Woman, where are those accusers of yours? Has no one condemned you?" 11 She said, "No one, Lord." And Jesus said to her, "Neither do I condemn you; go and sin no more" (John 8:1-11).

Christian Ethical Commentary

[1] The committee explains the process to the complainant, stressing the intent of the church to address the charges without delay. Joe E. Trull, and James E. Carter, *Minister Ethics: Moral Formation For Church Leaders*, (Baker Academic 2004), p.218.

[2] All parties maintain strict confidentiality. Joe E. Trull, and James E. Carter, *Minister Ethics: Moral Formation For Church Leaders*, (Baker Academic 2004), p.218.

[3] "When it comes right down to it, of course, there is no institutional substitute for personal integrity." H. Richard Uviller.

[4] Whether it is proper for a Christian Advocate defending a Cleric to question an adversary of a Cleric when it is known that the adversary has spoken the truth before the Tribunal; Whether it is proper for a Christian Advocate to present a witness to testify before the tribunal when the Christian Advocate knows the witness if presented will not be truthful; and Whether a Christian Advocate should provide good counsel to a Cleric believing that the good counsel will cause the Cleric to speak things that are untruthful before the Tribunal. Character and Context: What Virtue Theory Can Teach Us About A Prosecutor's Ethical Duty To "Seek Justice", R. Michael Cassidy, Notre Dame Law Review, Vol 82, Issue 2, Article 3, (2006), p.635.

[5] When is it proper for a Tribunal Advocate/Decision Maker to offer allegations or make a ruling or final decision concessions to a party, Cleric or accomplice in order to secure the testimony against a confidant? When, if ever, may a Tribunal Advocate/Decision Maker question negatively a person testifying on behalf of the accused Cleric, or party when the Tribunal Advocate/Decision Maker knows that person has presented testimony that is truthful without error, and how should the Tribunal Advocate/Decision Maker move forward in the questioning? When, or how should a Tribunal Advocate/Decision Maker respond when the Cleric's or person accused before the tribunal has a Christian Advocate who is not presenting the best representation for the defense of the Cleric or person accused before the Tribunal? Character and Context: What Virtue Theory Can Teach Us About A Prosecutor's Ethical Duty To "Seek Justice", R. Michael Cassidy, Notre Dame Law Review, Vol 82, Issue 2, Article 3, (2006), p.636.

Legal Example

[1] *Serbian Eastern Orthodox Diocese For The United States Of America And Canada et al. v. Milivojevich et al*

Issue: Who has the final authority to determine non-secular matters and affairs of the church concerning personnel, property, and provisions of the governing body and/or tribunal and documents for a religious institution or church?

Rule: Indeed, it is the essence of religious faith that ecclesiastical decisions are reached and are to be accepted as matters of faith whether or not rational or measurable by objective criteria. Constitutional concepts of due process, involving secular notions of "fundamental fairness" or impermissible objectives, are therefore hardly relevant to such matters of ecclesiastical cognizance.

The constitutional evils that attend upon any "arbitrariness" exception in the sense applied by the Illinois Supreme Court to justify civil court review of ecclesiastical decisions of final church tribunals are manifest in the instant case. The Supreme Court of Illinois recognized that all parties agree that the Serbian Orthodox Church is a hierarchical church, and that the sole power to appoint and remove Bishops of the Church resides in its highest ranking organs, the Holy Assembly and the Holy Synod. Indeed, final authority with respect to the promulgation and interpretation of all matters of church discipline and internal organization rests with the Holy Assembly, and even the written constitution of the Mother Church expressly provides:

"The Holy Assembly of Bishops, as the highest hierarchical body, is legislative authority in the matters of faith, officiation, church order (discipline) and internal organization of the Church, as well as the highest church juridical authority within its jurisdiction (Article 69 sec. 28)." Art. 57.

"All the decisions of the Holy Assembly of Bishops and of the Holy Synod of Bishops of canonical and church nature, in regard to faith, officiation, church order and internal organization of the church, are valid and final." Art. 64.

"The Holy Assembly of Bishops, whose purpose is noted in Article 57 of this Constitution:

310

.....

"9) interprets canonical-ecclesiastical rules, those which are general and obligatory, and particular ones, and publishes their collections;

.....

"12) prescribes the ecclesiastical-judicial procedure for all Ecclesiastical Courts;

.....

"26) settles disputes of jurisdiction between hierarchical and church-self-governing organs;

"27) ADJUDGES:

"A) In first and in final instances:

"a) disagreements between bishops and the Holy Synod, and between the bishops and the Patriarch;

"b) canonical offenses of the Patriarch;

"B) In the second and final instance:

"All matters which the Holy Synod of Bishops judged in the first instance." Art. 69.

Conclusion: In short, the First and Fourteenth Amendments permit hierarchical religious organizations to establish their own rules and regulations for internal discipline and government, and to create tribunals for adjudicating disputes over these matters. When this choice is exercised and ecclesiastical tribunals are created to decide disputes over the government and direction of subordinate bodies, the Constitution requires that civil courts accept their decisions as binding upon them. Reversed. *Serbian Eastern Orthodox Diocese For The United States Of America And Canada et al. v. Milivojevich et al, 426 U.S. 696 (1976) pp.713-717, 724-725.*

311

Rule 4.1 Truthfulness In Statements To Others

In the course of providing ministry services or advocating for another a cleric shall not knowingly make a false statement of fact material or minor, for it is against the laws of God, Thou Shalt Not Bear False Witness.

Comment

Misrepresentation

[1] A cleric is required to be truthful when dealing with others and when providing ministry services, or advocating for another, but generally has no affirmative duty to inform an opposing party of confidential facts given during confessions, or at the request for prayer. A misrepresentation can occur if the cleric incorporates or affirms a statement of another person that the cleric knows is false. Misrepresentation can also occur by partially true but misleading statements or omissions that are the equivalent of affirmative false statement. Part of the truth is a full lie. For dishonest conduct that does not amount to a false statement or for misrepresentation by a cleric other than in the course of providing ministry services or advocating for another, see Rule 8.4. Let no corrupt communication proceed out of your mouth, but that which is good to the use of edifying, that it may minister grace unto the hearers (Ephesians 4:29).

Statements Of Fact Before A Tribunal Or Decision Making Body

[2] This rule refers to statements of fact before a tribunal or decision-making body. Whether a particular statement should be regarded as one of fact can depend on the circumstances surrounding a matter that is before the body. Under general accepted conventions in negotiation, certain types of statement ordinarily are not taken as statements of material fact. Estimates of procedural outcomes, and a party's intentions as to an acceptable resolution of a matter are ordinarily in this category, and so is the existence of an undisclosed principal except where

nondisclosure of the principal would constitute unfairness, or could also constitute fraudulent behavior. Clerics should be mindful of their Spiritual and Social obligations under applicable church cannon, rules, bylaws, and those responsibilities found in the Holy Scriptures to avoid criminal, tortious, or irreparable harm by making misrepresentations. But let your communication be, Yea, yea; Nay, nay: for whatsoever is more than these comes of evil (Matthew 5:37).

[1] My little children, these things I write to you, so that you may not sin. And if anyone sins, we have an Advocate with the Father, Jesus Christ the righteous (1 John 2:1).

[2] "They advocate customs that are not lawful for us as Romans to accept or practice" (Act 16:21).

[3] A true witness delivers souls: but a deceitful witness speaks lies (Proverb 14:25).

Biblical Reference

[1] Absolutely not! Let God be true, even though everyone is a liar, as it is written: That you may be justified in your words and triumph when you judge.

[2] "You know the commandments: Do not murder; do not commit adultery; do not steal; do not bear false witness; do not defraud; honor your father and mother" (Mark 10:19).

[3] Do not give false testimony against your neighbor (Exodus 20:16).

[4] Beloved, never avenge yourselves, but leave it to the wrath of God, for it is written, "Vengeance is mine, I will repay, says the Lord" (Romans 12:19).

Christian Ethical Commentary

[1] According to Robert C. Roberts people have a character of truthfulness if: "a person has character if he or she is characterized by such traits as truthfulness, courage, justice and

compassion, especially if he or she is able to maintain virtuous action, emotion and thought despite pressures to slacken his or her measure." Robert C. Roberts, *"Character"*, in New Dictionary of Christian Ethics & Pastoral Theology, Illinois: InterVarsity Press, (1995).

[2] Ultimately, freedom means the ability to actualize potentials. It is to live day to day with the conviction that there is a way for [men and women] by which, if [they] live, . . . will become increasingly human, humane, and whole, full of health and peace. To choose such a way is to put at the disposal of the individual life the boundless resources of the Creator of life. Howard Thurman, "Freedom under God," (Feb 1955, St. Louis) in *The Papers of Howard Washington Thurman, Vol 4*, 117.

[3] Romans 12:19: "Some argue that Paul's language a few verses later suggests that violent vengeance may in fact be due to enemies: "Beloved, never avenge yourselves, but leave room for the wrath of God; for it is written, 'Vengeance is mine, I will repay, says the Lord.'" Then Paul continues: "No, 'if your enemies are hungry, feed them; if they are thirsty, give them something to drink; for by doing this you will heap burning coals upon their heads'" (12:19-20. Let us look more closely at these verses in context...If this story *[Elisha leading the Aramean army after God strikes them with blindness in 2 Kings 6:8-12, and then feeding them]* is read as a background to Romans 12:19-20, then the political overtones become clear. In a context of warfare, God chooses paradoxically generous means to relate to His enemies and bring peace. In addition, the vengeance of God is revealed to be deeply subversive of violent retaliation, for God's vengeance does not mirror the violence of the empire." *Character Ethics and the New Testament Moral Dimensions of Scripture*, Chapter 9, If Your Enemy Is Hungry Love and Subversive Politics in Romans 12-13, Sylvia C. Keesmaat, Robert L. Brawley, ed., Wesminister John Knox Press, Louisville-London, 2007, pp.146-147.

Legal Example

[1] *Serbian Eastern Orthodox Diocese For The United States Of America And Canada et al. v. Milivojevich et al*

Issue: Can a church tribunal make decisions devoid of fraud and collusion, which will be found to be supported and upheld by the First and Fourteenth Amendments of the United States Constitution?

Rule First Amendment: "the First Amendment severely circumscribes the role that civil courts may play in resolving church property disputes." *Presbyterian Church v. Hull Church, 393 U. S. 440, 449 (1969).* "First Amendment values are plainly jeopardized when church property litigation is made to turn on the resolution by civil courts of controversies over religious doctrine and practice. If civil courts undertake to resolve such controversies in order to adjudicate the property dispute, the hazards are ever present of inhibiting the free development of religious doctrine and of implicating secular interests in matters of purely ecclesiastical concern. . . . [T]he [First] Amendment therefore commands civil courts to decide church property disputes without resolving underlying controversies over religious doctrine." *Ibid.* This principle applies with equal force to church disputes over church polity and church administration."

Rule Fourteenth Amendment: The principles limiting the role of civil courts in the resolution of religious controversies that incidentally affect civil rights were initially fashioned in *Watson v. Jones, 13 Wall. 679 (1872),* a diversity case decided before the First Amendment had been rendered applicable to the States through the Fourteenth Amendment.[5] With respect to hierarchical churches, *Watson* held: "[T]he rule of action which should govern the civil courts . . . is, that, whenever the questions of discipline, or of faith, or ecclesiastical rule, custom, or law have been decided by the highest of these church judicatories to which the matter has been carried, the legal tribunals must accept such decisions as final, and as binding on them, in their application to the case before them." *Id., at 727.*

Rule First and Fourteenth Amendment: Consistently with the First and Fourteenth Amendments "civil courts do not inquire whether the relevant [hierarchical] church governing body has power under religious law [to decide such disputes]. . . . Such a determination . . . frequently necessitates the interpretation of ambiguous religious law and usage. To permit civil courts to probe deeply enough into the allocation of power within a [hierarchical] church so as to decide . . . religious law [governing church polity]. . . would violate the First Amendment in much the same manner as civil determination of religious doctrine." *Md. & Va. Churches v. Sharpsburg Church, 396 U. S. 367, 369 (1970)* (BRENNAN, J., concurring). For where resolution of the disputes cannot be made without extensive inquiry by civil courts into religious law and polity, the First and Fourteenth Amendments mandate that civil courts shall not disturb the decisions of the highest ecclesiastical tribunal within a church of hierarchical polity, but must accept such decisions as binding on them, in their application to the religious issues of doctrine or polity before them. *Ibid.*

Conclusion: Essentially, the court premised this determination on its view that the early history of the Diocese "manifested a clear intention to retain independence and autonomy in its administrative affairs while at the same time becoming ecclesiastically and judicially an organic part of the Serbian Orthodox Church," and its interpretation of the constitution of the American-Canadian Diocese as confirming this intention. It also interpreted the constitution of the Serbian Orthodox Church, which was adopted after the Diocesan constitution, in a manner consistent with this conclusion. *60 Ill. 2d, at 506-507, 328 N. E. 2d, at 283-284.* This conclusion was not, however, explicitly based on the *"fraud, collusion, or arbitrariness"* exception. Rather, the Illinois Supreme Court relied on purported "neutral principles" for resolving property disputes which would "not in any way

316

entangle this court in the determination of theological or doctrinal matters." *Id., at 505, 328 N. E. 2d, at 282.* Nevertheless, the Supreme Court of Illinois substituted its interpretation of the Diocesan and Mother Church constitutions for that of the highest ecclesiastical tribunals in which church law vests authority to make that interpretation. This the First and Fourteenth Amendments forbid. Reversed *Serbian Eastern Orthodox Diocese For The United States Of America And Canada et al. v. Milivojevich et al, 426 U.S. 696 (1976), pp.709-710, 719-721.*

Rule 4.2 Communication with Person Represented Or Being Advocated For By Another Cleric

In ministering services or advocating for another a cleric shall not communicate about the subject of the representation with a person the cleric knows to be represented by another cleric in a proceeding, unless the cleric has the consent of the other cleric or is authorized to do so by the bylaws, rules, or procedures of the church, or the denomination, or even by permission of the governing body, or decision-making body.

Comment

[1] This rule contributes to the proper performance of ministry services by protecting a person who has chosen to receive advocating services or ministry services on a matter by another cleric, then to have another cleric possibly overreach by participating in providing ministry services or advice in the same matter. Interference by a second cleric with the cleric-congregant or cleric-PINOMS, or cleric-Non-Profit Organization relationship can cause confusion, and conflicts of interest as well. For God is not the author of confusion but of peace, as in all the churches of the saints (1 Corinthians 14:33).

[2] This rule applies to communications with any person who is represented by an advocating cleric, or who is receiving ministry

services from a cleric concerning the matter to which the communication relates.

[3] The rule applies even though the congregant, or PINOMS, or Non-Profit initiates or consents to the communication with the cleric providing the ministry of advocacy or ministry services in a matter. A cleric must immediately terminate communications with a person, such as one receiving counseling, or court ordered counseling sessions with a cleric, if after commencing communication, the cleric learns that the person is on with whom communication is not permitted by this rule.

[4] This rule does not prohibit communication with a person receiving clerical assistance, or an employee of a ministry, or non-profit organization, or agent of such a person, concerning matters outside of the matter they are receiving ministry services, or clerical advocacy from another cleric. For example, the existence of a controversy between two organizations, does not prohibit a cleric for either from communicating with a non-represented congregant or PINOMS, or non-profit of the other regarding a separate matter. Nor does this rule preclude communication with a represented person who is seeking advice from a cleric who is not otherwise advocating for a congregant, PINOMS, or non-profit in the matter. A cleric may not make a communication prohibited by this rule through the acts of another. See Rule 8.4(a). Parties to a matter may communicate directly with each other, and a cleric is not prohibited from advising a congregant, or PINOMS, or non-profit organization concerning a communication that the congregant, or PINOMS, or non-profit organization is entitled to make by the procedure, or the rules, or the bylaws, or the governing body constitution.

[5] Communications authorized by the procedural rules may include communications by an advocating cleric on behalf of a congregant, PINOMS, or non-profit organization who is exercising a right given by the governing body's rules and procedures or constitution to communicate with the governing body. When communicating with a person accused of a violation

a cleric must comply with the rules, which protect the rights of the accused. The fact that a communication does not violate these rules, it is permissible.

[6] A cleric who is uncertain whether a communication with a congregant or PINOMS, or non-profit that already has a clergy advocate is permissible may seek a ruling from the governing body. A cleric may also seek a ruling in exceptional circumstances to authorize a communication that would otherwise be prohibited by this rule, for example, where communication with a person represented by another cleric is necessary to avoid reasonably certain injury.

[7] In case of a non-profit organization with cleric advocacy, this rule prohibits communications with a constituent of the organization who supervises, directs or regularly consults with the organization's advocate concerning the matter or has authority to obligate the organization with respect to the matter or whose act or omission in connection with the matter may be imputed to the organization for purposes of injury or liability. The term "constituent" is defined in Comment [1] to Rule 1.13. Consent of the organization's clergy advocate is not required for communication with the former constituent. If a constituent of the organization will be sufficient for purposes of this rule. Compare Rule 3.4(f). In communicating with a current or former congregant, PINOMS, or non-profit, a cleric must not use methods of obtaining evidence that violate the procedural rights of the organization. See Rule 4.4.

[8] The prohibition on communications with a represented person only applies in circumstances where the cleric knows that the person is in fact represented in the matter to be discussed. This means that the cleric has actual knowledge of the fact of the clergy advocate; but such actual knowledge may be inferred from the circumstances. See Rule 1.0(g). Thus, the cleric cannot evade the requirement of obtaining the consent of the advocating cleric by closing eyes to the obvious.

[9] In the event the person with whom the cleric communicates is not known to be represented by another clergy advocate in the matter, the cleric's communications are subject to Rule 4.3.

Biblical Reference

[1] But everything must be done in a proper and orderly manner (1 Corinthians 14:40).

[2] For God is not a God of disorder, but of peace--as in all the churches of the saints (1 Corinthians 14:33).

[3] For although I am absent from you in body, I am present with you in spirit, and I delight to see your orderly condition and firm faith in Christ (Colossians 2:5).

[4] "By the mouth of two or three witnesses every word shall be established" (2 Corinthians 13:1).

Christian Ethical Commentary

[1] "We have no really authentic records of a time when there was peace in the world; the most you can say is that we have records of those moments of treacherous quiet between armistices. Yet the human spirit constantly affirms its interest in, and the necessity of the logic of peace." Howard Thurman, *The Papers of Howard Washington Thurman: Volume 4, "The Power of the Spirit and the Powers of this World* Edited by Walter Fluker, et al. (Columbia, SC: University of South Carolina Press, 2017), 23.

[2] 12 Elements of doing things decently and orderly have been suggested as follows:

1. Provide orderly procedure

2. Give justice to all

3. Show courtesy to all

4. Uphold the rule of the majority

5. Recognize the rights of the minority

6. Encourage teamwork rather than individual agendas

7. Make the business meeting a time of joy and celebration

8. Remember that Jesus is the Head of the Church

9. Focus on the Lordship of Christ and His kingdom growth

10. Always ask what Jesus would want us to do

11. Pray for and about all decisions

12. Put off decisions to another meeting if a decision cannot be made until you have more information. SBC, *Transitional Pastor Ministry Training Manual, LifeWay Christian Resources of the Southern Baptist Convention*, (LifeWay Press, Nashville, TN, 2000), 36.

[3] In our advocating for another or in inspiring others the goal should always be upon the premise that Bishop Tutu wrote of: "somewhere deep inside us we seem to know that we are destined for something better." Desmond Tutu, *No Future Without Forgiveness* (New York: Doubleday, 1999), 264.

Rule 4.3 Dealing With Those Without Clergy Advocates

In dealing on behalf of a congregant, PINOMS, or non-profit who does not have a clergy advocate:

(a)   A cleric shall not state or imply that the cleric is disinterested;

(b)   A cleric shall clearly disclose that the congregant's or PINOMS's or non-profit's interests are adverse to the interest of the un-advocated for person, if the cleric knows or reasonably should know that the interests are adverse;

(c)   When a cleric knows or reasonably should know that the un-advocated for person misunderstands that cleric's role in the matter, the cleric shall make reasonable efforts to correct the misunderstanding; and

(d)   A cleric shall not give ministerial advice to the un-advocated for person in the matter before the tribunal, other than the advice to secure a cleric to advocate for them, if the cleric knows or reasonably knows or reasonably should know that the interests of the un-advocated for person are or have reasonable possibility of being in conflict with the interests of the congregant, PINOMS, or non-profit.

Comment

[1] An un-advocated for person, particularly one not experienced in dealing with religious tribunals or hearings, might assume that a cleric is disinterested in loyalties or is a disinterested authority on the procedural process even when the cleric represents a party. In order to avoid a misunderstanding, a cleric will typically need to identify the cleric's congregant, PINOMS, or non-profit and, where the cleric knows or reasonably should know that the interests are adverse, disclose that the congregant, PINOMS, or non-profit organization has interests opposed to those of the un-advocated for person. For misunderstanding that sometimes arise when a cleric for an organization deals with an un-advocated for person, see Rule 1.13(d).

[2] The rule distinguishes between situations involving un-advocated for persons whose interests may be adverse to those of the cleric's person they are representing, and those in which the person's interests are not in conflict with the person the cleric is representing. In the former situation, the possibility that the cleric will compromise the un-advocated for person's interest is so great that the rule prohibits the giving of any ministerial advice, apart from the advice to obtain a clergy advocate. Whether a cleric is giving impermissible advice may depend on the experience and sophistication of the un-advocated for person, as well as the setting in which the behavior and comments occur. This rule does not prohibit a cleric from negotiating the terms of a resolution to the matter before the tribunal with the non-advocated for person. So long as the cleric has explained that the cleric advocates for another party whose

interests are adverse and is not advocating for the person, the cleric may inform the person of the terms on which the cleric's congregant, PINOMS, or non-profit organization will enter into an agreement or settlement agreement, prepare documents, or resolve a matter that require the person's signature and explain the cleric's own view of the meaning of the document of the cleric's view of the underlying clerical obligations.

Biblical Reference

[1] Show yourself in all respects to be a model of good works, and in your teaching show integrity, dignity, and sound speech that cannot be condemned, so that an opponent may be put to shame, having nothing evil to say about us (Titus 2:7-8).

[2] But let your communication be, Yea, yea; Nay, nay: for whatsoever is more than these cometh of evil (Matthew 5:37).

[3] Whatever you do, work heartily, as for the Lord and not for men (Colossians 3:23).

[4] Let no corrupt communication proceed out of your mouth, but that which is good to the use of edifying, that it may minister grace unto the hearers (Ephesians 4:29).

Christian Ethical Commentary

[1] "We must search more and more creatively how to devise methods by which good may supplant evil, by which the hearts of men [and women] may be redeemed, and by which the world in which those hearts must function may be redeemed." Howard Thurman, *"The Kingdom of God,"* (lecture, June26,1938, Northfield, MA) in *The Papers of Howard Washington Thurman, Vol 2*, 170.

Rule 4.4 Respect for Rights of Third Persons

(a)   In representing a congregant, PINOMS, or non-profit organization shall not use means that have not substantial purpose other than to embarrass, delay, or burden a third-party person, or use methods of obtaining evidence that violate the procedural rights of such a person.

(b)   A cleric who receives a document or electronically stored information relating to the ministry services of the cleric's person they are advocating for and knows or reasonably should know that the document or electronically stored information was inadvertently sent shall promptly notify the sender.

[1] Responsibility to a congregant, PINOMS, or non-profit organization requires a cleric to subordinate the interests of others to those of the congregant, PINOMS, or non-profit organization, but that responsibility does not imply that a cleric may disregard the rights of third persons. It is impractical to catalogue all such procedural rights, but they include ministry restrictions or methods of obtaining evidence from third persons and unwarranted intrusions into privileged relationships, such as the cleric-congregant, cleric-PINOMS, and cleric-non-profit relationship.

[2] Paragraph (b) recognizes that clerics sometimes receive a document or electronically stored information that was mistakenly sent or produced by opposing parties or their clerics. A document or electronically stored information is inadvertently sent when it is accidentally transmitted, such as when and email or letter is misaddressed or document or electronically stored information is accidentally included with information that was intentionally transmitted. If a cleric knows or reasonably should know that such a document or electronically stored information was sent inadvertently, then this rule requires the cleric to promptly notify the sender in order to permit that person to take protective measures. Whether the cleric is required to take additional steps, such as returning or deleting the document or electronically stored information, is a matter of procedural rules, as in the question of whether the privileged status of a document or electronically stored information has been waived.

[3] Some clerics may choose to return a document or delete electronically stored information unread, for example, when the cleric learns before receiving it that it was inadvertently sent. Where a cleric is not required by applicable regulations to do so, the decision to voluntarily return such a document or electronically stored information is a matter of moral, and professional judgment ordinarily reserved to the cleric. See Rule 1.2 and 1.4.

Biblical Reference

[1] "So whatever you wish that others would do to you, do also to them, for this is the Law and the Prophets (Matthew 7:12).

[2] Love one another with brotherly affection. Outdo one another in showing honor (Romans 12:10).

Christian Ethical Commentary

[1] "If being Christian does not demand that all Christians love each other and thereby become deeply engaged in experiencing themselves as human beings, it would seem futile to expect that Christians as Christians would be concerned about the secular community in its gross practices of prejudice and discrimination." Howard Thurman, *The Luminous Darkness: A Personal Interpretation of the Anatomy of Segregation and the Ground of Hope* (New York: Harper & Row, 1965), 105.

[2] The tendency toward whole-making was at once self-defeating if it did not establish clear-cut and fixed boundaries. Without such boundaries freedom itself had no significance, so the reasoning ran. Therefore, it was only within fixed boundaries, self-determined–and that is the key word –that the goals of community could be experienced, achieved, or realized. The natural lines along which the boundaries should be set would be to separate those who had been historically victimized by society from those who had victimized them. Howard Thurman, *The Search for Common Ground: An Inquiry into the Basis of*

Man's Experience of Community. Richmond, IN: Friends United Press, (1986), 96.

[3] Implicit in the Christian message is a profoundly revolutionary ethic. This ethic appears as the binding relationship between [persons], conceived as children of a common . . . God. The ethic is revolutionary because the norms it establishes are in direct conflict with the relationship that obtains between [persons] in the modern world. It is a patent fact that attitudes of fellowship and sympathetic understanding across lines of separateness such as race, class, and creed are not characteristic of our age. Howard Thurman, *"Judgment and Hope in the Christian Message," in The Papers of Howard Washington Thurman, Vol 3*, 243.

[4] "In Romans 12 Paul draws out the implications of Jesus' death for the sake of His enemies: The Roman [church] community is called to be a blessing for those who persecute them. *Character Ethics and the New Testament Moral Dimensions of Scripture*, Chapter 9, If Your Enemy Is Hungry Love and Subversive Politics in Romans 12-13, Sylvia C. Keesmaat, Robert L. Brawley, ed., Wesminister John Knox Press, Louisville-London, 2007, p.147.

Rule 5.1 Responsibilities of a Senior Pastor or Associating Minister of the Gospel of Jesus Christ

(a)   A senior pastor or associated minister of the Gospel, and the cleric who individually or together with other clerics possesses comparable managerial authority in a ministry or non-profit, shall make reasonable efforts to ensure that the ministry has in effect measures giving reasonable assurance that all clerics I the ministry conform to the Rules of SMITH'S CHRISTIAN CLERGY PROFESSIONAL RULES OF ETHICS.

(b)   A cleric having direct supervisory authority over another cleric shall make reasonable efforts to ensure that the other cleric's conduct conforms to the Rules of SMITH'S

CHRISTIAN CLERGY PROFESSIONAL RULES OF ETHICS.

(c) A cleric shall be responsible for another cleric's violation of the Rules of SMITH'S CHRISTIAN CLERGY PROFESSIONAL RULES OF ETHICS if:

(1) the cleric orders or, with knowledge of the specific conduct, ratifies the conduct involved; or

(2) the cleric is an associated, or senior pastor, or has comparable managerial authority in the ministry or non-profit in which the cleric ministers, or has direct supervisory authority over the other cleric, and knows of the conduct at a time when its consequences can be avoided or mitigated but fails to take reasonable remedial action.

Comment

[1] Paragraph (a) applies to clerics who have managerial authority over the ministerial work of a ministry. See Rule 1.0(d). This includes members of a ministry, the board of trustees in a ministry organization as a standalone ministry, or a ministry that is incorporated, and members of other nonprofit organizations authorized to do nonprofit ministry; clerics having comparable managerial authority in a ministry services organization or a ministry department of an enterprise of a denominational or non-denominational governing body; and clerics who have intermediate managerial responsibilities in a ministry. Paragraph (b) applies to clerics who have supervisory authority over the ministry labors of love or work of other clerics in a ministry, or ministry organization, or nonprofit organization.

[2] Paragraph (a) requires clerics with managerial authority within a ministry to make reasonable efforts to establish internal policies and procedures designed to provide reasonable assurance that all clerics in the ministry will conform to the Rules of SMITH'S CHRISTIAN CLERGY PROFESSIONAL RULES OF ETHICS. Such policies and procedures include those designed to

detect and resolve conflicts of interest, identify dates by which actions must be taken in pending matters, account for ministry funds, and property, and ensure that inexperienced clerics are properly supervised.

[3] Other measures that may be required to fulfill the responsibility prescribed in paragraph (a) can depend on the ministry or nonprofit's structure and the nature of its ministry, such as a church, counseling, or services and the nature of its practices. In a small ministry of experienced clerics, informal supervision and periodic review of compliance with the required systems ordinarily will suffice. In a large ministry, or nonprofit, or in practice situations in which difficult ethical problems frequently arise, more elaborate measures may be necessary. Some ministries, for example, have a procedure whereby junior clerics can be confidential referral of ethical problems directly to a designated senior pastor or upper-level associate or special committee. See Rule 5.2. Ministries, whether large or small, may also rely on continuing ministry education in Christian ethics. In any event, the Christian ethical atmosphere of a ministry can influence the conduct of its members and the senior pastor, and the ministry associates may not assume that all clerics associated with the ministry will inevitably conform to the rules.

[4] Paragraph (c) expresses a general principle of personal responsibility for acts of another.

See also Rule 8.4(a).

[5] Paragraph (c)(2) defines the duty of an associate or other cleric having comparable managerial authority in a ministry, as well as a cleric who has direct supervisory authority over performance of specific ministry services and duties by another cleric. Whether a cleric has supervisory authority in particular circumstances in a question of fact. Associates and clerics with comparable authority have at least indirect responsibility for all ministry being done by the ministry, while an associate or senior pastor in charge of a particular matter ordinarily also has

328

supervisory responsibility for the work of other ministry clerics engaged in the matter. Appropriate remedial action by a senior pastor, or associate cleric, or managing cleric would depend on the immediacy of the cleric's involvement and the seriousness of the misconduct. A supervisor is required to intervene to prevent avoidable consequences of misconduct if the supervisor knows that the misconduct occurred. Thus, if a supervision cleric knows that a subordinate misrepresented a matter to an opposing party in a matter before a tribunal, deacon board, or trustee board or the like or in negotiations, or the supervisor as well as the subordinate has a duty to correct the resulting misapprehension.

[6] Professional misconduct by a cleric under supervision could reveal a violation of paragraph (b) on the part of the supervisory cleric even though it does not entail a violation of paragraph (c) because there was no direction, ratification or knowledge of the violation.

[7] Apart from this rule and Rule 8.4(a), a cleric does not have disciplinary liability for conduct of a senior pastor, associate minister or subordinate. Whether a cleric may be liable civilly or even criminally for another cleric's conduct is a question of morals and ethics beyond the scope of these rules.

Biblical Reference

[1] *Shepherd the Flock*: 1 The elders who are among you I exhort, I who am a fellow elder and a witness of the sufferings of Christ, and also a partaker of the glory that will be revealed: 2 Shepherd the flock of God which is among you, serving as overseers, not by compulsion but willingly, not for dishonest gain but eagerly; 3 nor as being lords over those entrusted to you, but being examples to the flock; 4 and when the Chief Shepherd appears, you will receive the crown of glory that does not fade away (1 Peter 5:1-4).

[2] Preach the word; be ready in season and out of season; correct, rebuke, and encourage with great patience and teaching (2 Timothy 4:2).

[3] 2 Timothy 5:19 Do not accept an accusation against an elder unless it can be confirmed by two or three witnesses. 20 Those guilty of sin must be rebuked before all, as a warning to the rest. 21 Before God and Christ Jesus and the elect angels, I solemnly charge you to carry out these commands without prejudice or favoritism of any kind. 22 Do not lay hands on anyone hastily and so identify with the sins of others. Keep yourself pure. 23 (Stop drinking just water, but use a little wine for your digestion and your frequent illnesses.) 24 The sins of some people are obvious, going before them into judgment, but for others, they show up later. 25 Similarly good works are also obvious, and the ones that are not cannot remain hidden (2 Timothy 5:19-25 NET).

[4] Not domineering over those in your charge, but being examples to the flock. And when the chief Shepherd appears, you will receive the unfading crown of glory. Likewise, you who are younger, be subject to the elders. Clothe yourselves, all of you, with humility toward one another, for "God opposes the proud but gives grace to the humble." Humble yourselves, therefore, under the mighty hand of God so that at the proper time he may exalt you (1 Peter 5:3-6).

[5] And John, calling to him two of his disciples, sent them to the Lord, saying, "Are you He who is to come, or shall we look for another?" And when the men had come to Him, they said, "John the Baptist has sent us to you, saying, 'Are you He who is to come, or shall we look for another?'" In that hour He cured many of diseases and plagues and evil spirits, and on many that were blind he bestowed sight. And He answered them, "Go and tell John what you have seen and heard: the blind receive their sight, the lame walk, lepers are cleansed, and the deaf hear, the dead are raised up, the poor have good news preached to them. And blessed is he who takes no offense at Me." (Luke 7:19-23).

[6] All Scripture is inspired by God and is profitable for teaching, for rebuking, for correcting, for training in righteousness (2 Timothy 3:16).

Christian Ethical Commentary

[1] "One of the central problems in human relations is applying the ethic of respect for personality in a way that is not governed by special categories." Howard Thurman, *The Luminous Darkness: A Personal Interpretation of the Anatomy of Segregation and the Ground of Hope.* (Richmond, IN: Friends United Press, 1965), 1.

[2] Chuck Phelps cites the following ethical behaviors as being the 10 most significant ethical systems in history, the tenth one should be a cleric's goal:

> 1. Might is right. Set forth by the Greek philosopher Thrasymachus, who said, "Justice is in the interest of the stronger party."

> 2. Mores are moral. Existing conditions form the basis of morality. "Right" is   what each community determines.

> 3. Man is the yardstick of what is right. Protagoras produced the statement, "Man is the measure of all things." This philosophy is individualistic. What is right for me is right.

> 4. Humanity is the yardstick of what is right. This system proposes that the entire human race is to be used in judging right from wrong.

> 5. Moderation is right. Aristotle's philosophy— Moderation is "the mean between indulgence and insensibility."

> 6. Pleasure is right. The Epicurean ethic of hedonism-- pleasure is good, and pain is evil.

> 7. Right is the greatest good for the greatest number of people in the long run. This is generally called utilitarianism. There are 2 divisions of this system:

>> (1) qualitative utilitarianism and

331

(2) quantitative utilitarianism.

8. Right is desirable for its own sake. Right becomes an end rather than a means to the end.

9. Right is indefinable. The philosophy of frustration.

10. Right is what God wills.

Chuck Phelps, Pastoral Ethics, Publisher Central Africa Baptist College, pp.5-7.

[3] John Dewey states that it is one's responsibility to study and have the "continual reorganization, reconstruction and transformation of experience." John Dewey, *Democracy and Education* (New York: Macmillan, 1961), 50.

[4] The main objective should be to point people to having a personal relationship with Jesus, as stated by WilliamJames without empathy for the cleric, "ecclesiastical organization, with its priest and sacraments and other go-betweens, . . . The relation goes direct from heart to heart, from soul to soul, between [one] and [one's]maker. . . . The personal religion will prove itself more fundamental than either theology or ecclesiasticism." William James, *The Varieties of Religious Experience: A Study in Human Nature* (New York: Penguin Books, 1982), 29-30.

[5] "When a pastor stumbles, we put him in a coffin and bury

him...many times they are walking wounded. The Christian army often not only shoots them, but we leave them to bleed to death in the field." Jeffrey Weiss, *Baptist Take over Program to Help, Wounded Heroes*, http://www.bibleteacher.org/wounded/wh-art2.htm (accessed February 2, 2010).

[6] "A minister drops out, his family suffers, a congregation is in disarray. The community is shocked. A generation of young people is lost because their role model crashed and burned...It impacts more than 31,200 family members, thousands of church members and hundreds of thousands in their communities." SBC

Life, January 1998, Journal of the Southern Baptist Convention, Nashville, 16.

[7] "The shepherd metaphor reflects how leaders guide, protect and provide. Resane (2014) expanded this function as follows: "The broader functions of the shepherd were to lead the sheep to pastures and water (Psalm 23:1) to protect them from wild animals (1 Samuel 17:34–35); and to guard them at night, whether in the open (Lk 2:8) or in sheepfolds (Zephaniah 2:6) where they counted them as they entered the fold (Jr 33:13). They took care of the sheep and even carried weak lambs in their arms (Isaiah 40:11). (p. 2). This means that the shepherd-leader directs the flock in areas of conduct and actions. They assist or lead the flock. The shepherd teaches the flock for restoration purposes and guides them in paths of righteousness. They are protected from erroneous dogma. Tenney (1975) highlighted this as follows: The life of the sheep was dependent upon the power and provision of the shepherd. Their recognition of him and his recognition of them established the relationship. Hearing his voice, following his leading, entering the fold through him, and the refusal to follow others was John's picture of belief. (p. 165)" Kelebogile Thomas Resane, *Servant leadership and shepherd leadership: The missing dynamic in pastoral integrity in South Africa today*, HTS Teologiese Studies/Theological Studies ISSN: (Online) 2072-8050, (Print) 0259-9422, p. 3.

[8] "Pastoral education should always have three fundamental objectives. These are: (1) ministerial formation; (2) spiritual/personal formation; and (3) academic formation. In following the learning theory known as Bloom's Taxonomy, the objectives must be expressed in and through hands, heart and head. In the first and second objective, the application is that of Christian standards. In the third objective, the application is that of the standards of the world. Pastoral training should never separate the academic from the practical, the head from the hands and leave the heart to the peripheral lifestyle. Resane (2018a) pointed to this as follows:

There is some symbiotic relationship between ministerial formation and moral formation. Knowledge comes through information, and that may lead to transformation. (p. 354)" Kelebogile Thomas Resane, *Servant leadership and shepherd leadership: The missing dynamic in pastoral integrity in South Africa today*, HTS Teologiese Studies/Theological Studies ISSN: (Online) 2072-8050, (Print) 0259-9422, p. 7.

[9] Naidoo has made the following appeal in reference to teaching: Teaching practices are the fundamental processes by which we learn and become who we are. Pedagogies of formation involve the integrated development of knowledge and spirituality, identity and integrity in the professional formation of clergy. Pedagogies of contextualization have to do with grounding pedagogies of formation in the interplay of historical and contemporary contextual influences. Marilyn Naidoo, '*Ministerial training: The need for pedagogies of formation and of contextualization in theological education*', *Missionalia* 38(3), (November 2010), (pp. 347–348).

[10] Chuck Phelps states the following clerics and those that they minister along with cited as: The Pastor and His Fellows

In the ministry we are surrounded by people…

The pastor walks regularly in the midst of other ministries. He must walk wisely (1 Cor. 4:1-4).

I. Our predecessors and successors

    A. Our predecessors—1 Cor. 3,10-15

        1. Loyalty is transferable as is criticism. Never willingly criticize or receive criticism about one's predecessor (Eph. 5:30-32).

        2. When possible, invite your predecessor to share in ministry with you. Paul looked forward to return visits to the churches he pastored and so should we (Acts 20).

3. Be willing to publicly share news regarding your predecessor's present ministry and family situations.

B. Our successors—Titus 1

1. Be open and approachable sharing information relevant to continuity of ministry.

2. Be careful not to damage your successor's willingness to work with certain individuals by sharing too much information.

3. Teach the people to follow God's man for the hour (Joshua1 : David & Solomon).

4. Never criticize or willingly hear criticism of your successor. Such willingness will cripple his ministry and is in direct disobedience to God's Word (1 Tim. 5).

5. Honor your successor by avoiding return engagements to conduct weddings and funerals. If the closeness to the individual absolutely merits a return it is customary and honorable to allow the present pastor to conduct the ceremony service while the former pastor assists.

6. If you plan to retire, you may want to plan to move or be booked out. The continued presence of the former pastor can be a genuine source of divided loyalty and intimidation. If you stay in the area, be sure to establish your loyalty to the new pastor. If you cannot be loyal and follow, at least be silent or move.

II. Office practices and staff

A. Set policies and follow them.

335

Set meetings and communicate.

It is the professor's [pastor's] observation that the #1 challenge in church staff relationships is communication.

1. Regularly scheduled meetings need to be maintained.

2. A mutual vision must be shared.

3. Lines of authority need to be established and respected.

B. Demonstrate the importance of the staff to the church family.

1. Plurality of leadership

2. Singularity of headship

C. General guidelines for good staff relationships

D. Hiring, firing, removing, and replacing the church staff

1. Follow the constitution carefully.

2. Be certain to treat the staff with utmost respect.

(What goes around comes around.)

3. Speak of "our" staff, not "my" staff.

E. General office considerations

1. Place your own phone calls.

2. Dress like a professional...

3. Establish office hours.

4. Never pirate software.

5. Use the telephone at the office for professional purposes and at home for personal purposes.

6. Maintain a spirit of diligence and dignity.

Examples of inappropriate behavior:

7. Establish basic protocols of professionalism.

    a. Space

    b. Expectations

    c. Reviews

8. Keep a clear desk.

9. Answer your phone calls and correspondence promptly.

10. Missionaries are people too.

11. Design to avoid doubt (windows, restrooms, amenities)."
Chuck Phelps, *Pastoral Ethics*, Publisher Central Africa Baptist College, pp.57-60.

[11] John the Baptist question to Christ Jesus, and Jesus' response provide a glimpse of not only ministry order, but the desired relationship even of one being a teacher, and the one being taught, which contains a dichotomous relationship as every good Christian teacher should desire that their students become greater teachers than they are themselves.

"The question of John in 7:19 (Σὺ εἶ ὁ ἐρχόμενος ἢ ἄλλον προσδοκῶμεν;--"Are you the one who is to come, or are we to wait for another?") allows Jesus to summarize His previous activity."' *Character Ethics and the New Testament Moral Dimensions of Scripture*, Chapter 3 "The Reorienting Potential of Biblical Narrative for Christian Ethos, with Special Reference to Luke

7:36-50" by Elna Mouton, Robert L. Brawley, ed., Wesminister John Knox Press, Louisville-London, 2007, p.41.

Christ Jesus' response was first an illustrative one, in which Christ Jesus performs the miracles that only the Messiah could perform, which the disciples of John, would have to recite as the past tense once they reached John to provide the answer to his question. Thus, Christ Jesus was citing the gifts and authority of the Messiah, which Christ Jesus Himself performed, which are listed in the Old Testament that provides John the Baptist with concrete evidence of Him being the One. Christ Jesus answers the question which would require John's disciples to point to that which had been demonstrated in His previous activity, which are the things the Messiah was to fulfill. However, in Christ Jesus' previous activity, John the Baptist baptized Christ Jesus in the River Jordan, thus, Christ Jesus submitting to the ministry of John the Baptist as the scripture was to be fulfilled. John the Baptist's own statement found in John 3:30 of "He [being Christ Jesus] must increase, but I must decrease" goes against the very question John the Baptist presented to Christ Jesus by what was still considered "John's disciples." "Are you the one who is to come, or are we to wait for another?" In Christ Jesus being the teacher's Teacher, the Riboni, said in John 14:12-14: "I tell you the truth, anyone who believes in me will do the same works I have done, and even greater works, because I am going to be with the Father. You can ask for anything in my name, and I will do it, so that the Son can bring glory to the Father. Yes, ask me for anything in my name, and I will do it!" This too for those who are the under-shepherds and disciples of Christ presents a dichotomous relationship, although those who are under-shepherds and disciples of Christ Jesus fully know that apart from Christ Jesus we can do nothing. (John 15:5-- "Yes, I am the vine; you are the branches. Those who remain in me, and I in them, will produce much fruit. For apart from me you can do nothing.")

Rule 5.2 Responsibilities of a Subordinate Cleric

(a)   A cleric is bound by the Rules of SMITH'S CHRISTIAN CLERGY PROFESSIONAL RULES OF ETHICS notwithstanding that the cleric acted at the direction of another person.

(b)   A subordinate cleric does not violate the Rules of SMITH'S CHRISTIAN CLERGY PROFESSIONAL RULES OF ETHICS if that cleric acts in accordance with a supervisory cleric's reasonable resolution of an arguably question of ministry service duty.

Comment

[1] Although a cleric is not relieved of responsibility for a violation by the fact that the cleric acted at the direction of a supervisor, and the fact may be relevant in determining whether a cleric had the knowledge required to render conduct a violation of the rules. For example, if a subordinate filed a frivolous report at the direction of supervisor, and subordinate would not be guilty of ministry violations unless the subordinate knew of the report's frivolous character.

[2] When clerics in a supervisor-subordinate relationship encounter a matter involving Christian moral judgment as to ethical duty, the supervisor may assume responsibility for making the judgment. Otherwise, a consistent course of action or position could not be taken. If the question can reasonably be answered only one way, the duty of both clerics is clear and they are equally responsible for fulfilling it. However, if the question is reasonably arguable, someone has to decide upon the course of action. That authority ordinarily responses in the supervisor, and a subordinate may be guided accordingly. For example, if a question arises whether the interests of two congregants' or two PINOMS, or two nonprofits' conflict under Rule 1.7, the supervisor's reasonable resolution of the question should protect the subordinate professionally in the resolution is subsequently challenged.

[3] Study to show yourself approved to God, a workman that needs not to be ashamed, rightly dividing the word of truth (2 Timothy 2:15).

[4] Then the mother of Zebedee's sons came to Him with her sons, kneeling down and asking something from Him. And He said to her, "What do you wish?" She said to Him, "Grant that these two sons of mine may sit, one on Your right hand and the other on the left, in Your kingdom." But Jesus answered and said, "You do not know what you ask. Are you able to drink the cup that I am about to drink, and be baptized with the baptism that I am baptized with?" They said to Him, "We are able." So He said to them, "You will indeed drink My cup, and be baptized with the baptism that I am baptized with; but to sit on My right hand and on My left is not Mine to give, but it is for those for whom it is prepared by My Father." And when the ten heard it, they were greatly displeased with the two brothers. But Jesus called them to Himself and said, "You know that the rulers of the Gentiles lord it over them, and those who are great exercise authority over them. "Yet it shall not be so among you; but whoever desires to become great among you, let him be your servant. "And whoever desires to be first among you, let him be your slave—"just as the Son of Man did not come to be served, but to serve, and to give His life a ransom for many" (Matthew 20:20-28).

Biblical Reference

[1] 2 To Timothy, my dearly beloved son: Grace, mercy, and peace, from God the Father and Christ Jesus our Lord. 3 I thank God, whom I serve from my forefathers with pure conscience, that without ceasing I have remembrance of thee in my prayers night and day; 4 Greatly desiring to see thee, being mindful of thy tears, that I may be filled with joy; 5 When I call to remembrance the unfeigned faith that is in thee, which dwelt first in thy grandmother Lois, and thy mother Eunice; and I am persuaded that in thee also. 6 Wherefore I put thee in remembrance that thou stir up the gift of God, which is in thee

by the putting on of my hands. 7 For God hath not given us the spirit of fear; but of power, and of love, and of a sound mind.

8 Be not thou therefore ashamed of the testimony of our Lord, nor of me his prisoner: but be thou partaker of the afflictions of the gospel according to the power of God; (2 Timothy 1:2-8).

Christian Ethical Commentary

[1] But there is another dimension of the encounter. It is at the level of [fellowship] and community with the children of God. This encounter is instinct with the demand that all broken harmonies with our fellows be repaired and restored. Where there is estrangement, there must be reconciliation. Wounds must be healed, crooked paths made straight, and the turbulence of human conflict subdued by the tranquility of forgiveness and the will to community. Hatreds upon which life has fed must be uprooted by great contrition and the felt necessity for forgiveness. Howard Thurman, *"The Twofold Encounter," in The Inward Journey*, Friends United Press (November 1, 2007), 137.

[2] In my effort to keep this fear from corroding my life and making me seek relief in shiftlessness, I sought help from God. I found that the more I turned to prayer, to what I discovered in later years to be meditation, the more time I spent alone in the woods or on the beach, the freer became my own spirit and the more realistic became my ambitions to get an education. Here at last was something I could do with my life. But it would call for a different emphasis in the religious life and experience from that which I saw around me in the community. Howard Thurman, *Footprints of a Dream: The Story of the Church of the Fellowship of All Peoples* (Eugene, Oregon: Wipf and Stock Publishers, 2009), 16.

[3] "There is a significant difference between knowing the number of the sheep and knowing the state of the flock. The good shepherd is concerned about even one sheep that has strayed away (Wiersbe 1991:45):...Shallow theology and false ideas derived from popular literature twist genuine spirituality and lead to the failure of the pastoral integrity and ministry. It is

important for pastors-in-training to receive theologically sound content that leads to life transparency, reflecting the character of Christ (Resane 2018): The moral conservatism or legalistic dictates on teaching and learning environment are powerful tools of the hidden curriculum. The legalism students imbibe at the college can easily be transported to the church life that the graduate will be teaching. (p. 8)

Shallow and a very narrow theology reduces the Christian faith to a private and personal concern of individuals and separates them from the needs and concerns of the wider society in which the flock resides (Kretzschmar 1997:313)." Kelebogile Thomas Resane, 'Leadership for the church: The shepherd model', HTS Teologiese Studies/Theological Studies 70(1), Art.# 2045. https://doi.org/10.4102/hts.v70i1.2045, 2014, (p. 6).

[4] Marilyn Naidoo is concerned about the training of ministers: The training of ministers involves the cognitive acquisition of appropriate knowledge, competence in required ministerial skill and personal character development. Marilyn Naidoo, *'Ministerial training: The need for pedagogies of formation and of contextualization in theological education', Missionalia* 38(3), (November 2010), (p. 349)

Rule 5.3 Responsibilities Regarding Non-Cleric Assistants

With respect to a non-cleric employed or in volunteering service in a ministry with a cleric supervising:

(a) a senior pastor, associate minister, trustee, or deacon board member or the like who individually or together with other clerics possess comparable managerial authority in a ministry organization, shall make reasonable efforts to ensure that the ministry has in effect measures giving reasonable assurance that the non-cleric's conduct is compatible with the ministry obligations of the cleric;

(b) a cleric having direct supervisory authority over the non-cleric shall make reasonable efforts to ensure that the person's conduct is compatible with the professional obligations of the cleric; and

(c) a cleric shall be responsible for the conduct of a non-cleric that would be a violation of the Rules of SMITH'S CHRISTIAN CLERGY PROFESSIONAL RULES OF ETHICS if engaged in by a cleric if:

(1) the cleric orders or, with the knowledge of the specific conduct, ratifies the conduct involved; or

(2) The clerics is a senior pastor, or an associate minister or member of the trustee board or has a comparable authority in the ministry in which the person is employed, or has direct supervisory authority over the person, and knows of the conduct at a time when its consequences can be avoided or mitigated by fails to take reasonable remedial action.

Comment

[1] Paragraph (a) requires clerics with managerial authority within a ministry to make reasonable efforts to ensure that the firm has in effect measures giving reasonable assurance that non-clerics in the ministry and non-clerics outside the ministry who serve in ministry matters act in a way compatible with the ministry obligations of the cleric. See Comment [6] to Rule 1.1 (obtaining clerics outside of the ministry) and Comment [1] to Rule 5.1 (responsibilities with respect to clerics within the ministry). Paragraph (b) applies to clerics who have supervisory responsibilities and authority over such non-clerics within or outside the ministry. Paragraph (c) specifies the circumstances in which a cleric is responsible for conduct of such non-clerics without or outside the ministry that would be a violation of Rules of SMITH'S CHRISTIAN CLERGY PROFESSIONAL RULES OF ETHICS if engaged in by a cleric.

[2] Clerics generally obtain the services of assistants in their ministry service, including secretaries, seminary interns, seminary

students, and those studying to become clerics. Such assistants, whether employees, or independent contractors, act for the cleric in rendition of the cleric's ministry services. A cleric must give assistants appropriate instructions and supervision concerning the ethical aspects of their employment, particularly regarding the obligation not to disclose information relating to representation of the congregation, church, board, or ministry, and should be responsible for their work product. The measures employed in supervision non-cleric should take account of the fact that they do not have or do not have completed ministry or seminary training and are not subject to ministry discipline such as losing licenses, or ordination documents.

[3] A cleric may use non-clerics outside of the ministry to assist the cleric in rendering ministry services to the congregant, PINOMS, or nonprofit organization. Examples include the obtaining secretarial help, copy and records preserving, and bookkeeping efforts. When using such services outside of the ministry, a cleric must make reasonable efforts to ensure that the services are provided in a manner that is compatible with the cleric's ministry obligations. The extent of this obligation will depend upon the circumstances, including the education, experience and reputation of the non-cleric; the nature of the services involved; the terms of any arrangements concerning the protection of ministry information; and the ministerial and ethical environments of the governing body, and any confidentiality that is involved. See also Rules 1.1 (competence), 1.2 (allocation of authority), 1.4 (communication with congregant, or PINOMS, or nonprofits), 1.6 (confidentiality), 5.4(a) (independence of the cleric), 5.5(a) (unauthorized or unlicensed practice of ministry). When retaining or directing a nonlawyer outside the ministry, a cleric should communicate directions appropriate under the circumstances to give reasonable assurance that the non-cleric's conduct is compatible with the ministry obligations of the cleric.

[4] Where the congregant, PINOMS, or non-profit directs the selection of a particular non-cleric service provider outside the ministry, the cleric ordinarily should agree with the congregant, PINOMS, or non-profit concerning the allocation of responsibility for monitoring as between the congregant, PINOMS, or non-profit and cleric. See Rule 1.2. When making such an allocation in a matter pending before a tribunal, clerics and parties may have additional obligations that are a matter of ministry ethics and ministry morals, which are beyond the scope of these Rules.

Biblical Reference

[1] For the administration of this service not only supplies the want of the saints, but is abundant also by many thanksgivings unto God; Whiles by the experiment of this ministration they glorify God for your professed subjection unto the gospel of Christ, and for your liberal distribution unto them, and unto all men; And by their prayer for you, which long after you for the exceeding grace of God in you. Thanks be unto God for his unspeakable gift (2 Corinthians 9:12-15).

Christian Ethical Commentary

[1] Tenney has stated the following concerning the non-cleric as follows:

The life of the sheep was dependent upon the power and provision of the shepherd. Their recognition of him and his recognition of them established the relationship. Hearing his voice, following his leading, entering the fold through him, and the refusal to follow others was John's picture of belief. Merrill C. Tenney, *John – The gospel of belief: An analytical study of the text*, *Wm. B. Eerdmans Publishing*, (Grand Rapids, Michigan 1975) (p. 165).

[2] Wessels correctly states the following concerning leaders and sheep of God's flock: In the Jeremiah text the metaphor of a shepherd is used to refer to the leaders in the Judean society (Jr

345

3:15; 6:3; 10:21; 12:10; 22:22; 23:1; 23:4; 25:34–36). The concept of a shepherd comes from the domain of rustic life where a person is given the responsibility to lead sheep into pastures, to watch over them, to keep them together, to protect them and to bring them back to safety. Wilhelm J. Wessels, 'Leader responsibility in the workplace: Exploring the shepherd metaphor in the book of Jeremiah', Koers – *Bulletin for Christian Scholarship* 79(2), Art.# 2121.
https://doi.org/10.4102/koers.v79i2.2121, (2004), (p. 2).

[3] Strobel has stated: "Ethical leadership behavior is both influenced by and a reflection of the internal ethical climate of an organization" Maria Strobel, Andranik Tumasjan, & Isabell M. Welpe, *Do business ethics pay off?: The influence of ethical leadership on organizational attractiveness*. Zeitschrift für Psychologie/Journal of Psychology, 218(4), (p.215).
https://doiorg.ezproxy.liberty.edu/10.1027/0044-3409/a000031

[4] The non-cleric is expected to participate fully in the ministry for some denominations: The principle of Congregational Church Government, namely, that a constituted church meeting is, under the Lordship of Jesus Christ, the highest court of authority for the local church; and that each individual member has the inalienable right and responsibility to participate fully in the life and government of the Church, including the appointment of its leaders. (Baptist Union of South Africa 1877:178)

[5] Administration: "Administrative ethics—Ex. 18:23-26; Acts 6:1-7; Acts 20:28; Heb. 13:7-The New Testament minister is referred to by titles: pastor, elder, teacher, [minister of the Gospel of Christ Jesus] preacher. He is also called "bishop" or episcopos. The word episcopos [bishop] was used for the office of supervision in the Greco-Roman world. Thayer says that the word describes "a man charged with the duty of seeing that things to be done by others are done rightly, any curator or guardian, or superintendent." (Acts 20:28; 1 Tim. 3:1-2; Heb. 13:7; 1 Peter 2:25). The leader (pastor) of the New Testament

church shoulders many burdens. There is one task that he must willingly and uniquely carry—He must be an administrator. In commenting on the N.T. minister's task, H. E. Dana said, "The chief function of this official (i.e. the pastor) was administrative. He was expected primarily to „rule well"—to be proficient in administration. He might sometimes labor „in the Word and in teaching," but not invariably. It startles—not to say agitates—the present day Baptist minister to remind him that the office of elder or bishop as presented in New Testament was primarily an administrative office and not a preaching function, but it takes bold and radical manipulation of the Scriptures to support any other conclusion." (H. E. Dana, A Manual of Ecclesiology, Kansas: Central Seminary Press, 1944).

A. Understand the people have great value (Phil. 2:3).

B. Recognize the work that others perform (1 Cor. 16:10-16).

C. Give away opportunities to serve (Phil. 3:10).

"Spectators become critic."

D. Promote with integrity.

E. Practice godly financial stewardship.

1. Designated contributions must go to designated causes.

2. Audits and controls are profitable for preserving integrity." Chuck Phelps, *Pastoral Ethics*, Publisher Central Africa Baptist College, p.53.

Rule 5.4 Professional Independence of a Cleric

(a) A cleric or ministry shall not share ministry fees with a non-cleric, except that:

(1) an agreement by a cleric with the cleric's ministry, senior pastor, or associate may provide for the payment of money, over a reasonable period of time after the cleric's death, to the cleric's estate or to one or mor specified persons;

(2) a cleric who is assigned or is given the ministry of a deceased, disabled, or disappeared cleric may, pursuant to the provisions of Rule 1.17, pay to the estate or other representative of the cleric the agreed-upon services fees;

(3) a cleric or ministry may include non-cleric employees in a compensation or retirement plan, even though the plan is based in whole or in part on a benevolent agreement;

(4) subject to full disclosure and denominational approval, or non-denominational approval, or church approval, a cleric may share ministry fees with a nonprofit organization that employed, or recommended employment of the cleric in the matter; and

(5) a cleric who undertakes to complete unfinished ministry business of a deceased cleric may pay to the estate of the deceased cleric the proportion of the total compensation that fairly represents the services rendered by the deceased cleric.

(b) A cleric shall not form a partnership with a non-cleric if any of the activities of the partnership consist of the ministry of the Gospel of Jesus Christ.

(c) A cleric shall not permit a person who recommends, employs, or pays the cleric to render ministry services for another to direct or regulate the cleric's ministry judgment in rendering such ministry services.

(d) A cleric shall not minister with or in the form of a ministry corporation or association authorized to minister for a profit, if:

(1) a non-cleric owns any interest therein, except that a fiduciary representative of the estate of a cleric may hold the benevolence interest of the cleric for a reasonable time during the administration;

(2) a non-cleric possesses denominational authority or governing body authority, unless permitted by the Ecclesiastical Body; or

(3) a non-cleric has the right to direct or control the ministry judgement of a cleric.

Comment

[1] The provisions of this rule express traditional limitations on sharing of ministry fees. These limitations are to protect the cleric's ministry independence of judgment. Where someone other than the congregant, PINOMS, or nonprofit organization pays the cleric's ministry fees or salary, or recommends employment of the cleric, that arrangement does not modify the cleric's obligation to the congregant, PINOMS, or nonprofit organization. As stated in paragraph (c), such arrangements should not interfere with the cleric's ministry judgment.

[2] This rule also expresses traditional limitations on permitting a third party to direct or regulate the cleric's ministry judgment in rendering ministry services to another. See also Rule 1.2(f).

Biblical Reference

[1] Elders who do their work well should be respected and paid well, especially those who work hard at both preaching and teaching. For the Scripture says, "You must not muzzle an ox to keep it from eating as it treads out the grain." And in another place, "Those who work deserve their pay!" (1 Timothy 5:17-18)

[2] But if we claim to know him and don't obey him, we are lying and the truth isn't in our hearts. We truly love God only when we obey him as we should, and then we know we belong to him. If we say we are his, we must follow the example of Christ (1 John 2:3-6).

[3] "We gave you strict orders not to teach in this name," he said. "Yet you have filled Jerusalem with your teaching and are determined to make us responsible for this man's blood." But Peter and the other apostles replied, "We must obey God rather than men. The God of our fathers raised up Jesus, whom you had killed by hanging Him on a tree" (Acts 5:28-30).

Christian Ethical Commentary

[1] [I]t is clear that the Old Testament conception of God sees two aspects in God's reign, which is part of his very essence. First, human beings are to orient themselves toward God vertically: i.e., the grandeur of divine filiation. Second, there is to be fellowship and reconciliation between human beings: i.e., [kinship]. And since God is inseparable from his 'reign,' both aspects are indissolubly linked as primary realities embodying our relationship to God and God's relationship to us. Jon Sobrino, *Christology at the Crossroads* (Maryknoll, NY: Orbis Books, 1982), 45.

[2] Fellowship With Other Churches And Possible Schisms

"Other parishes and schisms—Prov. 15:22; Luke 6:3

Because you will be a ministry in the midst of ministries, it is well to ponder your relationship to other churches.

A. Evangelical churches *[Other Churches]*

1. When possible, fellowship—when in doubt, don't!

2. Be careful not to compromise.

Explain:

3. Be careful not to compete

Explain:

4. Receive members from other evangelical churches with great care.

a. Respect the discipline of another church.

Explain:

b. Inform the former pastor/church when folk are coming.

350

c. Use caution in the promotion of new member's ("not a novice")

B. Compromised "Churches"—Gal. 1:9

1. Openly rebuke them when necessary.

Explain:

2. Avoid fellowship with them.

3. Reach their lost members with the Gospel! "

C. Consider your responsibility to fellow-pastors. Chuck Phelps, *Pastoral Ethics*, Publisher Central Africa Baptist College, pp.60-61.

Rule 5.5 Unlicensed and Unordain Ministry Services; Interdenominational Ministry

(a) A cleric shall not provide ministry service as a cleric in a denomination or ministry in violation of the tenants of a faith, or the regulations or procedures of a ministry, or assist another in doing so, except that a cleric ordained and licensed to minister in a ministry or denomination does not violate this rule by conduct in another denomination that is permitted in these Ministry Rules under Rule 5.5(c) and (d) for clerics not ordained and licensed to provide ministry services in a denomination, or ministry.

(b) A cleric who is not licensed or ordained in at denominational practice.

(1) except as authorized by these rules or other law, establish of an office or other systematic and continuous presence in a ministry or denomination for the ministry service of a Christian Doctrine; or

(2) hold out to the community or otherwise represent that the cleric is admitted to the service of ministry by the authority of a governing body as an ordained minister or one licensed by a

governing body, which has the authority to ordain or provide licenses;

(c) A cleric admitted in another ordaining body, and not defrocked our suspended from providing ministry services in a denomination, may provide ministry services on a temporary basis in a particular ministry:

(1)   Are undertaken in association with a cleric who is licensed or ordained to minister in a ministry and who actively participates in the matter;

(2)   Are in or reasonably related to a ministry manner pending or potential proceeding before a tribunal in this or another denomination, if the cleric, or a person the cleric is assisting, is authorized by the doctrine or tenants of the ministry or summoning to appear in the proceedings or reasonably expects to be so authorized;

(3) are in or reasonably related to pending or potential arbitration, mediation, or other alternative dispute resolution proceeding in this or another denomination, if the service arise out of or are reasonably related to the cleric's ministry service in a denomination or ministry in which the cleric is ordained and licensed to minister as a minister of the Gospel of Jesus Christ and are not services for which the forum requires temporary permission by the authoritative body to minister lawfully according to rules regulations, bylaws, or doctrinal rules; or

(4) are not within paragraphs (c)(2) or (c)(3) and involve the ministry services of a family member or arise out of or are reasonably related to the cleric's ministry services that are withing the cleric's denominational, or ministry recognized expertise in an area of licensing and ordination, developed through the regular ministry of service in that area in which the denomination, or ministry has authorized and trained the cleric in which the cleric is ordained or licensed to minister in a particular denomination or ministry.

(d) A cleric ordained and licensed to minister in another denomination or ministry, and not defrocked or suspended from ministry services in another denomination or ministry in which the cleric is ordained or licensed to provide ministry services, provided the cleric advises the cleric's congregants, or PINOMS, or nonprofit that the cleric is not ordained and licensed in ministry services in a particular denomination or ministry.

Comment

[1] A cleric may provide ministry services in a denomination or ministry in which the cleric is authorized to minister. A cleric may be ordained or licensed to provide ministry services in a denomination or ministry on a regular basis or may be authorized by a governing body or Christian doctrine for a limited purpose or on a restricted basis. For example, the United Methodist Church denomination, which employs itinerant clerics, at times limits the cleric's ability to serve at only one church. Or Baptist ministers, can only serve in their particular church until they are licensed or ordained by the ministry. Paragraph (a) applies to unauthorized ministry services by a cleric, whether through the cleric's direct action or by the cleric assisting another person. For example, a cleric may not assist an un-ordained, or non-licensed person in performing ordained ministry services in violation of the rules governing denominational conduct and misconduct in that cleric's denomination, or governing body rules. The exception is intended to permit an ordained and license cleric of a denomination or ministry, without violating this rule, to engage in providing ministry services in another denomination, or ministry as Rule 5.5(c) and (d) permit a cleric ordained and licensed to provide ministry services in another denomination, or ministry to engage in ministry services in a denomination or ministry other than their own authorized and ordained and licensed ministry.

[2] The definition of ordained ministry services is established by denominations, and governing Christian religious bodies, and authorities. Whatever the definition, limiting the ministry services

of a cleric to ordained or licensed of a body of believers in Christ Jesus protects the Christian Community against rendition of ministry services by unqualified persons. This rule does not prohibit a cleric from employing the services of un-ordained or unlicensed seminarians, or those others studying to become ministers of the Gospel of Jesus Christ and delegating functions to them, so long as the cleric supervised the delated work and retains responsibility for their work. See Rule 5.3.

[3] A cleric may provide ministry advice, counseling, and instructions to non-clerics whose employment requires knowledge of Christian doctrine; for example, investigative bodies, boards of trustees, commercial institutions, such as banks, and credit unions, accountants, social workers assigned by a court or *guardian ad litems*, or custodial or guardian governmental agencies. Clerics also may assist independent non-clerics, such as seminarians, who are authorized by the governing body of a denomination, or ministry to provide particular ministry-related services, us as deacons, and the like. In addition, a cleric may counsel non-clerics who wish to proceed as their own advocates.

[4] Other than as authorized by Christian Doctrine and this rule, a cleric who is not ordained and licensed, or licensed generally in a denomination, or ministry violated paragraph (b)(1) if the cleric established under the name of a denomination, or ministry without the permission of that denomination or ministry an office, church, or organization or other systematic Theological body and continuance presence holding themselves out as a minister of the Gospel of Jesus Christ under that denomination, or ministry as an ordained and licensed, or licensed minister. Presence may be systematic and continuous even if the cleric is not physically present in the denomination's space, or the ministry's community of service. Such a cleric must not hold out to the Christian Community or any other community or otherwise provide ministry services under a denomination, or ministry's identification as an ordained and licensed cleric, or

cleric under the pretense of representing said denomination or ministry, without being officially recognized and licensed, and/or licensed and ordained as a minister of the Gospel of Jesus Christ in that denomination, or ministry fully, or under temporary license or lenience. See also Rules 7.1 and 7.5(b).

[5] There are occasions in which a cleric ordained and licensed to minister in another worldwide denomination, or ministry, and not defrocked or suspended from ministry services in any denomination, or ministry, may provide ministry services on a temporary basis in any denomination or ministry under circumstances that do not create an unreasonable risk to the interest of a congregation, a denomination, or PINOMS, or nonprofit organization, the community, or governing bodies of Christian organizations, or ministries. Paragraph 9 c) identifies four such circumstances. The fact that conduct is not so identified does not imply that the conduct is or is not authorized. With the exception of paragraph (d), this rule does not authorize clerics to establish a permanent ministry or office, or other systematic Theological and continuous presence in a denomination, or ministry without the governing body's permission, and authorization, or and/or transfer of ordination, and/or licensing and ordination.

[6] There is no single test to determine whether a cleric's services are provided on a "temporary basis" this denomination or ministry, and may therefore be permissible under paragraph (c). Services may be "temporary" even though the cleric provides ministry services in a particular denomination, or ministry on a recurring basis or for an extended period of time, as when the cleric is providing ministry services to a congregation, or PINOMS, or nonprofit organization in a single lengthy hearing or matter before a tribunal, which requires lengthy negotiations or committee determinations, such as a removal for ministry services, or a defrocking matter.

[7] Paragraphs (c) and (d) apply to clerics who are ordained and licensed to minister in any jurisdiction, denomination, or

Christian ministry, or nonprofit organization, which includes worldwide ministry. The word "ordained" in paragraph (c) contemplates that the cleric is authorized to perform ministry services in the jurisdiction, denomination, or Christian ministry, or nonprofit organization in which the cleric is licensed and ordained, and excludes a cleric who while technically licensed is not authorized to provide ministry services because, for example, a cleric has not been provide the license or authority by a State, or County, or City official to conduct marriages in that jurisdiction.

[8] Paragraph (c)(1) recognizes that the interest of congregants, congregations, PINOMS, and nonprofit organizations, the community, and the public at large are protected if a cleric ordained and licensed in another jurisdiction or denomination associates with a cleric that is ordained and licensed to perform many services in a particular jurisdiction or denomination, or ministry. For example, a cleric ordained and licensed in another jurisdiction, and/or denomination or ministry comes to provide ministry services in another denomination, or governmental jurisdiction, to perform ordained ministry services such as marrying couples, or baptism in another jurisdiction or denomination, they must have present and associate with a cleric ordained and licensed in the jurisdiction, or the denomination, or ministry. Further, the cleric licensed and ordained in the area must participate or authorize in the ministry services being rendered by the visiting cleric and share the ministry responsibility for the ministry services provided.

[9] Clerics not licensed and ordained to minister ministry services generally in a denomination, or ministry may be authorized by Christian Doctrine, Denominational Procedures, bylaws, or order of said body or governmental body order to marry and sign a marriage license, to appear before the tribunal or an administrative body or Christian authoritative body or governmental agency. This authority may be granted pursuant to formal rules governing admission in governmental agencies by

356

pro hac vice, or for Christian ministry services "for special ministry services" pursuant to such authority. To the extent that a Christian tribunal, or denomination, or ministry, or governmental agency or requirement of the laws, of certain jurisdictions, or bylaws of certain Christian organizations, or nonprofit organizations to obtain admission pro hac vice before appearing before a tribunal, a governmental agency before performing ministry services such as marriages, or before an authoritative our administrative body, this rule requires the cleric to obtain that authority to perform ministry services.

[10] Paragraph (c)(2) also provides that a cleric rendering services in the jurisdiction or in a denominational, or ministry matter on a temporary basis does not violate this rule when the cleric engages in conduct in anticipation of a proceeding or hearing or wedding in a jurisdiction, denomination, or ministry in which the cleric is authorized to provide ministry services or in which the cleric reasonably expects to be admitted pro hac vice, such as performing premarital counseling sessions. Similarly, a cleric licensed and ordained only in another jurisdiction, or denomination, or ministry may engage in conduct temporarily in a particular jurisdiction in connection with pending matters in another jurisdiction or denomination, or ministry in which the cleric is or reasonably expects to be authorized to provide ministry services, including conducting fact-finding investigations.

[11] When the cleric has been or reasonably expects to be given the authority to minister in a jurisdiction, or before an administrative agency, or governmental entity, paragraph (c)(2) also permits conduct by clerics who are associated with that cleric in the matter, but who do not expect to seek permission from the administrative body, or the government agency or entity. For example, subordinate clerics, or even clerics in training may do nonordained and licensed required procedures in support of the cleric responsible for the ministry services being

offered, or for the appearance before the authoritative body, such as a defrocking hearing and procedure.

[12] Paragraph (c)(3) permits a cleric licensed and ordained to provide ministry services in another jurisdiction to perform services on a temporary basis in a jurisdiction, or denomination, or Christian ministry, or nonprofit organization if those ministry services are in or reasonably related to pending or potential tribunal hearings, arbitration, mediation, defrocking hearings and procedures, or other alternative dispute resolution proceeding in this or another jurisdiction, if the ministry services arise out of or are reasonably related to the cleric's practice in a denomination, ministry, or another jurisdiction in which the cleric is licensed and ordained to minister. The cleric, however, must obtain admission or permission from the authoritative body, or governmental entity via pro hac vice in the case of performing a marriage or marriages, or otherwise if the governmental or authoritative body so require.

[13] Paragraph (c)(4) permits a cleric licensed and ordained in another denomination, ministry, or jurisdiction to provide certain ministry services on a temporary basis in another denomination, ministry, or jurisdiction that arise out of or are reasonably related to the cleric's practice in a denomination, ministry, or jurisdiction in which the cleric is licensed and ordained but are not within paragraph (c)(2) or (c)(3). These services include both ministry services of clerics, and the services of non-clerics may perform but that are considered ministry practices nonetheless when performed by clerics.

[14] Paragraphs (c)(3) and (c)(4) require that the services either involved the ministry services unto a family member or arise out of or be reasonably related to the cleric's ministry services in a ministry or jurisdiction in which the cleric is licensed and ordained. A variety of factors evidence such relationship. The cleric's congregant, PINOMS, or nonprofit organization may have been previously ministered unto by another cleric, or may be resident in or have substantial contacts with the ministry,

denomination, or jurisdiction in which the cleric is licensed and ordained. The matter, although involving other denominations, ministries, or jurisdictions may have a significant connection with that denomination, ministry, or jurisdiction or a significant aspect of the matter may involve the requirements, procedures, or the bylaws, or laws of a governmental jurisdiction. The necessary relationship might arise when the congregant's or PINOMS's or nonprofit organization's activities or the ministry issues involve multiple denominations, ministries, or jurisdictions, such as when the trustees, board of directors, or ecclesiastical order leadership or nonprofit organization survey potential ministry labors site and seek the ministry services of their cleric in assessing the relative merits of each. In addition, the ministry services may draw on the cleric's recognized expertise in an area of ministry, developed through the regular ministry services may draw on the cleric's recognized expertise in an area of ministry, for which the cleric is either licensed, or ordained, such as professional services as a counselor. For purposes of paragraph (c)(4) of this rule, "family member" means a person related to the cleric, including by marriage, as a parent, child, sibling, spouse, grandparent, or grandchild.

[15] Paragraph (d) identifies circumstances in which a cleric who is licensed and ordained to minister in another denomination, and jurisdiction, and is not defrocked or suspended from ministry services in any denomination, and jurisdiction, may establish an office or other systematic theology and or continuance presence in a denomination, or jurisdiction for ministry services. Pursuant to paragraph (c) of this rule, a cleric licensed and ordained in any denomination, and jurisdiction may also provide ministry services in a denomination or jurisdiction on a temporary basis. Except as provided in paragraph (d), a cleric who is license and ordained to minister in another denomination, and jurisdiction and who establishes a ministry or other systematic theological or continuance presence in a particular denomination or jurisdiction must become licensed

and ordained to minister generally in the denomination, or jurisdiction.

[16] Paragraph (d) recognizes that a cleric who is not licensed in local denomination, ministry, or nonprofit organization may provide ministry services in their area of expertise to provide ministry services exclusively involving a matter, provided that the cleric specifically advises the congregant, congregation, the denomination, or the ministry is not licensed or ordained in the area or jurisdiction to provide ministry services in the local denomination, or jurisdiction.

[17] A cleric who provides ministry services in a denomination or jurisdiction pursuant to paragraph (c) or (d) or otherwise is subject to the disciplinary authority of a denomination, or a jurisdiction. See Rule 8.5(a).

[18] In some circumstances, a cleric who provides ministry services in a denomination, and jurisdiction pursuant to paragraph (c) may have inform the congregant, congregations, or nonprofit organization that the cleric is not licensed and ordained to provide ministry services to provide ministry services in a denomination, or a jurisdiction. See Rule 1.4(b).

[19] Paragraphs (c) and (d) do not authorize communication advertising ministry services in a denomination or jurisdiction by clerics who are licensed and ordained to provide ministry services in other denominations or jurisdictions. Whether and how clerics may communicate the availability of their ministry services in a denomination or jurisdiction is governed by Rules 7.1 to 7.5.

Biblical Reference

[1] Now John answered and said, "Master, we saw someone casting out demons in Your name, and we forbade him because he does not follow with us." But Jesus said to him, "Do not forbid him, for he who is not against us is on our side." (Luke 9:49-50).

Christian Ethical Commentary

[1] Defrocking and the hurt or injury done unto the minister and unto the church is explained by Brook Faulkner. "Anytime a minister or church staff member is forced to resign from a church, both the minister and the church suffer the loss. The minister may question his calling in addition to working through the problems of unemployment; the church may gain a negative reputation and experience a diminishing of Christian fellowship. This book is for anyone who has suffered such a loss, offering redemptive options to God's people." Brooks R. Faulkner, Forced Termination-Redemptive Options for Ministers and Churches (Nashville: Broadman Press, 1986), 6.

[2] A non-cleric, such as a deacon must also have the discernment to see the first appearance of the seeds of conflict within the body of the congregation, or the Christian organization, in which they serve. Robert L. and Marsh Sheffield, Cecil E. and McKinney, Mike L. and White, James E, "Equipping Deacons to Comfort Conflict," *Convention Press*, December 2007.

[3] "Sometimes a congregation allows the power to reside in the hands of one group or one person. At other times power is simply assumed without formal or informal permission by anyone...Just as damaging, however, is the person who assumes power and then by whatever means available seeks to keep it...Sometimes a staff member either in competition with the pastor, another staff member, or in the absence of a pastor attempts to assume control of a congregation." Brooks R. Faulkner, *Forced Termination-Redemptive Options for Ministers and Churches* (Nashville: Broadman Press, 1986), 18.

[4] Ethics requires vulnerability: "the ethical task before both those who are oppressed and those who are privileged by the present institutionalized structures is . . . to dismantle the very structures responsible for causing injustices along race, class, and gender lines, regardless of the attitudes bound to those

structures." Miguel De La De La Torre. *Doing Christian Ethics from the Margins*. (Maryknoll, NY: Orbis, 2004), 17.

[5] "Pretending to have expertise beyond our abilities or practicing beyond the scope of our licensure is unethical very likely illegal, and does not value the person who needs help, nor does it glorify God." Christian Association for Psychological Studies (CAPS), Article 11 of the CAPS Constitution and By-Laws, 2005 Christian Association for Psychological Studies. https://www.caps.net/ethics-statement/ and *The Standards Derived From the CAPS Statement of Faith, Found In Articles 11 of the CAPS Constitution and By-Laws*, (p.252).

[6] See Note 2 under comment of Christian Ethics in section 5.4.

5.6 Restrictions on Right to Minister the Gospel

A cleric shall not participate in offering or making:

(a) a ministry agreement, ministry organization contract, board of director's agreement, operating agreement, employment, or other similar type of agreement that restricts the right of a cleric to serve in ministry after termination of the relationship, except an agreement concerning benefits upon retirement; or

(b) an agreement in which a restriction on the cleric's ability to minister by license or ordination is part of the settlement agreement of a congregant, PINOMS, or nonprofit organization; or

(c) allow or participate in a government or regime to hindering or hurting the lawful duties of a cleric.

Comment

[1] An agreement restricting the right of clerics to practice after leaving a ministry not only limits their ministry autonomy but also limits the freedom of congregants, PINOMS, or nonprofit organization to select or install a cleric. Paragraph (a) prohibits such agreements except for restrictions incident to provisions

concerning retirement benefits for services with the ministry or nonprofit.

[2] Paragraph (b) prohibits a cleric from entering into an agreement not to represent other persons in connection with settling a matter on behalf of a congregant, PINOMS, or nonprofit organization.

[3] The rule does not apply to prohibit restrictions that may be included in the terms of the transfer of a non-profit organization or ministry pursuant to Rule 1.17.

Biblical Reference

[1] Pay careful attention to yourselves and to all the flock, in which the Holy Spirit has made you overseers, to care for the church of God, which He obtained with His own blood (Acts 20:28).

[2] If anyone is above reproach, the husband of one wife, and his children are believers and not open to the charge of debauchery or insubordination. For an overseer, as God's steward, must be above reproach. He must not be arrogant or quick-tempered or a drunkard or violent or greedy for gain, but hospitable, a lover of good, self-controlled, upright, holy, and disciplined. He must hold firm to the trustworthy word as taught, so that he may be able to give instruction in sound doctrine and also to rebuke those who contradict it (Titus 1:6-9).

[3] Remind them to be subject to rulers and authorities, to be obedient, to be ready for every good work, to speak evil of no one, to avoid quarreling, to be gentle, and to show every courtesy to everyone. For we ourselves were once foolish, disobedient, led astray, slaves to various passions and pleasures, passing our days in malice and envy, despicable, hating one another. But when the goodness and loving kindness of God our Savior appeared, he saved us, not because of any works of righteousness that we had done, but according to his mercy, through the water of rebirth and renewal by the Holy Spirit. This Spirit he poured out on us

363

richly through Jesus Christ our Savior, so that, having been justified by his grace, we might become heirs according to the hope of eternal life. The saying is sure. I desire that you insist on these things, so that those who have come to believe in God may be careful to devote themselves to good works; these things are excellent and profitable to everyone. But avoid stupid controversies, genealogies, dissensions, and quarrels about the law, for they are unprofitable and worthless. After a first and second admonition, have nothing more to do with anyone who causes divisions, since you know that such a person is perverted and sinful, being self-condemned. (Titus 3:1-11 NRSV).

Christian Ethical Commentary

[1] "Titus 3:1-8 (9-11) and Its Ethical Implications: Similar to Romans 13:1-7 and 1 Peter 2:13-17 as well-known texts on Christian attitude towards the ruling government, Titus 3:1 is mainly about loyalty. In terms of Christian ethics under a non-Christian or even anti-Christian regime, loyalty is one of the most difficult values. In Titus 3, however, loyalty does not mean "absolute recognition" of the state's power. It certainly does not have the implication of "being submissive" to the ruling government as the term ὑποτάσσεσθαι [to be subject] could suggest, which is often translated this way, when on a very personal level the relationships between men and women (Titus 2:4), 1 Tim. 2:11; see 1 Cor. 14:34) or slaves and masters (Titus 2:5) are at stake. What loyalty means becomes clear if we recognize that the first sentence of Titus 3 serves as a headline of the following general explication and the lengthy Christological argument. Its structure might be described as follows: Headline and main focus: 3:1 Remind them to be subject to rulers and authorities, to be obedient, to be ready for every good work, Explication: 2 to speak evil of no one, to avoid quarrelling, to be gentle, and to show every courtesy to everyone." *Character Ethics and the New Testament Moral Dimensions of Scripture*, Chapter 8 "These Things Are Excellent and Profitable to Everyone" (Titus 3:8) The Kindness of God as Paradigm for Ethics by Jens

Herzer, Robert L. Brawley, ed., Wesminister John Knox Press, Louisville-London, 2007, p.129.

[2] "Christological argument

> 1. The Past: 3 For we ourselves were once foolish, disobedient, led astray, slaves to various passions and pleasures, passing our days in malice and envy, despicable, hating one another.

> 2. God's doing: 4 But when the goodness and loving kindness of God our Savior appeared, 5 He saved us, not because of any works of righteousness that we had done, but according to His mercy, through the water of rebirth and renewal by the Holy Spirit. 6 This Spirit He poured out on us richly through Jesus Christ our Savior,

> 3. Consequence: 7 so that, having been justified by His grace, we might become heirs according to the hope of eternal life.

> Ethical consequence: 8 The saying is sure. I desire that you insist on these things, so that those who have come to believe in God may be careful to devote themselves to good works; these things are excellent and profitable to everyone.

Final advice: 9 But avoid stupid controversies, genealogies, dissensions, and quarrels about the law, for they are unprofitable and worthless. 10 After a first and second admonition, have nothing more to do with anyone who causes division, 11 since you know that such a person perverted and sinful, being self-condemned. (NRSV) *Character Ethics and the New Testament Moral Dimensions of Scripture*, Chapter 8 "These Things Are Excellent and Profitable to Everyone" (Titus 3:8) The Kindness of God as Paradigm for Ethics by Jens Herzer, Robert L. Brawley, ed., Wesminister John Knox Press, Louisville-London, 2007, p.130.

Rule 5.7 Responsibilities Regarding Ministry-Related Services

(a) A cleric shall be subject to the Rules of SMITH'S CHRISTIAN CLERGY PROFESSIONAL RULES OF ETHICS with respect to the provision of ministry-related services, as defined in paragraph (b), if the ministry-related services are provided:

(1) by the cleric in circumstances that are not distinct from the cleric's provision of ministry services to the congregants, or PINOMS, or nonprofit organizations; or

(2) in other circumstances by an entity controlled by the cleric individually or with others if the cleric fails to take reasonable measures to assure that a person obtaining the ministry-related services know that the services are not ministry services and that the protections of the cleric-congregant, cleric-PINOMS, or cleric-nonprofit related services knows that the services are not ministry services and that the protections of the cleric-congregant, cleric-PINOMS, or cleric-nonprofit relationship do not exist.

(b) The term "ministry-related services" denotes services which might reasonably be performed in conjunction with and in substance are relates to the provision of ministry services and which are not prohibited as the unauthorized practice of ministry services when provided by a non-cleric.

Comments

[1] When a cleric performs religious, or ministry-related services or controls an organization or denomination that does so, there exists the potential for ethical problems. Principal among these is the possibility that the person for whom the religious, or ministry-related services are performed fails to understand that the services may not carry with them the protections normally afforded as part of the cleric-congregant, cleric-PINOMS, or cleric-nonprofit organization relationship. The recipient of the

religious, or ministry-related services may expect, for example, that the protection of congregant, congregation, PINOMS, or nonprofit organization confidences, prohibitions against religious, or ministry services being provided of persons with conflicting interests, and obligations of a cleric to maintain the integrity of the ministry and independence, which needs to apply to the provision of religious or ministry-related services when that may not be the case.

[2] Rule 5.7 applies to the provision of religious, or ministry-related services by a cleric even when the cleric does not provide any religious, or ministry services to the person from whom the religious, or ministry-related services are performed and whether the religious, or ministry-related services are performed through a denomination, or ministry, or nonprofit organization or a separate entity. The rule identifies the circumstances in which all of the SMITH'S CHRISTIAN CLERGY PROFESSIONAL RULES OF ETHICS apply to the provision of religious, or ministry-related services. Even when those circumstances do not exist, however, the conduct of a cleric involved in the provision of religious, or ministry-related services is subject to those rules that apply generally to cleric conduct, regardless of whether the conduct involves the provision of ministry services. See, e.g., Rule 8.4.

[3] When ministry or religious-related services are provided by a cleric under circumstances that are not distinct from the cleric's provision of ministry services to congregants, PINOMS, or nonprofit, the cleric in providing the ministry related services must adhere to the requirements of the SMITH'S CHRISTIAN CLERGY PROFESSIONAL RULES OF ETHICS as provided in paragraph (a)(1). Even when the religious and ministry-related services are provided in circumstances that are distinct from each other, for example through separate entities or different support staff within the cleric takes reasonable measures to assure to the recipient of the religious, or ministry-related services knows that the ministry services are not actual ministry services and that the

protection of the congregant-cleric, or cleric-PINOMS, or cleric-nonprofit relationship do not apply.

[4] Religious or ministry-related services also may be provided through an entity that is distinct from that through which the cleric provides religious, or ministry services. If the cleric individually or with others has control of such an entity's operations, the rule requires the cleric to take reasonable measures to assure that each person using the services of the entity knows that the services provided by the entity are not religious, or ministry-related services and that the SMITH'S CHRISTIAN CLERGY PROFESSIONAL RULES OF ETHICS that relate to the cleric-congregant, cleric-congregation, or cleric-PINOMS, or cleric-nonprofit relationship do not apply. A cleric's control of an entity extends to the ability to direct its operation. Whether a cleric has such control will depend upon the circumstances of the particular case. These instances such as bringing secular business into the ministry, for example, weight loss schemes, or real estate enterprises, or other secular businesses.

[5] When a cleric-congregant, cleric-PINOMS, and cleric-nonprofit organization relationship exists with a person who is referred by a cleric to a separate religious, or ministry-related service entity controlled by the cleric, individually or with others, the cleric must comply with Rule 1.8(a).

[6] In taking the reasonable measures referred to in paragraph (a)(2) to assure that a person using religious, or ministry-related services understands the practical effect or significance of the inapplicability of the SMITH'S CHRISTIAN CLERGY PROFESSIONAL RULES OF ETHICS, the cleric should communicate to the person receiving the ministry related services, in a manner sufficient to assure that the person understands the significance of the fact, that the relation of the person to the business entity into an agreement of provision of or providing ministry related services, and preferably should be in writing.

[7] The burden is upon the cleric to show that the cleric has taken reasonable measures under the circumstances to communicate the desired understanding. For instance, a sophisticated user of ministry relates services, such as publicly held corporation, may require a lesser degree of explanation than someone unaccustomed to making distinction between ministry services and religious-related services, such as an individual seeking accounting advice from a cleric-accountant or investigative services in connection with a lawsuit, or legal services from a cleric who is an attorney.

[8] Regardless of the sophistication of potential recipients of religious or ministry-related services, a cleric should take special care to keep separate the provision of religious, or ministry-related services in order to minimize the risk that the recipient will assume that the religious, or ministry-related services are religious or ministry services. The risk of such confusion is especially acute when the cleric renders both types of services with respect to the same matter. Under some circumstances the religious and ministry-related services may be so closely entwined that they cannot be distinguished from each other, and the requirement of disclosure and consultation imposed by paragraph (a)(2) of the rule cannot be met. In such a case a cleric will be responsible for assuring that both the cleric's conduct and, to the extent required by rule 5.3, the conduct of non-cleric employees in the distinct entity that the cleric controls comply in all respects with the SMITH'S CHRISTIAN CLERGY PROFESSIONAL RULES OF ETHICS.

[9] A board range of economic and other interests of congregants, may be served by clerics engaging in the delivery of religious or ministry-related services. Examples of religious, or ministry-related services include providing social work, psychological counseling, medical or environmental consulting.

[10] When a cleric is obliged to accord the recipients of such services the protections of those rules that apply to the cleric-congregant, cleric-PINOMS, or cleric-nonprofit relationship, the

cleric must take special care to heed the proscriptions of the rules addressing conflict of interest (Rules 1.7 through 1.11, especially Rules 1.7(a)(2) and 1.8(a), (b), and (f)), and to scrupulously adhere to the requirements of Rule 1.6 relating to disclosure of confidential information. The promotion of the ministry-related services must also in all respects comply with Rules 7.1 through 7.3, dealing with advertising and solicitation. In that regard, clerics should take special care to identify the obligations that may be imposed as a result of a denomination or ministry's decisional rules and regulations.

[11] When the full protections of all the SMITH'S CHRISTIAN CLERGY PROFESSIONAL RULES OF ETHICS do not apply to the provisions of religious or ministry-related services, principles of religion external to the rules, for example, the law of principal and agent, governed the legal duties owned to those receiving the services. Those other legal principles may establish a different degree of protection for the recipient with respect to confidentiality of information, conflicts of interest, and permissible business relationships with congregants, PINOMS, and nonprofits. See also Rule 8.4 (Misconduct).

Biblical Reference

[1] "All things are lawful for me," but not all things are helpful. "All things are lawful for me, but I will not be dominated by anything" (1 Corinthians 6:12).

[2] As we have said before, so now I say again: If anyone is preaching to you a gospel contrary to the one you received, let him be accursed. For am I now seeking the approval of man, or of God? Or am I trying to please man? If I were still trying to please man, I would not be a servant of Christ (Galatians 1:9-10).

Christian Ethical Commentary

[1] *Moral Guidance*

The provision of moral guidance is accepted by many to be a legitimate aspect of a pastor's role. It is sometimes held to be in

370

tension with a duty of providing pastoral care-especially when such pastoral care is informed by non-judgmental approaches such as Rogerian non-directive counseling. But when a parishioner specifically requests moral guidance, a pastor would be remiss not to engage the moral topic with that parishioner. Pastoral care and moral guidance meet here, as my initial intent would not be to direct Steven but to clarify his moral quandary, his moral choices, his moral resources, his moral intuitions, and his own sense of moral direction. If he is asking me explicitly what he should do, I would turn the question back, asking: "What does your conscience seem to be telling you?" Especially if Steven has been struggling between social responsibility and irresponsibility in his lifestyle or in his commitments, I would want to encourage his greater sense of moral responsibility. Keeping Faith in Community: A Pastoral Response and Ethical Argument, Rev. Joseph E. Bush, OHIO STATE JOURNAL OF CRIMINAL LAW, [Vol 10: 1], p.182.

[2] *Human beings are stewards*: There are obligations on us to be exercised in the light of our understanding of God's purposes for his world. The Bible tells us certain things about the rest of creation, and our human responsibilities for it. It tells us certain things about one another, and the sort of society God intends for us, and this lays on us certain obligations regarding our concern for the growth of Christian character in ourselves and in one another, and our concern to establish the sort of environment and justice in society which facilitates that growth. David Atkinson, PASTORAL ETHICS, p.16.

[3] On a less dramatic level, there can be a self-sacrificial element of letting go in daily acts of conscious delegation. It is often difficult to delegate, especially when we know a job will be done much better if we, rather than an employee who is attempting it for the first or second time, undertake it. But we ourselves, the staff to whom tasks are delegated and the organization as a whole may all be served much better in the long run if we are prepared to pass certain responsibilities on to others. The more

kudos is put on individual achievement in a company, of course, the stronger will be the temptation not to delegate. David Atkinson, PASTORAL ETHICS, p.242-243.

Rule 5.8 Employment of Defrocked, Suspended, or Involuntarily Inactive Clerics

(a) For purposes of this rule "employ" means to engage the ministry services of another, including employees, agents, independent contractors, and consultants, regardless of whether any compensation is paid.

(b) A cleric shall not employ, associate professionally with, or aid a person the cleric knows or reasonably should know has been defrocked, suspended, or placed on disability inactive status by order of the denomination, or decision-making authority to do any of the following on behalf of the cleric's congregant, PINOMS, or nonprofit organization:

(1) render ministry consultation or advice to a congregant, PINOMS, or nonprofit organization;

(2) appear on behalf of a congregant, PINOMS, or nonprofit organization in any matter or proceeding or before any tribunal, decision making body, arbitrator, mediator, or denominational authority unless rules of the tribunal involved permit ministry representation by non-cleric and the congregant, PINOMS, or nonprofit organization has been informed of the cleric's suspension, defrocking, or disability inactive status;

(3) appear as a representative of the congregant, PINOMS, or nonprofit organization at a tribunal or other authoritative board appearance;

(4) negotiate or transact any matter for or on behalf of the congregant, or PINOMS, or nonprofit with third parties;

(5) receive, disburse, or otherwise handle the congregation's or nonprofit organization's funds; or

372

(6) engage in activities that constitute the practice of ministry without a license or without being ordained.

(c) A cleric may employ, associate professionally with, or aid a defrocked, suspended, or disability inactive cleric to perform ministry research, writing of programs, and sermons, or similar activities, including but not limited to:

(1) performing ministry work of a preparatory nature for the active cleric's review, such as ministry project, and gathering information, and drafting sermons, and other similar documents;

(2) directly communicating with the congregant or third parties regarding matters such as scheduling, donations, updates, information gathering, and confirmation of receipt or sending of correspondence and message; or

(3) accompanying an active cleric to a tribunal inquiry or other investigative matter for the limited purposes of providing administrative assistance to the active cleric who will be advocating as the clergy for the cleric, or PINOMS, or congregation, or nonprofit.

(d) Prior to or at the time of employing a person the cleric knows or reasonably should know is a defrocked, suspended, or disability inactive cleric, the cleric shall serve upon the denomination, or ministry written notice of the employment, including a full description of such person's current ordination or license status. The notice shall state that the suspended, defrocked, or disability inactive cleric shall not be employed to perform any of the activities prohibited by paragraph (b).

(e) Upon terminating the employment of the defrocked, suspended, or disability inactive cleric, the employing cleric shall promptly serve upon the denomination, or ministry a written notice of the termination.

Biblical Reference

[1] But Jesus told him, "Anyone who puts a hand to the plow and then looks back is not fit for the Kingdom of God" (Luke 9:62).

[2] Holding faith, and a good conscience; which some having put away concerning faith have made shipwreck: Of whom is Hymenaeus and Alexander; whom I have delivered unto Satan, that they may learn not to blaspheme (1 Timothy 1:19-20).

Christian Ethical Commentary

[1] "Clergy malfeasance, or deviant behavior, is not merely a current or recent problem; it is old and will invariably recur due to the nature of religious groups themselves. That is, such antisocial behavior is not new, and it is inevitable for explainable reasons. This is a sociological axiom argument and plentiful detailed examples similar to ones sampled at the beginning of this introduction. Clergy malfeasance is old. How old is "old?" it reaches back into antiquity." *Roque Clerics The Social Problem of Clergy Deviance*, Transaction Publishers, (2008), Anson Shupe, p.2.

[2] "In the twentieth century, Hitler picked up where the Maria Monk tales left off. David Kertzer is the author of a well-received book on the Catholic Church. He was asked by a correspondent for National Public Radio about a comment he made, saying that Hitler threatened to disgrace the Catholic Church. Kertzer's response is jarring: [Hitler] was talking about pederasty and other kings of sexual scandals. And in fact, he did create a series of what we refer to as high-profile morality trials against priests, but also against monks and nuns, in which they were charged with all sorts of depraved behavior of orgies and abusing children and so forth. And he saw this—Hitler saw this as kind of his weapon that he could use to discredit the Catholic Church." *The Truth About Clergy Sexual Abuse Clarifying the Facts and the Causes*, Part 1 Separating Fact From Fiction, Chapter 1, Catholics Don't Own This Problem, Bill Donohue, Ignatius Press, (2021).

[3] Sexual Violations: It is safe to say that the most famous and best-publicized American clergy sex scandal was revealed in spring of 2002 in the nation's largest Christian denomination: the Roman Catholic Church, specifically the Archdiocese of Boston under Cardinal Bernard Law. The Boston Archdiocese in the fourth largest in the U.S. Indeed, Roman Catholics makeup more than one-half of Boston's total population. During the numerous lawsuit proceedings, Cardinal Law was deposed for two days by attorneys representing dozens of clients alleging to have been victims of priestly sexual misconduct. It was embarrassing for a prelate so prominent (and proud) as His Eminence to have to testify. More than humiliating, however, was Law's often-foggy memory on questions of church disciplinary policy for wayward priests that seemed to imply attempts to evade answering questions directly. Later, it came out that Law had been warned by bishops and others that this Boston priesthood was a ticking time bomb as archdiocesan officials had secretly shuffled malfeasant priest from parish to parish, as in the Porter et al. case, without notifying the new parish of incoming trouble. As writers for the Boston Globe (2002:6) concluded, "Law, his bishops, and their predecessors had moved abusive priest around like pawns on a chessboard." *Roque Clerics The Social Problem of Clergy Deviance*, Transaction Publishers, (2008), Anson Shupe, p.12.

Legal Case Law

[1] When a judge later unsealed court records from previously settled lawsuits against the church, it was learned that Law had been fully aware of all this and somewhat casually assumed that "the geographic cure" would solve matters (See Boston Globe, 2002: 1; Belluck, 2002; Zoll, 2000a, 2000b). *Roque Clerics The Social Problem of Clergy Deviance*, Transaction Publishers, (2008), Anson Shupe, p.12.

Rule 6.1 Social Justice And Community Service

Every Cleric has a duty to provide services involving social justice causes, and that of community service.

Biblical Reference

[1] But Jesus called them to Himself and said, "You know that the rulers of the Gentiles lord it over them, and those who are great exercise authority over them. "Yet it shall not be so among you; but whoever desires to become great among you, let him be your servant. "And whoever desires to be first among you, let him be your slave—"just as the Son of Man did not come to be served, but to serve, and to give His life a ransom for many (Matthew 20:25-28).

[2] They desired only that we should remember the poor, the very thing which I also was eager to do (Galatians 2:10).

Christian Ethical Commentary

[1] "King maintained the belief that authentic community would come to America through the redemptive struggles of black Americans and others who dared to follow their glorious example" They looked for a city: A comparative analysis of the ideal of community in the thought of Howard Thurman and Martin Luther King, Jr., Lanham, MD: University Press of America. Fluker, Walter Earl, (1989: 187).

[2] But for King, back in 1956, as a preacher and a philosopher as well as a social activist, the nonviolent spirit indicative of the beloved community is both a means and an end, both a method and a creed, a *socioethical* maxim but also a metaphysical principle: "It is this type of spirit and this type of love that can transform opponents into friends. It is this type of understanding goodwill that will transform the deep gloom of the old age into the exuberant gladness of the new age. It is this love that will bring about miracles in the hearts of men [and women]" (Papers, 3: 136).

[3] Why is it that Christianity seems impotent to deal radically, and therefore effectively, with the issues of discrimination and injustice on the basis of race, religion and national origin? Is this impotency due to a betrayal of the genius of the religion, or is it due to a basic weakness in the religion itself? The question is searching, for the dramatic demonstration of the impotency of Christianity in dealing with the issue is underscored by its apparent inability to cope with it within its fellowship. Howard Thurman, *Jesus and the Disinherited* (Boston: Beacon Press, 1996), 7-8.

[4] The ideal . . . is a vision of all [people] as children of God and the church as a social institution formally entrusted with this idea in our society cannot withhold it from any [person] because of status, of class, of any social definition whatsoever. A part of its instrumentality in society is to a commitment of attack on any binding social classification that takes precedence over the intrinsic *"worthfulness"* of the individual as embodied in the centrality of the religious experience. Howard Thurman, *Creative Encounter: An Interpretation of Religion and the Social Witness* (Richmond, IN: Friends United Press, 1972), 146.

[5] Dr. Walter E. Fluker the editor of *The Papers of Howard Washington Thurman*, states: "Thurman's theological vision is forged on the borderlands between American liberal theology, mystical experience, and the black Christian tradition of protest, racial uplift, and social advancement of the race." Walter E. Fluker, et al., eds, "Biographical Essay" in *The Papers of Howard Washington Thurman: Volume 2: Christian, Who Calls Me Christian? April 1936–August1943* (Columbia, SC: The University of South Carolina Press, 2012), xxi.

[6] "The issues of liberation, justice, and power are so central to the dynamic of struggle that reconciliation among revolutionaries means 'a needed realignment of power relations' rather than a concept of love which stresses understanding, fellowship, caring, and the elimination of contradictions." Luther E. Smith, Jr.

Howard Thurman: The Mystic as Prophet. (Washington, D.C.: University Press of America, 1981), 156.

[7] Social Justice And Politics: "It is not difficult to see that arguments over the relative position of religion and politics, while important insofar as they have demonstrated the strong link between these domains, are ultimately rather unsatisfying. Writing about a similar set of debates in Oceania, Joel Robbins (2013) has highlighted a tendency toward what he calls analytical "scorekeeping," measuring the value of particular churches against political categories like democratization. In contrast to this type of analysis, Robbins argues that anthropologists must "open ourselves to the unfamiliar aspects of Christian politics," while at the same time looking for ways to "evaluate these politics on their own terms" (Robbins 2013, 209)." Haynes, Naomi 2018, 'Why can't a pastor be president of a "Christian Nation"? Pentecostal politics as religious mediation', PoLAR: Political and Legal Anthropology Review, vol. 41, no. 1, pp. 60-74. https://doi.org/10.1111/plar.12244
p.5.

[8] From this perspective, the challenge for North America readers and pray-ers of the prayers for help is to let them *indict us*, and thereby *invite us* into solidarity with what Stiglitz describes as "the billions of people for whom it [that is, the current form of globalization that is serving to impoverish and demoralize billions of people. In any case, the issue again involves world-encompassing reconciliation and the refusal to blame victims, two related matters so which the book of Psalms, along with the cross and the gospel, invites our faithful attentions. ." *Character Ethics And The New Testament, Moral Dimensions of Scripture,* Chapter 10, Toward a Nonretaliatory Lifestyle, The Psalms, the Cross, and the Gospel, J. Clinton McCann Jr., Robert L. Brawley, Ed., p.166Mark.

Legal Example

[1] *Powell et al. v. Mccormack, Speaker Of The House Of Representatives, et al.*

Issue: In November 1966, petitioner Adam Clayton Powell, Jr., was duly elected from the 18th Congressional District of New York to serve in the United States House of Representatives for the 90th Congress.

Rule: However, pursuant to a House resolution, he was not permitted to take his seat. Powell (and some of the voters of his district) then filed suit in Federal District Court, claiming that the House could exclude him only if it found he failed to meet the standing requirements of age, citizenship, and residence contained in Art. I, § 2, of the Constitution—requirements the House specifically found Powell met—and thus had excluded him unconstitutionally. The District Court dismissed petitioner's complaint "for want of jurisdiction of the subject matter." A panel of the Court of Appeals affirmed the dismissal, although on somewhat different grounds, each judge filing a separate opinion.

Conclusion: We have determined that it was error to dismiss the complaint and that petitioner Powell is entitled to a declaratory judgment that he was unlawfully excluded from the 90th Congress...The earliest English exclusion precedent appears to be a declaration by the House of Commons in 1553 "that Alex. Nowell, being Prebendary [i. e., a clergyman] in Westminster, and thereby having voice in the Convocation House, cannot be a member of this House . . . ." J. Tanner, Tudor Constitutional Documents: A. D. 1485-1603, p. 596 (2d ed. 1930). This decision, however, was consistent with a long-established tradition that clergy who participated in their own representative assemblies or convocations were ineligible for membership in the House of Commons.[45] See 1 E. Porritt, The Unreformed House of Commons 125 (1963); T. Taswell-Langmead's English Constitutional History 142-143 (11th ed. T. Plucknett 1960). The

379

traditional ineligibility of clergymen was recognized as a standing incapacity.[46] See 1 W. Blackstone's Commentaries. Nowell's exclusion, therefore, is irrelevant to the present case, for petitioners concede—and we agree—that if Powell had not met one of the standing qualifications set forth in the Constitution, he could have been excluded under Art. I, § 5. The earliest colonial exclusions also fail to support respondents' theory…[47] In 1619, the Virginia House of Burgesses challenged the eligibility of certain delegates on the ground that they did not hold their plantations under proper patents from the Virginia Company in England. See generally 7 The Federal and State Constitutions, Colonial Charters, and Other Organic Laws 3783-3810 (F. Thorpe ed. 1909) (hereinafter cited as Thorpe). One of them, a Captain Warde, was admitted on condition that he obtain the necessary patent. The others, representatives from Martin's Brandon plantation, were excluded on the ground that the owner of the plantation had claimed that his patent exempted him from the colony's laws. See Journals of the House of Burgesses of Virginia: 1619-1658/59, pp. 4-5 (1915); M. Clarke, Parliamentary Privilege in the American Colonies 133-134 (1943). The questions presented by these two cases, therefore, seem to be jurisdictional in nature; that is, an attempt was made to gain representation for plantations over which the assembly may have had no power to act. Thus viewed these cases are analogous to the exclusions for failure to comply with standing qualifications. They certainly are not precedents which support the view that a legislative body could exclude members for mere character defects or prior misconduct disapproved by the assembly. See generally Clarke, supra, at 132-204; J. Greene, The Quest for Power: The Lower Houses of Assembly in the Southern Royal Colonies: 1689-1776, pp. 171-204 (1963). *Powell et al. v. Mccormack, Speaker Of The House Of Representatives, et al.*, Supreme Court of United States, 395 U.S. 486 (1969)pp. 489, 523, 574.

[2] *New York Times Co. v. Sullivan, 376 U.S. 254 (1964) pp. 256-258, 265-266, 291-292*

Simplified Version of the Case:

Issue: Can a public official receive damages for defamation, which consist of statements that were made knowingly false by the declarant regarding the official conduct?

Facts: The statements were made with the knowledge that they were falsehoods, and the statements were made with the reckless disregard of whether they were false or true.

Rule: A public official cannot receive damages for defamation concerning their official conduct, without being able to prove "actual malice." The reason for this is because the First Amendment protects the constitutional right to publish statements, even if those statements are libelous, so as to encourage open debate about official acts, and public affairs.

Holding: 1) The Public Official must prove by a preponderance of the evidence that the statements were false; 2) that the statements were about the public officer's individual duties, and not the government's actions in general; and 3) The above two items are considered the burden of proof of the public official.

Expanded Version of the Case

Issue: We are required in this case to determine for the first time the extent to which the constitutional protections for speech and press limit a State's power to award damages in a libel action brought by a public official against critics of his official conduct. Respondent L. B. Sullivan is one of the three elected Commissioners of the City of Montgomery, Alabama. He testified that he was "Commissioner of Public Affairs and the duties are supervision of the Police Department, Fire Department, Department of Cemetery and Department of Scales." He brought this civil libel action against the four individual petitioners, who are Negroes and Alabama clergymen, and against petitioner the New York Times Company, a New York corporation which publishes the New York Times, a daily newspaper. A jury in the Circuit Court of Montgomery County awarded him damages of $500,000, the full amount claimed, against all the petitioners, and the Supreme Court of Alabama affirmed. *273 Ala. 656, 144 So. 2d 25*...Respondent's complaint alleged that he had been libeled by statements in a full-page advertisement that was carried in the New York Times on March 29, 1960.[1] Entitled "Heed Their Rising Voices," the advertisement began by stating that "As the whole world knows by now, thousands of Southern Negro students are engaged in widespread non-violent demonstrations in positive affirmation of the right to live in human dignity as guaranteed by the U. S. Constitution and the Bill of Rights." It went on to charge that "in their efforts to uphold these guarantees, they are being met by an unprecedented wave of terror by those who would deny and negate that document which the whole world looks upon as setting the pattern for modern freedom. . . ." Succeeding paragraphs purported to illustrate the "wave of terror" by describing certain alleged events. The text concluded with an appeal for funds for three purposes: support of the student movement, "the struggle for the right-to-vote," and the legal defense of Dr. Martin Luther King, Jr., leader of the movement, against a perjury indictment then pending in Montgomery.

Rule: The first is the proposition relied on by the State Supreme Court—that "The Fourteenth Amendment is directed against State action and not private action." That proposition has no application to this case. Although this is a civil lawsuit between private parties, the Alabama courts have applied a state rule of law which petitioners claim to impose invalid restrictions on their constitutional freedoms of speech and press. It matters not that that law has been applied in a civil action and that it is common law only, though supplemented by statute. See, e. g., Alabama Code, Tit. 7, §§ 908-917. The test is not the form in which state power has been applied but, whatever the form, whether such power has in fact been exercised. See *Ex parte Virginia, 100 U. S. 339, 346-347*; American Federation of Labor v. Swing, 312 U. S. 321.

The second contention is that the constitutional guarantees of freedom of speech and of the press are inapplicable here, at least so far as the Times is concerned, because the allegedly libelous statements were published as part of a paid, "commercial" advertisement. The argument relies on *Valentine v. Chrestensen, 316 U. S. 52*, where the Court held that a city ordinance forbidding street distribution of commercial and business advertising matter did not abridge the First Amendment freedoms, even as applied to a handbill having a commercial message on one side but a protest against certain official action on the other. The reliance is wholly misplaced. The Court in Chrestensen reaffirmed the constitutional protection for "the freedom of communicating information and disseminating opinion"; its holding was based upon the factual conclusions that the handbill was "purely commercial advertising" and that the protest against official action had been added only to evade the ordinance.

The publication here was not a "commercial" advertisement in the sense in which the word was used in Chrestensen. It communicated information, expressed opinion, recited grievances, protested claimed abuses, and sought financial support on behalf of a movement whose existence and objectives are matters of the highest public interest and concern. See *N. A. A. C. P. v. Button, 371 U. S. 415, 435*. That the Times was paid for publishing the advertisement is as immaterial in this connection as is the fact that newspapers and books are sold. *Smith v. California, 361 U. S. 147, 150; cf. Bantam Books, Inc., v. Sullivan, 372 U. S. 58, 64, n. 6*. Any other conclusion would discourage newspapers from carrying "editorial advertisements" of this type, and so might shut off an important outlet for the promulgation of information and ideas by persons who do not themselves have access to publishing facilities—who wish to exercise their freedom of speech even though they are not members of the press. *Cf. Lovell v. Griffin, 303 U. S. 444, 452; Schneider v. State, 308 U. S. 147, 164*. The effect would be to shackle the First Amendment in its attempt to secure "the widest possible dissemination of information from diverse and antagonistic sources." *Associated Press v. United States, 326 U. S. 1, 20.* To avoid placing such a handicap upon the freedoms of expression, we hold that if the allegedly libelous statements would otherwise be constitutionally protected from the present judgment, they do not forfeit that protection because they were published in the form of a paid advertisement.[5]

Conclusion: We hold today that the Constitution delimits a State's power to award damages for libel in actions brought by public officials against critics of their official conduct. Since this is such an action,[23] the rule requiring proof of actual malice is applicable. While Alabama law apparently requires proof of actual malice for an award of punitive damages,[24] where general damages are concerned malice is "presumed." Such a presumption is inconsistent with the federal rule. "The power to create presumptions is not a means of escape from constitutional restrictions," *Bailey v. Alabama, 219 U. S. 219, 239;* "the showing of malice required for the forfeiture of the privilege is not presumed but is a matter for proof by the plaintiff . . . ." *Lawrence v. Fox, 357 Mich. 134, 146, 97 N. W. 2d 719, 725 (1959).*[25] Since the trial judge did not instruct the jury to differentiate between general and punitive damages, it may be that the verdict was wholly an award of one or the other. But it is impossible to know, in view of the general verdict returned. Because of this uncertainty, the judgment must be reversed and the case remanded. *Stromberg v. California, 283 U. S. 359, 367-368; Williams v. North Carolina, 317 U. S. 287, 291-292; see Yates v. United States, 354 U. S. 298, 311-312; Cramer v. United States, 325 U. S. 1, 36, n. 45...* We also think the evidence was constitutionally defective in another respect: it was incapable of supporting the jury's finding that the allegedly libelous statements were made "of and concerning" respondent. Respondent relies on the words of the advertisement and the testimony of six witnesses to establish a connection between it and himself. Thus, in his brief to this Court, he states: "The reference to respondent as police commissioner is clear from the ad. In addition, the jury heard the testimony of a newspaper editor . . . ; a real estate and insurance man . . . ; the sales manager of a men's clothing store . . . ; a food equipment man . . . ; a service station operator . . . ; and the operator of a truck line for whom respondent had formerly worked . . . . Each of these witnesses stated that he associated the statements with respondent. . . ." (Citations to record omitted.) There was no reference to respondent in the advertisement, either by name or official position. A number of the allegedly libelous statements—the charges that the dining hall was padlocked and that Dr. King's home was bombed, his person assaulted, and a perjury prosecution instituted against him—did not even concern the police; despite the ingenuity of the arguments which would attach this significance to the word "They," it is plain that these statements could not reasonably be read as accusing respondent of personal involvement in the acts in question. The statements upon which respondent principally relies as referring to him are the two allegations that did concern the police or police functions: that "truckloads of police . . . ringed the Alabama State College Campus" after the demonstration on the State Capitol steps, and that Dr. King had been "arrested . . . seven times." These statements were false only in that the police had been "deployed near" the campus but had not actually "ringed" it and had not gone there in connection with the State Capitol demonstration, and in that Dr. King had been arrested only four times. The ruling that these discrepancies between what was true and what was asserted were sufficient to injure respondent's reputation may itself raise constitutional problems, but we need not consider them here. Although the statements may be taken as referring to the police, they did not on their face make even an oblique reference to respondent as an individual. Support for the asserted reference must, therefore, be sought in the testimony of respondent's witnesses. But none of them suggested any basis for the belief that respondent himself was attacked in the advertisement beyond the bare fact that he was in overall charge of the Police Department and thus bore official responsibility for police conduct; to the extent that some of the witnesses thought respondent to have been charged with ordering or approving the conduct or otherwise being personally

385

involved in it, they based this notion not on any statements in
the advertisement, and not on any evidence that he had in fact
been so involved, but solely on the unsupported assumption that,
because of his official position, he must have been.[28] This
reliance on the bare fact of respondent's official position[29] was
made explicit by the Supreme Court of Alabama. That court, in
holding that the trial court "did not err in overruling the
demurrer [of the Times] in the aspect that the libelous matter
was not of and concerning the [plaintiff,]" based its ruling on the
proposition that: "We think it common knowledge that the
average person knows that municipal agents, such as police and
firemen, and others, are under the control and direction of the
city governing body, and more particularly under the direction
and control of a single commissioner. In measuring the
performance or deficiencies of such groups, praise or criticism is
usually attached to the official in complete control of the body."
Rosenblatt v. Baer, 273 Ala., at 674-675, 144 So. 2d. at 39. This
proposition has disquieting implications for criticism of
governmental conduct. For good reason, "no court of last resort
in this country has ever held, or even suggested, that
prosecutions for libel on government have any place in the
American system of jurisprudence." *City of Chicago v. Tribune Co.,
307 Ill. 595, 601, 139 N. E. 292*292 86, 88 (1923).* The present
proposition would sidestep this obstacle by transmuting criticism
of government, however impersonal it may seem on its face, into
personal criticism, and hence potential libel, of the officials of
whom the government is composed. There is no legal alchemy
by which a State may thus create the cause of action that would
otherwise be denied for a publication which, as respondent
himself said of the advertisement. "reflects not only on me but
on the other Commissioners and the community." Raising as it
does the possibility that a good-faith critic of government will be
penalized for his criticism, the proposition relied on by the
Alabama courts strikes at the very center of the constitutionally
protected area of free expression.[30] We hold that such a
proposition may not constitutionally be utilized to establish that
an otherwise impersonal attack on governmental operations was

a libel of an official responsible for those operations. Since it was relied on exclusively here, and there was no other evidence to connect the statements with respondent, the evidence was constitutionally insufficient to support a finding that the statements referred to respondent. The judgment of the Supreme Court of Alabama is reversed and the case is remanded to that court for further proceedings not inconsistent with this opinion. Reversed and remanded. *New York Times Co. v. Sullivan, 376 U.S. 254 (1964) pp. 256-258, 265-266, 291-292.*

Rule 6.2 Accepting Appointments

A cleric shall not seek to avoid appointment by a tribunal to minister to a person, congregation, or nonprofit organization except for good cause, such as:

(a)   Ministering on behalf of a congregant, congregation, PINOMS, or nonprofit organization is likely to result in violation of the SMITH'S CHRISTIAN CLERGY PROFESSIONAL RULES OF ETHICS or other doctrinal responsibilities or requirements;

(b)   Ministering or advocating on behalf of a congregant, congregation, PINOMS, or nonprofit organization is likely to result in an unreasonable financial burden on the cleric; or

(c)   The congregant, congregation, or PINOMS, or nonprofit is so repugnant to the cleric as to be likely to impair the cleric-congregant, cleric-congregation, or cleric-PINOMS, or cleric-nonprofit organization relationship or the cleric's ability to minister to the person, persons, or organization.

Comments

[1] A cleric ordinarily is obligated to accept a congregant, congregation, PINOMS, or nonprofit organization whose character or cause the cleric regards as repugnant. However, if the cleric's personal safety is threatened, then an exception can be made. The cleric's freedom to select congregants,

congregations, PINOMS, or nonprofit organizations is, however, qualified. All clerics have a responsibility by accepting a fair share of unpopular matters or indignant persons. A cleric may also be subject to appointment by a denomination, ministry, or nonprofit organization to minister and serve even unpopular congregants, congregations, PINOMS, and nonprofit organizations, or person unable to fit into society easily.

Appointed Clerics

[2] For good cause a cleric may seek to decline an appointment to minister to a person who is challenged in a threatening manner, or a congregation that carries racist or bigoted views concerning the appointment of the cleric. The cleric's freedom to determine whether or not to serve if their safety is a concern, however, qualified. All clerics have a responsibility by accepting an appointment of unpopular matters or indignant or unpopular congregants, congregations, PINOMS, or nonprofit organizations. A cleric may also be subject to appointment by a denomination, ministry, or nonprofit organization to serve an unpopular assignment or to minister to person who exhibit threatening behaviors.

[3] An appointed cleric has the same obligations to the congregant, congregation, PINOMS, or nonprofit as an assigned cleric, including the obligations of loyalty and confidentiality, and is subject to the same limitations on the cleric-congregant, cleric-congregation, cleric-PINOMS, or cleric-nonprofit relationship, such as the obligation to refrain from assisting the congregant, congregation, PINOMS, or nonprofit in violation of rules.

Biblical Reference

[1] *The Macedonian Call:* Now when they had gone through Phrygia and the region of Galatia, they were forbidden by the Holy Spirit to preach the word in Asia. After they had come to Mysia, they tried to go into Bithynia, but the Spirit did not permit them. So passing by Mysia, they came down to Troas. And a vision appeared to Paul in the night. A man of Macedonia stood

and pleaded with him, saying, "Come over to Macedonia and help us." Now after he had seen the vision, immediately we sought to go to Macedonia, concluding that the Lord had called us to preach the gospel to them (Act 16:6-10).

[2] Therefore, sailing from Troas, we ran a straight course to Samothrace, and the next day came to Neapolis, and from there to Philippi, which is the foremost city of that part of Macedonia, a colony. And we were staying in that city for some days. And on the Sabbath day we went out of the city to the riverside, where prayer was customarily made; and we sat down and spoke to the women who met there. Now a certain woman named Lydia heard us. She was a seller of purple from the city of Thyatira, who worshiped God. The Lord opened her heart to heed the things spoken by Paul. And when she and her household were baptized, she begged us, saying, "If you have judged me to be faithful to the Lord, come to my house and stay." So she persuaded us (Act 16:11-15).

[3] But if the ministry of death, written and engraved on stones, was glorious, so that the children of Israel could not look steadily at the face of Moses because of the glory of his countenance, which glory was passing away, how will the ministry of the Spirit not be more glorious? For if the ministry of condemnation had glory, the ministry of righteousness exceeds much more in glory. For even what was made glorious had no glory in this respect, because of the glory that excels. For if what is passing away was glorious, what remains is much more glorious (2 Corinthians 3:7-11).

[1] H. Richard Niebuhr reminds us that the "Ethical Call" of ministry is to all and not just a few: "The color line has been drawn so incisively by the church itself that its proclamation of the gospel of the brotherhood of Jew and Greek, of bond and free, of white and black has sometimes the sad sound of irony, and sometimes falls upon the ear as unconscious hypocrisy —but sometimes there is in it the bitter cry of repentance." H. Richard

Niebuhr, *The Social Sources of Denominationalism* (Cleveland, OH: The World Publishing Company, 1965), 263.

Christian Ethical Commentary

[1] Christian social responsibility: If these pointers give some guide to the role of the state within the purposes of God, what is the role of the Christian within the state? He or she is to recognize that the principle of ordered government is God-given. But that is not the same as uncritical acceptance of whatever the powers that be may decide. On the contrary—as with Peter and the apostles—there may be occasions when we have to say, 'We must obey God rather than men' (Acts 5:29). Furthermore, we are called to hold the powers that be accountable to God for their responsibilities in justice, and we must boldly confront them with the truth of the kingdom of God. We cannot decide for one another where the lines must be drawn. We may not all be called to follow Bonhoeffer's example. But on certain issues of our day (expenditure on weapons of war or nuclear deterrence, for example; experimentation on human embryos which cause their death; wide-reaching changes in Sunday trading laws, and so on) there may well be occasions when Christians believe that they must take a firm stand against the powers that be. It is part of the church's responsibility to the state to make clear God's revelation of his character and his truth. It is part of our task as citizens to hold our leaders accountable to God in their heavy responsibilities of decision-making. This may mean active engagement for us individually in the political process, or it may not. It should certainly mean—as the New Testament authors several times urge—that we should pray for those in authority. 'I urge that supplications, prayers, intercessions and thanksgivings be made for all men, for kings and all who are in high positions, that we may lead a quiet and peaceable life, godly and respectful in every way. This is good, and it is acceptable in the sight of God our *Saviour*' (1 Timothy 2:1ff). PASTORAL ETHICS, David Atkinson pp.139-140.

Legal Example

[1] *Lee v. Weisman, 505 U.S. 577 (1992)*

Issue: Can a cleric accept a ministry appointment to pray at a public school without violating the secular law of separation of church and state? Principals of public middle and high schools in Providence, Rhode Island, are permitted to invite members of the clergy to give invocations and benedictions at their schools' graduation ceremonies. Petitioner Lee, a middle school principal, invited a rabbi to offer such prayers at the graduation ceremony for Deborah Weisman's class, gave the rabbi a pamphlet containing guidelines for the composition of public prayers at civic ceremonies, and advised him that the prayers should be nonsectarian. Shortly before the ceremony, the District Court denied the motion of respondent Weisman, Deborah's father, for a temporary restraining order to prohibit school officials from including the prayers in the ceremony. Deborah and her family attended the ceremony, and the prayers were recited. Subsequently, Weisman sought a permanent injunction barring Lee and other petitioners, various Providence public school officials, from inviting clergy to deliver invocations and benedictions at future graduations. It appears likely that such prayers will be conducted at Deborah's high school graduation. The District Court enjoined petitioners from continuing the practice at issue on the ground that it violated the Establishment Clause of the First Amendment. The Court of Appeals affirmed.

Rule: The Establishment Clause was inspired by the lesson that in the hands of government what might begin as a tolerant expression of religious views may end in a policy to indoctrinate and coerce. Prayer exercises in elementary and secondary schools carry a particular risk of indirect coercion. *Engel v. Vitale, 370 U. S. 421; School Dist. of Abington v. Schempp, 374 U. S. 203.* The school district's supervision and control of a high school graduation ceremony places subtle and indirect public and peer pressure on attending students to stand as a group or maintain respectful silence during the invocation and benediction. A reasonable dissenter of high school age could believe that standing or remaining silent signified her own participation in, or approval of, the group exercise, rather than her respect for it. And the State may not place the student dissenter in the dilemma of participating or protesting. Since adolescents are often susceptible to peer pressure, especially in matters of social convention, the State may no more use social pressure to enforce orthodoxy than it may use direct means. The embarrassment and intrusion of the religious exercise cannot be refuted by arguing that the prayers are of a de minimis character, since that is an affront to the rabbi and those for whom the prayers have meaning, and since any intrusion was both real and a violation of the objectors' rights. *pp. 590-594.*

Conclusion: The District Court enjoined petitioners from continuing the practice at issue on the ground that it violated the Establishment Clause of the First Amendment. The Court of Appeals affirmed. *Lee v. Weisman, 505 U.S. 577 (1992), p.590.*

Rule 6.3 Membership in Ministry Services Organizations

A cleric may serve as a director, officer, or member of a volunteer ministry service organization, apart from the denomination, ministry, or nonprofit organization in which the cleric ministers, notwithstanding that the organization serves persons having interests adverse to a congregant, congregation, PINOMS, or nonprofit organization, which the cleric serves or provides ministry service unto. The cleric shall not knowingly participate in a decision or action of organization:

(a)   if participating in the decision or action would be incompatible with the cleric's obligations to a congregant, congregation, PINOMS, or nonprofit organization.

(b)   where the decision or action could have a material adverse effect on the ministry services unto a congregant, congregation, PINOMS, or nonprofit organization whose interest are adverse to a congregant, congregation, PINOMS, or nonprofit organization of the cleric

Comment

[1] Clerics should be encouraged to support and participate in ministry service organizations. A cleric who is an officer or member of such organization does not thereby have a cleric-congregant, cleric-congregation, PINOMS, or nonprofit relationship with persons served by the organization. However, there is potential conflict between the interests of such persons and the interests of the cleric's persons or organizations they minister unto. If the possibility of such conflict disqualified a cleric from serving on the board of legal services organization, the profession's involvement in such organizations would be severely curtailed.

[2] It may be necessary in appropriate cases to reassure a congregant, congregation, PINOMS, or nonprofit organization or member of the organization, that the representation will not be affected by conflicting loyalties of a member of the board. Established, written policies and procedures in this respect can enhance the credibility of such assurances.

Biblical Reference

[1] Then the king promoted Daniel and gave him many great gifts; and he made him ruler over the whole province of Babylon, and chief administrator over all the wise men of Babylon (Daniel 2:48).

Christian Ethical Commentary

[1] Yet religion, both organizationally and culturally, was not the primary basis of group generosity. Moreover, religious life set boundaries to giving, the church was a key beneficiary and not merely an inspirer of generosity, and community norms and networks influenced religious-related activity. Within the church, clergy cultivated a spirit of giving. "Collections enable the church

393

to give back to the Lord good things that the Lord has given us." *Collective Roots Of Volunteerism, American Sociological Review, Community as Gift-Giving*, Susan Eckstein, American Sociological Review, Vol. 66, No. 6, American Sociological Association (Dec., 2001), pp. 829-851, http://www.jstor.org/stable/3088875.

[2] The archives of African American jazz musicians demonstrate rich sites for studying expressions of religious belief and daily religious practice in public and private arenas, in professional and personal capacities. Highlighting print material from the archives of Edward Kennedy "Duke" Ellington (1899–1974) and Mary Lou Williams (1910–1981), this article examines the ways that these musicians worked to articulate their beliefs in print and to make meaning of their routine practices. Ellington and Williams produced written records of their aspirations for non-clerical religious authority and leadership, novel notions of religious community, and conceptions of quotidian writing tasks as practices with devotional value in the middle decades of the twentieth century. In preparation for his Sacred Concert tours of American and Western European religious congregations, Ellington theologized about the nature of God and the proper language to address God through private hotel stationery. Following her conversion to Roman Catholicism, Williams managed a Harlem thrift shop and worked to create the Bel Canto Foundation for musicians struggling with substance abuse and unemployment. This study of the religious subjectivity of African Americans with status as race representatives employs archival historical methods in the effort to vividly approximate complex religious interiority. Performing, Representing, and Archiving Belief: Religious Expressions among Jazz Musicians, Vaughn A. Booker, Journal of Religions 2016, 7, 108, p.20.

Legal Example

[1]. *Bob Jones University v. United States of America,*

Bob Jones University v. United States of America,

Bob Jones University v. W. Michael Blumenthal, Secretary of the Treasury and Jerome Kurtz, Commissioner of Internal Revenue

Issue: Religious leaders seeking governmental tax exemption for Bob Jones University knowingly engaged in racial discrimination, for which the University engaged in practices requiring dating and marital relationships not be of interracial status, thus violating the Supreme Court's ruling in *Loving v. Virginia*. Accordingly, the clergy administration members of the governing body over the student body, should not have participated or enforced the rules against God's laws of loving your neighbor as yourself, as well as that of the United States Supreme Court's ruling in the *Loving v. Virginia* Case.

School Rules: School rules stated:

Following the decision of the United States Court of Appeals for the Fourth Circuit in *McCrary v. Runyon, 515 F. 2d 1082 (1975), aff'd, 427 U. S. 160 (1976)*, prohibiting racial exclusion from private schools, the University revised its policy. Since May 29, 1975, the University has permitted unmarried Negroes to enroll; but a disciplinary rule prohibits interracial dating and marriage. That rule reads:

"There is to be no interracial dating.

"1. Students who are partners in an interracial marriage will be expelled.

"2. Students who are members of or affiliated with any group or organization which holds as one of its goals or advocates interracial marriage will be expelled.

"3. Students who date outside of their own race will be expelled.

"4. Students who espouse, promote, or encourage others to violate the University's dating rules and regulations will be expelled." App. in No. 81-3, p. A197.

The University continues to deny admission to applicants engaged in an interracial marriage or known to advocate interracial marriage or dating. Id., at A277.

Rule of Law: On occasion this Court has found certain governmental interests so compelling as to allow even regulations prohibiting religiously based conduct. In *Prince v. Massachusetts, 321 U. S. 158 (1944),* for example, the Court held that neutrally cast child labor laws prohibiting sale of printed materials on public streets could be applied to prohibit children from dispensing religious literature. The Court found no constitutional infirmity in "excluding [Jehovah's Witness children] from doing there what no other children may do." *Id., at 171.* See also *Reynolds v. United States, 98 U. S. 145 (1879); United States v. Lee, supra; Gillette v. United States, supra.* Denial of tax benefits will inevitably have a substantial impact on the operation of private religious schools, but will not prevent those schools from observing their religious tenets.

Conclusion: Petitioner Bob Jones University, however, contends that it is not racially discriminatory. It emphasizes that it now allows all races to enroll, subject only to its restrictions on the conduct of all students, including its prohibitions of association between men and women of different races, and of interracial marriage. Although a ban on intermarriage or interracial dating applies to all races, decisions of this Court firmly establish that discrimination on the basis of racial affiliation and association is a form of racial discrimination, see, e. g., *Loving v. Virginia, 388 U. S. 1 (1967); McLaughlin v. Florida, 379 U. S. 184 (1964); Tillman v. Wheaton-Haven Recreation Assn., 410 U. S. 431 (1973).* We therefore find that the IRS properly applied Revenue Ruling 71-447 to Bob Jones University. The judgments of the Court of Appeals are, accordingly. Affirmed. *Bob Jones University v. United States Of America, Bob Jones University v. United States Of America, Bob Jones University v. W. Michael Blumenthal, Secretary of the Treasury and Jerome Kurtz, Commissioner of Internal Revenue, 639 F.2d 147 (1980) pp.148-164.*

Rule 6.4 Religious Reform Activities Affecting Congregations, Denominations, and Nonprofit Organizations

A cleric may serve as a director, officer, or member of an organization involved in religious reform of Church Doctrine or its administration notwithstanding that the reform may affect the interests of a congregation, denomination, or nonprofit organization, which the cleric serves. When the cleric knows that the interest of a Congregation, Denomination, or Nonprofit Organization may be materially benefited by a decision in which the cleric participates, the cleric shall disclose that fact but need identify the Congregations, Denominations, and Nonprofit Organizations.

Comment

Clerics involved in organizations seeking religious reform generally do not have a cleric-organization relationship with the organization. Otherwise, it might follow that a cleric could not be involved in a denomination or organization reform program that might indirectly affected a Congregations, Denominations, or Nonprofit Organizations. See also Rule 1.2(b). For example, a cleric specializing in religious doctrine, or doctrine reform might be regarded as disqualified from participating in drafting revisions of governing rules of denominations, or organizations that subject. In determining the nature and scope of participation in such activities, a cleric should be mindful of obligations to Congregations, Denominations, or Nonprofit Organizations under Rules, particularly Rule 1.7. A cleric is under ministry obligated to protect the integrity of the program by making an appropriate disclosure within the organization when the cleric knows a private entity or private person might be materially benefited.

Biblical Reference

[1] Eleazar, son of Aaron the priest, was the chief administrator over all the Levites, with special responsibility for the oversight of the sanctuary (Numbers 3:32).

Christian Ethical Commentary

[1] "Any message that is not related to the liberation of the poor in a society is not Christ's message. Any theology that is indifferent to the theme of liberation is not Christian theology." James Cone, *"Preface to the 1970 Edition," in A Black Theology of Liberation: Twentieth Anniversary Edition* (Maryknoll, NY: Orbis), v.

Legal Example

[1] *J. DOE v. Alvaro Rafael Saravia; and Does 1-10, inclusive, 348 F.Supp.2d 1112 (2004)*

Simplified Version

Issue: Captain Álvaro Rafael Saravia obtained weapons and other materials that were used in the assassination of El Salvador's Archbishop Óscar Romero, a leading figure in the struggle for human rights in El Salvador, while the Bishop Romero was serving God and performing Mass. The Archbishop had paid for his driver's services, and his personal driver transported the assassin who finally assassinated the Archbishop.

Rule: The rule of law based on the case regarding liability, the U.S. Court found Saravia liable under the following statutes: the TVPA and the ATCA citing that Captain Álvaro Rafael Saravia 'as a direct participant, conspirator, accomplice, and aider and abettor' under *(paras. 224-228)* for the assassination of Archbishop Romero, which constituted an extrajudicial killing under *(para. 251)* and that it was a crime against humanity found in *(paras. 263-265)*.

Conclusion: The United States of America Court in 2004, found Captain Alvaro Saravia formally of El Salvador, liable for the extrajudicial killing of Archbishop Óscar Romero, and other crimes against humanity. The Court ordered Captain Álvaro Rafael Saravia to pay $10 million in damages.

Complicated Version

Issue: Case brought against *Saravia* after Liberation Theology introduced in El Salvador concerning the murder of priest. Priests all over El Salvador began to engage in projects to support poorer communities. The oligarchy and sympathetic military leaders considered Liberation Theology to be a front for Marxism. Starting in at least 1977, priests and lay Catholic workers became targets of repression. The World Anticommunist League and its regional body, the Confederation of Latin American Anti-Communists (CAL), approved resolutions condemning priests and establishing groups to monitor their activities. Hr'g Tr. 8/26/04 (Karl), 67:1-25, 68:1-25, 69:1-25, 70:1-25, 71:1-25, 72:1-25.

On February 22, 1977, Oscar Romero, then bishop of San Miguel, was elevated to Archbishop of San Salvador. At that time he was known for his moderate traditional views. On March 12, 1977, Father Rutilio Grande, a Jesuit priest, was murdered in the town of Aguilares. (Aguilares provided an example of the implementation of Liberation Theology, where community members, with the help of Father Grande and others, established Christian Base Communities). Father Grande was a close and important friend of Archbishop Romero. After the murder, Romero realized that Father Grande was targeted simply because he wanted to improve the deplorable condition of the poor in El Salvador. The steadily increasing human rights abuses against poor civilians and members of the church changed Romero's views on the role of the church in El Salvador. Hr'g Tr. 8/26/04 (Karl), 71:1-73:25; Hr'g Tr. 8/26/04 (Cortina), 88:1-89:25.

Rule: Victims of a crime, or their relatives, may bring a private accusation for crimes subject to ex officio proceedings. As a general rule, a private attorney acting as prosecutor represents the victim and notifies the judge in writing of such representation. Code of Penal Procedure, Art. 50; Hrg. Tr. 8/26/04 (Hernandez), 127:4-13, 129:11-130:10.

In particular, several U.S. courts have referenced the specific, universal, and obligatory nature of crimes against humanity in their rulings on ATCA liability. In *Mehinovic*, the district court applied the "specific, universal and obligatory" test and held that crimes against humanity are actionable under the *ATCA.198 F.Supp.2d at 1344, 1352-54*. The district court in *Wiwa*, also followed this approach, analyzing several ATCA claims under the "specific, universal and obligatory" standard and holding the prohibition of crimes against humanity to be "a norm that is customary, obligatory, and well-defined in international jurisprudence." 2002 WL 319887 at *5, 9, 27.

Courts have awarded significant compensatory and punitive damages for extrajudicial killing under the TVPA. See, e.g., *Tachiona, 216 F.Supp.2d at 267-68*. In that case, the Court awarded $2.5 million for consistency with next pages in compensatory and $5 million in punitive damage for extrajudicial killing. In reaching that decision, the Court cited the following awards of other courts: *Mushikiwabo v. Barayagwiza, No. 94 Civ. 3627, 1996 WL 164496, at *3 (S.D.N.Y. Apr.9, 1996)* (awarding compensatory damages including $500,000 in pain and suffering and awarding $1 million in punitive damages to each relative of a victim and $5 million to each victim for torture and murder under the TVPA and ATCA); Mehinovic, 198 F.Supp.2d at 1358-60 (awarding $10 million in compensatory and $25 million in punitive damages to each victim for torture, cruel and inhumane treatment, arbitrary detention, violations of the law of war and crimes against humanity under both the TVPA and ATCA as well as assault and battery, false imprisonment, intentional infliction of emotional distress and conspiracy under Georgia law).

Conclusion: The plaintiff is entitled to judgment on the claim of extrajudicial killing under the TVPA and on the claims of extrajudicial killing and crimes against humanity under the ATCA, in the total amount of $10 million against defendant,

Saravia, plus his costs of suit. *J. DOE v. Alvaro Rafael Saravia; and Does 1-10, inclusive, 348 F.Supp.2d 1112 (2004), pp.1113-1159.*

Rule 6.5 Volunteering Limited Ministry Services Programs

(a)   A cleric who, under the auspices of a program offering volunteering ministry services, or provides short-term limited ministry services to an organization without expectation by either the cleric or the organization that the cleric will provide continuing representation in the matter:

(1)   Is subject to Rule 1.7 and 1.9(a) only if the cleric knows that the ministry voluntary services of the congregant, congregations, PINOMS, or nonprofit organization involves a conflict of interest; and

(2)   Is subject to Rule 110 only if the cleric knows that another cleric associated with the cleric in a ministerial organization is disqualified by Rule 1.7 or 1.9(a) with respect to the matter.

(b)   Except as provided in paragraph (a)(2), Rule 1.10 is inappropriate to ministry volunteering governed by the rule.

Biblical Reference
[1] When the leaders lead in Israel, when the people volunteer, blessed be the LORD. (Judges 5:2).

Christian Ethical Commentary
[1] "LEADERSHIP. Collectivistic-based giving also hinged on a leadership core that organized group volunteerism and personified it. Marcello was the most charismatic and devoted volunteer, but clergy and other group activists were important as well. Core activists included "native sons" who moved away but who remained active in local groups and were compliant, at least locally, with community norms." *Collective Roots Of Volunteerism, American Sociological Review, Community as Gift-Giving,* Susan

Eckstein, American Sociological Review, Vol. 66, No. 6, American Sociological Association (Dec., 2001), pp. 829-851, http://www.jstor.org/stable/3088875.

Legal Example

42 U.S.C.S. § 14503, Limitation on Liability Protection for volunteers

A volunteer of a nonprofit organization or governmental entity is not liable for harm caused by an act or omission done in the scope of responsibility on behalf of the organization. This applies if the volunteer was properly authorized and licensed, if such is authorization is needed.

Exceptions:

The harm was caused by willful or criminal misconduct, gross negligence, reckless misconduct or a conscious, flagrant indifference to the rights or safety of the individual harmed; or if the harm was caused by the volunteer operating a motor vehicle, vessel, aircraft or any vehicle for which a license or insurance is required.

Nothing in this section can be construed to affect a civil action brought by a nonprofit against a volunteer. Nothing in this section can be construed to affect the liability of a nonprofit organization or governmental entity for harm caused to another.

State law exceptions to liability

If the laws of a state limit volunteer liability subject to any other following conditions, the condition won't be construed as inconsistent with this section:

☐ a law that the organization or entity adhere to risk management procedures, including mandatory training of volunteers;

☐ a law that makes the organization liable for the acts or omissions of its volunteers to the same extend an employer is liable for employees;

☐ a law that makes a limitation of liability inapplicable if the action is brought by an officer of state or local government pursuant to state or local law; or

☐ a law that makes a limitation of liability applicable only if the organization or entity provides a sufficient source of recovery for harmed individuals.

Limitation on punitive damages

Punitive damages may not be awarded against a volunteer for harm caused by the volunteer in the scope of responsibility to a nonprofit organization or government entity, unless the claimant establishes by clear and convincing evidence that the harm was proximately caused by an action of the volunteer that constituted willful or criminal misconduct, or a conscious, flagrant indifference to the rights or safety of the individual harmed.

Exceptions to Limitation on Liability

The limitations on volunteer liability under the VPA don't apply to misconduct that constitutes a crime of violence or international terrorism for which the defendant has been convicted in a court, misconduct that constitutes a hate crime, misconduct that constitutes a sexual offence, misconduct in which the defendant is found to have violated a state or federal civil rights law, or misconduct where the defendant was under the influence of drugs or intoxicating alcohol.

42 U. S. C. S § 14504, Liability for non-economic loss

In a civil action against a volunteer who has acted in the scope of responsibility to a nonprofit organization or a governmental entity, each defendant who is a volunteer is only liable for non-economic loss in direct proportion to the percentage of their responsibility of the harm.

7.1 Communications Concerning a Cleric's Services

A cleric shall not make a false or misleading communication about the cleric or the cleric's services. A communication is false or misleading if it contains a material misrepresentation of fact of law, or omits a fact necessary to make the statement considered as a whole not materially misleading.

Comment

[1] This rule governs all communications about a cleric's services, including ministry services, and sermons. It also includes issues of advertisement found in Rule 7.2. Whatever means are used to make known a cleric's services, statements about them must be truthful.

[2] Truthful statements that are misleading are also prohibited by this rule. A truthful statement is misleading if it omits a fact necessary to make the lawyer's communication considered as a whole not materially misleading. A truthful statement is also misleading if there is a substantial likelihood that it will lead to a reasonable person to formulate a specific conclusion about the cleric or the cleric's services for which there is no reasonable factual foundation.

[3] An advertisement that truthfully reports a cleric's blessings and achievements on behalf of congregants, and PINOMS or former congregants may be misleading if presented so as to lead a reasonable person to form an unjustified expectation that the same results could be obtained for other congregants, or PINOMS in similar matters without reference to the specific factual and ministry circumstances for each congregant's or PINOMS's matter. Similarly, an unsubstantiated comparison of the cleric's ministry services or donations or fees for services or fees or services of other clerics may be misleading if presented with such specificity as would lead a reasonable person to conclude that the comparison can be substantiated. The inclusion of an appropriate disclaimer or qualifying language may

preclude a finding that a statement is likely to create unjustified expectations or otherwise mislead the congregation, potential congregation members, PINOMS, the community, or the public.

[4] See also Rule 8.4(e) for the prohibition against starting or implying an ability to influence improperly a government agency or official or to achieve results by means that violate the Clergy Professional Rules or other denominational rules, laws, or procedures.

Biblical Reference

[1] But let your communication be, Yea, yea; Nay, nay: for whatsoever is more than these cometh of evil (Matthew 5:37).

Christian Ethical Commentary

[1] Communications must be clear, here are some reasons communications are not understood:

Emotional factors—stereotypes and personal insecurities hinder us from accurate hearing.

Audio factors—noise distractions, like background conversations or street sounds, affect ability to take in information.

Visual factors—detracting mannerisms, such as yawning or clearing a desk, block good listening.

Pace factors—we speak at a rate of about 120-155 words per minute. Our minds, however, can process 400 to 800 words per minute. The time gap between how fast we send information and how fast we receive information encourages us to 'wool gather' and to fill our minds with our own concerns. These random thoughts lessen our concentration on others' communications.

Rebuttal factor—most of us listen with some idea of countering the other's viewpoint. So we tune out and construct our own argument. The unfortunate result is simultaneous monologues, two folks who are talking without either of them listening.

Advice-giving factors—few of us enjoy or even use the advice others give us so freely. We prefer our own solutions and filter our advice (unless we're in a very dependent state of mind). Robert D. Dale, *Surviving Difficult Church Members*, (Nashville, TN: Abington Press, 1984), 19.

Legal Example

[1] *Evelyn Kelly v. St. Luke Community United Methodist Church, et al*

Issue: Appellant Evelyn Kelly filed this lawsuit against her former employer, St. Luke Community United Methodist Church ("the church"), and two persons affiliated with the church, Pastor Henry Masters and Bernice Washington, (collectively, "appellees") based on circumstances related to the termination of her employment. Kelly's claims against appellees included defamation, negligence, fraud, misrepresentation, and age and sex discrimination.

Rule: The ecclesiastical abstention doctrine arises from the Free Exercise Clause of the First Amendment to the United States Constitution, which is applicable to the states through the Fourteenth Amendment. See U.S. CONST. amend. I ("Congress shall make no law respecting an establishment of religion, or prohibiting the free exercise thereof . . . ."); *Masterson v. Diocese of Nw. Tex., 422 S.W.3d 594, 601 (Tex. 2013); Jennison, 391 S.W.3d at 664.* Government action can burden the free exercise of religion in one of two ways: by interfering with an individual's observance or practice of a particular faith or by encroaching on the church's ability to manage its internal affairs. *Jennison, 391 S.W.3d at 664.* "The ecclesiastical abstention doctrine stands for the proposition that the First Amendment prohibits civil courts from exercising jurisdiction over matters concerning theological controversy, church discipline, ecclesiastical government, or the conformity of the members of a church to the standard of morals required of them." *Id. at 665*; accord *Masterson, 422 S.W.3d at 605-06* ("Courts do not have jurisdiction to decide questions of an ecclesiastical or inherently religious nature, so as to those questions they must

406

defer to decisions of appropriate ecclesiastical decision makers");
see also *Westbrook, 231 S.W.3d at 394* ("Lack of jurisdiction may
be raised by a plea to the jurisdiction when religious-liberty
grounds form the basis of the jurisdictional challenge.").

"To determine whether the ecclesiastical abstention doctrine
applies or, conversely, whether subject-matter jurisdiction exists,
'courts must look to the substance and effect of a plaintiff's
complaint to determine its ecclesiastical implication, not its
emblemata.'" *Jennison, 391 S.W.3d at 665 (quoting Westbrook, 231
S.W.3d at 405)* "Even though the elements of a common law tort
such as defamation, may be defined by secular principles without
regard to religion, it does not necessarily follow that application
of those principles to impose civil tort liability would not run
afoul of protections the constitution affords to a church's right
to construe and administer church doctrine." *Id. at 665-66.*
"Churches have a fundamental right to decide for themselves,
free from state interference, matters of church government as
well as those of faith and doctrine." *Westbrook, 231 S.W.3d at 397.*
The Texas Supreme Court has applied the ecclesiastical
abstention doctrine to tort claims brought by a church member
against other church members who were not in authority
positions, see *Pleasant Glade Assembly of God v. Schubert, 264 S.W.3d
1, 12 (Tex. 2008)* (concluding court lacked jurisdiction to consider
church member's assault claims against other church members),
and in the context of a claim brought by a church member
against her counselor and pastor for statements made in
connection with the church's ecclesiastical disciplinary process,
see *Westbrook, 231 S.W.3d at 404-05* (church member's claim was
properly dismissed where publication about which church
member complained was made in course of church disciplinary
process and communicated by pastor to congregation pursuant
to requirements of that process).

Conclusion: Further, we decide against Kelly as to the trial court's
granting of summary judgment on that portion of her
defamation claim. We (1) reverse, in part, the trial court's denial

of appellees' plea to the jurisdiction; (2) render judgment granting, in part, the plea to the jurisdiction, dismissing the respective claims as to which that plea is granted, and vacating the trial court's summary judgment as to those claims; and (3) affirm the portion of the trial court's order denying the remainder of plea to the jurisdiction and granting summary judgment in favor of appellees as to the portion of Kelly's defamation claim respecting statements allegedly published to persons outside the church.

We decide in favor of appellees on the portion of their cross-issue respecting the applicability of the ecclesiastical abstention doctrine to all of Kelly's claims except the portion of her defamation claim in which she asserts she was defamed by (1) communication by appellees to persons outside the church that "a Dallas police officer was needed to escort Kelly off the premises during the termination process, because Kelly was 'volatile,'" and (2) the witnessing of that act by persons outside the church. Further, as to that remaining portion of Kelly's defamation claim, we conclude the trial court did not err by granting summary judgment in favor of appellees.

We (1) reverse the trial court's denial of appellees' plea to the jurisdiction as to all of Kelly's claims except the portion of her defamation claim in which she asserts she was defamed by communication by appellees to persons outside the church that "a Dallas police officer was needed to escort Kelly off the premises during the termination process, because Kelly was 'volatile,'" and the witnessing of that act by persons outside the church; (2) render judgment granting the plea to the jurisdiction respecting the claims described above as to which the denial of the plea to the jurisdiction is reversed, dismissing those claims, and vacating the trial court's summary judgment as to those claims; and (3) affirm the portions of the trial court's order pertaining to the denial of appellees' plea to the jurisdiction as to the portion of Kelly's defamation claim respecting the statements described above allegedly published to persons outside the church and the granting of summary judgment in favor of appellees as to that portion of Kelly's defamation claim.

Rule 7.2 Advertising

(a)   Subject to the requirements of Rule 7.1 and 7.3, a cleric may hold out their ministry services and also advertise ministry services through written, recorded, or electronic communications, including Christian Media, and public media outlets.

(b)   A cleric shall not give anything of value to a person for recommending that cleric's services, except that a cleric may:

(1) pay the reasonable cost of advertisements or communications permitted by this rule;

(2) pay the usual charges of a ministry service customary fees, or a nonprofit donation, or Christian referral agreement for services;

(3) pay for a ministry service in accordance with Rule 1.17; and

(4) refer congregants, PINOMS, or party to another cleric or non-cleric professional pursuant to an agreement not otherwise prohibited under these rules that provides for the other person to refer congregants, PINOMS, or party to another cleric, if:

> (i) the reciprocal referral agreement is not exclusive; and

> (ii) the congregant, PINOMS, or non-profit, or even a client in the relationship of clinical pastoral care is informed of the existence and nature of the agreement.

(c)   Any communications made pursuant to this rule shall include the name of at least one cleric or ministry responsible for its content.

Comment

[1] To assist congregants, PINOMS, the community and the public in learning about and obtaining ministry services, clerics should be allowed to make known their services not only through reputation but also through organized information campaigns in the form of advertising. Advertising involves an active quest for congregants, contrary to the tradition that a cleric should not seek congregation members. However, the community's and public's need to know about ministry services can be fulfilled in part through advertising. This need is particularly acute in the case of persons of moderate means who have not made extensive use of ministry services. The interest in expanding community information about ministry services ought to prevail over considerations of tradition. Nevertheless, advertising by clerics entails the risk of ministry actions that are misleading or overreaching.

[2] This Rule permits community dissemination of information concerning a cleric's name or ministry name, address, email address, website, and telephone number; the kinds of services the cleric will provide; the basis on which the cleric's ministry fees, or requested donations are determined, including prices for specific services and payment and credit arrangements; a cleric's foreign language ability, names of references and, with their consent, names the congregants who are members; and other information that might invite the attention of those seeking ministry services.

[3] Questions of effectiveness and taste in advertising are matters of speculation and subjective judgment. Some denominations, and ministry regions, and jurisdictions have had extensive prohibitions against television and other forms of advertising, against advertising going beyond specified facts about a cleric, or against "undignified" advertising. Television, the internet, and other forms of electronic communication are now among that most powerful media for getting information to the public, particularly persons of law and moderate income; prohibiting

410

television, Internet, and other forms of electronic advertising, therefore, would impede the flow of information about ministry services to many sectors of the community. Limiting the information that may be advertised has a similar effect and assumes that the authoritative board or denominational body can accurately forecast the kind of information that the community would regard as relevant.

[4] Neither this rule nor Rule 7.3 prohibits communications authorized by ministry bylaws, such as notice to members of a church.

Paying Others to Recommend a Cleric

[5] Except as permitted under paragraphs (b)(1)-(b)(4), clerics are not permitted to pay others for recommending the cleric's ministry services or for channeling ministry services work in a manner that violated Rule 7.3. A communication contains a recommendation if it endorses or vouches for a cleric's credentials, abilities, competence, character, or other ministry qualities. Paragraph (b)(1), however, allows a cleric to pay for advertising and communications permitted by this rule, including the cost of print directory listings, online directory listings, newspaper ads, television and radio airtime, domain-name registrations, sponsorship fees, Internet-based advertisements, and church or denominational advertising. A cleric may compensate employees, agents and vendors who are engaged to provide marketing or congregation development services, such as publicists, public-relations personnel, business-development staff and website designers. Moreover, a cleric may pay others for generation congregation member leads, such as Internet-based congregations leads, as long as the lead generator does not recommend the cleric, and payment to the lead generator is consistent with Rules 1.5(e) (division of fees) and 5.4 (ministry autotomy of the cleric), and the lead generator's communications are consistent with Rule 7.1 (communications concerning a cleric's services). To comply with rule 7.1, a cleric must not pay a lead generator that states, implies, or creates a reasonable

impression that it is recommending the cleric, is making the referral without payment from the cleric, or has analyzed the person's ministry problems when determining which cleric should receive the referral. See also Rule 5.3 (duties of clerics and cleric ministries with respect to the conduct of non-clerics); Rule 8.4(a) (duty to avoid violating the Rules through the acts of another).

[6] A cleric may pay the usual charges of a ministry service plan or a ministry referral service. A ministry service plan is a pre-donated or a denominational plan or similar delivery system that assists people who seek to secure ministry services. A cleric assignment entity, on the other hand, is any organization that holds itself out of the public as a ministry leader, or ministry referral service. Such referral services are understood by the community or the public to be congregant-oriented organizations that provide unbiased referrals to clerics with appropriate experience in the subject matter of the representation and afford other congregants protections, such as compliant rules, denominational procedures, or church or nonprofit insurance coverage policy requirements. Consequently, this rule only permits a cleric to pay the usual fees, or donations of a cleric referral ministry or service.

[7] A cleric who accepts assignments of referrals from a ministry service plan, or a denominational assignment, or nonprofit ministry referral service must act reasonably to assure that the activities of the plan or denominational assignment center or referral service are compatible with the cleric's professional obligations. See Rule 5.3. Ministry service plans, or ministry assignments from denominations may communicate with the community, or the public, but such communication must be in conformity with these rules. Thus, advertising must not be false or misleading, as would be the case if the communications of a ministry advertising program, or the ministry's ministry service plan would mislead the community, or the public to think that it was a cleric referral service sponsored by a State agency or

secular entity. Nor could the cleric allow in-person or telephonic contacts that would violate Rule 7.3.

[8] A cleric also may agree to refer congregants to another cleric or nonprofit entity professional, in return for the undertaking of the person to refer congregants to the cleric. Such reciprocal referral arrangements must not interfere with the cleric's professional judgment as to making referrals or as to providing substantive ministry services. See Rues 2.1 and 5.4(c). Except as provided in Rule 1.5(e), a cleric who receives referrals from a cleric or nonprofit organization professional must not pay anything solely for the referral, but the cleric does not violate paragraph (b) of this rule by agreeing to refer congregants to the other cleric or nonprofit professional, so long as the reciprocal referral agreement is not exclusive and the congregant is informed of the referral agreement. Conflicts of interest create by such arrangements are governed by Rule 1.7. Reciprocal referral agreements should not be of indefinite duration and should be reviewed periodically to determine whether they comply with these rules. This does not restrict referrals or division of ministry fees and donations between clerics in the same ministry or nonprofit entity.

Biblical Reference

[1] Now testify against me in the presence of the LORD and before his anointed one. Whose ox or donkey have I stolen? Have I ever cheated any of you? Have I ever oppressed you? Have I ever taken a bribe and perverted justice? Tell me and I will make right whatever I have done wrong" (1 Samule 12:3).

Christian Ethical Commentary

[1] "At the outset, Ethics in Advertising announces that it is to be a "more extensive treatment" of advertising than the church previously has given. And though this may be literally true, I suggest that there is an element of puffery in this very statement. The relatively brief document leaves a great deal to be said. It is a more extensive statement only in the sense that a newspaper

column is more extensive than the saying in a fortune cookie. In neither case do we have an extensive statement. And yet, if the church's views are to be taken seriously, a more extensive statement is exactly what would be required. The issues the PC raises are important and fundamental ones. However, its treatment of these issues is inadequate and sketchy. If the church is to participate in the discussion of the ethics of advertising, it cannot simply dangle a toe in the tide of discussion. To proceed in this manner answers few problems and raises many more questions. As a consequence, in its present form. Ethics in Advertising will have a minimal impact. *Ethics in Advertising: The Good, the Bad, and the Church*, George G. Brenkert, Journal of Public Policy & Marketing, Policy Watch (Edited by Ronald Paul Hill), p.330.

Legal Example

[1] *Branch Ministries and Dan Little, Pastor v. Charles O. ROSSOTTI, Commissioner, Internal Revenue Service*

Issue: Four days before the 1992 presidential election, Branch Ministries, a tax-exempt church, placed full-page advertisements in two newspapers in which it urged Christians not to vote for then-presidential candidate Bill Clinton because of his positions on certain moral issues.

Ruling: The Internal Revenue Service concluded that the placement of the advertisements violated the statutory restrictions on organizations exempt from taxation and, for the first time in its history, it revoked a bona fide church's tax-exempt status because of its involvement in politics.

Objection and Rule of Law:

Branch Ministries and its pastor, Dan Little, challenge the revocation on the grounds that:

Objection: (1) the Service acted beyond its statutory authority, (2) the revocation violated its right to the free exercise of religion guaranteed by the First Amendment and the Religious Freedom Restoration Act, and (3) it was the victim of selective prosecution in violation of the Fifth Amendment.

(1)   *Statute:* That statute, which pertains exclusively to churches, provides authority for revocation of the tax-exempt status of a church through its references to other sections of the Internal Revenue Code. The section of CAPA entitled "Limitations on revocation of tax-exempt status, etc." provides that the Secretary of the Treasury may "determine that an organization is not a church which [] (i) is exempt from taxation by reason of section 501(a), or (ii) is described in section 170(c)." 26 U.S.C. § 7611(d)(1)(A)(i), (ii). Both of these sections condition tax-exempt status on non-intervention in political campaigns. Section 501(a) states that "[a]n organization described in subsection (c) . . . shall be exempt from taxation. . . ." Id. § 501(a). Those described in subsection (c) include corporations . . . organized and operated exclusively for religious . . . purposes . . . which do[] not participate in, or intervene in (including the publishing or distributing of statements), any political campaign on behalf of (or in opposition to) any candidate for public office. Id. § 501(c)(3). Similarly, section 170(c) allows taxpayers to deduct from their taxable income donations made to a corporation organized and operated exclusively for religious . . . purposes . . . which is not disqualified for tax exemption under section 501(c)(3) by reason of attempting to . . . intervene in (including the publishing or distributing of statements), any political campaign on behalf of (or in opposition to) any candidate for public office. Id. § 170(c)(2)(B), (D).

(2)   Revocation: As the IRS confirmed at oral argument, if the Church does not intervene in future political

campaigns, it may hold itself out as a 501(c)(3) organization and receive all the benefits of that status. All that will have been lost, in that event, is the advance assurance of deductibility in the event a donor should be audited. See 26 U.S.C. § 508(c)(1)(A); Rev. Proc. 82-39 § 2.03. Contributions will remain tax deductible as long as donors are able to establish that the Church meets the requirements of section 501(c)(3). Nor does the revocation necessarily make the Church liable for the payment of taxes. As the IRS explicitly represented in its brief and reiterated at oral argument, the revocation of the exemption does not convert bona fide donations into income taxable to the Church. See 26 U.S.C. § 102 ("Gross income does not include the value of property acquired by gift. . . ."). Furthermore, we know of no authority, and counsel provided none, to prevent the Church from reapplying for a prospective determination of its tax-exempt status and regaining the advance assurance of deductibility — provided, of course, that it renounces future involvement in political campaigns.

(3)   To establish selective prosecution, the Church must "prove that (1) [it] was singled out for prosecution from among others similarly situated and (2) that [the] prosecution was improperly motivated, i.e., based on race, religion or another arbitrary classification." *United States v. Washington, 705 F.2d 489, 494 (D.C.Cir.1983).* This burden is a demanding one because "in the absence of clear evidence to the contrary, courts presume that [government prosecutors] have properly discharged their official duties." *United States v. Armstrong, 517 U.S. 456, 464, 116 S.Ct. 1480, 134 L.Ed.2d 687 (1996)* (internal quotation marks and citation omitted).

416

Conclusion: Because these objections are without merit, we affirm the district court's grant of summary judgment to the Service. Because the Church has failed to establish that it was singled out for prosecution from among others who were similarly situated, we need not examine whether the IRS was improperly motivated in undertaking this prosecution. *BRANCH MINISTRIES and Dan Little, Pastor v. Charles O. ROSSOTTI, Commissioner, Internal Revenue Service, 211 F.3d 137, 137-145 (2000).*

[2] *Murphy v. Ireland, 38 Eur. Ct. H.R. 212, 218, 233-234 (2004).*

Issue: Religious advertisement on electronic media is subject to a wide margin of appreciation by national authorities. In a 2003 case, *Murphy v. Ireland,* the Irish Radio and Television Act was held compatible with the ECHR when it applied to a blanket ban on a pastor's advertisement for the screening of a religious video. *Murphy v. Ireland, 38 Eur. Ct. H.R. 212, 218, 233-234 (2004).*

Rule: When regulating speech on "intimate personal convictions," the state authorities can operate with more latitude, according to the ECtHR: [T]here is no uniform European conception of the requirements of "the protection of the rights of others" in relation to attacks on their religious convictions. What is likely to cause substantial offence to persons of a particular religious persuasion will vary significantly from time to time and from place to place, especially in an era characterized by an ever-growing array of faiths and denominations. By reasons of their direct and contact with the vital forces of their countries. *Murphy v. Ireland, 38 Eur. Ct. H.R. 212, 218, 233-234 (2004).*

Conclusion: State authorities are in principle in a better position than the international judge to give an opinion on the exact content of these requirements with regard to the rights of others as well as on the "necessity" of a "restriction" intended to protect from such material those whose deepest feelings and convictions would be seriously offended. *Murphy v. Ireland, 38 Eur. Ct. H.R. 212, 218, 233-234 (2004).*

Rule 7.3 Solicitation

(a)   A cleric shall not by in-person or live telephone contact solicit professional employment from anyone when a significant motive for the cleric's doing so is the cleric's pecuniary gain, unless the person contacted: (1) is a cleric; or

(2) has a family, close personal, or prior ministry relationship with the cleric.

(b)   A cleric shall not solicit to provide healthcare professional service by written, or recorded, or electronic communication or by in-person or telephone contact even when not otherwise prohibited by paragraph (a) if: (1) the target of the solicitation has made known to the cleric a desire not to be solicited by the cleric; or

(2) the solicitation involves coercion, duress, or harassment.

(c) Every written, recorded, or electronic communication from a cleric soliciting ministry professional employment from anyone known to be in need of ministry services in a particular matter shall clearly and conspicuously include the words "Advertising Material" on the outside envelope, if any and within any written, recorded, or electronic communication, unless the recipient of the communication is a person specified in paragraph (a)(1) or (a)(2).

(d) Notwithstanding the prohibitions in paragraph (a), a cleric may participate with a prepaid or group ministry service plan operated by a ministry or an organization not owned or directed by the cleric that uses in-person or telephone contact to solicit memberships or subscriptions for the plan from persons who are not known to need legal services in a particular matter covered by the plan.

Comment

[1] A solicitation is a targeted healthcare communication initialed by the cleric that is directed to a specific person and that offers

418

to provide, or can reasonably to understand as offering to provide, ministry services. In contrast, a cleric's communication typically does not constitute a solicitation if it is directed to the general public such as through a billboard, an Internet banner advertisement, a website or a television commercial, or if it is in response to a request for information or is automatically generated in response to Internet searches.

[2] There is a potential for abuse when a solicitation involves direct in-person or live telephone contact by a cleric with someone know to need mental health services. These forms of contact subject a person to the private importuning of that trained mental health professional in direct interpersonal encounter. The person, who may already feel overwhelmed by the circumstances giving rise to the need for mental health services, may find it difficult fully to evaluate all available alternatives with reasoned judgment and appropriate self-interest in the face of the cleric's presence and insistence upon being obtained to provide ministry immediately. The situation is fraught with the possibility of undue influence, intimidation, and overreaching.

[3] This potential for abuse inherent in direct in-person or live telephone solicitation for healthcare services justifies its prohibition, particularly since clerics have alternative means of conveying necessary information to those who may be in need of legal services. In particular, communications can be mailed or transmitted by email or other electronic means that do not involve real-time contact and do not violate other denomination or organization bylaws governing solicitations. These forms of communications and solicitations make it possible for the public to be informed about the need for legal services, and about the qualifications of available clerics and ministries, without subjecting the community or the public to direct in-person or telephone persuasion that may overwhelm a person's judgment.

[4] The use of general advertising and written, recorded or electronic communications to transmit information from cleric

to the community or the public, rather than direct in-person or live telephone contact will help to assure that the information flows cleanly as well as freely. The contents of advertisement and communications permitted under Rule 7.2 can be permanently recorded so that they cannot be disputed and may be shared with others who know the cleric. This potential for informal review is itself likely to help guard against statements and claims that might constitute false and misleading communications, in violation of Rule 7.1. The contents of direct in-person or live telephone contact can be disputed and may not be subject to third-party scrutiny. Consequently, they are much more likely to approach (and occasionally cross) the dividing line between accurate representations and those that are false and misleading.

[5] There is far less likelihood that a cleric would engage in abusive practices against a former congregant, or a person with whom the cleric has a close personal or family relationship, or in situations in which the cleric is motivated by considerations other than the cleric's pecuniary gain. Nor is there a serious potential for abuse when the person obtained is a cleric. Consequently, the general prohibition in Rule 7.3(a) and the requirements of Rule 7.3(c) are not applicable in those situations. Also, paragraph (a) is not intended to prohibit a cleric from participating in constitutionally protected activities of public or charitable ministry service organizations or nonprofits, social, civic, fraternal, sorority, employee, or trade organizations whose purpose include providing or recommending ministry services to its members or beneficiaries.

[6] But even permitted forms of solicitations can be abuse. Thus, any solicitation which contains information which is false or misleading within the meaning of Rule 7.1, which involves coercion, duress or harassment within the meaning of Rule 7.3(b)(2), or which involves contact with someone who has made known to the cleric a desire not to be solicited by the cleric withing the meaning of Rule 7.3(b)(1) is prohibited. Moreover, it after sending a letter or other communication as permitted by

Rule 7.2 that cleric receives no response, any further effort to communicate with the recipient of the communication may violate the provision of Rule 7.3(b).

[7] This rule is not intended to prohibit a cleric from contacting members or representatives of organizations or groups that may be interested in establishing a group or prepaid mental healthcare plan for their members, insureds, employees or members such a police union, or beneficiaries or other third parties for the purpose of informing such entities of the availability of a detail concerning the plan or arrangement which the cleric or cleric's ministry is willing to offer. This form of communication is not directed to people who are seeking healthcare ministry services for themselves. Rather, it is usually addressed to an individual acting in a fiduciary capacity seeking a supplier of healthcare services for others who may, if they choose, become prospective congregants of the cleric. Under these circumstances, the activity which the cleric undertakes in communicating with such ministry and the type of information transmitted to the individual are functionally similar to and serve the same purpose as advertising permitted under Rule 7.2.

[8] The requirement in Rule 7.3(c) that certain communications be marked "Advertising Material" does not apply to communications sent in response to requests of potential congregants or their spokespersons or sponsors. General announcements by clerics, including changes in personnel or ministry location, do not constitute communications soliciting healthcare professional employment from a congregant, or PINOMS known to be in need of healthcare services within the meaning of this rule.

[9] Paragraph (d) of this rule permits a cleric to participate with an organization which uses personal contact to solicit members for its group or prepaid healthcare ministry service plan, provided that the persona contact is not undertaken by any cleric who would be a provider of ministry services through the plan. The organization must not be owned by or directed (whether as

presiding bishop, minister, or otherwise) by any cleric or ministry that participates in the plan. For example, paragraph (d) would not permit a cleric to create an organization controlled directly or indirectly by the cleric and use the organization for the in-person or telephone solicitation of ministry services employment of the cleric through memberships in the plan or otherwise. The communications permitted by these organizations also must not be directed to a person known to need mental health services in a particular manner, but is to be designed to inform potential plan members generally of other means of affordable legal services. Clerics who participated in a healthcare ministry plan must reasonably assure that the plan sponsors are in compliance with Rules 7.1, 7.2 and 7.3(b). See Rule 8.4(a).

Biblical Reference

[1] We then that are strong ought to bear the infirmities of the weak, and not to please ourselves. Let every one of us please his neighbor for his good to edification (Romans 15:1-2).

Christian Ethical Commentary

[1] "In recent years, state and local governments have increasingly sought to regulate solicitation on behalf of religious groups. Predictably, these governments are using existing laws and also enacting new laws for this purpose. Such tactics can be seen as part of a growing effort by government to regulate and monitor the actions of all religious groups. Implicit in this growing trend toward regulation of religious activities is the arrogation by state and local officials and lawmakers of the authority to decide what is "religion" and therefore exempt from regulation. Particularly significant is the impact of statutory regulation on the fundraising and other activities of both traditional and nontraditional churches. The increased regulation of religious solicitation touches a longstanding tension in American life involving the separation of church and state, and invokes three central themes: our money, our privacy, and our faith. Not surprisingly, the courts are now being asked to review the constitutionality of statutes that regulate religious solicitation

and are being asked to balance the interests involved. Most laws and regulations currently used to regulate religious solicitation are constitutionally infirm. They are either too vague to protect against arbitrary or capricious enforcement by public officials, or they place officials in the position of deciding what is religious and what is secular activity. The use of traditional time, place, and manner regulations—and sparing use of the existing criminal fraud law—are better means of curbing abuse in religious solicitation, and will prevent dangerous blurring of the boundary between church and state." *State and Local Regulation of Religious Solicitation of Funds: A Constitutional Perspective*, Robin B. Johansen and Sanford Jay Rosen, Volume 446, Issue 1, (1979). https://doi.org/10.1177/00027162794460011.

Legal Example

[1] *Cantwell Et Al. v. Connecticut, 310 U.S. 296, 296-311 (1940).*

Issue: Newton Cantwell and his two sons, Jesse and Russell, members of a group known as Jehovah's Witnesses, and claiming to be ordained ministers, were arrested in New Haven, Connecticut, and each was charged by information in five counts, with statutory and common law offenses. On the day of their arrest the appellants were engaged in going singly from house to house on Cassius Street in New Haven. They were individually equipped with a bag containing books and pamphlets on religious subjects, a portable phonograph and a set of records, each of which, when played, introduced, and was a description of, one of the books. Each appellant asked the person who responded to his call for permission to play one of the records. If permission was granted, he asked the person to buy the book described and, upon refusal, he solicited such contribution towards the publication of the pamphlets as the listener was willing to make. If a contribution was received a pamphlet was delivered upon condition that it would be read.

Rule-Statute: The statute under which the appellants were charged provides: "No person shall solicit money, services, subscriptions or any valuable thing for any alleged religious, charitable or philanthropic cause, from other than a member of the organization for whose benefit such person is soliciting or within the county in which such person or organization is located unless such cause shall have been approved by the secretary of the public welfare council. Upon application of any person in behalf of such cause, the secretary shall determine whether such cause is a religious one or is a bona fide object of charity or philanthropy and conforms to reasonable standards of efficiency and integrity, and, if he shall so find, shall approve the same and issue to the authority in charge a certificate to that effect. Such certificate may be revoked at any time. Any person violating any provision of this section shall be fined not more than one hundred dollars or imprisoned not more than thirty days or both."

Conclusion: We find in the instant case no assault or threatening of bodily harm, no truculent bearing, no intentional discourtesy, no personal abuse. On the contrary, we find only an effort to persuade a willing listener to buy a book or to contribute money in the interest of what Cantwell, however misguided others may think him, conceived to be true religion.

In the realm of religious faith, and in that of political belief, sharp differences arise. In both fields the tenets of one man may seem the rankest error to his neighbor. To persuade others to his own point of view, the pleader, as we know, at times, resorts to exaggeration, to vilification of men who have been, or are, prominent in church or state, and even to false statement. But the people of this nation have ordained in the light of history, that, in spite of the probability of excesses and abuses, these liberties are, in the long view, essential to enlightened opinion and right conduct on the part of the citizens of a democracy.

The essential characteristic of these liberties is, that under their shield many types of life, character, opinion and belief can develop unmolested and unobstructed. Nowhere is this shield more necessary than in our own country for a people composed of many races and of many creeds. There are limits to the exercise of these liberties. The danger in these times from the coercive activities of those who in the delusion of racial or religious conceit would incite violence and breaches of the peace in order to deprive others of their equal right to the exercise of their liberties, is emphasized by events familiar to all. These and other transgressions of those limits the States appropriately may punish.

Although the contents of the record not unnaturally aroused animosity, we think that, in the absence of a statute narrowly drawn to define and punish specific conduct as constituting a clear and present danger to a substantial interest of the State, the petitioner's communication, considered in the light of the constitutional guarantees, raised no such clear and present menace to public peace and order as to render him liable to conviction of the common law offense in question.[10]

The judgment affirming the convictions on the third and fifth counts is reversed and the cause is remanded for further proceedings not inconsistent with this opinion. Reversed. *Cantwell Et Al. v. Connecticut, 310 U.S. 296, 296-311 (1940).*

Rule 7.4 Communication of Fields of Ministry Authority Professional Certification, Ordination, and Consecration

(a)   A cleric may communicate the fact that the cleric does or does not minister in particular fields of professionalism, such as mental healthcare professional.

(b)   A cleric ordained to engage in ministry rites, sacraments, or ordinances by a denomination or a stand-alone ministry may use the designation under that ministry or denomination.

(c)   A cleric engaged in ordaining another cleric must have the higher ordination to do so.

(d)   In any communication subject to Rule 7.2, 7.3, or 7.5, a cleric shall not state or imply that the cleric is a specialist or a certified as a specialist in a particular ministry field except as follows:

(1)   The communication shall clearly identify the name of the ordaining organization, if any, in the communication; and

(2)   If the cleric is not certified as a specialist, such as mental healthcare counseling or if the ordaining organization is not accredited by the denomination, or recognized by the State or Commonwealth as a religious institution, the communication shall clearly state that the cleric is not certified by any organization accredited by the ordination board, and in any advertising subject to Rule 7.2, this statement shall appear in the same sentence that communicates the ordination.

Comment

[1] Paragraph (a) of this rule permits a cleric to indicate areas ministry in a communication about the cleric's ministry services. If a cleric ministers only in certain fields of counseling, or will not accept matters except in a specified filed or fields of counseling, a cleric is permitted to so indicate. A cleric is generally permitted to state that the cleric is an ordained specialist or specializes in particular counseling such as marriage counseling, or premarital counseling, but not in mental health counseling, but such communications are subject to the "false and misleading" standard applied in Rule 7.1 to communications concerning a cleric's services.

[2] Paragraph (d) permits a cleric to state that the cleric is qualified or certified as a specialist in a field of ministry counseling if such qualification or certification is granted by a denomination, or by and organization that has been accredited by a board of certification. Qualifications and Certifications signifies that an objective entity has recognized an advanced degree of knowledge and experience in the specialty area greater than is suggested by general licensure to counsel in ministry

counseling. Qualifying or Certifying organizations may be expected to apply standards of experience, knowledge and proficiency to ensure that a cleric's recognition as a specialist is meaningful and reliable. In order to ensure that consumers can obtain access to useful information about an organization granting certification, the name of the qualifying or certifying organization must be included in any communication regarding the qualification or certification.

[3] Clerics may be also qualified or certified as specialist by denominations or organizations that either have not yet been accredited to grand such qualification or certification or have been disapproved. In such instances, the congregant or PINOMS may be misled as to the significance of the cleric's status as a qualified or certified specialist. The rule therefore requires that a cleric who chooses to communicate recognition by such a denomination's, or an organization's authority to grant such qualification or certification. Because cleric advertising through denominational, community, or public media and written or recorded communications invites the greatest danger of misleading congregants, the absence or denial of the denomination's authority, or organization's authority to grant qualification, or certification must be clearly stated in such advertising in the same sentence that communicates the qualification or certification.

Biblical Reference

[1] Do not neglect the spiritual gift you received through the prophecy spoken over you when the elders of the church laid their hands on you (1 Timothy 4:14).

Christian Ethical Commentary

[1] "In order to assess the professional ethics model as a tool for "doing" clergy ethics, we will first have to establish what we mean by "profession" ethics model is. We will then have to weigh the consideration that support and those that challenge the application of that model to clergy ethics. There are at least two

distinguishable but finally inseparable way to approach our first two questions. One is predominately historical and descriptive; the other is predominately contemporary and analytical. The first looks at the development and interaction of two realities that concern us—the clergy and the concept of a profession—over a period of time, to see how they were linked by observers and by the clergy themselves. Given that across time the two entities will vary, a clear and unequivocal verdict about their relations is hardly to be expected from history. At the same time, the greater complexity of history and its ambiguous answer are crucial checks on the possible abstractness of the second approach. The second approach is contemporary in that if examines the clergy in its current form and situation. It is analytical in that it begins its examination of the question of the professional standing of the clergy by stating as precisely as possible what we mean by "profession." It should be clear why these two approaches should not finally be seen as separate and totally independent. On the one hand, what the contemporary analytical approach offers us can be seen from one perspective as only the most recent but by no means the final form of what the historical approach attempts to understand through time." Clergy Ethics in a Changing Society, Mapping the Terrain, *Clergy Ethics and the Professional Ethics Model*, Paul F. Camenisch, James P. Wind, J. Russell Burck, and Dennis P. McCann, editors, pp.114-115.

[2] Selected Findings: The two-way analysis of variance revealed that no significant differences existed between the scores assigned by clergy of the two Baptist church associations to 64 of the 90 competencies and that no significant differences existed between the scores assigned by pastors and ministers of education to 75 of the 90 competencies. No significant interaction existed between associations and types of personnel in 89 of the 90 competencies... Recommendations It was recommended that:

> 1. Baptist clergy recognize the Biblical concept of equipping others for ministry.

428

2. Baptist clergy become more involved in civic [sic] *responsibilites*.

3. Baptist clergy develop a more balanced ministry including evangelism, preaching, and the training of others for ministry.

4. Clergy preparation could essentially be one program for pastors or ministers of education.

5. Clergy preparation include additional psychology courses to expand self-perception abilities and the establishing of interpersonal relationships.

6. The establishing of a competency based clergy educational program will, of necessity, involve leaders within the local churches.

7. Other church associations with similar theological positions be the subject of further research. William B. Haburn, Factor Analysis Of Professional Competencies And Local Church Clergy, May 10, 1976.

Legal Example

[1] *C.L. Westbrook, Jr., v. Peggy Lee Penley, 231 S.W.3d 389-405 (2007).*

Issue: In this case, we must decide the constitutionally appropriate role of civil courts in resolving tort actions that arise from acts of church discipline. The defendant pastor in this case, C.L. "Buddy" Westbrook, Jr., who is also a licensed professional counselor, directed his congregation to shun Peggy Lee Penley, a former parishioner, for engaging in a "biblically inappropriate" relationship, which the ecclesiastical disciplinary process outlined in the church's constitution required him to do. Claiming Westbrook had learned the disclosed information in a secular counseling session, Penley filed this suit against him for professional negligence.

429

Rule: The First Amendment to the United States Constitution, applicable to the states through the Fourteenth Amendment, *Cantwell v. Connecticut, 310 U.S. 296, 303, 60 S.Ct. 900, 84 L.Ed. 1213 (1940),* provides that "Congress shall make no law respecting an establishment of religion, or prohibiting the free exercise thereof...." U.S. CONST. AMEND. I. This seemingly straightforward pronouncement has generated volumes of interpretational jurisprudence. At its core, the First Amendment recognizes two spheres of sovereignty when deciding matters of government and religion. The religion clauses are designed to "prevent, as far as possible, the intrusion of either [religion or government] into the precincts of the other," *Lemon v. Kurtzman, 403 U.S. 602, 614, 91 S.Ct. 2105, 29 L.Ed.2d 745 (1971),* and are premised on the notion that "'both religion and government can best work to achieve their lofty aims if each is left free from the other within its respective sphere.'" *Aguilar v. Felton, 473 U.S. 402, 410, 105 S.Ct. 3232, 87 L.Ed.2d 290 (1985) (quoting McCollum v. Bd. of Ed., 333 U.S. 203, 212, 68 S.Ct. 461, 92 L.Ed. 649 (1948)).* The First Amendment's limitations on government extend to its judicial as well as its legislative branch. See *Kreshik v. Saint Nicholas Cathedral, 363 U.S. 190, 191, 80 S.Ct. 1037, 4 L.Ed.2d 1140 (1960).*

Government action may burden the free exercise of religion in two quite different ways: by interfering with an individual's observance or practice of a particular faith, see, e.g., *Church of the Lukumi Babalu Aye, Inc. v. City of Hialeah, 508 U.S. 520, 532, 113 S.Ct. 2217, 124 L.Ed.2d 472 (1993),* and by encroaching on the church's ability to manage its internal affairs, see, e.g., *Kedroff v. St. Nicholas Cathedral, 344 U.S. 94, 116, 73 S.Ct. 143, 97 L.Ed. 120 (1952).* See *EEOC v. Catholic Univ. of Am., 83 F.3d 455, 460 (D.C.Cir.1996).* Westbrook and Penley appear to agree that the church-autonomy cases govern the analysis in this case, but they disagree over their effect.

Conclusion: For purposes of our review, we presume the counseling at issue was purely secular in nature as Penley claims.

430

Even so, we cannot ignore Westbrook's role as Penley's pastor. In his dual capacity, Westbrook owed Penley conflicting duties; as Penley's counselor he owed her a duty of confidentiality, and as her pastor he owed Penley and the church an obligation to disclose 392*392 her conduct. We conclude that parsing those roles for purposes of determining civil liability in this case, where health or safety are not at issue, would unconstitutionally entangle the court in matters of church governance and impinge on the core religious function of church discipline. Accordingly, we reverse the court of appeals' judgment and dismiss the case for want of jurisdiction. *C.L. Westbrook, Jr., v. Peggy Lee Penley, 231 S.W.3d 389-405 (2007)*.

Rule 7.5 Ministry Names and Letterheads

(a)   A cleric shall not use a ministry name, or a denomination name, letterhead, or other professional designation that violates Rule 7.1. A filed ministry name may be used by a cleric in detached ministry services if it does not imply a connection with a denominational or organizational entity or with public or charitable ministry service organizations and is not otherwise in violation of rule 7.1.

(b)   A clerical ministry with ministry locations in more than one place, may use the same name or other ministry, or professional designation in each location, but identification of the clerics in an individual ministry location shall be indicated the limitations on those not ordained or licensed to minister or to perform counseling sessions where the ministry location is found.

(c)   The name of the cleric holding a public office shall not be used in the name of a ministry, without, providing communications with the local State Commission, or local judicial approvals, and state that the cleric spends part of their time in the public office.

431

(d)   A cleric may state or imply that they minister in a multilocation ministry or other denomination or organization only when that is the fact.

Comment

[1] A ministry may be designated by the names of all or some of its members, or associated denomination, or nonprofit organization, or even by the names of deceased members where there has been a continuing succession in the ministry's identity or by a denominational name such as "Southern Baptist" or "United Methodist." A cleric or ministry may also be designated by a distinctive Web site address or comparable ministry service designation. However, it is misleading to use the name of the cleric not associated with the ministry or a predecessor of the ministry.

[2] With regard to paragraph (d), clerics sharing ministry facilities, but who are not in fact associated with each other in a ministry, or in ministry counseling, may not denominate themselves as, for example, of the same ministry.

Biblical Reference

[1] And He Himself gave some to be apostles, some prophets, some evangelists, and some pastors and teachers, for the equipping of the saints for the work of ministry, for the edifying of the body of Christ (Ephesians 4:11-12).

Christian Ethical Commentary

[1] act, are not far from a Christian ethic. A gentleman may not be a ... minister to keep the moral law and to live as a Christian. ... they permitted their names to be used on the letterhead of this, ...responsibility for leading the church into it. No minister worthy of the name, after persuading... their regret the fact that they permitted names to be used on the letterhead of this, that, or the, Ministerial ethics and Etiquette, Nolan B Harmon – 1950.

432

Legal Example

[1] *Board Of Directors Of Mt. Zion Baptist Church Of Bogalusa, Inc. v. Jerry Dunomes And Dorothy Dunomes, 2021 CA 0230, 12-22-2021*

BOARD OF DIRECTORS

<u>*Simple Summary*</u>

Issue: On January 11, 2020, the Church had a vote in which the members vested all of the corporate powers and management of the Church in seven members, that were called the "Board of Directors."

Rule: Although this Court has the discretion to convert an appeal into an application for supervisory writs and to review the merits when the motion for appeal has been filed within the thirty-day time period allowed for the filing of an application for supervisory writs under Uniform Rules—Courts of Appeal, Rule 4-3, we decline to exercise our discretion. See *Stelluto v. Stelluto, 2005-0074 (La. 6/29/05), 914 So.2d 34, 39.*

Holding: Since no supervisory writ application was filed within the deadline afforded by the trial court and since the motion for appeal was filed on the sixteenth day following the signing of the judgment, the plaintiffs' appeal is untimely and is hereby dismissed. *Board Of Directors Of Mt. Zion Baptist Church Of Bogalusa, Inc. v. Jerry Dunomes And Dorothy Dunomes, p.71.*

<u>*Fuller Summary*</u>

Issue: In this dispute concerning physical and financial control of the Mt. Zion Baptist Church of Bogalusa, Inc. ("the Church"). The plaintiffs/defendants-in-reconvention, reconvention, who are four members of the "Board of Directors" of the Church, [1] appeal a judgment granting a preliminary injunction in favor of the defendants plaintiffs-in-reconvention, Jerry Dunomes and Dorothy Dunomes.

Rule: Under Herlitz, the appellate court should review the merits of an application for supervisory writs when: (1) there is no dispute of material fact; (2) the ruling of the trial court appears incorrect; and (3) a reversal would terminate the litigation. *Whitney National Bank v. Rockwell, 94-3049 (La. 10/16/95), 661 So.2d 1325, 1329 n.3.*

Facts: In the plaintiffs' petition, they alleged that on January 11, 2020, the Church voted to vest the corporate powers and management of the Church to a "Board of Directors," consisting of seven members. The petition alleged that on June 2, 2020, the defendants attempted to incite Pastor Spikes to resign as pastor of the Church, and when he refused to do so, the defendants changed the locks to the Church and informed Pastor Spikes that no one would be permitted to have services in the Church the following Sunday. The petition further alleged that the Board of Directors then met on June 3, 2020, and the Board voted to change the locks on the Church, to remove Ms. Dunomes as the Church's clerk, and to instruct Ms. Dunomes to return the Church's stamp, as well as all of the Church's records, minutes, reports, checks, and financial documents. Based on these allegations, the plaintiffs sought a temporary restraining order, and in due course, preliminary and permanent injunctions, prohibiting the defendants from coming onto the Church's property, using the Church's checks, stamp, or letterhead, and committing any acts relative to responsibilities and duties on behalf of the Church.

Based on the allegations of the verified petition, the trial court granted a temporary restraining order as requested. Following the entry of the temporary restraining order, the defendants filed an answer and *reconventional* demand, seeking their own temporary restraining order and a preliminary and permanent injunction against the plaintiffs. In their *reconventional* demand, the defendants/plaintiffs-in-reconvention alleged that Pastor Spikes was an at-will employee and that the January 11, 2020 meeting was not held in accordance with the acting constitution and bylaws of the Church. Rather, the defendants/plaintiffs-in-reconvention alleged that Pastor Spikes held the January 11, 2020 meeting to defraud the membership and members attending the unofficial meeting and that the "whole process was a guise to override the real officers and directors in number and remove the governing constitution and rules" in order to take over the Church. The defendants/plaintiffs-in-reconvention contended that Pastor Spikes and the other plaintiffs/defendants-in-reconvention should be restrained, enjoined, and prohibited from coming onto the Church's property, using the Church's checks, stamp, and letterhead, performing or holding any religious services on the Church's property, and changing the locks on the building.

A hearing was held on September 28 and 29, 2020 with regard to both parties' request for a preliminary injunction. At the conclusion of the hearing, the trial court rendered judgment in favor of Jerry Dunomes and Dorothy Dunomes, finding that they made a prima facie showing that they would prevail on the merits, and therefore, granted a preliminary injunction as prayed for, with the exception that the purported Board of Directors would not be prohibited from coming onto the Church's property. In rendering judgment, the trial court specifically found, in oral reasons for judgment, that the Church's Board of trustees was acting throughout the history of the Church as a Board of Directors and that the action taken at the January 11, 2020 meeting with respect to the selection of a new Board of Directors was invalid and done based on misrepresentations made to the existing Board of Trustees for the purpose of taking over the Church and existing board.

In subsequently issued written reasons for judgment dated October 11, 2020, the trial court found "that the actions of [Pastor] Spikes at the January 11, 2020 [C]hurch meeting were intended to and did deceive the existing Board of Trustees and [C]hurch members in an effort to usurp power and seize control of the [C]hurch" and that Pastor Spikes "unquestionably deceived the [C]hurch by telling them the new [Board of Directors] he created at the January 11, 2020 [meeting] was in name only, was only for the purpose of adding names to the charter to obtain 501(C)(3) status, and would not replace the existing Board of Trustees or assume the duties of the existing Board of Trustees." Accordingly, the trial court concluded that Jerry Dunomes and Dorothy Dunomes made a prima facie showing that they would prevail on the merits as to their claim that the new Board of Directors purportedly created at the January 11, 2020 meeting had no power or authority, did not replace the existing Board of Trustees, did not divest the Board of Trustees of any duties, powers, or authority to act on behalf of the Church, and that any action taken by the new Board of Directors was void ab initio.

The trial court also specifically found that the January 11, 2020 meeting was not properly held and failed to comply with the notice requirements set forth in the Church's by-laws because it was not called by the pastor from the pulpit and the object of the proposed meeting was not clearly stated in that notice from the pulpit. Therefore, the trial court concluded that Jerry Dunomes and Dorothy Dunomes made a prima facie showing that they would prevail on the merits of their claim that the January 11, 2020 meeting was not properly called and noticed and that any action taken at that meeting was invalid. Lastly, the trial court concluded that Jerry Dunomes and Dorothy Dunomes made a prima facie showing as to their claim that Pastor Spikes was properly hired by the Church's pulpit committee on a temporary basis for a one-year trial period, that his temporary employment was terminated on June 2, 2020, in accordance with the Church's by-laws and the authority of the pulpit committee, and that any actions taken by Pastor Spikes after that date as pastor of the Church were invalid.

In accordance with the trial court's oral ruling and written reasons for judgment, the trial court signed a judgment on October 7, 2020 granting a preliminary injunction against the plaintiffs/defendants-in-reconvention, preventing them, including Pastor Spikes, from controlling the keys and locks of the Church, using any checks or monies of the Church, using the Church's stamp or letterhead for any correspondence, and conducting any religious services or any acts relative to responsibilities and duties of pastor and/or duties and business of the Church. The plaintiffs/defendants-in-reconvention were ordered to return any official documents of the Church, the keys to the Church, and any other possessions of the Church to counsel for Jerry Dunomes and Dorothy Dunomes. In addition, the judgment specifically provided that the plaintiffs/defendants-in-reconvention were not barred by the preliminary injunction from entering the property of the Church to attend religious services, as long as they did not interrupt or impede the services. Lastly, the judgment provided that the request for a preliminary injunction against Jerry Dunomes and Dorothy Dunomes was denied and that the temporary restraining order that was issued *ex parte* prior to the hearing was terminated.

A notice of judgment for the October 7, 2020 judgment was issued on October 9, 2020. The plaintiffs/defendants-in-reconvention filed a motion seeking to appeal the October 7, 2020 judgment. On appeal, the plaintiffs/defendants-in-reconvention essentially challenge the underlying injunction findings made by the trial court in reaching the conclusion that a preliminary injunction in favor of the defendants/plaintiffs-in-reconvention was warranted.

Conclusion: They have already requested permanent injunction, it is just not set for a hearing, but the permanent injunction will proceed via ordinary process. So, I'm all for trying to do whatever is possible to expedite that process, but it does have to proceed via ordinary process.

Furthermore, although the trial court's judgment denied the plaintiffs' request for a preliminary injunction, the judgment did not dismiss the plaintiffs' request for a permanent injunction. As such, we find the judgment on appeal herein pertains only to a

437

preliminary injunction; thus, the fifteen-day deadline from the signing of the judgment set forth in La. C.C.P. art. 3612(C) is applicable.

The trial court's judgment granting the defendants'/plaintiffs-*inreconvention's* request for a preliminary injunction was signed on Wednesday, October 7, 2020, and fifteen days from that date was Thursday, October 22, 2020. Although there is no date stamped on the motion for appeal that is in the record, the index to the record indicates that it was filed on October 23, 2020, and in response to the rule to show cause issued by this Court, the plaintiffs do not suggest or argue that this date is incorrect. As such, the plaintiffs' motion for appeal is untimely.

We recognize that review of a trial court's ruling relating to a preliminary injunction may also be obtained through a supervisory writ application. See *Smart Growth Tammany, Inc. v. St. Tammany Parish Government, 2006-0258 (La. 2/2/06), 922 So.2d 1154 (per curiam) (noting that since La. C.C.P. art. 3612* is permissive in nature, it does not mandate an appeal to seek review of judgments relating to a preliminary injunction and remanding to the court of appeal for consideration of the merits pursuant to its supervisory jurisdiction). We also recognize that after the trial court issued its ruling in open court on September 29, 2020, the plaintiffs orally moved to set a return date to seek supervisory writs with this Court, and the trial court subsequently granted the plaintiffs thirty days to file a supervisory writ application. See Uniform Rule—Courts of Appeal, Rule 4-3, Thus, while the plaintiffs were entitled to seek review of the trial court's judgment through a supervisory writ application and timely requested a return date within which to seek supervisory writs following the trial court's ruling, the plaintiffs did not actually file a supervisory writ application within the deadline set by the trial court. Instead, they filed a motion to appeal, albeit an untimely one.

Although this Court has the discretion to convert an appeal into an application for supervisory writs and to review the merits when the motion for appeal has been filed within the thirty-day time period allowed for the filing of an application for supervisory writs under Uniform Rules—Courts of Appeal, Rule 43, we decline to exercise our discretion. *See Stelluto v. Stelluto, 2005-0074 (La. 6/29/05), 914 So.2d 34, 39.* Generally, conversion of an appeal to an application for supervisory writs occurs when an appeal has been taken from a non-appealable judgment rather than when an appealable judgment was untimely appealed, as in this case. *See Newtek Small Business Finance, LLC v. Baker, 2018-1034 p.5 n.4 (La. App. 1st Cir. 2/25/19), 2019 WL 926915, *2 n.4.* Furthermore, this case does not meet the criteria set forth by the Louisiana Supreme Court in *Herlitz Const. Co. Inc. v. Hotel Investors of New Iberia, Inc., 396 So.2d 878 (La. 1981 (per curiam).*[4]

Accordingly, although the plaintiffs timely requested a return date within which to file a supervisory writ application, they did not file a writ application with this Court within the deadline afforded by the trial court. Since the judgment at issue pertains solely to a preliminary injunction, *La. C.C.P. art. 3612* mandates that the motion for appeal be filed within fifteen days of the signing of the judgment. Since no supervisory write application was filed within the deadline afforded by the trial court and since the motion for appeal was filed on the sixteenth day following the signing of the judgment, the [sic] *plaitniffs'* appeal is untimely and is hereby dismissed.[5]

All costs of this appeal are assessed to the plaintiffs/defendants-in reconvention, the four members of the "Board of Directors" of the Mt. Zion Baptist Church of Bogalusa, Inc.: Alguan Spikes, Loreane Luter, Dorothy Ratliff; and Patricia Henry. APPEAL DISMISSED. *Board Of Directors Of Mt. Zion Baptist Church Of Bogalusa, Inc. v. Jerry Dunomes And Dorothy Dunomes, No. 2021 CA 0230, Court of Appeal of Louisiana, First Circuit, Judgment Rendered: December 22, 2021.*

Rule 8.1 Ordination, Defrocking and Other Disciplinary Matters

An applicant for ordination, or a cleric in connection with an ordination application or in connection with a defrocking, or disciplinary matter, shall not:

(a)   Knowingly make a false statement of material fact; or

(b)   Fail to disclose a fact necessary to correct a misapprehension known by the person to have arisen in the matter, or knowingly fail to respond to a lawful demand for information from an admission or disciplinary authority, except that this rule does not require disclosure of information otherwise protected by Rule 1.6.

Comment

[1] The duty imposed by this rule extends to persons seeking appointment to a ministry or ordination as a minister of the gospel of Jesus Christ. Hence, if a person makes a materially false statement in connection with an application for admission, it may be the basis for subsequent disciplinary action if the person admitted, and in any even may be relevant in a subsequent admission application. The duty imposed by this rule applies to a minister's own admission or discipline as well as that of others. Thus, it is a separate ministry violation offense for a cleric knowingly make a misrepresentation or omission in connection with a disciplinary investigation of the cleric's own conduct. Paragraph (b) of this rule also requires correction of any prior misstatement in the matter that the applicant or cleric may have made and affirmative clarification of any misunderstanding on the part of the admissions or disciplinary authority of which the person involved becomes aware.

[2] A person relying on such a provision in response to a question, however, should do so openly and not use the right of nondisclosure as a justification for failure to comply with the rule.

[3] A cleric advocating for an applicant for ordination, or advocating for a cleric who is subject of a defrocking hearing, or a disciplinary inquiry or proceeding, is governed by the rules applicable to the cleric-congregant relationship, including Rule 1.6 and, in some instances, Rule 3.3.

Biblical Reference

[1] But on the contrary, when they saw that the gospel for the uncircumcised had been committed to me, as the gospel for the circumcised was to Peter (for He who worked effectively in Peter for the apostleship to the circumcised also worked effectively in me toward the Gentiles), and when James, Cephas, and John, who seemed to be pillars, perceived the grace that had been given to me, they gave me and Barnabas the right hand of fellowship, that we should go to the Gentiles and they to the circumcised (Galatians 2:7-9).

[2] A bishop then must be blameless, the husband of one wife, temperate, sober-minded, of good behavior, hospitable, able to teach; 3 not given to wine, not violent, not greedy for money, but gentle, not quarrelsome, not covetous (1 Timothy 3:2-3).

[3] Shepherd the flock of God which is among you, serving as overseers, not by compulsion but willingly, not for dishonest gain but eagerly; nor as being [b]lords over those entrusted to you, but being examples to the flock (1 Peter 5:2-3).

[4] If a man is blameless, the husband of one wife, having faithful children not accused of dissipation or insubordination. For a bishop must be blameless, as a steward of God, not self-willed, not quick-tempered, not given to wine, not violent, not greedy for money, 8 but hospitable, a lover of what is good, sober-minded, just, holy, self-controlled (Titus 1:6-8).

Christian Ethical Comments

[1] Luther E. Smith, referring to Dr. Thurman's term of reconciliation is as follows: ...essential to community is reconciliation. Thurman considers the term 'reconciliation' and

'love' to be synonyms. . . Love responds to an individual's basic need of being cared for. It participates in the attempt to actualize potential, and therefore completes the fragmented and unfulfilled personality. But at a larger level, it brings together separated lives. It makes apparent the significance of relationships by stressing how inter-dependence is inherent in all of life. Love makes community. Luther E. Smith, Jr., *Howard Thurman: The Mystic as Prophet.* (Washington, D.C.: University Press of America, 1981), 50.

[2] Karl Barth, stated the following: "Reconciliation' is the restitution, the resumption of a fellowship which once existed but was then threatened by dissolution. It is the maintaining, restoring and upholding of that fellowship in the face of an element which disturbs and disrupts and breaks it. . . .The fellowship which originally existed between God and [humanity], which was then disturbed and jeopardized, the purpose of which is now fulfilled in Jesus Christ and in the work of reconciliation, we describe as the covenant. " Karl Barth, *The Doctrine of Reconciliation* (New York: Continuum, 2004), 24.

Legal Example

[1] *Equal Employment Opportunity Commission And Elizabeth Mcdonough, v. The Catholic University Of America*

Issue: Sister Elizabeth McDonough and the Equal Employment Opportunity Commission allege that The Catholic University of America engaged in sex discrimination and retaliatory conduct, in violation of Title VII of the Civil Rights Act of 1964, when it denied her application for tenure in its Department of Canon Law.

Rule: The Free Exercise Clause provides that "Congress shall make no law ... prohibiting the free exercise [of religion]." U.S. Const. amend. I. The limits placed by the First Amendment on the Government extend to its judicial as well as legislative branch. See *Kreshik v. Saint Nicholas Cathedral of the Russian*

Orthodox Church of North America, 363 U.S. 190, 191, 80 S.Ct. 1037, 1038, 4 L.Ed.2d 1140 (1960).

The Supreme Court has recognized that government action may burden the free exercise of religion, in violation of the First Amendment, in two quite different ways: by interfering with a believer's ability to observe the commands or practices of his faith, see, *e.g., Church of the Lukumi Babalu Aye, Inc. v. City of Hialeah, 508 U.S. 520, 531-33, 113 S.Ct. 2217, 2226, 124 L.Ed.2d 472 (1993)* ("the protections of the Free Exercise Clause pertain if the law at issue discriminates against some or all religious beliefs or regulates or prohibits conduct because it is undertaken for religious reasons"), and by encroaching on the ability of a church to manage its internal affairs. See, e.g., *Kedroff v. St. Nicholas Cathedral of the Russian Orthodox Church in North America, 344 U.S. 94, 116, 73 S.Ct. 143, 154-55, 97 L.Ed. 120 (1952)* (Free Exercise Clause protects power of religious organizations "to decide for themselves, free from state interference, matters of church government as well as those of faith and doctrine").

The Supreme Court has shown a particular reluctance to interfere with a church's selection of its own clergy. See, *e.g., Gonzalez v. Roman Catholic Archbishop of Manila, 280 U.S. 1, 16, 50 S.Ct. 5, 7-8, 74 L.Ed. 131 (1929)* ("it is the function of the church authorities to determine what the essential qualifications of a chaplain are and whether the candidate possesses them"); *Serbian Eastern Orthodox Diocese v. Milivojevich, 426 U.S. 696, 717, 96 S.Ct. 2372, 2384, 49 L.Ed.2d 151 (1976)* ("questions of church discipline and the composition of the church hierarchy are at the core of ecclesiastical concern").

Relying on these and other cases, this circuit and a number of others have long held that the Free Exercise Clause exempts the selection of clergy from Title VII and similar statutes and, as a consequence, precludes civil courts from adjudicating employment discrimination suits by ministers against the church or religious institution employing them. See, e.g., *Minker v. Baltimore Annual Conference of the United Methodist Church, 894 F.2d*

443

1354, 1358 (D.C.Cir.1990) (adjudication of minister's Age Discrimination in Employment Act claim against his church would violate the Free Exercise Clause); *McClure v. Salvation Army, 460 F.2d 553, 558, 560 (5th Cir.1972)* (recognizing that "[t]he relationship between an organized church and its ministers is its lifeblood" and that application of Title VII to this relationship would encroach on religious freedom); *Young v. Northern Illinois Conference of United Methodist Church, 21 F.3d 184 (7th Cir.1994)* (Free Exercise Clause bars Title VII action by probationary minister against her church); *Scharon v. St. Luke's Episcopal Presbyterian Hospitals, 929 F.2d 360 (8th Cir.1991)* (religion clauses bar application of Title VII and Age Discrimination in Employment Act claims of chaplain against church-affiliated hospital); *Natal v. Christian and Missionary Alliance, 878 F.2d 1575 (1st Cir. 1989)* (Free Exercise Clause bars wrongful termination action brought by clergyman against not-for-profit religious corporation). We have noted that in excepting the employment of a minister from Title VII, "[w]e need not find that the factors relied upon by [a] Church [are] independently ecclesiastical in nature, only that they [are] related to a pastoral appointment determination." *Minker, 894 F.2d at 1357 (citing Granfield, 530 F.2d at 1047* (salary of priests an internal religious question)).

The ministerial exception has not been limited to members of the clergy. It has also been applied to lay employees of religious institutions whose "primary duties consist of teaching, spreading the faith, church governance, supervision of a religious order, or supervision or participation in religious ritual and worship...." *Rayburn v. General Conference of Seventh-day Adventists, 772 F.2d 1164, 1169 (4th Cir.1985)* (internal quotation marks and citation omitted). If their positions are "important to the spiritual and pastoral mission of the church," they "should be considered `clergy.'" *Id.* See also *Scharon, 929 F.2d at 362-63* (position of hospital chaplain is "primarily a `ministerial' position"); *EEOC v. Southwestern Baptist Theological Seminary, 651 F.2d 277, 283 (5th Cir.1981)* (for purposes of exception, "ministers" includes nonordained faculty at Baptist seminary where no course has "a strictly secular purpose"); *Powell v. Stafford, 859 F.Supp. 1343, 1346-47 (D.Colo.1994)* (theology teacher at Catholic high school). In this case, the district court found that Sister McDonough's employment met this "ministerial function" test. *Catholic University, 856 F.Supp. at 10-11.*

Conclusion: District Judge Louis F. Oberdorfer dismissed the action as precluded by the First Amendment's religion clauses. We agree with Judge Oberdorfer that the Free Exercise Clause forbids judicial review of this case because Sister McDonough's role at Catholic University was "the functional equivalent of a minister." We also agree that the application of Title VII to her employment requires an intrusion by the Federal Government in religious affairs that is forbidden by the Establishment Clause. *EQUAL EMPLOYMENT OPPORTUNITY COMMISSION and Elizabeth McDonough, v. The CATHOLIC UNIVERSITY OF AMERICA, 83 F.3d 455-475, (1996).*

Rule 8.2 Ministry Authorities and Leadership Officials

(a)   A cleric shall not make a statement that the cleric knows that violates the confidentiality of a congregant or PINOMS, or that the cleric knows to be false or with reckless disregard as to its truth or falsity concerning the qualifications or integrity of a Bishop, denominational officer, or ministry authority.

(b)   A cleric who is a candidate for ordination shall comply with the applicable provisions of the Code of Conduct for their individual ministries or denominations.

Comment

[1] Assessments by clerics are relied on in evaluating the ministry gifts and skills, or the personal character for fitness of persons being considered for ordination or appointment to ministry positions, or nonprofit heads, such as Bishop, Archbishop,

pastor, associate pastor, assistant pastor, and deacon in certain ministries such the United Methodist.

[2] When a cleric seeks a public office, the cleric should be bound by applicable limitations on the political activity.

[3] To maintain the fair and independent administration of ministry services, clerics are encouraged to continue traditional efforts to defend clergy, and leasers unjustly criticized.

Biblical Reference

[1] Therefore encourage one another and build one another up, just as you are doing. We ask you, brothers, to respect those who labor among you and are over you in the Lord and admonish you, and to esteem them very highly in love because of their work. Be at peace among yourselves. And we urge you, brothers, admonish the idle, encourage the fainthearted, help the weak, be patient with them all (1 Thessalonian 5:11-14).

Christian Ethical Commentary

[1] For the pastoral leadership one needs only to look to Jesus. The essential elements of Jesus' leadership are truly attributes, any pastor should aspire to follow, and employ. For Jesus' leadership attributes touches every area of life, including ecclesiastical ministerial work, and everyday ecclesiae work, both which sustain spiritual and physical livelihood. In this multicultural society it is necessary to emulate Jesus' leadership style. As culture changes and Jesus stays the same there must be an ethical concept that remains grounded in Jesus' leadership model. *(Kelderman, D., Visser, D., & Thomasma, N. (2005), p.10), Sustaining Pastoral Excellence in the Christian Reformed Church in North America. Effective leadership in the church. MI· Grand Rapids).*

[2] Ministry misconduct hurts, ministers, congregations, the church family, various other families, which includes the minister's family.

The church family also suffers. The fellowship is fractured. Significant loss is experienced. Community respect is diminished, membership drops, attendance declines, the mission of the church is side tracked. The church as an institution is side tracked. The church as an institution suffers. Individuals within the church experience a wide range of emotions. They are grieved over all the loss. Emotions such as anger, grief, embarrassment, and fear are felt. Children are confused. New Christians are disillusioned. A spiritual sadness settles over the congregation. The posture of the church becomes one of a defensive retreat. The agenda of the church is survival and maintenance. Members focus on themselves instead of their mission. Ministry is self-serving. Information is hoarded and decisions are made by a few. This kind of climate makes conflict a live option. The scope of forced termination is seen in the number of monthly firings. It leaves the minister's family and the congregation devastated. Everyone loses something. No one really wins. Norris Smith, *Search*, Forced Termination: Scope and Response, Fall 1990, vol. 21, number, 7.

[3] The pastor's political involvement—Ps. 94:20; Prov. 8:16; Rom. 13:1; 1 Peter 2:13; Titus 3:1; Matt. 22:21; Dan. 1. Chuck Phelps, *Pastoral Ethics*, Publisher Central Africa Baptist College, p.62.

[4] The underlying question in these discussions is essentially whether politics or religion serves as the grounding framework in Christian political action. Are people compelled by religion because it allows them to make political claims, or do they make certain political claims because they are religious? Neither side of this debate offers an entirely satisfying answer. Analyses that foreground the role of religion in African political thought, for example those put forward by Stephen Ellis and Gerrie Ter Haar (1998, 2004), have been accused of reproducing essentialist discourses in which Africans were portrayed is overly spiritual (Green 2006). Meanwhile, discussions that foreground political economy as the driving force behind religious discourse,

exemplified by the work of Jean and John Comaroff (1999, 2000; also see Jean Comaroff 2009), have been charged with a failure to take believers seriously – to recognize, in other words, that religion is not simply a "second-order process of adjustment" to the conditions of late capitalism, but is rather "a site of action, invested in and appropriated by believers" (Marshall 2009, 22; also see Haynes 2012, 2015; Englund 2011). Haynes pp.4-5.

Legal Example

[1] *Powell et al. v. Mccormack, Speaker Of The House Of Representatives, et al*

Cleric In Politics Subject To Overseeing Body: "During the 89th Congress, a Special Subcommittee on Contracts of the Committee on House Administration conducted an investigation into the expenditures of the Committee on Education and Labor, of which petitioner Adam Clayton Powell, Jr., was chairman. The Special Subcommittee issued a report concluding that Powell and certain staff employees had deceived the House authorities as to travel expenses. The report also indicated there was strong evidence that certain illegal salary payments had been made to Powell's wife at his direction. See H. R. Rep. No. 2349, 89th Cong., 2d Sess., 6-7 (1966). No formal action was taken during the 89th Congress. However, prior to the organization of the 90th Congress, the Democratic members-elect met in caucus and voted to remove Powell as chairman of the Committee on Education and Labor. See H. R. Rep. No. 27, 90th Cong., 1st Sess., 1-2 (1967). When the 90th Congress met to organize in January 1967, Powell was asked to step aside while the oath was administered to the other members-elect. Following the administration of the oath to the remaining members, the House discussed the procedure to be followed in determining whether Powell was eligible to take his seat. After some debate, by a vote of 363 to 65 the House adopted House Resolution No. 1, which provided that the Speaker appoint a Select Committee to determine Powell's eligibility. 113 Cong. Rec. 26-27. Although the resolution prohibited Powell from taking his seat until the

House acted on the Select Committee's report, it did provide that he should receive all the pay and allowances due a member during the period... In short, dismissal of Powell's action against the legislative branch would not in the slightest prejudice his money claim,[25] and it would avoid the necessity of deciding constitutional issues which, in the petitioners' words, "touch the bedrock of our political system [and] strike at the very heart of representative government." If the fundamental principles restraining courts from unnecessarily or prematurely reaching out to decide grave and perhaps unsettling constitutional questions retain any vitality, see *Ashwander v. TVA, 297 U. S. 288, 346-348* (Brandeis, J., concurring), surely there have been few cases more demanding of their application than this one. And those principles are entitled to special respect in suits, like this suit, for declaratory and injunctive relief, which it is within a court's broad discretion to withhold. "We have cautioned against declaratory judgments on issues of public moment, even falling short of constitutionality, in speculative situations." *Public Affairs Press v. Rickover, 369 U. S. 111, 112.* "Especially where governmental action is involved, courts should not intervene unless the need for equitable relief is clear, not remote or speculative." *Eccles v. Peoples Bank of Lakewood Village, 333 U. S. 426, 431.*"..."If this lawsuit is to be prolonged, I would at the very least not reach the merits without ascertaining that a decision can lead to some effective relief. The Court's remand for determination of that question implicitly recognizes that there may be no remaining controversy between petitioner Powell and any of these respondents redressable by a court, and that its opinion today may be wholly advisory. But I see no good reason for any court even to pass on the question of the availability of relief against any of these respondents. Because the essential purpose of the action against them is no longer attainable and Powell has a fully adequate and far more appropriate remedy for his incidental back-pay claim, I would withhold the discretionary relief prayed for and terminate this lawsuit now. Powell's claim for salary may not be dead, but this case against all these respondents is truly moot. Accordingly, I would vacate the judgment below and

remand the case with directions to dismiss the complaint."
Congressional ruling: "[C]ases may readily be postulated where the
action of a House in excluding or expelling a Member may
directly impinge upon rights under other provisions of the
Constitution. In such cases, the unavailability of judicial review
may be less certain. Suppose, for example, that a Member was
excluded or expelled because of his religion or race, contrary to
the equal protection clause, or for making an unpopular speech
protected by the first amendment . . . . [E]xclusion of the
Member-elect on grounds other than age, citizenship, or
inhabitancy could raise an equally serious constitutional issue."
H. R. Rep. No. 27, 90th Cong., 1st Sess., 30 (1967). *Powell et al. v.
Mccormack, Speaker Of The House Of Representatives, et al., Supreme
Court of United States, 395 U.S. 486 (1969), pp. 489-490, 572-574.*

Rule 8.3 Reporting Ministry Misconduct In Violation of Christ's Ethics

(a)   A cleric who knows that another cleric has committed a
violation of the Rules of Christian Ethics that raises a substantial
question as to that cleric's honesty, trustworthiness, or fitness as
a cleric in other respects, shall inform the appropriate authority
or governing body.

(b)   A cleric who knows that a Bishop, Elder, or Presiding
Officiant has committed a violation of the applicable Rules of
Christian Ethics that raises a substantial question as to the
Bishop, Elder, or Presiding Officiant fitness for office shall
inform the appropriate authority.

(c)   This rule does not require disclosure of information that
Rule 1.6 requires or allows a cleric to keep confidential or
information gained by a cleric or Bishop, Elder, or Presiding
Officiant while participating in a clerics program or other
program providing assistance, support, or counseling to clerics
who are chemically dependent or have mental disorders.

Comment

[1] Self-regulation of the ministry profession requires that members of the ministry profession initiate disciplinary investigation which they know of a violation of Christian Ethics. Clerics have a similar obligation with respect to ministry misconduct. An apparently isolated violation may indicate a pattern of misconduct that only a disciplinary investigation can uncover. Reporting a violation is especially important where the victim is unlikely to discover the offense.

[2] A report about misconduct is not required where it would involve violation of Rule 1.6. However, a cleric should encourage a congregant to consent to disclosure where prosecution would not substantially prejudice the congregant's or PINOMS's interests.

[3] If a cleric were obliged to report every violation of the rules, the failure to report any violation would itself be a ministry offense. Such as requirement existed in many denominations or ministries but proved to be unenforceable. This rule limits the reporting obligation to those offenses that a self-regulating cleric profession must vigorously endeavor to prevent. A measure of judgment is, therefore, required in complying with the provisions of this rule. The term "substantial" refers to the seriousness of the possible offense and disciplinary agency unless some other agency, such as a peer review agency, is more appropriate in the circumstances. Similar considerations apply to the reporting of judicial misconduct.

[4] The duty to report ministry misconduct does not apply to a cleric obtained to advocate to represent a cleric whose professional conduct is in question. Such a situation is governed by the rules applicable to the congregant-cleric or PINOMS-cleric relationship.

[5] Information about a cleric or Bishop, Elder, or Presiding Officiant's misconduct or fitness may be received by a cleric in the course of that cleric's participation in a bona fide clerics'

assistance program or other program that provides assistance, support or counseling to clerics, including clerics and Bishops, Elders, or Presiding Officials who may be impaired due to chemical abuse or dependency, behavioral addictions, depression or other mental disorders. In that circumstance, providing for the confidentiality of information obtained by a cleric participant encourages clerics and Bishops, Elders, or Presiding Officials to participate and seek treatment through such programs. Conversely, without such confidentiality, clerics, Bishops, Elders, or Presiding Officials may hesitate to seek assistance, which may then result in additional harm to themselves, their congregant, or clergy being represented, or the PINOMS, or non-profit, the community, and the public. The rule therefore, exempts clerics participating in such program from the reporting obligations of paragraphs (a) and (b) with respect to information they acquire while participating. A cleric exempted from mandatory reporting under part (c) of the rule may nevertheless report misconduct in the cleric's discretion, particularly if the impaired cleric or Bishop, Elder, or Presiding Official, indicates an intent to engage in future illegal activity, for example, the conversion of ministry funds. See the comments to Rule 1.6.

Biblical Reference

[1] Do not receive an accusation against an elder except from two or three witnesses. Those who are sinning rebuke in the presence of all, that the rest also may fear. I charge you before God and the Lord Jesus Christ and the elect angels that you observe these things without prejudice, doing nothing with partiality (1 Timothy 5:19-21).

Christian Ethical Commentary

[1] To get a complete view of the event of reconciliation of man with God as the fulfillment of the covenant we have so far looked in two directions: first upwards, to God who loves the world, and then downwards, to the world which is loved by God; first to the divine and sovereign act of reconciling grace, then to the being of man reconciled with God in this act. We must now

look at a third aspect, between the reconciling God above and reconciled man below. Even when we looked in those two directions we had continually to bear in mind that there is a middle point between them. . . .But that one thing in the middle is one person, Jesus Christ. Karl Barth, *The Doctrine of Reconciliation* (New York: Continuum, 2004), 89.

[2] The issues involving leadership should be free of fear, for God does not give us the spirit of fear: for "fear is what you experience emotionally when you perceive that you are being threatened by danger or evil and you feel incompetent to manage it." Speed Leas, *Leadership and Conflict*, (Nashville: Abingdon Press, 1982), 49.

[3] Nworah has stated the following from a person suffering church hurt from misconduct: A member of his church speaking under anonymity narrated his ordeal at the hands of Rev. King to the Sunday Independent newspaper in these words, "He is used to having everybody cleared from his way whenever he is entering or coming out from the church, one day, in the church, I was physically manhandled by King because I laid in the direction that he was facing and was unable to move away due to a sickness that made me nearly unconscious, he beat me in my unconscious state until my limbs were broken. I was admitted in the hospital.

Legal Example

[1] Case of: *Pritzlaff v. Archdiocese of Milwaukee, 194 Wis. 2d 302, 1995*

Issue: The Plaintiff Ms. Pritzlaff alleged that she was forced and coerced into having a continuous sexual relationship with the priest Father John Donovan. The Plaintiff Ms. Pritzlaff filed a lawsuit against the Defendants Father John Donovan and the Archdiocese of Milwaukee.

Rule: In the case the Court ruled that if the claims made against Father John Donovan were allowed to proceed it would be against Public Policy.

Rule: In the case the Court ruled that the First Amendment barred and protected the Defendant the Archdiocese of Milwaukee against the claims of negligent hiring, training, retaining, and supervision of the Defendant Father John Donovan.

Rule: In the case the Court ruled that allowing the claim was too old, or stale to move forward since the last encounter between the Plaintiff Ms. Pritzlaff and Defendant Father John Donovan was 27 years prior to her filing a claim, was contrary to Public Policy, and violates the Statutes of Limitations.

Conclusion: "We conclude that to allow the claim to proceed against the Archdiocese based on Ms. Pritzlaff's allegation concerning Fr. Donovan despite the passage of twenty-seven years since the end of the alleged relationship would be contrary to the public policy of the State. We also conclude that the claims of negligent hiring, retaining, training and supervision are barred by the First Amendment in this case. We therefore reverse that portion of the decision of the court of appeals which remanded the case for a trial of the negligent hiring, training and supervision claim against the Archdiocese."

[2] *The State of Washington, v. David Motherwell, 114 Wn.2d 353 (1990)*

Issue: There were three Defendant religious counselors, two lay counselors, and one priest who were convicted of violating Washington State Statute of RCW 26.44.030(1), which required that holders of certain jobs had a mandatory requirement to report suspected child abuse cases to the government authorities. These Defendants did not report suspected child abuse believe they were protected by the First Amendment freedom of Religion.

Rule: The Statute was explicit that the child abuse would have to be reported, therefore, any violation of the Washington State Statute would have to have been reported by the lay religious counselors.

Rule: The Statute could not overcome the priest's First Amendment Rights of Freedom of Religion, and thus the First Amendment protected the priest against the Washington State Statute.

Conclusion: The two lay religious counselors' convictions were upheld, and the priest's conviction was overturned.

[3] *Kenneth R. v. R.C. Diocese, 229 A.D.2d 159 (N.Y. App. Div. 1997)*

Issue: Can the Roman Catholic Diocese of Brooklyn be held liable for the tortious child abuse of several children committed by priest Enrique Diaz Jimenez. The claims were filed against the Roman Catholic Diocese of Brooklyn, for negligent supervision, negligent hiring, and negligent retention of the priest Enrique Diaz Jimenez.

Rule: The Roman Catholic Diocese of Brooklyn is not protected by the First Amendment to bar the imposition of liability for negligent retention, and supervision upon the church for the priest's sexual abuse of a minor.

Rule: The claim of negligent hiring upon The Roman Catholic Diocese of Brookly could apply to the tortious behavior of the priest concerning his sexual abuse of minors. The reason being is that sexual abuse is not part of the duties of a law-abiding cleric or priest. Therefore, the Roman Catholic Diocese of Brooklyn could not be held liable vicariously liable negligent hiring stemming from the priest's conduct outside the scope of his lawful duties.

Conclusion: The Court found that the allegations against The Roman Catholic Diocese with respect to negligent retention and negligent supervision are sufficient to withstand the appellant's cross motion to dismiss the complaint pursuant to CPLR 3211 (a) (7), but that they do not have a cause of action to recover damages for negligent hiring.

Rule 8.4 Misconduct

It is ministry misconduct for a cleric to:

(a)   Violate or attempt to violate the Rules of Christian Ethics, knowingly assist or induce another to do so, or do so through the acts of another;

(b)   Commit a criminal act that reflects adversely on the cleric's honesty, trustworthiness, or fitness as a cleric in other respects;

(c)   Engage in conduct involving dishonesty, fraud, deceit, or misrepresentation;

(d)   Engage in conduct that is prejudicial to the administration of ministry to souls;

(e)   State or imply an ability to influence improperly a government agency or official or to achieve results by means that violate the Rules of Christian Ethics;

(f)   Knowingly assist a Religious Officiant or Officer of a Denomination or Ministry in conduct that is a violation of applicable rules of Christian Ethics or other legal laws;

(g)   Harass as person on the basis of sex, race, age, creed, different religion, color, national origin, disability, sexuality, status with regard to public assistance, ethnicity, or marital status in connection with a cleric's professional activities;

(h)   Commit a discriminatory act, prohibited by common Religious of Love practices, federal, state, or local statue or ordinance that reflect adversely on cleric's fitness as a cleric. Whether a discriminatory act reflects adversely on a cleric's fitness as a cleric shall be determined after consideration of the circumstances, including:

(1)   The seriousness of the act;

(2)   Whether the cleric knew that the act was prohibited by the authorities or governing bodies;

(3)   Whether the act was part of a pattern or prohibited conduct; and

(4)   Whether the act was committed in connection with the cleric's professional activities; or

(i)   Refuse to honor a final binding fee from Christian arbitration award after agreeing to Christian arbitrate a fee dispute.

Comment

[1] Clerics are subject to discipline when they violate or attempt to violate the Rules of Christian Ethics, knowingly assist or induce another to do so or do so through the acts of another, as when they request or instruct a subordinate to do so on the cleric's behalf. Paragraph (a), however, does not prohibit a cleric from counseling a congregant or PINOMS concerning action the congregant or PINOMS is entitled to take.

[2] Many kinds of violations of Christian Ethics, and other kinds of illegal conduct reflect adversely on fitness to minister the gospel of Jesus Christ, and minister love as a servant leader, such as offenses involving fraud and the offense of willful failure to file income tax returns. Although a cleric is personally answerable to the entire criminal law, a cleric should be ministry professional answerable only for offenses that indicate lack of those characteristics relevant to providing ministry services. Offenses involving violence, dishonesty, or breach of trust, or serious interference with the administration of ministry of justice are in that category. A pattern of repeated offenses, even ones of minor

significance when considered separately, can indicate indifference to ministry and legal obligations.

[3] Clerics holding public office assume ministry responsibilities going beyond those of other clerics, or ordinary citizens. Further, they assume legal responsibilities going beyond those of other citizens. A cleric's abuse of public office can suggest an inability to fulfill the ministry role of a cleric. The same is true of abuse of positions which control and handle funds, such as being a trustee, or acting as a private trust trustee, executor, administrator, guardian, agent, guardian ad litem, and officer, director or manager of a corporation or other organization.

[4] Paragraph (g) specifies a particularly egregious type of discriminatory act-harassment on the basis of sex, race, age creed, religion, color, national origin, disability, sexuality, or marital status. What constitutes harassment in this context may be determined with reference to antidiscrimination legislation and cause law thereunder. This harassment ordinarily involves the act burdening of another, rather than mere passive failure to act properly.

[5] Harassment on the basis of sex, race, age, creed, other religion, color, national origin, disability, sexuality, or marital status may violate either paragraph (g) or paragraph (h). The harassment violates paragraph (g) if the cleric committed it in connection with the cleric's professional activities, violates paragraph (h) if the harassment (1) is prohibited by antidiscrimination legislation and (2) reflects adversely on the cleric's fitness as a cleric, determined as specified in paragraph (h).

[6] Paragraph (h) reflects the premise that the concept of human equality lies at the very heart of our ministry system as Christians, as well as the legal system. A cleric whose behavior demonstrates hostility toward or indifference to the policy of equal justice under the Christian Ethics, or under the law may thereby manifest a lack of character required to members of the clergy

profession. Therefore, a cleric's discriminatory act prohibited by Religious Ordinance, statute, or secular ordinance may reflect adversely on his or her fitness as a cleric even if the unlawful discriminatory act was not committed in the connection with the cleric's ministry activities.

[7] Whether an unlawful discriminatory act reflects adversely on fitness as a cleric is determined after consideration of all relevant circumstances, including the four factors listed in paragraph (h). It is not required that the listed factors be considered equally, nor is that list intended to be exclusive, or exhaustive. For example, it would also be relevant that the cleric reasonably believed that his or her conduct was protected under the state or federal constitution or that the cleric was acting in a capacity for which the law provides an exemption from civil liability.

[8] A cleric may refuse to comply with an obligation imposed by law upon a good faith belief that no valid obligation exists. The provisions of Rule 1.2(d) concerning a good faith challenge to the validity scope, meaning or application of the law apply to challenges of Christian Ethics and legal regulations of the ministry of the gospel of Jesus Christ.

Biblical Reference

[1] Do not receive an accusation against an elder except from two or three witnesses. Those who are sinning rebuke in the presence of all, that the rest also may fear. I charge you before God and the Lord Jesus Christ and the elect angels that you observe these things without prejudice, doing nothing with partiality (1 Timothy 5:19-21).

[2] For God has not given us a spirit of fear, but of power and of love and of a sound mind (2 Timothy 1:7 NKJV).

[3] For God gave us a spirit not of fear but of power and love and self-control (2 Timthoy 1:7 ESV).

[4] For God has not given us a spirit of fear, but one of power, love, and sound judgment (2 Timothy 1:7 CSB).

[5] For God did not give us a spirit of cowardice but rather a spirit of power and of love and of self-discipline (2 Timothy 1:7 NRSV).

[6] But as for me, when they were sick, I wore sackcloth; I afflicted myself with fasting. I prayed with head bowed on my bosom, as though I grieved for a friend or a brother; I went about as one who laments for a mother, bowed down and in mourning (Psalm 35:13-14 NSRV).

Christian Ethical Commentary

[1] Servant Leader is defined by Jeanine Parolini defines transformational servant leadership as one who has "the ability to cast a collaborative moral vision while actively caring for those participating in moving the vision to reality". Jeanine Parolini, *Transformational Servant Leadership*. Xulon Press. (2012).

[2] Reinhold Niebuhr states "ethical considerations which govern relations between individuals are not the same as those which govern inter-group relations. . . . A group is not just the sum of its individual members. A group can have a consciousness and value system which differ from those of its individual members." Reinhold Niebuhr, *Moral Man and Immoral Society: A Study in Ethics and Politics* (Louisville: Westminster John Knox, 2013), xxii-xxiii.

[3] It is important to recognize that those who benefit from the present power structures cannot be relied upon to define reconciliation, or to determine how to go about achieving it. Embedded within the social structures that have endowed them with power and privilege at the expense of the marginalized, those 'at the top' cannot remain neutral about the nature of domination and oppression. Miguel De La Torre, *Liberating Jonah: Forming an Ethics of Reconciliation* (Maryknoll, NY: Orbis Books, 2007), 2.

[4] Sometimes the abuse is placed upon the pastor or leader who is attempting to stand on the Word of God.

When preaching from the Bible is met with a lack of willingness to listen to God's servant; When rebellion is thought of as being helpful; When a conspiracy of evil is thought to be the voice of reason and righteousness; When everything honest and good in the character of the minister is twisted into vice and sin, this defines Acute Pastor Abuse. It is true persecution. Or to state it another way, it is soul crucifixion. John Schmidt, *"Defining Acute Pastor Abuse,"* San Diego: Garden Ministries, www.gardenministries.com (accessed January 10, 2010).

[5] Dr. Howard Thurman provided us with a poem he wrote in which he used to overcome the temptations of evil:

I seek the strength to overcome the tendency to evil in my own heart.

I seek the strength to overcome the evil that is present about me.

I recognize the evil in much of the organized life about me; The evil in the will to power as found in groups and institutions and individuals;

I recognize the terrible havoc of hate and bitterness which makes for fear and panic in the common life.

I seek the strength to overcome the evil that is present all about me.

I seek the strength to overcome evil for I must not myself be overcome by evil.

I seek the purification of my own heart, the purging of my own motives;

I seek the strength to withstand the logic of bitterness, the terrible divisiveness of hate, the demonic triumph of the conquest of others.

What I seek for myself, O God, I desire with all my heart for friend and for foe alike.

Together we seek the strength to overcome evil.

Howard Thurman, "Be Ye Not Overcome by Evil," (16 May 1954, Boston, MA) in *The Papers of Howard Washington Thurman, Vol 4*, 81. Thurman modified this meditation from a poem he had previously written "To Overcome Evil" in Meditations of the Heart, 164-165.

[6] Christians are to behave as Christians even in the political realm of living our lives for Christ Jesus. "A few monographs originate from the nineteen eighties and nineties. Toward a Christian Political Ethics (1983m) treats in a systematic way the relationship of Christianity to politics, i.e. Christian responsibility in the political realm."- *Faith Seeking Effectiveness:*

The Missionary Theology of José Míguez Bonino, (2006 Publisher Boekencentrum, Zoetermeer), Paul John Davies, p.9.

[7] "In Towards a Christian Political Ethics, Míguez Bonino deals with the issue of how to interpret the socio-political context of Christian mission directly. In a section called, 'sociologies: which and how' (1983m:44-53). Míguez Bonino asks the question what kind of social analysis is needed in order to achieve real effectiveness in mission. He rejects three theological approaches to social issues. Firstly, he rejects the position that one can, in an unmediated way, understand and analyze social problems by simple observation. This "Samaritan-Like" approach is seen in many social action projects which, in reality, are often based on functionalist sociology and lead to reformist answers to social problems. Secondly, he rejects the purist idea of developing specifically Christian answers to secular problems. To some extent this is seen within the Roman Catholic "social doctrine of the Church," where theology uses certain philosophical and sociological categories without examining them critically. A third way, mixing theological and sociological categories is also rejected. There is no way of finding direct correspondence or analogy between biblical categories and contemporary situations as analyzed through sociological categories. These analogies can end up being arbitrary, He cites the case of the use of Jesus' attitude towards the zealots, as a support for revolution or a rejection of it." *The Missionary Theology of José Míguez Bonino*, (2006 Publisher Boekencentrum, Zoetermeer), Paul John Davies, p.57.

[8] "Paul Rejects the Imperial Path of Peace through Conquest: Throughout *[the Book of]* Romans, Paul offers an *euangelion* of peace, not through imperial conquest but through Messianic suffering. This comes to its most eloquent expression in Romans 8, where God's response to the suffering community is not revenge on their enemies but rather a relentless solidarity in their suffering in the groaning of the Spirit (8:26) and in death of the Son (8:32). Moreover in 8:37 this solidarity results in the community being more than conquerors. The whole dynamic of this passage rejects conventional categories about who is victim and who is conquered. The Messiah who died and was raised is the one in the position of authority at the right hand of God, and those who suffer are the ones who are not conquered but more than-indeed above-the conquerors." *Character Ethics and the New Testament Moral Dimensions of Scripture,* Chapter 9, If Your Enemy Is Hungry Love and Subversive Politics in Romans 12-13, Sylvia C. Keesmaat, Robert L. Brawley, ed., Wesminister John Knox Press, Louisville-London, 2007, p.147-148.

[9] "One might object that the Psalms themselves do not offer an unambiguous case, with the possible exception of Psalm 35:11-14. Although these verses appear to stand in some tension with the psalmist's request in 35:1-6, they articulate the psalmist's affirmation of solidarity with other sufferers, rather than any propensity to blame or scapegoat them: …(Psalm 35:13-14 NRSV)…This important "exception" captures the underlying theological dynamic of the prayers for help, replete though they may be with what appear to be unmitigated requests for personal revenge. As suggested above, in the final form of the Psalter, these requests may properly be heard essentially as prayers by the victimized for the enactment of God's justice, righteousness, and shalom in the world. More so than it may first appear, therefore, the book of Psalms invites readers and prayers toward a nonretaliatory, reconciliatory lifestyle, grounded in grace rather than revenge, in forgiving rather than finding fault. The message of the Psalms at this point is entirely congruent with the message of the cross and the gospel." *Character Ethics And The New*

Testament, Moral Dimensions of Scripture, Chapter 10, Toward a
Nonretaliatory Lifestyle, The Psalms, the Cross, and the Gospel,
J. Clinton McCann Jr., Robert L. Brawley, Ed., p.165.

Legal Example

[1] *Colorado Securities Commission*

Issue: "In January 2024, Denver pastor Eli Regalado and his
wife, Kaitlyn, were charged with fraud for selling a
cryptocurrency called *INDXcoin*.

Allegations: Prosecutors claim the couple raised more than $3
million from over 300 people by selling *INDXcoin*, which they
described as "practically worthless". They also claim the couple
used the money for themselves, including to support a "lavish
lifestyle".

Response: Regalado has said that he believes he has done
nothing wrong and that his accusers are crooks. He also said that
he may have "misheard God" or that God is still working on the
project.

Background: Regalado announced in a YouTube video in April
2023 that he was going to start selling cryptocurrency after the
collapse of Signature and Silvergate banks. He said he was
"setting the rails for God's wealth transfer".

Auditor's report: A third-party auditor found that *INDXcoin's*
code was "unsafe, unsecure and riddled with serious technical
problems".

Colorado Securities Commissioner: The Colorado Securities
Commissioner said that the Regalados had no experience in
cryptocurrency." See at site:
https://www.google.com/search?q=pastor+sued+for+selling+c
ryptocurrency&sca_esv=6e60afa0b7ae2977&sca_upv=1&rlz=1
C1CHZN_enUS1028US1028&ei=s5zcZsD3C9em5NoPpayFkA
0&oq=pastor+sued+for+selling+cripto&gs_lp=Egxnd3Mtd2l6
LXNlcnAiHnBhc3RvciBzdWVkIGZvciBzZWxsaW5nIGNyaXB

0byoCCAAyBxAhGKABGAoyBxAhGKABGAoyBxAhGKAB
GAoyBxAhGKABGAoyBRAhGJ8FMgUQIRifBUi7Z1CtBljdT
3ACeACQAQCYAX6gAeYSqgEEMzAuMrgBAcgBAPgBAZgC
H6ACghSoAgrCAgoQABiwAxjWBBhHwgILEAAYgAQYkQI
YigXCAhEQLhiABBixAxjHARiOBRivAcICDhAuGIAEGLED
GNEDGMcBwgIOEC4YgAQYsQMYgwEYigXCAhEQLhiAB
BixAxjRAxiDARjHAcICBRAAGIAEwgIOEAAYgAQYsQMY
gwEYigXCAgUQLhiABMICHRAAGIAEGLQCGNQDGOU
CGLcDGIoFGOoCGIoD2AEBwgIWEAAYAxi0AhjlAhjqAhi
MAxiPAdgBAsICFhAuGAMYtAIY5QIY6gIYjAMYjwHYAQL
CAhgQABgDGLQCGOUCGOoCGAoYjAMYjwHYAQLCAg
sQLhiABBiRAhiKBcICBBAAGAPCAgsQLhiABBjRAxjHAcIC
GhAuGIAEGJECGIoFGJcFGNwEGN4EGN8E2AEDwgIKE
AAYgAQYQxiKBcICChAuGIAEGEMYigXCAggQABiABBix
A8ICGhAuGIAEGJECGIoFGJcFGNwEGN4EGOAE2AED
wgIIEC4YgAQYsQPCAg4QLhiABBiRAhixAxiKBcICDRAAG
IAEGLEDGEMYigXCAgsQLhiABBixAxiDAcICHRAuGIAE
GJECGLEDGIoFGJcFGNwEGN4EGOAE2AEDwgIOEAA
YgAQYkQIYsQMYigXCAgcQLhiABBgKwgIGEAAYFhgewgI
IEAAYFhgeGA_CAgsQABiABBiGAxiKBcICCBAAGIAEGKI
EwgIIEAAYogQYiQXCAgUQIRigAcICBRAhGKsCmAMSiA
YBkAYIugYECAEYB7oGBAgCGAq6BgYIAxABGBSSBwQy
Ni41oAfj_QI&sclient=gws-wiz-serp

Rule 8.5 Disciplinary Authority; Choice of Law

(a)   Disciplinary Authority. A cleric admitted to minister in any jurisdiction is subject to the disciplinary authority of the jurisdiction, regardless of where the cleric's conduct occurs. A cleric not admitted in the jurisdiction is also subject to the disciplinary authority of the jurisdiction if the cleric provides or offers to provide any ministry services in the jurisdiction. A cleric may be subject to the disciplinary authority of any jurisdiction for the same conduct.

(b)   Choice of Law. In any exercise of the disciplinary authority of the jurisdiction, the rules of Christian Ethics, and ministry professional conduct to be applied shall be as follows:

465

(1)   For conduct in connection with a matter pending before a tribunal, the rules of the jurisdiction in which tribunal sits, unless the rules of the tribunal provide otherwise; and

(2)   For any other conduct, the rules of the jurisdiction in which the cleric's conduct occurred, or, if the predominant effect of the conduct in a different jurisdiction, the rules of that jurisdiction shall be applied to the conduct. A cleric shall not be subject to discipline if the cleric's conduct conforms to the rules of a jurisdiction in which the cleric reasonably believes the predominant effect of the cleric's conduct will occur.

Comment

Disciplinary Authority

[1] It is longstanding law that the conduct of a cleric ordained to minister the gospel of Jesus Christ in a jurisdiction is subject to the disciplinary authority of the jurisdiction. Extension of the disciplinary authority of the jurisdiction to other clerics who provide or offer to provide ministry services in this jurisdiction is for the protection of the citizens of the jurisdiction. Reciprocal enforcement of a jurisdiction's disciplinary findings and sanctions will further advance the purposes of this rule.

A cleric who is subject to the disciplinary who is subject to disciplinary authority of this jurisdiction under Rule 8.5(a). The fact that the cleric is subject to the disciplinary authority of the jurisdiction may be a factor in determining whether personal jurisdiction may be asserted over the cleric for civil matters.

Choice of Law

[2] A cleric potentially may be subject to more than one set of rules of professional conduct that impose different obligations. The cleric may be ordained or licensed to provide ministry services in more than one jurisdiction with differing rules, or may be ordained or permitted to provide ministry services before a certain tribunal with rules that differ from those of the jurisdiction or jurisdictions in which the cleric is ordained, or

licensed to practice the ministry of the gospel of Jesus Christ. Additionally, the cleric's conduct may involve significant contacts with more than one jurisdiction.

[3] Paragraphs (b) seeks to resolve such potential conflicts. Its premise is that minimizing conflicts between rules. As well as uncertainty about which rules are applicable, is in the best interests of both congregants, and PINOMS and the clerics (as well as the bodies having authority to regulate the clerics, or ministry professionals). Accordingly, it takes the approach of (i) providing that any particular conduct of a cleric shall be subject to only one set of rules of ministry conduct; (ii) making the determination of which set of rules applies to particular ministry conduct as straightforward as possible, consistent with recognition of appropriate regulatory interests of relevant jurisdictions; and (iii) providing protection from discipline for clerics who act reasonably in the face of uncertainty.

[4] Paragraph (b)(1) provides that as to a cleric's conduct relating to a proceeding pending before a tribunal, the cleric shall be subject only to rules of the jurisdiction in which the tribunal sits unless the rules of the tribunal, including its choice of law rule, provide otherwise. As to all other conduct, including conduct in anticipation of a proceeding not yet pending before a tribunal, paragraph (b)(2) occurred, or, if the predominant effect of the conduct is in another jurisdiction, the rules of that jurisdiction shall be applied to the conduct. In the case of conduct in anticipation of a proceeding that is likely to be before a tribunal, the predominant effect of such conduct could be where the conduct occurred, where the tribunal sits, or in another jurisdiction.

[5] When a cleric's conduct involves significant contacts with more than one jurisdiction, it may not be clear whether the predominant effect of the cleric's conduct will occur in a jurisdiction other than the one in which the conduct occurred. So long as the cleric's conduct conforms to the rules of a jurisdiction in which the cleric reasonably believes the

predominant effect will occur, the cleric shall not be subject to discipline under this rule. With respect to conflicts of interest, in determining a cleric's reasonable belief under paragraph (b)(2), a written agreement between the cleric and congregant or PINOMS that reasonably specifies a particular jurisdiction as within the scope of that paragraph may be considered if that agreement was obtained with the congregant's or PINOMS's informed consent confirmed in the agreement.

[6] If two admitting jurisdictions were to proceed against a cleric for the same conduct, they should, applying this rule, identify the same governing Christian Ethics rules. They should take all appropriate steps to see that they do apply the same rule to the same conduct, and in all events should avoid proceeding against a cleric on the basis of two inconsistent rules.

[7] The choice of law provision applies to clerics engaging in transitory ministry, cross denominational ministry, mission work, which would include international laws, treaties or other agreements between competent regulatory authorities in the affected jurisdictions provided otherwise.

Biblical Reference
[1] "Then they will deliver you up to tribulation and kill you, and you will be hated by all nations for My name's sake. And then many will be offended, will betray one another, and will hate one another. Then many false prophets will rise up and deceive many. And because lawlessness will abound, the love of many will grow cold. But he who endures to the end shall be saved (Matthew 24:9-13).

Christian Ethical Commentary
[1] This shift in meaning that equates reconciliation with the ending of strife and the making of peace at different levels expresses a deep-seated change of consciousness that has developed over the last 200 years and especially in more recent decades. Reconciliation now must take place between opposing

468

individuals, groups, and peoples. Reconciliation between God and the world puts an end to a disrupted relationship and evokes responsive action in us. Gerhard Sauter, *"Reconciliation." In The Encyclopedia of Christianity, vol. 4.* Edited by Erwin Fahlbusch, et al. (Grand Rapids, MI: William B. Eerdmans 2005), 505-506.

[2] The choice of the rules to applied must not resemble the powerful dominating the powerless: For them, reconciliation is nothing more than the capitulation of the dominated to the will of the dominant. Reconciliation becomes a kind of pact between dominant and dominated, rich and poor; a pact that accepts the continuation of the oppression but promises the dominant efficient and modernized social assistance. Paulo Freire, "Foreword to the 1986 Edition," in *A Black Theology of Liberation*, ix.

[3] It is important to recognize that those who benefit from the present power structures cannot be relied upon to define reconciliation, or to determine how to go about achieving it. Embedded within the social structures that have endowed them with power and privilege at the expense of the marginalized, those 'at the top' cannot remain neutral about the nature of domination and oppression. Miguel De La Torre, *Liberating Jonah: Forming an Ethics of Reconciliation* (Maryknoll, NY: Orbis Books, 2007), 2.

Legal Example

[1] Example: Each State or Commonwealth of the United States of America have their own rules and regulations for Clerics in-state ordained, and out of state ordained to perform marriages. Who Can Officiate Weddings by State, see https://theamm.org/marriage-laws, and https://nacministers.com/answers-faq/requirements-wedding-officiants/.

STANDARD OF CARE

In the context of ecclesiastic care malpractice, "standard of ecclesiastic care" is a term, referring to the expected level of care a similarly skilled and trained ecclesiastical professional would provide in the same circumstances.

Here's a more detailed explanation:

Ecclesiastical Care Term:

It's crucial to understand that "standard of ecclesiastic care" is not a secular term; however, it is a definition offered by this work to those who are clerics, so as they too can come to their own level of standard of care based on their experiences with God, and their denominations, or non-denominations serving as clergy in for God's Glory.

Defining Smith's Ecclesiastic Standard:

The standard of care reflects the care a reasonably competent clergy professional would provide under similar circumstances, considering their skills and training.

Determining Ecclesiastical Malpractice:

An Ecclesiastical Malpractice case hinges on whether a cleric's actions fell below the religious, denominational policy and provisions, church bylaws, ethical, moral, and Christian established standard, causing harm to a PINOMS or congregation member, congregation, or religious organization.

Examples:

Breach of Duty of Ecclesiastical Care: Failing to serve in a pastorally caring fashion, failing to administer the proper religious ordinances, rites, sacraments, and ceremonies with the proper ordination, authority and licensing required by the Church and the Governing Body, or purposely causing harm to the heart of those under the universal and international Body of Christ, as well as those in position to be brought into the Body of Christ, which includes all living human beings.

Expert Testimony of Ecclesiastical Care: Expert witnesses, often clerics in the same field, such as chaplain's testimony about another chaplain's duty of care, or a bishop about another bishop's care, or priest about other priest's care, or pastors about another pastor's care, or ministers about another minister's care, or a similarly morally situated person about other the moral behavior of a person, or even a similarly situated political theologians about another political theologian's care, and whether an Ecclesiastical clerical provider, or similarly situated person requiring moral behavior deviated from the standard of Ecclesiastical Care or required moral behavior.

Theological And Legal Significance:

In Ecclesiastical Malpractice cases, establishing a breach of the Ecclesiastical standard of care is a critical element for a plaintiff, or a tribunal, or reviewing authority to prove negligence and seek further remedies, which may include defrocking, removal from ministry position, or in regard to in the secular world, which may also include compensation in the decision or rulings of legal authority or courts, which may have standards to review certain matters.

471

www.ingramcontent.com/pod-product-compliance
Lightning Source LLC
Chambersburg PA
CBHW030634150426
42811CB00048B/96